HANDBOOK OF U.S. Theologies *of* Liberation

HANDBOOK OF U.S. Theologies *of* Liberation

Miguel A. De La Torre, editor

CHALICE PRESS
ST. LOUIS, MISSOURI

Cover and interior design: Elizabeth Wright

This book is printed on acid-free, recycled paper.

Visit Chalice Press on the World Wide Web at
www.chalicepress.com

10 9 8 7 6 5 4 3 2 1 04 05 06 07 08 09

Library of Congress Cataloging-in-Publication Data

Handbook of U.S. theologies of liberation / Miguel A. De La Torre, editor.
p. cm.
Includes bibliographical references.
ISBN 978-0-827214-48-0 (pbk. : alk. paper)
1. Theology, Doctrinal–United States. I. Title: Handbook of United States theologies of liberation. II. De La Torre, Miguel A.
BT30.U6.H36 2004
230'.0464'0973–dc22

2004011562

Printed in the United States of America

To my daughter Victoria
Whose in-depth questions make her the true theologian of the family.
May you never lose your hunger for justice!

Contents

PART 2: CONTEXTUAL ESSAYS

Contributors

Edwin David Aponte is associate professor of Christianity and culture at Perkins School of Theology, Southern Methodist University. He is the author of "Hispanic/Latino Protestantism in Philadelphia," in *Re-Forming the Center: American Protestantism 1900 to the Present* (1998); *¡Santo! Varieties of Latino Spirituality* (forthcoming); "Music and the U.S. Latina and Latino Experience," in *Introduction to the U.S. Latina and Latino Religious Experience* (2004); and the co-author of *Introducing Latino/a Theologies* with Miguel A. De La Torre (2001).

Karen Baker-Fletcher is associate professor of systematic theology at Perkins School of Theology. She is the author of *A Singing Something: Womanist Reflections on Anna Julia Cooper* (1994); and *Sisters of Dust, Sisters of Spirit: Womanist Wordings on God and Creation* (1998); and the coauthor of *My Sister, My Brother: Womanist and Xodus God-Talk* with Garth Kasimu Baker-Fletcher (1997). She has also published several articles and chapters in books on womanist and eco-womanist theology.

Phillip Berryman has authored numerous books, among them: *The Religious Roots of Rebellion: Christians in Central American Revolutions* (1984); *Inside Central America: The Essential Facts Past and Present on El Salvador, Nicaragua, Honduras, Guatemala, and Costa Rica* (1985); *Liberation Theology: The Essential Facts About the Revolutionary Movement in Latin America and Beyond* (1987); *Our Unfinished Business: The U.S. Catholic Bishops' Letters on Peace and the Economy* (1989); *Stubborn Hope: Religion, Politics, and Revolution in Central America* (1995); *Religion in the Megacity: Catholic and Protestant Portraits from Latin America* (1996); and has translated into English over twenty works by leading Latin American liberation theologians.

Steven Bouma-Prediger is the Jacobson Professor of Religion at Hope College. He is the author of *The Greening of Theology: The Ecological Models of Rosemary Radford Ruether, Joseph Sittler, and Jürgen Moltmann* (1995); *For the Beauty of the Earth: A Christian Vision for Creation Care* (2001); and coeditor of *Evocations of Grace: The Writings of Joseph Sittler on Ecology, Theology, and Ethics* with Peter Bakken (2000).

Will Coleman is cofounder and chief executive officer/president of the BT Forum, Inc., a theological think tank and corporation of intellectuals that focuses on research, writing and consultation on matters pertaining to African American religious life. He is also a cofounder and codirector of the Black Kabbalah Institute, Inc., a nonsectarian organization designed to teach and apply principles of the Kabbalah for the enrichment of African American spiritual and psychological health. He is the author of *Tribal Talk: Black Theology, Hermeneutics and African/American Ways of Telling the Story* (2000).

Elizabeth Conde-Frazier is associate professor of religious education at the Claremont School of Theology. She has written "Hispanic Protestant Spirituality," in *Teología en Conjunto: A Collaborative Hispanic Protestant Theology* (1997); *A Many Colored Kindom: Multicultural Dynamics for Spiritual Formation* (2004); as well as articles on varied subjects in theology and religious education and the histories of Protestant Latinas in ministry. Her current projects are on Bible institutes in the Hispanic community (forthcoming).

Miguel A. De La Torre is assistant professor at Hope College. He is the author of several books, among them: *The Quest for the Cuban Christ: A Historical Search* (2002); *Reading the Bible from the Margins* (2002); *Santería: The Beliefs and Rituals of a Growing Religion in America* (2004); *La Lucha for Cuba: Religion and Politics on the Streets of Miami* (2003); *Doing Ethics from the Margins* (2004); and the coauthor of *Introducing Latino/a Theologies* with Edwin D. Aponte (2001). He has also published several articles and chapters in books and is presently working on *Rethinking Latino/a Religion and Ethnicity*, to be coedited with Gaston Espinosa; and *Handbook on Latino/a Theologies*, to be coedited with Edwin Aponte.

Musa W. Dube is an assistant professor at Scripps College. She has authored *Postcolonial Feminist Interpretation of the Bible* (2000); edited *Other Ways of Reading: African Women and the Bible* (2001); and coedited *The Bible in Africa: Transactions, Trajectories, and Trends* (1999) with Gerald O. West; *John and Postcolonialism: Travel, Space and Power* (2002) with Jeffrey L. Staley; and *Reading the Bible in the Global Village: Cape Town* (2002) with Justin S. Ukpong et al.

Stacey M. Floyd-Thomas is assistant professor of ethics and black church studies, Brite Divinity School, Texas Christian University. She is currently working on two book projects, *Mining the Motherlode: A Sourcebook of Methods in Womanist Ethics* and *Making It Plain: Doing Black Theology in Community.*

Justo L. González is a former professor at the Evangelical Seminary of Puerto Rico and at Candler School of Theology. He has authored more than eighty books, mostly on the history of theology, church history, biblical interpretation, the devotional life, and Hispanic theology. He has also served as the founding President of the Association for Hispanic Theological Education (AETH), the first Director of the Hispanic Summer Program

(HSP), and the first Executive Director of the Hispanic Theological Initiative (HTI).

Carter Heyward is the Robbins Professor of Theology at the Episcopal Divinity School. She is the author of several books. Among her most recent books are: *Saving Jesus From Those Who Are Right: Rethinking What It Means to be Christian* (1999) and *God in the Balance: Christian Spirituality in Times of Terror* (2002).

Dwight N. Hopkins teaches theology at the University of Chicago Divinity School. He is the author of several books, among them: *Introducing Black Theology of Liberation* (1999); *Down, Up & Over: Slave Religion and Black Theology* (1999); *Shoes That Fit Our Feet: Sources for a Constructive Black Theology* (2000); *Black Faith and Public Talk: Critical Essays on James H. Cone's Black Theology and Black Power* (2000); *Heart and Head: Black Theology Past, Present, and Future* (2002); *Cut Loose Your Stammering Tongue* (2003); *On Being Human: Black Theology Looks at Culture, Self, and Race* (forthcoming); and coedited *Global Voices for Gender Justice* with Ana Maria Tepedino and Ramathate T. H. Dolamo (2001).

Deborah W. Little is founder and director of Ecclesia Ministries and Common Cathedral in Boston, which welcome homeless and housed people in Bible study, art, healing groups, and teaching. She is the author of *Home Care for the Dying* (1985), and her dissertation *Church Under the Tree* is being prepared for publication.

Fumitaka Matsuoka is professor of theology at Pacific School of Religion, and executive director of PANA Institute (The Institute for Leadership Development and the Study of Pacific and Asian North American Religion). He is the author of *Out of Silence: Emerging Themes in Asian American Churches* (1995); *Color of Faith: Building Communities in a Multiracial Society* (1998); and coedited *Realizing the America of Our Hearts* with Eleazar Fernandez (2003).

Andrew Sung Park is professor of theology at United Theological Seminary. He is the author of several books, among them: *The Wounded Heart of God: The Asian Concept of Han and the Christian Doctrine of Sin* (1993); *Racial Conflict and Healing: An Asian-American Theological Perspective* (1996); *From Hurt to Healing: A Theology of the Wounded* (2004); and the coeditor of *The Other Side of Sin* (2001) with Susan Nelson.

Luis G. Pedraja is the former academic dean and professor of theology at Memphis Theological Seminary. He is the author of *Jesus Is My Uncle: Christology from a Hispanic Perspective* (1999); *Teología: An Introduction to Hispanic Theology* (2004); a forthcoming book about the theology of faith from Chalice Press, and editor of *Más Voces: Reflexione Teológicas de la Iglesia Hispana* (2001).

Luis N. Rivera-Pagan is the Henry Winters Luce Professor of Ecumenics at Princeton Theological Seminary. He is the author of several books, among them: *A Violent Evangelism: The Political and Religious Conquest of the Americas* (1992); *Mito, exilio y demonios: literatura y teología en América Latina* (1996); *Diálogos y polifonías: perspectivas y reseñas* (1999); and *Essays from the Diaspora* (2002).

Karen K. Seat is an assistant professor in the religious studies program at The University of Arizona. She specializes in U.S. religious history and women's history (and their interconnections). She is completing a book manuscript on nineteenth-century American women's mission movements, in which she examines how these missions both promoted and challenged imperialist American assumptions about gender, race, Christianity and civilization.

Andrea Smith, a member of the Cherokee nation, is assistant professor in American culture and women's studies at the University of Michigan. She also sits on the steering committee of the American Indian Boarding School Healing Project.

Daniel T. Spencer is associate professor of religion and ethics at Drake University. He is the author of *Gay and Gaia: Ethics, Ecology and the Erotic* (1996).

JoAnne Marie Terrell is associate professor of theology and ethics at Chicago Theological Seminary and assistant pastor at Greater Walters AME Zion Church (Chicago). She has authored *Power in the Blood? The Cross in the African American Experience* (1998).

Tink Tinker, a member of the Osage Nation, is professor of American Indian cultures and religious traditions at Iliff School of Theology. He is the author of *Missionary Conquest: The Gospel and Native American Genocide* (1993); *Spirit and Resistance: Political Theology and American Indian Liberation* (2004); coauthor of *Native American Theology* (2001) with Clara Sue Kidwell and Homer Noley; and coeditor of *Native Voices: American Indian Identity and Resistance* (2003) with Richard A. Grounds and David E. Wilkins.

Darryl M. Trimiew is The John Price Crozer Chair in Christian Social Ethics at Colgate Rochester Crozer Divinity School. He has authored *Voices of the Silenced: The Responsible Self in a Marginalized Community* (1993) and *God Bless the Child That's Got Its Own: The Economic Rights Debate* (1997); has edited *Out of Mighty Waters: Sermons by African-American Disciples*; and has coedited *Living Responsibly in Community* with Frederick E. Glennon and Gary S. Hauk.

Seung Ai Yang is an associate professor of Old Testament at Saint Paul Seminary School of Divinity of the University of St. Thomas. Her current research projects include Asian American biblical hermeneutics and theology of the book of Job.

Introduction

"Introduction to Theology" is the typical name for a course taught at most religious studies departments in colleges throughout the United States and Canada. Usually, it fulfills the humanitics portion of the core courses needed for graduation. The college at which I teach is no different. When I was first asked to teach this course, I surveyed how my predecessors had taught the class. Not surprisingly, the theological concepts explored had one common denominator–they were based on the opinions and interpretations formulated by mainly Western theologians, specifically Eurocentric male theologians. It was as if other groups simply did not exist, and if mentioned, their contributions to the overall theological discourse were usually relegated to either the footnotes, or to other "interesting" perspectives. The canon was set! To deviate from Luther, Calvin, or Barth endangered the course, opening it to the accusation of lacking scholastic rigor.

In many institutions, a professor who wishes to teach a course on theology from a perspective other than white male European is forced to transform the subject of the course into an adjective. Hence, the subject Asian American, Native American, Black or Latino/a becomes an adjective before the topic "Theology." Such courses are usually offered as electives, not a requirement for obtaining a degree. This means students of the dominant culture are able to be deemed properly prepared in the area of theological thought without ever having to listen to or consider the voices of scholars relegated to the margins of academia. The center is secured, for seldom is the subject "European" transformed into an adjective. Few schools, if any, offer an introductory course in "Eurocentric Male Theologies." This is because the European male perspectives have become the norm for all cultures, legitimized as objective. Theological perspectives from other ethnic or racial groups are usually dismissed as an interesting view but regrettably, too subjective.

If every theological perspective is constructed from a particular social location, then the idea of theologizing from a position of complete "objectivity" is a myth constructed to protect the privileged space of those with the power to determine how the discipline is to be defined. In short, objectivity is the dominant culture's subjectivity, cloaked as academically or spiritually purer than the theology produced from the periphery of power. Yet, theological thought does not occur in a social vacuum. All theologies are constructed by human beings attempting to understand the infinite; yet all are limited by their finite identities within a particular society, culture, and history. Every theology is contextual, a product of an ongoing communal process. Therefore, theologies constructed by Eurocentric men will substantially differ from the theologies done by women, African Americans, or Asian/Pacific Islander Americans. Yet Eurocentric theologies have historically positioned themselves as the "center" of worldwide theological thought, as though they were somehow more objective and thus more legitimate.

To see through the eyes of the dominant culture contributes to the ongoing error of relegating theologies as constructed by historically disenfranchised groups to the "special interest" courses of the curricula assuming such theologies are only relevant to the members of those specific marginalized groups. In reality the perspectives of marginalized groups contribute an often ignored voice to the current theological discourse. This voice challenges the Eurocentric perspectives presented as normative in our universities, colleges, and seminaries. Conventional authoritative paradigms are unmasked as these voices from "the underside" assert themselves in the general colloquy. For this reason, books such as this one expand the attempt to construct a systematic theological position as relevant to the Eurocentric reader as it is to the historically marginalized communities. A revealing window into a world fraught with the consequences of oppressive structures provides a fundamental basis for future works in constructing a theology relevant to all people. This new theology will empower the marginalized while challenging the theology of the dominant culture–the one usually highlighted in our academic and religious centers.

The purpose of this handbook is to introduce the reader to Christian concepts from the perspective of U.S. marginalized communities by surveying various manifestations presented by leading religious scholars. This task is accomplished through the process of surveying different manifestations of liberation theology as conducted within the United States, specifically, the theologies rooted in the African American, Amerindian, Asian American, feminist, gay/lesbian, and Hispanic experiences. Special attention is given to the history, nature, sources, and development of these U.S. theologies of liberation and the theologians who contributed to the formation of each one. Prominent theologians are discussed, as are significant and recurring themes found in the different expressions of these theologies of liberation. Additionally, this work considers the relationship between these different theological concepts and the identity of the individual groups that gave rise to these perspectives. It explores the interrelationship among religion, community, and culture in the social context of different marginalized groups as well as their impact on the development and nature of theologies of liberation. One important factor of this study is that it clearly distinguishes both the differences and similarities between these U.S. theologies and their Latin American counterparts.

The handbook is divided into two major sections. The first part, "Thematic Essays," consists of compositions that provide a general overview of a specific theological theme from the perspectives of different marginalized groups, highlighting the similarities and differences that exist among these groups. The second section of the handbook, "Contextual Essays," attempts to focus on the specific contributions provided by scholars from various racial, ethnic, and gender backgrounds so that the reader can avoid the pitfall of perceiving the different theological perspectives as monolithic. Special care was given to the uniqueness of each separate theology.

It is important to note that the writers of these traditions are not, nor do they claim to be, the "official spokesperson" for their entire race, ethnicity, gender, or orientation. In effect, there is no such thing as one unified theological perspective arising from the marginalized spaces within the U.S. There are instead many variations, due to a number of diverse factors among and within marginalized groups. Hence, the contributors in this volume write of the perspectives they detect to be common among marginalized groups in the hopes that such observations resonate with others.

Although only my name appears as the editor, the reality is that this book was a joint project that cut across race, ethnic, and gender lines. The error should never be made that this book is solely the effort of one person. Rather it was birthed by a community of scholars who find solidarity due to the oppressive societal structures that presently exist. We are part of a larger community of religious scholars who find common purpose in our joint struggle for justice. Hence it would be reprehensible of me if I did not acknowledge the effort they exerted in getting the chapters to me on time. I am honored to work among those who have intellectually mentored me through the different books they have written and the many lives they have touched through the "doing" of theology.

PART 1

THEMATIC ESSAYS

1

God

JoAnne Marie Terrell

God is love.

(1 Jn. 4:8)

God specializes in things impossible, and He can do what no other power can do.

—Gospel song[1]

We have as much right biblically and otherwise to believe that God is a Negro, as you buckra,[2] or white people have to believe that God is a fine-looking symmetrical and ornamented white man.

—Henry McNeal Turner (Redkey 1971,176)

Christ [God] is a black woman.

—Jacquelyn Grant (1989, 219)

[1]"God Specializes" is an African American Gospel song published on the Savoy Label. A Chicago-based group, the Roberta Martin Singers, popularized it in 1958, and several sources credit Gloria Griffin as the songwriter. Today it is a standard in many black congregations.

[2]"Buckra" is a post-Civil War Southern slang term for whites. According to my black elders, it was not a term of derision, but since in the post-slavery ethos social relaitons did not signficantly change, it was rather a "hidden description" blacks used as a form of social resistance in order to talk about whites in their presence with impunity.

God provided Hagar with a resource. God gave her new vision to see survival resources where she had seen none before. Liberation in the Hagar stories is not given by God; it finds its source in human initiative.
—DELORES S. WILLIAMS (1993, 5)

God is as Christ does.
—KELLY BROWN DOUGLAS (1989, 7–16)

God has got a lot of explaining to do.
—JAMES H. CONE[3]

The Aseity of God

Orthodox Christian doctrine affirms that God is, having no origin but having *aseity*. Aseity is "a characteristic of being self-derived in contrast to being derived from or dependent on another. It is a technical term for the judgment that the existence of God is necessary in contrast to contingent. Karl Barth (1886–1968) interprets aseity as 'the freedom of God.'"[4] In the theism of orthodox and neoorthodox perspectives, God is frequently described as the One alone who has aseity, sovereignty, agency, ultimacy, and inexhaustible mystery.[5]

This understanding serves to highlight the woeful nonnecessity, irrelevance, powerlessness, bondage, and banality of human beings. These common features of human existence morally level us and point to the transcendence of God as the sovereign Creator. They show our ongoing need for God as an able Redeemer. They stress the immanence of God as our Companion/Sustainer all along our journey throughout the finitude, vulnerability, and meaninglessness that lend themselves to pride and sinfulness. Indeed this is the theological anthropology that Augustine systematized in his explication of the consequences of and remedy for original sin, which Christians have inherited, both to our blessing and detriment. Given this assessment of the Necessary Being[6] of God in contrast to the contingent character of human existence in orthodox and neoorthodox perspectives, it is easy to assent to Barth's oft-cited claim that there is an "infinite, qualitative difference" between humans and God.

Nonetheless, human freedom, or capacity for transcendence, is self-evident in the independent thought, sensation, desire, and mobility that we as living beings possess. These discrete dimensions of our existence–relating to our knowing, being, and doing–owe their vitality to a Reality

---

[3]Per telephone conversation with Professor James H. Cone of Union Theological Seminary (New York) in October 2002. Quoted with permission.

[4]Van Austin Harvey, "aseity" in *A Handbook of Theological Terms.*

[5]See Kaufman, *In Face of Mystery.*

[6]Necessary Being is "traditionally defined as that being whose essence it is to exist or that cannot not exist," in Harvey, "necessary being," in *A Handbook of Theological Terms.*

and a Power in and beyond us. That Reality and Power is commonly called God, upon whom we depend immediately for the breath and natural processes that quickened, and that sustain, our individual and common life. Although the Trinitarian formula for the Deity–Father, Son, and Holy Spirit–is commonplace in orthodox confession, the acknowledgment of God as our Creator, Redeemer and Sustainer sheds light on the contingency of all creaturely existence: we owe the very idea of us, the fact of our coming into being and what agency we experience to One who is more than us. What capacity for transcendence or individuation we also experience is God's gift to us. What initiative we demonstrate in discovering the length and breadth of that ability is our gift to God, to the world we inhabit, and to ourselves.

Liberation Theology's God-talk

Theology is God-*talk*, but it is not God talking; it is we humans who are doing the talking. Theology is a human enterprise filled with competing claims about who God is, about who we are, and about the world of vast resources God has created–it is presumed–for human companionship, stewardship, and consumption (Gen. 1:27ff.). Within the human family, there is splendid diversity of race, gender and sexual orientation. Christians are able to affirm God's "foreseeing care" for and "guardianship"[7] of the finite, dependent creatures we happen to be in the gift of each other, and we certainly attribute to God's providence the gift of God's own son, Jesus, both as a sacrifice and as an exemplar of sacrificial love. This is perhaps the reason it is consistently signified within Christian scriptural and preaching traditions that God is, that "God is love," and that God loves us.[8] The love of God for us (*pro nobis*) is at once transcendent and immediate, spontaneous and gratuitous (*'ahabah*=Hebrew; *agape*=Greek), and produces a response of mutual (*phileo*) and embodied love (*eros*) in us.[9]

Orthodox perspectives that begin with the Bible are akin to theistic liberation perspectives that affirm the sovereignty of God over that of putative authorities. Liberation God-talk also speaks of God as Creator, Redeemer, Sustainer; as Giver and Gift. That is, liberation God-talk speaks of the love and providence of God, but it does so not only mystically and scripturally, but also *historically*. Liberation God-talk speaks of the ways in which humankind has experienced the gifts of God and interpreted the significance of both the giving and the given-ness. Liberation God-talk does *not* speak abstractly, apart from the concrete realities of people who are stratified favorably and unfavorably by the race, gender, sexual orientation, able-bodiedness, etc., with which they are endowed, and by the social class

---

[7] *Webster's Encyclopedic and Unabridged Dictionary of the English Language*, s.v. "providence."

[8] See Deut. 7:8, 33:3; 1 Kings 10:9; 2 Chr. 2:11, 9:8; Sg; Jn. 3:16ff; 1 Jn. 4:8.

[9] Harvey, "Agape and Eros" in *A Handbook of Theological Terms*.

arrangements of the cultures and economies in which they live and work. Liberation God-talk from the lower tiers–the "underside"–of human history and experience attempts to demystify interpretations and arrogations of the Reality and Power in and beyond us that reify and contribute to the oppression of individuals and whole classes of people.

Black, Hispanic, womanist and feminist theologians therefore have not attempted to create logical proofs for the existence, essence, and activity of God as an object of abstract contemplation.[10] Rather, the survival and creative self-expression of theologies of liberation conducted on the margins of U.S. society emerged out of reflection on their people's struggles for freedom and ontological recognition as beneficiaries, agents, and interpreters of God's love and providence in the midst of their common experience of oppression.

Power for the Impossible

Consonant with orthodox faith in the Bible as a source of revelation, theologians from the underside of U.S. society begin with the affirmation that God *is*. For many, the radical personalism of the God of their experience at once comports with the evangelical heritage of, for example, the Black Church and flies in the face of the standalone God who is characterized by aseity and transcendence. In a variety of ways they attest to the character of their Ultimate Concern as creative, generative, relational, authoritative, ethical, transrational Power, who "can do what no other power can do." Rooted in the faith traditions, and confessional utterances of their communities of accountability, they point to divine providence in, through, beyond, and despite the natural, social, economic, and political orders, and to divine empowerment to do "things impossible." For them, "theology is the second step" in the experience, reflection, praxis model for doing theology. Thus the antecedent of the confession is the personal and collective experience of *requiring* the practically impossible–in managing, resisting, and overcoming, for example, the absurdities of the power dynamics in slavery and Jim-and-Jane-Crow America.

*God specializes in things impossible...*This theological understanding is consistent with the confessional posture of historically tyrannized groups like the Black Church[11] that was forged in oppression and in the evangelical

[10]See Hood, *Must God Remain Greek?*

[11]See Lincoln and Mamiya, *The Black Church*. The book is the work of sociologists of religion. The authors define the Black Church as the seven historically black denominations, which are the African Methodist Episcopal Church, African Methodist Episcopal Zion Church, Christian Methodist Episcopal Church, the National Baptist Convention, National Baptist Convention-USA, Progressive Baptist Convention, and the Churches of God in Christ. I have not as narrowly construed the Black Church but rather include black congregations in white denominations and other bodies that are sourced by black culture and community.

ethos of awakening, antebellum America.[12] While the management of evil and suffering (and the celebration of the good) lies in back of all religiosity, marginalized theologians construe their work as deeply theodical,[13] that is, inquiring of God concerning the remediation of the evil and suffering they experience personally and collectively. The primacy of experience in their theologies suggests that the most significant corollary doctrine for reflection on the idea of God is that of humanity.

Liberation Theodicy

The classic formulation of the question of theodicy is, If God is perfectly good and perfectly just, then why does God permit evil and suffering to exist? This is the perennial question of humankind from age to age and culture to culture. It is a question about how to manage the vicissitudes of life and have some assurance about the place from where help will come. The human experience of living in the question of theodicy is responsible for the generation of myths to explain the origins of social structures and world orders that presently define us. Creation stories, for example, are theodicies, in that they seek to explain the origin of the good that exists, the ubiquity and intransigence of evil, and how to manage all of it intellectually and spiritually, individually and communally.

Any discussion of God–if it is to be liberating for humanity–must include the question of evil, addressing forthrightly the suffering and injustice that pervade human life. Evil involves the conscious and unconscious exercise of individual and/or systemic agency toward injurious consequences for others. Since such evil exercise involves intent, it is fundamentally unjust–a violation of human rights and an undermining of the respect each person is due in consequence of his and her finitude and vulnerability.

Suffering may be unrelated to the issue of justice (and therefore unrelated to evil), as in the case of illness, accidents, or natural disasters. But even so, such types of suffering may well be unjust, and therefore evil. Illness and accidents may stem from prolonged or brief exposure to structural oppression and to thought patterns that wreak havoc on the lives of individuals and classes of people, chronically debilitating and acutely delimiting their capacity for healthy development. In addition, the complexes of interdiction to which the poor of the world are subject comprise a system of "steal, kill, destroy." In such a system advantaged classes take resources from communities and countries. In so doing they limit others' life chances, destroy sub- and whole cultures, and exploit micro- and macroeconomies to promote their own interests. Although natural

[12]To some extent, black faith in the God of the Bible gave to the emergent civil religion its emphasis on the experiential nature of religious truth.

[13]See Terrell, *Power in the Blood?*

disasters such as drought may not be averted, the way that first-world economies are structured to support dictatorial regimes or require debt repayment in the two-thirds world rather than provide resources for drought management promotes evil and suffering.

In any case, whatever precipitates it, pain–whether personal or communal, accidental or systemic–is part of the "*is*-ness" of life, a consequence of living under the conditions of mortality. Since pain *is*, what do we confess about God's role in it? The questions of theodicy implicate the Creator God for the vulnerability to pain that fundamentally defines human existence. The liberationist asks: What does what we confess about God make us do about pain? How do we respond lovingly, creatively, ethically, and reasonably to the pain of oppression given the demands made on us by our relationship with a God whom we claim *is* love and who is also generative, ethical, and transrational? What does God's own suffering (in Christ) speak to us about how we are to manage our own and others' suffering?

Only sociopaths feel *only* their own pain. Liberation God-talk believes God is love. Such talk echoes what Charles Hartshorne, a process theologian, has affirmed, "God is the most affected being in the universe, the One who experiences everything"; indeed, "God is the one who matters to all things and to whom all things matter."[14] Such belief makes it imperative for any theologian or preacher who purports to speak of and for God to address the causes and remedies for the suffering and pain in the world. And if God's magnanimous and providential love evokes a response of mutual and embodied love in us, we must think not only of what it will take to remedy our pain but of what it will take to remedy others' as well. Feminist theologian Susan B. Thistlethwaite avers that, "Good theology begins where the pain is."[15]

Many U.S. theologians of liberation are confessing people with varying degrees and kinds of participation in both the work of the Church and the pain and struggles of the community. This makes them zealous to protect notions of the love of God for the people of God; of the inviolate nature of God's justice in relationship to God's love and in the working out of God's purposes for creation; and of the sovereignty of God over the whole created order. In assiduously affirming God and tracing the roots of oppression to

[14]I am grateful to my friend and colleague, Theo Walker, of Perkins School of Theology, Southern Methodist University for his insight on the ways process theology can benefit Black and Womanist theologies by helping to construct a concept of God that is attentive to the issue of theodicy at the same time it portends the deepened articulation of eschatological hope. I am also grateful to Tolonda Henderson, a graduate student at Chicago Theological Seminary, for pointing me to some other resources linking black theology and process thought. I have been open to this because of my long-standing, deep affinity with Taoism and Hinduism. My very inchoate reflections include a bent towards a kind of pantheism.

[15]Quoted from her university lectures.

their human, systemic causes, these theologians have effectively reworked the questions of theodicy into questions of anthropodicy.[16]

God as Liberator

Black theologians, in particular, have based their claims in the covenantal and prophetic traditions of the Bible, for they have seen in it a mirror image of their own world. Just as the Exodus from Egyptian slavery signaled the beginning of peoplehood for the children of Israel, so deliverance from American slavery was the beginning of peoplehood for African Americans. Just as the God of the Bible gave victory to David over Goliath, delivered Daniel from the lion's den, rescued the three Hebrew children from Nebuchadnezzar's fiery furnace, and raised Jesus from the dead, so black theologians attribute the personal and collective victories of black people from slavery to the present to the hand of God.

Because the God of the Bible made and makes impossible things possible, God continuously demonstrates love for God's people, asserts the justice of God beyond the will of their oppressors, and maintains for God's sovereignty over their enemies. The liberating activity of the God of the Bible and the experiences of God's people resonated with black theologians (as well as other theologians from historically marginalized groups), and they characterized their Redeemer from the structural sins of racism and classism as a Liberator. Through the prophets, this Liberator God preached woes to the rich, signifying a "preferential option for the poor" and marginalized.

For some marginalized theologians the correlation of the biblical stories and prophetic traditions with the history and experience of oppression justifies the belief that "God is on the side of the oppressed." They understand this faith-claim as a gift of divine assistance that also evokes the faithful and creative exercise of agency on the part of the oppressed. For blacks, this included the profoundly important task of reimagining the color of God in an attempt to wrest control of the commonly signified metaphor of a glorified white male from dominant art and the public mentality.[17] Kelly Brown Douglas traces this work of nascent black theologians to the late nineteenth and early twentieth century, when Robert Alexander Young and African Methodist Episcopal (AME) Bishop Henry McNeal Turner argued for the ontological blackness of God, linking it to God's opposition to oppression (1994, 31). Bishop Turner's remarks (cited at the beginning of the chapter) are notable, not only because they are consistent with the Judeo-Christian tradition of anthropomorphizing God, but also because they are ontologically affirming and have the serendipitous effect of

---

[16]See Terrell, *Power in the Blood?*, 143, in which I raise the question of anthropodicy in this God-affirming way: "Since God is good, why are people evil?"

[17]See Major Jones, *The Color of God.*

theomorphizing black people in their own assessment. In the context of late-1960s America, empowered by the reimaging, some black theologians affirmed the full range of humanly possible responses to the violence of race and class oppression.[18] Others agitated for civil rights and full participation in the American dream as part of a larger cosmic vision, while testifying to the hope of reconciliation that has been part and parcel of the love ethic and survivalist sensibilities of the African American community.[19]

Some womanist theologians have been reticent to identify God as a Liberator, in light of Delores S. Williams's explication of Hagar's story. Williams's study provides an alternative scriptural paradigm for understanding race, class, gender, and sexual oppression in black women's experience and God's response to it. Just as the biblical heroes Abraham and Sarah abused and exploited the Egyptian slave woman sexually, so whites abused and sexually exploited black children, women, and men, who were unable to resist fully on account of their status as slaves. Yet in and beyond slavery, black women have been and are subject to as unyielding and devastating a hierarchy within their own families, churches, and social and civic organizations on account of racism, poverty, sexism, and heterosexism. Just as Hagar did not experience God's deliverance but rather God's empowerment to endure, survive, and effect a meaningful "quality of life" for her son, herself and, ultimately, their community, so black women place a premium on this enabling.

In light of their lived experience of interstructured oppression[20] coming from outside as well as from *within* the African American community, womanists place into sharper relief the questions of theodicy/anthropodicy that have arisen out of black humanity's ongoing struggle against oppression. They question not only the aptness of the liberation motif in black theology but also the efficacy of the reworked image of God as black and *male* for black women to have a sense of themselves as being fully empowered by the Christian God. These questions are also being raised by women within the Hispanic, Asian, and Native American communities.

Liberation Theology and Christ

For black people generally, any discussion of Christ impinges on the doctrine of God, so closely held are the traditional, Trinitarian beliefs concerning the relationship between the Father (Creator), Son (Redeemer), and Holy Spirit (Sustainer). Jacquelyn Grant, Delores Williams, and Kelly Brown Douglas entered theological discourse by way of critiques of classical

[18]See James Cone, *Black Theology and Black Power;* Cleage, *The Black Messiah;* Wilmore, *Black Religion and Black Radicalism;* and Wilmore and Cone, *Black Theology.*

[19]See King, *Stride Toward Freedom,* and *Strength to Love.* Also see Roberts, *Liberation and Reconciliation.*

[20]See Riggs, *Awake, Arise, Act.*

and black christologies and their deployment of Jesus'/God's maleness and color in furtherance of their strategies of domination and resistance. In so doing, the premier womanists identified with the exponentially charged significance of Jesus Christ who is "very God of very God" in the confession of black folks.

For Grant, the assertion that "Christ [God] is a black woman" radicalizes black women's conceptual apparatus for imaging God and carries a step further black theologians' notion of the blackness of God. Beyond black theology's signification of the Liberator God, she lifts up an additional image of Christ or God as the "divine co-sufferer." This recognizes the efficacy of the cross as a symbol of the pain and suffering in black life and acknowledges the Spirit's intercession on black humanity's behalf. Douglas's retort that "God is as Christ does" encourages Grant and other womanists to be ever more inclusive in defining the very humanity for whom God in Christ incarnated, lived, struggled, died, and presently intercedes. In so doing God in Christ provided a moral standard for believers that is paradoxically binding and liberative for all of humanity, even as it affirms the freedom of God.

Williams's survivalist paradigm and black women's lived experience offer insight on the ways that the Black Church and the African American community must really struggle to find appropriate images and God-concepts that do not ratify male oppression or mimic white power dynamics but that are accountable ultimately to the work of human liberation.

Other theologians from the United States margins stop short of indicting God for the pain of existence. Some embrace a radical humanism as an additional faith option that constitutes not so much a rejection of a divine principle but of the God-concept of the Christian church–its fantastical, often contradictory claims and exclusivist posture. William R. Jones was among the first to critique black theology's overreliance on the theme of theodicy, identifying it as a rhetorical prison that does not permit black theologians to question seriously the idea of God's goodness and power.[21] Anthony Pinn argues for the existence of a long-standing, deep-rooted humanist tradition[22] within black life and for an intellectual discourse that does not simply rely on the confessional posture of the predominantly Christian African American community, which sees itself as "churched" and "super-churched."[23]

Building on the cultural and religious heritage of Africa and displaced African cultures in the United States, the Caribbean, and other places, Pinn, Dianne Stewart[24] and others have begun to question the Christian

[21]See William R. Jones, *Is God a White Racist?*
[22]See Pinn, *Why Lord?*
[23]See Lincoln and Mamiya, *The Black Church.*
[24]Stewart, *Three Eyes for the Journey.*

God-concept (its emphasis on a suffering God), that forces African Americans in particular to deal with questions of theodicy and agency in peculiar, often disempowering, ways. Moreover, we are faced with the pervasiveness of evil in human experience manifested in the genocidal conflicts in places around the globe, in terrorism and counterterrorism, and in the insatiable capacity of our nation, the last remaining superpower, to wage merciless war. These discussions of the place of theodicy in theology today provide the context for the last epigram, James Cone's quip: "God has got a lot of explaining to do."

With the people of their communities, disenfranchised by the present status quo, Christian theologians speak and act as sacramental witnesses to the Reality and Power in and beyond all of us. Attempting to be faithful signifiers of "God-with-all-of-us," they celebrate the love of God proclaimed in scripture, maintain the freedom of God illuminated in their inherited theological traditions, and defy the shameful arrogations of the sovereignty of God in their own lives and in the lives of others on the underside of human experience. Clothed, like the rest of creation, in mortality, they have experienced the extremes of vulnerability. Having accepted the ethical challenges respecting their own and others' finitude, they rigorously affirm the exercise of human agency in thoughtful, sustained interaction with the Bible and all the social, economic, and cultural tools at their disposal, to the ends of survival, liberation, and creative self-expression.

2

Christ

Carter Heyward

The identity of Jesus Christ–who he or she is among us today–provides the key to understanding Christian liberation theology even when, in some cases, little explicit theological attention is given it. This second chapter focuses on Jesus Christ in an attempt to show in what distinctive ways Jesus Christ is presented by liberation theologians. How does the "Jesus Christ" of liberation theology differ from the "Jesus Christ" of other theological traditions and movements throughout Christian history?

Information on theological terminology is often put in endnotes, but in this case the word choices are too important to the content of the chapter to be explained at the end. Readers need to be clear at the outset what the words mean to the author. The words "Jesus Christ," when used together, refer to *both* Jesus of Nazareth, the human brother, a young Jewish male and itinerant teacher, who lived in Israel/Palestine some two millennia ago *and* the "christic"–sacred, redemptive, indeed liberating–spirit that Christians often associate with Jesus. When I speak in these pages simply of "Jesus," the reference is to the human brother. When I speak of "Christ," I am talking about "christic spirit," a term I personally prefer on the theological grounds that the sacred power, the "divinity" that Christians have encountered through Jesus, is a Spirit by no means limited to the earthly or heavenly life of Jesus of Nazareth.

The Question of Identity

Who is Jesus Christ among us today? This is the basic christological question raised by liberation theologians in the United States and elsewhere during the last four decades of the twentieth century.[1] The different constituencies that liberation theologians represent, such as African Americans and Native Americans, have offered various images of Jesus Christ that reflect their diverse historical experiences. We will explore these differing images with the recognition that a general consensus prevails among liberation theologians in the United States about the identity of Jesus Christ.

The Collective Christ

Liberation theology sharpens the traditionally catholic understanding of Christ as a collective Body of humanity. Jesus Christ is not simply one person, past or present. Jesus Christ is not simply Jesus of Nazareth, the Jewish teacher who lived in Palestine/Israel. Furthermore, Jesus Christ is not simply Jesus of Nazareth as a resurrected divine "person" accessible to individual believers through prayer and mystical experience. In liberation theology, Jesus Christ is the poor, the marginalized, the outcast and disregarded, those at the margins of society and those at the bottom of the margins. Thus, in liberation theology, the identity of Jesus Christ is collective. Biblical images of Jesus of Nazareth and Jesus Christ function as historical springboards into collective identities of groups and movements in today's world and throughout history.

More in keeping with traditional christological assumptions, Jesus Christ refers not only to the oppressed but also to those who liberate the oppressed. Jesus Christ is in solidarity with those who are poor, abused, violated. Here, too, the identity is primarily collective. Jesus Christ–in liturgical language, the Body of Christ–is both those who suffer and those who bring relief from suffering. In liberation theology, the collective emphasis is on the suffering that is brought about by systems of injustice–such as white racism, male gender supremacy, and economic exploitation–and on the struggles for social and economic justice.

The question of who Jesus Christ is often cannot be easily answered. This is because "identity" is not, for liberation theologians, a static concept. It is a question about who is suffering today, and where, and why, and what can be done to relieve the suffering. To identify Jesus Christ is to notice the suffering among those we know and those we don't know and to realize that most suffering in the world is the result of many overlapping forces. Poor black women, for example, are never simply African American,

---

[1]Traditionally in Christian theology, "christology" is the study of the "person and work of Jesus Christ." It usually refers to the conclusion reached at the Council of Chalcedon in 451 C.E. that Jesus Christ was "fully human and fully divine."

or female, or poor. Their identities are shaped by all of these "social locations." Hence, Jesus Christ lives and dies, breathes and cries out from many different social locations all in the same moment and often in and among the same people and creatures. Wherever and whoever, Jesus Christ calls out to us from the margins of our life together.

Below are some of the many marginal social locations that shape Jesus Christ today in the United States:

1. race and cultural oppression (Arab American, African American, Native American, Latino, Asian American, and certain European American "tribes" in particular situations–such as being Irish, Greek, or Italian American in communities that are largely Anglo and Protestant)
2. class and economic exploitation (poverty across race, culture, and gender); sexual and gender injustice (queerness and femaleness across race, culture, and class)[2]
3. religious marginalization (Islam, Wicca, Judaism, and other spiritual traditions that are not Christian)
4. age discrimination (being very old or very young across race, culture, class, and gender–especially among the poor)
5. marginalization and disempowerment because of disability or illness across race, culture, class, and gender–but especially among the poor
6. the exploitation by humans of the earth and "creaturekind."[3] Indeed the Body of Christ can be the body of the earth and of other creatures

Near the outset of a new century, liberation theologians increasingly are aware of this immensely significant expansion of our understandings of who and what Jesus Christ is among us today.[4]

The Immanent Jesus

Liberation theologians not only articulate a catholic understanding of Jesus Christ as essentially a collective spirit, they sharpen this understanding by bringing Christ down to earth. Liberation theologians do not care much, if at all, about images of Jesus Christ sitting in heaven at the right hand of the Father. What matters much more is that Jesus Christ is a baby girl

---

[2]"Queer" is an inclusive term that, in this essay, refers not only to gay, lesbian, bisexual, transgendered. and other gender and sexual nonconformists but also to those who are publicly in solidarity with us.

[3]In this chapter, "creaturekind" refers to all creatures that are other than human–animals, plants, minerals. Of course, the term literally includes humans, but I am searching for language that avoids defining animals, plants, minerals, and earth primarily as "other" (the problem with terms like "other-kind" and "other-than-human").

[4]For Christian liberation resources on ecojustice, see Rasmussen, *Earth Community, Earth Ethics;* McFague, *Super, Natural Christians;* Fox, *The Boundless Circle;* Spencer, *Gay and Gaia;* Adams, *Neither Man Nor Beast;* Heyward, *Saving Jesus from Those Who are Right;* and Clark, *Erotic Ecology.*

hooked on crack and that she is also the power to transform structures of urban poverty and despair. The Jesus Christ of liberation theology does not occupy a throne. He is a political prisoner, and he is also the struggle for liberation from political repression.

Illuminating an understanding of Jesus Christ as the poor and marginalized of the world, three other theological themes characterize liberation christology: (1) the centrality of physical bodies in the realm of God to which Jesus Christ bears witness; (2) participation in struggle for social change as embodiment of solidarity with the poor and marginalized; and (3) authorization by the poor and marginalized, rather than by ecclesiastical authority, to speak theologically. These characteristics understandably have often placed liberation theologians in conflict with authorities of both church and state.

Centrality of Body

Outside liberation theology, the "Body of Christ" has tended to be spiritualized by Christians, referring to the consecrated bread in the service of Holy Communion or to the belief in the resurrected presence of Jesus Christ as a spiritual power dwelling "above" with the Father and the Spirit as part of the Trinity. The real human body, in its physicality, and the real world, in its materiality, have been subjected under Christ. Throughout Christian history, "the body" has been experienced and understood to be distinctly inferior to "the spirit." As such, human bodies and the body of the earth itself have been placed under the control of Christian dogma and moral theology. In fact, it can be fairly argued that Christian ethics and moral teachings have been largely focused on controlling human bodies–especially women's bodies, which traditionally have been experienced by male churchmen and theologians as the *most* physical–sensual, sexual, out of control, and spiritually dangerous–bodies.[5]

Not only have human bodies been put down and subjected to spiritual control. In much traditional Christianity, the same has been true of the material character of poverty and the physicality of the earth and its many creatures. Poverty has been spiritualized–lifted up throughout Christian history as a mark of spiritual blessing. The biblical suggestion that the poor will always be with us, and other related texts, have been interpreted as evidence that God has created poverty as a special vocation to which "the poor" are called.[6] Liberation theologians reject this interpretation as contrary to who God is and how God acts. Moreover, liberation theologians indict the Christian church for upholding structures of social injustice through its peddling of oppressive theologies that support unjust social,

[5]For excellent treatment of connections between Christian history and the history of misogyny (woman hating) see Harrison, *Our Right to Choose*, and *Making the Connections*.

[6]See Mt. 26:11 and Mk. 14:7.

political, and economic systems, especially global capitalism in the late twentieth century.[7]

As for the earth and creaturekind, the church historically has viewed "creation," much like the human body, as an appropriate object of domination and use for human purposes.[8] Though a relative latecomer to liberation theologies in United States and elsewhere, an interest in eco-justice at the heart of all liberation increasingly has characterized the work of theologians with special commitments to the sustainability of the earth and the well-being of creaturekind. This emphasis has been strengthened by feminist and queer liberation theologians[9] joining our voices with Native American theologians who, among all Christian theologians, historically have been the clearest and most unequivocal in their ongoing commitments to the earth.[10] The christological effect of these commitments to earth and creaturekind has been to de-anthropocentrize Jesus Christ–that is, to show that humankind is not the center of God's realm any more than the earth is the center of the universe. We humans are participants with many other creatures, all of us together at the center of God's love. Thus, Christ is as much a pelican, an elephant, and a tree as she is our brother from Nazareth.

Struggle for Social Change

Because liberation theologians are in a sense scribes for activist communities of Christians who believe that the church is called by God to help generate justice and build peace, most liberation theologians frequently find ourselves at odds with governments of both church and state. Most liberation theologians assume that this is the way it will be here on earth as long as a capitalist political economy, or any other global structure of human greed and fear, is hanging over the planet like a sword. Indeed, the poor *will* always be with us–as long as there is capitalism and as long as there is greed. And as long as poverty and other forms of human and creature exploitation exists on the earth, our world will need liberation theology and the social activism in which it is rooted. For liberation theology is never simply an academic exercise. It takes root in struggle, community-building, networking, organizing. The liberation theologian–Black, feminist, womanist, Native, whatever his or her social location–is therefore never a solitary thinker. They are giving voice to those with whom they stand either

---

[7]See McAfee Brown, *Spirituality and Liberation.*

[8]See especially Rasmussen, op. cit. and Spencer, op. cit.

[9]Two gay/queer liberation theologians who have made especially strong theological connections between sexual and ecological exploitation are Daniel Spencer and J. Michael Clark.

[10]See Kidwell, et al., *A Native American Theology.* I am also grateful to my colleague and friend Steven Charleston, a Choctaw Indian and President of the Episcopal Divinity School in Cambridge, Mass., for conversation about eco-justice, sexuality, and God.

through identity or solidarity. The fruits of their labor bear witness to the integrity of their voices and to the authenticity of their identity or solidarity.

Authorized through Community

But who gives liberation theologians the authority to speak so boldly of what God is doing in history? For liberation theologians, the authority to speak of God, Jesus Christ, and the struggle for justice as sacred struggle is given by God through the communities and networks with whom the theologians stand. The authority does not come from bishops, priests, pastors, church councils, or "tradition" defined narrowly as what the church has most often taught about Jesus Christ, women, poverty, sexuality, and other pressing matters. This doesn't mean that liberation theologians always stand against church authorities or traditional Christian teachings. It does mean that, where there is conflict between "tradition' and social justice liberation theology will be advocating justice. For example, in the matter of women's ordination liberation theology seeks ways, theologically, to address the misogynist, tradition upon which patriarchal theological practices (such as a male-only priesthood) are held in place.

Of course, this willingness to stand at odds with the church means that liberation theologians must be willing to work at the margins, rather than at the center, of public life. Often liberation theologians oppose the state as well, such as the stand they took against the invasion and occupation of Iraq in 2003.[11] This is because the state–in our case, the government of the United States–will not allow social, political, or economic dissent a strong public voice. Like other voices of political disruption in the United States today, liberation theologians can be tolerated only at the margins. For us and our communities and networks, this poses a challenge–how shall our voices be heard? It also presents an opportunity for us to help strengthen these marginalized communities and networks while the principalities and powers of our time are looking the other way, occupied with more important business than social justice and, hence, with more important people than us.

Jesus Christ Is Born in Particular Contexts

No one image of Jesus Christ prevails among liberation theologies in the United States. This reflects the assumption that Jesus Christ literally

[11]During the fall of 2002 and spring of 2003, the Bush administration made its case for war against Iraq. Protestant church leaders of theologically/socially so-called "liberal" denominations, such as the Episcopal, Lutheran, Quaker, United Church of Christ, Unitarian Universalist, along with various bodies within Roman Catholicism voiced public opposition to this so-called "war." These church officials called it an invasion and occupation. Many liberation theologians in the United States opposed the war and spoke out through public addresses, op-ed pieces, and television appearances.

comes to life in specific contexts, times, places, and circumstances in our life together on this earth. Christic power is not an abstraction nor a spiritual power that can simply be "applied" from one context to another. Christ is rooted in particular historical situations. He is a liberator in the struggles for civil rights and in movements against racism and economic exploitation. She is an angry advocate of children who have been abused, and she is a leader in the movements for gender and sexual justice. He is our active commitment to building a sustainable ecosystem. She is our promise to make no peace with oppression of any kind for any reason.

Still, among the many varied presentations of Jesus Christ abounding in liberation theology in the United States during the last third of the twentieth century and into the twenty-first, it could be argued that three particular perspectives or images stand out:

1. Jesus Christ as Black Messiah/Liberator
2. Erotic power as christic power
3. Earth community as Body of Christ

Each of these christological images represents significant social movement and commitment in the late twentieth century in the United States of America. Each of these images of Jesus Christ is distinctly "American," a product of our collective history in the United States. For whereas liberation from slavery, erotic power, and earth community are by no means simply American themes, they have taken particular shapes as liberation theological images, shapes that are American and not, for example, Brazilian, German, Kenyan, or Korean. In each case, the image of Jesus Christ conveys not only something about a particular group's spirituality but also about the history of the particular group in the United States. It becomes clear that, for liberation theologians, theological truth is born and cultivated in real human life in the world. Liberation theologians thus speak of doing theology "from below." Let's turn now to the three contexts and see how some particular groups of people understand Jesus Christ.

The *Blackness* of Jesus

Liberation theology in the United States was born in the civil rights movement. This pre-dated the term *liberation theology* (borrowed from Latin America's *teología de liberacion*) by more than a decade. The term was popularized by the 1972 English publication of the now classic book by Peruvian priest Gustavo Gutiérrez (*A Theology of Liberation: History, Politics, and Salvation*). The civil rights movement in the United States articulated a "theology from below." Through the labor of clergy and lay leaders in the Black Church, most notably Martin Luther King Jr., God's liberating love was being celebrated as a rising social force in the United States.

King's "Letter from Birmingham Jail" is an example of liberation theology. In this piece, written to his "fellow clergymen," King presents

Jesus as "an extremist in love"(1986, 297). Throughout his life as leader of the civil rights movement, King's theological and social emphasis was on love as God's way and on non-violence as a manifestation of this divine love. Speaking in Atlanta to the interracial Fellowship of the Concerned in 1961, King urged the grounding of the struggle against racism in agapic love:

> *Agape* is more than romantic love, *agape* is more than friendship. *Agape* is understanding, creative, redemptive, good will to all men. It is an overflowing love which seeks nothing in return. Theologians would say that it is the love of God operating in the human heart. So that when one rises to love on this level, he loves men not because he likes them, not because their ways appeal to him, but he loves every man because God loves him. And he rises to the point of loving the person who does an evil deed while hating the deed that the person does. I think this is what Jesus meant when he said "love your enemies" (47).

Although he didn't identify himself as a "theologian" (a term too limited in its academic connotation), Martin Luther King Jr. was a liberation theologian who, more than any other person in the United States, sharpened the identification of God and Jesus with love. King understood divine love to be an energy for justice. Drawing on this spiritual energy, King himself emerged as a prophetic figure comparable in his own mind not to Jesus but to Moses, whom God had also chosen to help lead people from bondage to freedom. Thus, the exodus became a foundational theme for liberation theology in the United States.

In the period following the 1968 assassination of King (and the assassination in 1965 of Malcolm X), Christian theologians Albert B. Cleage Jr., Gayraud Wilmore, James H. Cone, and others continued to illuminate the theme of God's love voiced so passionately by King. Malcolm X interrogated this theme strongly , since he did not believe non-violence would lead to liberation for Black Americans. Wrestling in the tension between "Martin and Malcolm," as Black liberation theologians did throughout the last part of the twentieth century, James Cone asked,

> How then does a black Christian preacher and theologian like me understand and communicate the religious message of a Black Muslim minister like Malcolm? The most important thing we have in common was also the source of his faith: *the experience of being black in a white, racist society*.... As much as I am persuaded by the truth of the gospel of Jesus, I am equally persuaded that living and preaching Jesus' gospel in America requires the exacting test of Malcolm's nationalist critique (1991, 152).

In the decade following the deaths of Malcolm X and Martin Luther King, Cone and other black theologians de-emphasized King's focus on the universality of God's love, but they stopped short of endorsing violence as a means to achieve racial justice. Rather, black theologians emphasized the *blackness* of Jesus as liberator. In Cleage's words, Jesus was the "Black Messiah."[12] James Cone was clear from his earliest theological work, in the late 1960s, that the blackness of Christ is essential to his redemptive efficacy for black Americans. By whiteness Cone meant the enslavement of Black minds and bodies through immersion in white racist culture. Such whiteness is not only sinful; such whiteness is the "anti-Christ." Only a Black Christ can save Black people–and perhaps white people too, though Cone was not especially concerned about white people–from this "anti-Christ."

The primary contribution of Black liberation theology to the Black community and to the rest of America from the late 1960s on was that Jesus Christ is *Black*. The Blackness of Jesus Christ is not only good for Black Americans; it is good for us all. It's important to recognize, however, that despite the prominence of the assumption that Christ is Black, neither Black theologians nor most other Christian liberation theologians who work primarily in relation to racial or ethnic minority communities are concerned much with christology. In the Black Church, Jesus Christ is experienced as so central and pivotal a spiritual force that most Black theologians see little need to explain his life, death, and resurrection to anyone. In fact, most Black theologians have little to say *about* Jesus Christ; they speak and write as if their audiences assume that Jesus is Lord and that Jesus Christ is, of course, the central spiritual force in their lives as Christians.[13]

Christic Power as Erotic Power

Liberation theologians, like everyone, see truth only partially and thus have written about Jesus Christ as if his maleness were simply a fact. As Black theology developed during the 1970s and 1980s, Black women theologians like Kelly Brown Douglas and Delores S. Williams would name the sexist assumptions embedded in the work of their Black brother theologians like Cone and King. Along with other women theologians–white women and other racial/ethnic women like Ada María Isasi-Díaz and Rita Nakashima Brock–Black women theologians, some calling themselves "womanists," were clear that the Christ who lives and breathes among us today is not a man.[14] Few women or men dispute the fact of Jesus of Nazareth's maleness. But since Jesus' christic power transcends his

[12]See Cleage, *The Black Messiah;* also his *Black Christian Nationalism.*

[13]Several notable exceptions to this are Thurman, *Jesus and the Disinherited;* Grant, *White Women's Christ and Black Women's Jesus,* and Douglas, *The Black Christ.*

[14]"Womanism" is a term Alice Walker based on an old saying in the Black community, "you're actin' womanish." See Walker, *In Search of Our Mothers' Gardens,* xi-xii.

gender, no feminist, womanist, or *mujerista* liberation theologian has taught that Jesus Christ is necessarily male.[15] These women theologians have insisted that Jesus' christic power, the spiritual energy that sparked between him and others, transcends the bounds of gender just as it does race and ethnicity.

Even more than most Black and Hispanic male theologians, most women of color who are Christian theologians of liberation do not focus much on Jesus Christ in their work. This may be because, like their male colleagues, the women theologians realize the huge significance of Christ among their communities of color and assume, therefore, that the presence of Jesus Christ needs no explanation. Then again it may be, and often is, something else, as Cuban-American theologian Ada María Isasi-Díaz notes,

> In the case of Jesus...we ask, Why is it that the majority of Hispanic Women do not relate to Jesus? What does this mean about their understanding of the divine and the presence of the divine in their lives? *Mujerista* theology...often becomes a subversive act by enabling Hispanic Women to be suspicious of what we have not participated in defining (1993, 74).

Isasi-Díaz is raising an issue that goes to the heart of the concerns of most feminist, womanist, and *mujerista* theologians–the experience of exclusion, of having been left out of the shaping of traditional Christian theologies regardless of ethnic or cultural context. It is not simply a case of hurt feelings or resentment (though sometimes both apply). The problem from the perspective of being a woman in patriarchal religion is that our experiences of the sacred have not been represented historically in the shaping of Christian teachings and worship. Thus, our God-experiences, the deepest and most compelling dimensions of our lives, are rendered invisible in the religion we have been taught to practice. For this reason, Christian women theologians of liberation have refused to attempt simply to adapt to our own lives the theologies of liberation being done by men. Rather, they have boldly claimed theological authority to shape our spiritualities and our Christian religion on the basis of our shared experiences of God, Jesus Christ, and other holy matters.

This theological authorization by communities and networks of women has generated the specifically christological work of a number of women liberation theologians, including womanist Kelly Brown Douglas, Asian/Latina Rita Nakashima Brock, and my own work on Jesus Christ. Interestingly, the three of us–women who have written extensively about Christ–have also emphasized the sacred character of the sexuality and erotic power to which the Jesus story points us. In imaging Christ or christic

[15]"Mujerista" refers to Hispanic women's experience. Ada María Isasi-Díaz began to use the term in the early 1990s in her theological work.

power as erotic power, Brock, Douglas, and others of us are "transcending" (crossing over) two millennia of the dis-valuation of both women and sexuality that has been intrinsic to Christian patriarchy. Just as Black male theologians like Cleage and Cone were unwilling to accept the "whiteness" of Christ, many feminist and womanist theologians are unwilling to accept the patriarchal character of Christ.

Thus, addressing the Black community within the Christian Church, Douglas writes on behalf of sexual and gender inclusivity. She emphasizes, "By perfectly manifesting agape, Jesus' life and ministry, as the presence of God in the world, reinforce the understanding that to reflect the image of God is to do nothing less than nurture loving relationships. This, then, brings us to human sexuality" (1999, 115). Douglas proceeds to commend the affirmation of gay and lesbian Christians, much as in an earlier book she had joined Cone and other black colleagues in commending the blackness of Christ.

Brock and I, interestingly enough, working independently of each other during the same time frame in the late 1980s, connect Jesus with "erotic power." In Brock's words:

> [Erotic power is] the fundamental power of life, born into us. [It] heals, makes whole, empowers, and liberates. Its manifold forms create and emerge from heart, that graceful, passionate mystery at the center of ourselves and each other. This power heals brokenheartedness and gives courage to the fainthearted (1988, 25).

Focusing both on Jesus as presented in the gospel of Mark and on what she names the "Christa/Community" of disciples that grew up around him before and after his death and resurrection, Brock elaborates:

> [T]hrough the heart within ourselves, through the image of erotic power in our very being, we are led to liberation and to the miraculous recreation of Christa/Community by our heartfelt connection to others. Erotic power creates life in the midst of the ambiguity of existence by making heart possible (88).

Working along the same lines, I warned, "We must keep in mind...that the body of Christa cannot be, and should never become, an exclusively or uniquely christian body. Hers can be merely a christian name for the universal body of diverse people, religions, nations, and species-beings formed and reformed by the sacred and erotic power of mutual relation" (1989, 117).

To those outside the currents of feminism and womanism, it may seem odd that women of different races and cultures working in different parts of the church in the United States, would choose, almost serendipitously, it would appear, to shape our understandings of Jesus Christ around our experiences of erotic power! To understand this connection, one would need to have experienced being both female and sexual–sexual women–in the context of a woman-fearing, sex-phobic religious tradition and, in the case of womanism, the context also of white racism. To have been a feminist or womanist liberation theologian in the late twentieth-century United States is to have participated gladly in an effort to subvert and transform a racist, patriarchal Christianity that also functions pornographically–to sacralize, make sacred, sexual violence, especially against women. The Christian theological process of women's liberation will take many lifetimes of work across many cultures and gender identities.

A vibrant, fast moving tributary of this feminist movement to affirm sexual bodies has been the "LGBT"–lesbian, gay, bisexual, transgender–movement within Protestant and Catholic churches in the United States during the last quarter of the twentieth century and now into the twenty-first. The gay liberation theologian best known for his work on Jesus Christ has been former Jesuit Robert Goss:

> On Easter, God made Jesus queer in his solidarity with us. In other words, Jesus "came out of the closet" and became the "queer" Christ. Jesus the Christ becomes actively queer through his solidarity with our struggles for liberation. Jesus becomes gay/lesbian rather than gay because of his solidarity with lesbians as well...If the Christ is not queer, then the incarnation has no meaning for our sexuality (1993, 84–85).

Goss reflects on the "scandal of particularity" that characterizes all christology, but especially that done in the service of liberation:

> It is the particularity of Jesus the Christ, his particular identification with the sexually oppressed, that enables us to understand Christ as black, queer, female, Asian, African, a South American peasant, Jewish, a transsexual, and so forth. It is the scandal of particularity that is the message of Easter, the particular context of struggle where God's solidarity is practiced (85).

Earth Community as Body of Christ

Moving toward the twenty-first century, most liberation theologians in the United States were probably agreeing that our planet Earth is in serious trouble and is much in need of advocacy, solidarity, and liberation. Hence, liberation theologians increasingly are struggling with eco-justice and environmental racism. One of the first Christian liberation theologians to address these issues theologically was Sallie McFague, at the time a white feminist professor and dean of Vanderbilt Divinity School. Writing in the early 1990s, McFague spoke of God's body being shaped by the "Christic paradigm," which she defined as "God's liberating, healing, and inclusive love" (1993, 129). McFague calls the world "the sacrament of God, the visible, physical bodily presence of God." She continues, "The cosmic Christ metaphor suggests that Jesus' paradigmatic ministry is not limited to the years 1–30 C.E., nor to the church, as in the model of the church as the mystical body of Christ, but is available to us throughout nature" (182).

Another voice for ecojustice among Christian liberation theologians has been the creative work of Kwok Pui-lan, a native of Hong Kong who has spent most of her professional life teaching theology in the United States. In her passion for creation, McFague joins other Christian voices in the United States like Jay McDaniel, Daniel Spencer, and J. Michael Clark, gay and straight white male theologians and ethicists who themselves have intentionally joined up with feminist theologians as advocates for the earth and creature-kind. As McDaniel contends:

> Assuming that the divine Consciousness is Jesus-like, we cannot rest content with [an assumption] that God watches falling sparrows and flailing pelicans from a very great distance. Such a God would lack depth. Rather, we must try to understand how God's unlimited love extends even to the smallest of creatures, even to "the least of these" (1989, 23).

Theologically, these ecological liberation theologians identify Christ with creation and not merely with humans and God. It is not simply that creation is sacred or important to God. It is rather, for eco-liberation theologians, that the earth and all creatures are embedded deeply in God and that God–in her christic paradigm–reveals herself through all creatures great and small. Christ is the pelican, the sparrow, the tree, and the water, just as Christ is the subjugated human. These theologians of liberation are mindful that social justice and eco-justice are interdependent, and that racism, sexism, economic exploitation, and other forms of systemic evil contribute to, and too often require, the devastation of earth and other creatures.

Ecospirituality is, of course, nothing new to Native Americans who were, in relation to earth and creature-kind, the first liberation theologians in the Americas. Writing in the early 1970s, Vine Deloria Jr. expressed doubts that

> "the Western Christian can change his understanding of creation at this point in his existence. His religion is firmly grounded in his escape from a 'fallen' nature, and it is highly unlikely to suppose at this late date that he can find a reconciliation with nature while maintaining the remainder of his theological understanding of salvation (1973, 105).

Almost thirty years later, another generation of Native theologians would agree with Deloria's negative assessment of white religious sensibilities but would go further in suggesting that Native Christians, nonetheless, must be true to their own spiritual heritages:

> Indian Christians will want to struggle in the coming generations to understand their Christian commitments increasingly on their own terms in ways that incorporate their own cultural traditions of the sacred. The Christian Indian interpretation of Jesus the Christ will eventually differ considerably from the interpretation offered in the colonizer churches and hierarchies (Kidwell et al. 2001, 83).

Whether in Native contexts or from other Christian liberation perspectives, the christological opportunities that lie ahead are multiple and potentially creative, healing, and liberating. These creative opportunities include Christ as Corn Mother (79–83), Christ as horse (Heyward 2002, 92–104), Jesus as fully dust (Baker-Fletcher 1998, 18), and fully spirit (González 1990, 151–54); Christ as divine for-otherness. We face so many possibilities, so many truths born of experiences that are fully human, fully creaturely, fully divine.

Christ "in the Form of our Sister"

Probably the most prolific theologian of liberation in the United States and undoubtedly one of the most strongly committed to the task of justice-building has been Rosemary Radford Ruether, a white feminist professor and scholar for whom christology has been a primary interest all along. For Ruether, Christ is always being shaped by an ethic of solidarity. She maintains that "we can encounter Christ *in the form of our sister.* [She, the liberated community] is not confined to a static perfection of one person two thousand years ago. Rather, redemptive humanity goes ahead of us, calling us to yet incomplete dimensions of human liberation" (1983, 70).

Ruether's great strength as a liberation theologian has been in her ability to connect the dots, make the connections among the many structures of oppression and possibilities for liberation. She has taken on this work with courage, speaking out repeatedly on issues that were not "popular"–Christian anti-Semitism (which Ruether calls the "left hand of christology"), women's liberation and ordination within Roman Catholicism, the violence being done to the Palestinian people by the state of Israel. These are just a few of the public stands Ruether has taken as a theologian, a feminist, and a Christian activist.

What then of the future? Who will Jesus Christ be tomorrow from one liberation context to another? And how will we know? Several progressive theological movements have been growing globally and in the United States during these early years of the twenty-first century. Movements in environmental and eco-justice, queer theory, and postcolonial theology are probably the best known. One of the strongest voices for postcolonialism as well as feminism and eco liberation among Christians is that of Kwok

Pui-lan, who even as a heterosexual woman, is committed to queer theology.[16]

Might it be that Jesus Christ will become better known in years to come through the care and cultivation of trees and rivers? Through experiences of, and struggles for, gender and sexual integrity? Through advocacy of diversities of peoples and cultures? And through the decentering of any one image of Jesus Christ as the only way to God?

The terrible events of September 11, 2001, and the horrendous backlash, engineered by an unelected Commander in Chief with no moral depth or trustworthy spirituality, make dreadfully clear the stakes if the United States continues to fuel global fires of violence, revenge, greed, and arrogance. Christians who are aware of these problems and who want to act toward just and peaceful resolution are needed in the public discourse now more than ever–to embody the christic power being offered to us through

the Iraqi child who lost her legs
–is her name Christa?

the band of camels fleeing the bombs
–could they be Christ for us today?

the prisoners of "the war against terrorism" being held at Guantanamo Bay
–what if they are Jesus Christ and Guantanamo is their Golgotha?

the young suicide bombers in Palestine/Israel
–what if they are Jesus, too?

and the U.S. soldiers who yearn for peace
–do they, too, embody Jesus Christ for us today?

like the many folks who picket and pray
morning by morning and day by day
who surely are Christ for us today.
and what of the Israelis and United States citizens who love justice
and so desperately want to build peace?
Truly, they are the Daughters and Sons of God.

[16]See Kwok Pui-lan, *Discovering the Bible in the Non-Biblical World;* and *Introducing Asian Feminist Theology.* My gratitude goes out to Kwok Pui-lan for her ongoing friendship and collegiality as a sister theologian and sister professor at the Episcopal Divinity School. Her life and work are a source of inspiration to me!

3

The Holy Spirit

Elizabeth Conde-Frazier

Introduction

Liberation theologies take an inductive approach and use terms such as *experience* and *context* as their source of theology or as the *locus theologicus.* This is because the only way to comprehend God, the unembraceable Infinite, is if God reveals or unveils Godself. This revelation is historical in nature. This historical locus of theology is found in the everyday. Within the framework of liberation theologies, Christian praxis is committed to the day-to-day liberation process of people.[1] It is within this theological framework that we will give consideration to the understandings of the Holy Spirit.

I will begin by looking at the classical understandings of the Holy Spirit. These categories are employed by liberation theologians as they expand and deepen the theological understandings of the Holy Spirit. It is therefore important for our discussion to have an understanding of these categories. After this discussion, each section of the chapter will explore the understanding of the Holy Spirit in different liberation theologies. I will discuss the direct writings about the Holy Spirit whenever these are

[1] For further discussion see Dussel, *History and the Theology of Liberation*, chapter 1.

present and will explore the writings on the Trinity, in particular the insights on the third person of the Godhead. I will then explore the possibilities of an articulation about the Holy Spirit by discussing the areas of revelation, and experience.

The Holy Spirit in Classical Theology

In classical theology the Holy Spirit is the particular person of the Trinity through whom the entire Triune Godhead works in us (Erikson 1985, 846). The doctrine of the Spirit formulated at Constantinople in 381 described the Spirit as "Lord and giver of life" and as proceeding from the Father and worshiped and glorified with the Father and the Son. The Spirit was responsible for creating, renewing, and sanctifying. The Spirit was seen as performing functions that were specific to God. To follow this argument is to say that the Holy Spirit also shares in the divine nature (283).

It is also important to note that the Holy Spirit is a person, not an impersonal force. Descriptions of the Spirit show the Spirit possessing certain personal characteristics such as intelligence (Jn. 14:26), will (1 Cor. 12:11), and emotions (Eph. 4:30). The Holy Spirit is referred to as a person when we are warned not to grieve the Spirit. One can resist a force but not grieve it. The Spirit also engages in ministries that can only be performed by a person such as teaching, regenerating, searching (1 Cor. 2:10), speaking, interceding (Rom. 8:26), guiding, illuminating, and revealing.

As the doctrine of the Holy Spirit has evolved, the work of the Spirit has been understood to focus on three broad areas: revelation, salvation, and the Christian life. The Spirit has a role in how the scriptures came to us (2 Tim. 3:16). The work of the Spirit moves us toward conversion (Jn. 16:8–11), and the Spirit's work in us continues the work of transformation giving us the power to witness of Jesus (Acts 1:8). This work of conversion and transformation through sanctification relates directly to the doctrine of salvation. The Spirit's work takes place in persons as the result of indwelling the believers whereby the Spirit can then lead us into all truth (Jn. 16:14) and bring to remembrance the teachings of Jesus (Jn. 14:26). The third person also empowers believers as individuals and as the body in their Christian life and service. Augustine and Cyril of Alexandria are only two of the many who have stressed the role of the Spirit in binding together the believers in the unity of the church. The experiential aspect of the Christian life is also connected to the work of the Holy Spirit and is seen as the special domain of the Holy Spirit.

These dimensions of the Spirit will be discussed in light of liberation theologies. At first glance, liberation theologies have not said very much directly about the Holy Spirit. This seeming absence of the Spirit in liberation writings is not unlike the first centuries of the church. Liberation theologies have emphasized Christology, ecclesiology, the nature of revelation, and praxis but have not found it imperative to give direct attention to the person and work of the Holy Spirit. However, if we take into consideration the work of the Holy Spirit in the areas of revelation, praxis, and the experiential aspect of the Christian life, then we may imagine an outline for the construction of this aspect of liberation theology.

Latin American Liberation Theology

In this section I will explore the understandings of the Holy Spirit within Latin American liberation theology represented in the work of José Comblin. The perspectives of the Holy Sprit within the Trinity offered by Leonardo Boff and María Clara Bingemer will also be discussed.

José Comblin

José Comblin begins his chapter on the Holy Spirit by acknowledging that Latin American theology has not developed a specific theology of the Holy Spirit. He proceeds to speak of such a theology by departing from the basics of Latin American theology and projecting where it might go. The presence of the God of liberation is felt in the midst of the people, their actions, and commitments. Comblin names the *Dios liberador* (God of liberation) as the Holy Spirit. The *Dios liberador* does not deliver the people by the force of God's will but by the "means of the enlightenment and prophetic charisma of mighty leaders, by means of the union and solidarity of living communities and by means of the enthusiasm of the multitudes that these communities and prophets succeed in arousing." The power of the resurrection and transformation (the work of the Holy Sprit) resides in these. When one sees the collective action of the poor in the world, one can be sure that the Holy Spirit is acting. Comblin assures the reader that this action is not sheer social forces at work, but that it proceeds from the presence of the Holy Spirit (1996, 146–47). The Holy Spirit's work is seen in the experiences of historical actions toward liberation.

To understand the work of the Spirit in Latin American theology one must understand the context, because it is a spirit at work in the experience of history. Comblin describes a history of passivity for many centuries–masses of isolated individuals whose native peoples were destroyed. Their efforts to re-establish community ties have been systematically prevented. They have been deprived of the memory of the past and forbidden to imagine a future. However, the gospel accounts and the liberative action of God in the Hebrew Scriptures are the means through which the Holy Spirit breathes the birth of new action and genuine resurrection in the lives of the poor. The miracle accounts of the lame walking, the deaf hearing, the dead rising, and the blind seeing have brought persons to awareness, new consciousness to where they have been empowered to form communities (147). This takes expression in the cooperation among neighbors, meetings to take particular action or celebrations of events. These are ways that the power of the Holy Spirit is active in the people. Through them, renewed strength and initiative is restored in the people.

The emphasis of Latin American theology is on the charisms or gifts that build community rather than those that show forth only inward satisfaction but produce no outward fruit (1 Cor. 14:4, 12). It is on Jesus' promise to the disciples that those "who have faith in me will do the works I do, and greater far than these" (Jn. 14:12, author's translation). This is the superhuman strength needed to overcome the layers of conquest and total domination of the multitudes in Latin America. Such domination came not only from Latin American governments and elites but from the forces of globalization that produce exclusion, unemployment, loss of culture, identity, unequal distribution of wealth, and ecological crisis.

The Holy Spirit also transforms the people's experience of freedom from flight to participation and responsibility expressed in coming together to think, to organize, and to seek common objectives through creative struggle. Comblin names this the freedom to fight for freedom. This is the people's interpretation of freedom in the light of the Bible which includes freedom from any religion of slavery (2 Cor. 3:17). The Spirit and freedom are connected in the Gospel of John and the Pauline letters. These are the biblical passages that inform Latin American theology's understanding of the Holy Spirit (Jn. 3:6–8, 4: 23–24; Gal. 5:1, 13). Comblin suggests that those who are not poor are not genuinely free in the spirit and are afraid of freedom so that a theology of the Holy Spirit which comes from the experience of freedom, "can emerge only from the praxis of a free Christian people" (149–50).

Freedom includes the freedom to come out of the silence of fear and of the lie of the systems of domination. To speak truth is an "extraordinary impression of liberation. The word is the first expression of rebellion against domination" (Comblin 1996, 150). This is because the word is an expression of personhood and is self-assertion. It is the will to exist and an expression of dignity. This word may take form as an outcry inspired by the Spirit. This is the cry of the oppressed of Egypt, of those in exile, and of Jesus on the cross. Comblin asserts: "The Holy Spirit is at the root of the cry of the Christian people groaning in the hope of the resurrection" (Rom. 8:14–27). It is clearly the work of the Holy Spirit to produce words (151).

Within the open spaces of dissolved ties and uprootedness (migration), the Spirit creates new kinds of associations for survival. These associations resist the forces of domination with the bonding power of the spirit. It is the Holy Spirit that creates the bonds of unity for forming community. This is what births genuine community life in the crammed mines, the outskirts of teeming cities, and the rural slums. The renewal of community is what Comblin calls "a sensible sign of the Spirit in the world." The miracle of the Spirit is not only the ability to re-birth community but to found the relationships in that community upon kinship rather than domination (152).

Comblin then points out that this community is communion and that communion proceeds from charity or solidarity, the first fruit of the Sprit and the most excellent charism of all (1 Cor. 12:30–13: 13; Gal. 5:22–25). Finally, the communities created by the Spirit not only renew the shape of the church but also, the structure of society which then represents "the communion engendered of all nations by the Spirit (Eph. 2:11–22, 4:2–4)" (153).

It is the Spirit that can raise the dead (Ezek. 37) so that it is a Spirit with the power of life. The Nicaeo-Constantinopolitan creed professes "We believe in the Holy Spirit...the giver of life." Latin American theology understands that life to bear its first fruits on earth. Their hope is that the Spirit produces vital life in the people even when they are physically broken and that the people can become "vessels of the energies of the Spirit" (Comblin 1996, 154). If this is so, and if the purpose of the Spirit is to shape the world into a communion of all nations, then the Holy Spirit is active in ecclesiastical space as well as in the movements of the world itself. For this purpose, the various charisms are given to the church for its service. Comblin asserts that the church opens itself to serve the needs of all of the people. The meaning of service or Christian vocation goes beyond being an expression of paternalism by the privileged toward their victims to being the expression of the solidarity of the poor (158).

Leonardo Boff

Leonardo Boff brings a different perspective of the Holy Spirit as he writes about the Trinity. Boff begins with John Paul II's opening address to the Latin American bishops who assembled at Puebla January 28, 1979. The statement was as follows:

> Our God, in his most intimate mystery, is not a solitude, but a family. For he intrinsically contains paternity, filiation, and the essence of the family that is love: this love in the divine family is the Holy Spirit (Boff 1996, 75).

For Boff, the assertion of communion where "nothing exists only in itself and for itself" but is in relational interplay with everything else is the central understanding to be reopened from the doctrine of the Holy Spirit (75). The Trinity constitutes the prototype of the universal communion among all living beings. For Boff communion is the "first and last word of the mystery of God and the mystery of the world" (77). When we fail to act within the Trinitarian framework of communion, it affects the church at all levels as well as society. Boff claims that historically belief in a monistic god has led to oppression and injustice. Emphasis on the Father leads to monarchical and hierarchical societies. Emphasis on the importance of the Son denies the existence of the transcendent, and stress on the Spirit alone results in otherworldliness.

Within the Trinitarian mystery the person of the Holy Spirit is the unity of the divine persons. "It is the power of union within all beings." The power of the Holy Spirit irrupts into history with new things. These new things anticipate the substance of the reign of the Holy Trinity. Liberation is one of these new things. Liberation is becoming free from all that diminishes life. It is also freedom that allows differences to emerge; these are seen in the variety of gifts. The freedom of the Spirit prevents differences from degenerating into inequalities and discrimination because it maintains all things in communion. Finally, Boff sees the work of the Holy Spirit related to revelation and the authority of scriptures since it stirs our memory of Jesus by not allowing the words of Christ to become "dead Letter" but instead in their rereading the Holy Spirit helps us to gain new meanings and to be inspired to liberative practices (87).

María Clara Bingemer

Latin American feminists have made their own contributions to the doctrine of the Trinity. María Clara Bingemer of Brazil speaks of "The threefold God in a female perspective" (1994, 314–18). She points out that: "To say that God is Father, Son and Holy Spirit is not and cannot be, in any way equivalent to saying that the divine community is composed of three persons identified as male." Instead, she explains how women theologians in Latin America seek to recover the Hebrew word "*rahamin*" or womb to refer to God's love as the biblical root of the experience of God. It is the Spirit, the divine "*ruach*" who in labor of creation hatches the cosmos that brings forth the primitive chaos. The Spirit is also "sent like a loving mother to console the children left orphaned by Jesus' departure (Jn. 14:18, 26)." Lastly, Bingemer claims that the work of women doing theology is a call to bear witness to the God of compassion. She does this with her body, actions, and life (315). It reminds us that it is the Holy Spirit that gives us the power to be witnesses (Acts 1:8).

Black Liberation Theology

In this section I will show the places where the work of the Holy Spirit can be seen within the theology articulated by Black Liberation theologians. These are possible places for furthering the conversation about the Holy Spirit. I will look briefly at such places within the work of James Cone and Delores Williams.

The Origins of Black Theology

In the 1960s Malcolm X called for a new system of reason devised by those who are at the bottom. He was speaking of a system that is not from the oppressor but from the exploited (Epps 1968, 133). Black theology can be said to be such a system. This liberation has influenced persons of color in North America as well as South Africa and the Pan-African world. The founder and major leader of this liberation theology is Martin Luther King Jr. Its origins can be traced to the day Rosa Parks sat down in the part of the bus reserved for whites in Montgomery, Alabama. This led to the bus boycott from which emerged the civil rights movement. The theology emerges from the praxis of demonstrations, imprisonments, sermons, and speeches.

James H. Cone

In the world of academic theologies these speeches, sermons, and praxis of struggles toward liberation need to be placed in the form of academic theology. James H. Cone, professor of systematic theology at Union Theological Seminary in New York City, has brought together the elements that have shaped Black theology. He names six sources of Black theology:

1. black experience
2. black history
3. black culture
4. revelation
5. scripture
6. tradition

When speaking of revelation, Cone argues that revelation cannot be apprehended unless it has a concrete manifestation in the black experience, history, culture, and community. Regarding scripture, he insists that the meaning of scripture is not in the words themselves but in the power that such words have to point beyond themselves to God. For Cone, this is synonymous with pointing toward black liberation. In similar fashion, the Bible is inspired because of what it inspires us to do. Our encounter with God in the Bible inspires us to risk all for the struggle for freedom (1970, 69). In this, we can see the work of the Holy Spirit in leading one to truth. This truth leads one toward liberation.

Black theology is concerned with those traditions that can be used in this struggle. The hermeneutical principle Cone claims for Black theology is that "The norm of all God talk which seeks to be black talk is the manifestation of Jesus as the Black Christ who provides the necessary soul for black liberation" (80). The Holy Spirit manifests Jesus to us. We could say therefore that the work of the Holy Spirit can be found in the hermeneutical principle of Black theology.

Cone's work *Martin and Malcolm and America* links together three important and interlocking issues in liberation theology: racism, poverty, and sexism.[2] Cone traces the treatment that both men give to these issues. He also further defines how the two shaped their thought and work by

[2]This work brings together the biographical details of the lives of both men alongside the theological concepts and narrative of their lives and thought.

maintaining a dialectic between theory and practice. The practice consisted of the various sit-ins, demonstrations, boycotts, and imprisonments as well as the search for efficacious strategies and policies to address the struggle for justice and freedom. These practices refined the eloquent speeches, sermons, and other forms of communication of both men.

This can be considered the theory of the movement that, in turn, inspired and informed the continued practices. This dialectic is the core of theologies of liberation. Theory is refined by the social analysis of one's actions and vice versa. The place of reflection between theory and practice is where we can pinpoint the signs of the work of the Holy Spirit. The practice is the visible work of the Spirit in the world, while the theory is the work of the Sprit leading into truth.

This dialectical process was important, for it led King to expand his vision. King's vision became more global as he made connections between the freedom of the black community in the United States and the liberation of oppressed persons in the third world. He expanded the understanding of equality between blacks and whites in the United States to mean equality for all peoples of the world who are poverty-stricken and affected by the perils of war. King's links between poverty and racism caused him to assault militarism. He proclaimed the United States to be the "greatest purveyor of violence in the world today" (Cone 1991, 237). This extension of the understanding of love beyond his own community is a manifestation of the work of the Holy Spirit. As the first-century church was led by the Holy Sprit, it, too, began to extend its boundaries beyond the first group of believers. The challenges of this expansion shaped its theology. The work of the Spirit was a revolution of love.

Dr. King presented justice as the other side of love: "Justice is love correcting that which would work against love."[3] Establishing this relationship between justice and love was important as the civil rights movement began because most of the rhetoric before this emphasized love bereft of the tools of justice for carrying out that love. As the understanding of love grows into justice, protest against oppression becomes a faithful and biblical expression of Christian love as it is also a constitutional right. In this understanding of justice and in its praxis the work of the Holy Spirit is present.[4]

---

[3]Martin Luther King Jr., "Address to the Initial Mass Meeting of the Montgomery Improvement Association" at the Holt Street Baptist Church on December 5, 1955. The tape and printed copy of this address are located in the Martin Luther King, Jr. Papers, Center for Non-Violent Social Change, Atlanta. See also Cone, *Martin and Malcolm and America,* 61–62.

[4]Let us remember that during the 1940s and 1950s Christian theology had not emphasized these links. They viewed such actions toward justice as too radical.

Delores Williams

African American feminists use the term *womanist* to identify themselves.[5] Womanist Delores Williams asserts that theology of the Spirit where the locus of the Spirit's action is black women's political action. It stresses the beginning of revelation with the Spirit coming upon Mary (Lk. 1:35). This is a part of the tradition that can be traced back to Sojourner Truth, a feminist abolitionist of the nineteenth century. She confronted a preacher on the subject of equal rights for women and men by reminding him that the origins of Jesus were from God and a woman and that "man had nothing to do wid Him!" (Williams 1991, 63).

The womanists point out that "the Divine Spirit connects us all" (Williams 1991, 63). Certainly, this is true as we see Black theology reaching out to theologians from the third world. In 1976, a meeting convened in Nairobi, Kenya. The group has become known as the Ecumenical Association of Third World Theologians (EATWOT). Again, the dialectic of theory and practice is observed as the world's poor enter into political and theological solidarity with the purpose of breaking the forces of oppression.

North American Feminist Liberation Theology

In this section I begin with Catherine Mowry LaCugna's feminist doctrine of the Trinity and her discussion of the third person of the Godhead. This is to introduce the reader to an evolution of thought that births a feminist constructive theology of the Holy Spirit. Overcoming the dualisms of mind/body, spirit/matter, and male/female is a central project of feminist theology and central to the discussion of pneumatology from a feminist perspective. These themes will emerge throughout the discussion.

Catherine Mowry LaCugna

Among the North American feminists, Catherine Mowry LaCugna reformulated the doctrine of the Trinity based on the idea of persons in communion, with attention to the doctrine's spiritual, ethical, and ecclesial implications. Among the issues related to the Trinity, she discusses the question of how to address God in public prayer and the exclusively masculine imagery for God. LaCugna offers different strategies for a solution. One of these explores the concept of the Holy Spirit as feminine. This is an argument based on the recovery of Syriac materials that used feminine imagery for the Spirit.[6]

---

[5]The name *womanist* derives from Black folk culture. It describes a woman who displays willful behavior or who is in charge and serious.

[6]For further discussion, see Murray, *Symbols of Church and Kingdom;* Schaup, *Woman;* Congar, "Motherhood in God," in *I Believe in the Holy Spirit;* and Grey, "Where Does the Wild Goose Fly," in *New Blackfriars.*

Wisdom was often associated with the Holy Spirit and portrayed as a female personification of God. LaCugna sees this as a promising line of thought since the Holy Spirit is God's healing, caring, loving presence in creation and history. However, she also cautions that the Spirit's activities should not be stereotyped according to gender -determined roles for women. Another observation she makes along those lines is that according to subordinationist Trinitarian theology, the Spirit is third. To associate feminine imagery solely with the Spirit could reinforce the subordination of women in church and society (1991, 105). She concludes that a variety of images for God is appropriate because God is incomprehensible, inexpressible mystery; therefore, no one image expresses the totality of God's sacred mystery. Also, no one image or name of God may be turned into an idol (108). She reminds us that the Holy Spirit speaks through many voices and reformist movements.

Mary Grey

Mary Grey claims that feminist theology seeks to develop a theology of the Spirit as a means of redeeming the oppressive structures of patriarchal theology and church. The question she tackles is how re-envisioning the role of the Holy Spirit can reconnect the church's scriptural roots with a liberating force for the world of today. She begins to explore this interrogative by naming the difficulties of how the Spirit has been perceived. The Spirit had been contrasted in dualistic manner with the flesh. Woman has been identified with flesh and man with spirit so that the life of the Spirit is seen as more authentically male. Women, on the other hand, are identified with the physical, the bodily, and the earthy and thus with the impediment of attaining holiness associated with a spiritual life (1991, 89–90). As we follow this argument, the Spirit directs us "away from the earth to focus on all that is heavenly." This makes the material world secondary or unimportant.

The last difficulty arises from ascribing to the Spirit the female qualities of the Godhead as Yves Congar and Leonardo Boff have done.[7] Congar describes the Spirit as a mother who guides us in coming to know Father God and our brother Jesus through a communication of feeling (1983, 161–62). Boff makes a link between the Holy Spirit and Mary, the mother of God. These arguments ignore the nurturing qualities of God and Jesus. Boff's argument could reinforce the societal norm for women to bear children and assume the nurturing roles that place her within the societal pattern of obedience and passivity.

Where, then, can we turn to reap an understanding of the Spirit that is liberating to women? Grey attempts a three-pronged approach. Grey moves

---

[7]See Congar, *I Believe in the Holy Spirit;* and Boff, *The Maternal Face of God.*

to a discourse of connection–"every living system of the universe is interdependent and interconnected" (Grey 1991, 92). This she claims as the metaphor that highlights what Christian theology means by the Holy Spirit.

As she points to the places of connection related to the Spirit, Grey speaks of the image of the Spirit of God hovering over the face of the earth. The word of God in that setting has power as it "spills forth from the energy of connection and mutuality" over what had been chaotic and is now seeking living expression. Mutuality is restored to the word through the Spirit's relational energy. It is the drive to communicate, connect, relate, and to respond empathetically that gives the Word authority (Grey 1991, 93).

Rebecca Button Prichard

Rebecca Button Prichard wrote the first theology of the Holy Spirit from a feminist perspective. She uses the five senses as a central metaphor in her work. The metaphor becomes a hermeneutical scheme that she focuses on the embodied life of the Spirit. This pneumatology places attention on the created world and on bodily existence (1999, 5).

For example, Prichard portrays hearing as the image of new birth and the breath of life when we hear crying, the mighty wind, and the still, small voice, creation and word. "God's Spirit gives prophetic utterance and faith-filled hearing." When the Spirit bears witness with our spirits, it makes possible our own speech, testimony, proclamation, and praise. The spirit does not stop at words. It inspires prophetic action as well so that it is an integrating force that unites the breath of life (*nephesh*), heart (*levav*) and soul, spirit and body. This divine speech and integration are the empowerment of the Spirit. This allows her to break into oppressive history and tradition. This is sometimes done through the teachings from orthodoxy as well as from the margins (123–24).

Prichard also connects the fire of the Spirit to a zeal for justice and reconciliation. The touch of fire, God's anger kindles our passion and compassion. I want to point to the link between the Spirit's relationship to us through her indwelling and our empowerment through passion and compassion. It is passion and compassion that make our daily encounters into relationships where the "other" becomes neighbor. It is this initial transformation in our relationships from a state of alienation (other) to a sense of human connectedness (neighbor) that begins the work of justice and reconciliation.

It is not necessary to summarize the other metaphors and images that Prichard conjures for us. We can see that her emphasis is that of connectedness. Her method of theology draws from experience and embodiment. She therefore presents her theology not only through the rich layers of the metaphor of the five senses but also by drawing from the creeds and hymns of the church. These sources capture the connecting experiences of the church's *leitourgia* and *koinonia* not always reflected in theology.

Hispanic American Liberation Theology

The context that has shaped Hispanic American liberation theology has been the experiences of conquest, colonialism, migration, and biculturalism. Hispanic Americans are shaped by the experience of becoming uprooted from their culture and all personal relationships. This entails economic and social hardship. In this context a theology emerges that is different than both the mainstream United States theology and the Latin American theology of liberation. What is the place of the Holy Spirit within this theological framework? What does the Spirit have to do with salvation, justice, and the work of transformation?

Samuel Solivan

Pentecostal theologian Samuel Solivan begins to address the issues of pneumatology within a Hispanic American theology by examining the depersonalization of the Holy Spirit and her important role in affirming and empowering diversity.[8] By depersonalization Solivan means the practice of referring to the Spirit as a force, an influence, or an energy. This, he claims, serves the interests of those who would employ a divine image to further their own desires of control. Persons and groups are more easily subjected to control if one can reduce them from subject to object. On the other hand, the personalization of the Spirit in a context where Latinos/as experience being treated as non-persons can provide a "transformative model of personhood and self-esteem"(1997, 53). The Holy Spirit then empowers Latino/as as they confront the powers that dehumanize and objectify them.

The *imago Dei* is the direct linkage between the Holy Spirit and ourselves because whatever the Spirit shares with us as part of the Trinity draws us into community with the Godhead. The *imago Dei* is restored within all persons through the agency of the Spirit. In her relationship to the Godhead, the Holy Spirit reflects the personality of the Godhead. Because God as Spirit is life, human life is subject and not object (Solivan 1998, 143). The depersonalization of the Spirit also renders it impossible for a non-personal Spirit to reveal Christ who is person. Therefore, Solivan concludes that "nothing less than full personhood of the Spirit is sufficient to reflect the

---

[8]See Solivan, "The Holy Spirit-Personalization" in *Teología en Conjunto,* 50–65.

I must clarify that Hispanic Pentecostalism does not consider its beliefs, practices, and theological framework to be in complete congruence with liberation theology. However, the theologians who have come forth from the Pentecostal tradition that are featured in this section formulate their theology in dialogue with liberation theology, finding within it helpful dimensions for the formation of a North American Hispanic theology.

testimonies of the scriptures and the needs of the Hispanic community and the world" (55).

How does this understanding relate to liberation? It is the Spirit that is the bearer of the gifts of life and humanization. These are the gifts of wholeness, faith, hope, and love. These gifts have the power to overcome the work of evil. This evil is manifested in the daily experiences of suffering of the Hispanic community and all those who suffer. The gifts of the Spirit, however, empower us to restore the full humanity of all of God's creatures through her transforming power and presence. This makes it possible for the oppressed to overcome oppressive forces that work to dehumanize them. Also, to liberate the oppressor since the Holy Spirit gives power to overcome the sinful tendency to oppress others (Solivan 1998, 63).

How does this take place? Solivan addresses the matter of suffering by examining the theological paradigm of *orthopathos*. Orthopathos makes use of the two terms *ortho* and *pathos*. *Pathos* in the classical Greek understanding refers to self-alienation. Generally, it refers to the experience of suffering or anguish that can result in self-alienation. In the Latino/a context it may relate to being alienated as a result of discrimination and/or racism as well as being alienated from one's culture. In the early Christian tradition the understanding of *pathos* was self-empowering particularly as presented in the climax of the Christian message where God is the one who loves to the point of suffering. The term *orthopathos* makes the distinction between suffering that results in self-alienation and suffering that becomes a source for liberation and social transformation. It is looking for a way to transform human suffering into a resource for liberation (1993, 103).

Solivan points out that theological orthodoxy is usually uninformed by the suffering of oppressed persons and by the pathos of God. Orthopathos serves as a corrective to this by pointing to how the Holy Spirit works in and through our brokenness to bring us the benefits of Christ. Orthopathos grounds orthodoxy by addressing a different set of questions that come from the people's context of pain and suffering. This brings a different perspective to doctrinal construction. Orthopathos also grounds praxis in action. It becomes the third leg of a new theological triad bridging orthodoxy and orthopraxis. This link is a witness to the liberating power of the Holy Spirit in and through the lives of suffering people (1998, 147–48).

Solivan believes that the transformation of the suffering of the people takes place in spite of the systemic presence of evil. As such, it does not require that the structures be overcome first in order for our pathos to be transformed. Once the power of the Holy Spirit is manifested in the persons who had been suffering, their weakness is transformed into power for liberation. This power takes the form of the hope of overcoming the structures of evil in our society. It is this hope that empowers persons' gifts and persevering strength for carrying out the work of structural transformation. This is why Solivan argues that conversion is an early stage of praxis. It serves as a catalytic agent for change. It is the process of being empowered in the inner person by reconnecting with God and self that further empowers a person for praxis. Praxis involves reconnecting with the neighbor through relationships that reflect justice. Thus, "the orthopathic event of conversion sets in motion a series of other conversions which move us toward God and our neighbor" (145).

María Pilar Aquino

Latina feminist María Pilar Aquino speaks of the importance of *lo cotidiano*, the everyday life as a source of theology. She claims that it is in *lo cotidiano* that we experience the salvific experience of God here and now in our "daily struggles for humanization, for a better quality of life and for greater social justice."[9] In liberation theology, experience is a source for theology. *Lo cotidiano* is where we will go to trace the work of the Holy Spirit. *Testimonios*, or the stories of our faith experiences, reflect a dimension of *lo cotidiano*. In them, we observe how the work of the Holy Spirit has proven to affirm the tradition as well as reform it. On the side of reforming the tradition, *testimonios* have led the Hispanic American community of faith to re-evaluate and expand its theological understanding pertaining to political involvement toward social justice. The testimonies of women in particular have shown how the Holy Spirit moves in them through the movement of compassion turning it into passion for healing the wounds of their communities. In another writing I have commented on this:

> The courage and creativity in a woman are a strength that comes from seeking God in her struggles and finding her voice in prayer. The moans and groans of the Spirit in and through us become a power of social action or justice. Our passion in prayer is informed by meditation and Bible study. This has been the way that women have dared to hold beliefs that differ from some of the traditions of their communities of faith...about the forms of ministry. When theology has dichotomized the religious and the secular, the world and the church, women's experiences have led them to understand the scriptures in a way that prophetically moves us to go beyond those boundaries. We have sat on boards and organized the community; in short, we have taken political action. The Holy Spirit has been the one to lead us and empower us (1997, 140–41).

Harold Recinos defines testimony as a knowledge system that "meaningfully integrates social experiences and historical events in lives that are ongoing and always raising questions about the role of God in human affairs. They are reminders to take seriously the thought and life-struggle of

---

[9]See Aquino, "Theological Method in U.S. Latino/a Theology," in *From the Heart of Our People*, 39. *Lo cotidiano* is the Spanish term used for the everyday.

Latino/as" (2001, 123). The Holy Spirit brings us to all truth–the truth of "suffering and oppression in the context of political belief" (128). This truth takes the traditional symbols and biblical texts and gives those suffering subversive power in relation to hegemonic social contexts. The work of the Holy Spirit brings persons from innocence to awareness–conscientization. Conscientization is the work of the Holy Spirit leading one to the truth of one's situation and thus to an understanding of one's call or to action in that situation. The communal action is the mission of the church. This awareness re-shapes biblical understandings of death as structural injustice and life, or resurrection, as the struggle toward humanization and freedom.

Conclusion

Liberation theologies have brought out the life-giving aspects of the Spirit. In these aspects reside the power of resurrection and transformation. These theologians have emphasized the Spirit's work of bringing one into truth and into connectedness and mutuality for the purpose of creating communion and building community. This is important for transforming domination, marginalization, and dehumanization into freedom and life. The Spirit also empowers the oppressed so that agency, speech, and political action become a part of their daily experiences. Her work is seen in the bringing forth from innocence to awareness (conscientization) and in the dialectic between theory and practice.

4

Trinity

Luis G. Pedraja

God as Trinity: A View from the Margins

Solidarity is an important theme in theologies emerging from the margins of society, expressing the belief that God stands with us and is for us. Through our readings of the prophets, we get a sense of God's solidarity with the poor and with those who suffer under the burden of injustices. However, while the voices of the prophets show God's concern for us, the Incarnation shows God's full solidarity with us. The Incarnation is the difference between speaking on behalf of those at the margins and living in solidarity with those at the margins. Through the Incarnation, God stands with us as one of us, becoming vulnerable to the same forces of violence and oppression that we face. Both the Incarnation and Pentecost bring God to us.

The doctrine of the Trinity is at the heart of our understanding of God as being for us. It is where we truly can begin to speak in a doctrinal sense of God as our God–as the One who comes to us and becomes part of our history. It is also central to most Christian faiths and particularly essential to marginalized groups (African Americans, Latino/as, etc.), where Pentecostalism and our unique understanding of Jesus play critical roles in the way we understand God. At the same time, it is necessary to acknowledge that not all Christians believe in the doctrine of the Trinity, including some

Pentecostals. Likewise, it is also necessary to recognize that while the scriptures speak of God in triune ways, they make no mention of the trinity per se.[1] So why is the doctrine of the Trinity important to us? It is important for what it signifies to us.

Our basic understanding of God as triune comes not so much from philosophical interpretations–those would come later–but from the way people experience God. At its core, the doctrine of the Trinity comes out of human experience. Through it we understand that we must ground even our understanding of God in the ways in which we experience God as human beings. In that sense, the doctrine of the Trinity expresses doctrinally how it is that God has and continues to come for us. It also ruptures any attempts we may make at reducing God into a fixed definition, forcing us to contend with the mystery of unity and plurality in our understandings of God (Boff 1988a, 2–3).

The early church had to contend with a unique set of circumstances in its understanding of God. They had come to understand Jesus as divine, as God's revelation manifested in the flesh. At the same time, their faith in Jesus was grounded to a great extent in the Hebrew faith, with its strong monotheistic beliefs in Yahweh, the one true God. Jesus spoke of Yahweh in parental terms, redefining the relationship between God and humanity in terms of parental love. But Jesus and Yahweh were clearly not the same person. When Jesus prayed, he did not pray to himself. To compound the problem, Jesus spoke of the Holy Spirit, whom the disciples had experienced as the indwelling of God in their lives. How could they preserve their monotheistic faith and acknowledge the different ways in which they had experienced God? Thus the early church formulated the concept of the Trinity to address these issues as a way to understand how these experiences of God are connected. At the same time, the male imagery inherent in the articulation of these experiences through the doctrine also presented us with some difficulties that are still difficult to avoid. Marginalized groups like Latino/as, Asian Americans, Amerindians, and African Americans are not exempt from the domination of such language, and more often than not use male imagery in speaking about the Trinity. In expressing the classical arguments, I will use the traditional terms commonly used to avoid confusion. But we need to remember that the terms are primarily an expression of relationship and not of biology or gender.

Trying to Understand God: Traditional Approaches to the Trinity

For us to comprehend the complex problem presented by Trinitarian language, we need to take a brief look at some of the history of this doctrine. To understand their threefold experience of God and the Trinitarian

[1] Note Justo González's account of the biblical use of Trinitarian language as early as Paul's epistles (1 Thess. 1:2–5) and in the baptismal formulas (Acts 8:16), (1990, 102–3).

language of scripture, the early church turned to philosophy for help. While the problems inherent in understanding how Jesus' humanity and divinity could coexist with each other led to the christological controversies, the problem presented by the Trinity was in trying to understand how Jesus' divinity related to the monotheistic God of Israel, the one whom Jesus called Father.

Jesus as Logos

At the heart of the controversies lay a common problem–relationships. But underlying the problem of relationships was an even more significant problem. How could something as frail, changeable, and limited as human nature be in any way connected with all the philosophical and theological preconceptions of a powerful, immutable, limitless God? The problem underlying both the Trinitarian and christological controversies that affected the early church was rooted in reconciling preconceptions of God with the actual ways people experienced God in history. The solution came by linking Jesus to the *logos* or word. This connection allowed the church and theologians to move away from some of the problematic aspects of the Incarnation–dealing with the historical reality of a flesh-and-bone human being who was subject to changes and passions.[2] If these problems regarding Jesus could be resolved, understanding the Spirit as God was then fairly easy since the Spirit was free of such problematic entanglements.

Averting Tritheism

However, the emphasis on the three distinct ways of speaking about God raised the fear that it would lead to tritheism, the belief in three gods. Thus, preserving the unity of God was an issue of great concern to the earliest theologians.

Monarchianism

At times, their zeal for protecting the unity of God led them to err in the opposite direction, failing to recognize any diversity in God. For instance, some proposed to preserve the unity of God by asserting that the three manners of experiencing God were simply three ways or modes of experiencing the same reality, the one true God. This was the position chosen by Monarchian Modalism that was accepted by many, including several popes, that would later be deemed heretical (Rusch 1980, 11). While Monarchianism and other forms of modalism sought to preserve monotheism, they did not recognize any differences in the persons. Each

[2]González argues that with the equation of *logos* with Jesus in the gospel of John, it became possible to delve into philosophical understandings of Jesus without necessarily having to deal with some of the more complicated aspects of Jesus' humanity and historical reality, thus bridging the gap between biblical revelation and classical philosophy (1990, 104).

person was merely a name by which we referred to the same God. However, this went counter to the language of scripture, which seemed to indicate a distinction. After all, some would ask, was Jesus just talking to himself when he prayed to the Father? And why would Jesus speak of the Spirit as another whom he would send? Why not say that he was the one coming?

Adoptionism

Others, argued that Jesus was merely human, adopted by God or a prophet in whom God's spirit dwelt, thus solving the problem by denying Jesus' full divinity. For instance, the Ebionites, with roots in Essenian Judaism and Judaizing Christianity, maintained that Jesus was a prophet or an angel. Adoptionism, sometimes called dynamic Monarchianism, believed Jesus to be adopted by God and indwelt by the Holy Spirit. Others would argue that Jesus was simply a prophet (González 1970, 122–126).

Arianism

On the other hand, some attempts to achieve a balance between unity and diversity verged on tritheism. One prevailing way of understanding the problem of the Trinity was Arianism, named after Arius, its leading proponent. Arianism made a clear distinction between God the Father and Jesus the Son. They argued that if Jesus came from the Father, as the only begotten Son, then the Son was "generated" (*genetos*) while the Father was "ungenerated" (*agenetos*). Hence, according to Arius and his followers, the Father had to be greater than the son, for only the Father was ungenerated, which was deemed as better by order of priority (was first) and necessity (was not derivative). In other words, they assumed that Jesus coming after and from the Father made him substantially different.

Naturally, to arrive at this conclusion, Arius made some assumptions. First, underlying Arius's view was a tacit and unquestioned assumption that God was impassible, and hence Jesus' suffering could not belong to God (LaCugna 1991, 34–35). He also assumed other categories of Greek philosophical thought, such as the belief that perfection meant that God was not subject to change, something that Jesus was subject to as a human being. The result was a hierarchical understanding of the Trinity that made Jesus and the Holy Spirit subordinate to the Father and hence, lesser deities of a different nature.

Subordination, however, was not the main problem of Arius's teaching–subordination was widely accepted in the church until the middle of the fourth century and might even be substantiated by scripture. The problem was that he argued that the natures were different (LaCugna 1991, 23–24). This was problematic for the church and for its understanding of salvation. That the One who suffered with us was indeed God was essential to the church's understanding of salvation. As we will see, it is especially important to those of us who live at the margins of society and who identify with

Jesus, because we know that through Jesus' suffering, God can understand our own suffering.

In the course of history many approaches to understanding the Trinity, including those mentioned above, were branded as heretical. This does not necessarily mean that they were inherently evil and wrong. I believe they were honest attempts by Christian thinkers at understanding the mystery of God. But, they did miss the point. They left something out leading to other problems. Thus, the church rejected them. They had failed to capture what God meant to us. Yet many of these views still prevail in different forms throughout some strands of Christianity and among individual believers throughout our churches.

The Origins of Orthodoxy

Tertullian

Astonishingly enough, the earliest attempt at articulating a doctrine of the Trinity came out of a heretical group. Tertullian was the first to introduce the Latin term, *trinitas.* Arguing against the Monarchian modalists at the end of the second century, Tertullian, a lawyer by training, articulated a doctrine of the Trinity framed in terms of one divine substance in three persons. This became one of the most enduring and prevailing ways of understanding the Trinity in the Western church. Yet Tertullian, at the time he framed this doctrine, was a Montanist, a member of a radical group eventually deemed heretical! That goes to show that, sometimes, even heretics get it right.

The term "substance" in Tertullian's argument is that which stands (*stance*) under (*sub*) the appearances and particularities of something, making it what it is. That is, substance is the nature or essence of something that makes it what it is. For Tertullian, the substance of all three persons of the Trinity is the same divine nature.[3] At the same time, each person has a different mode of being. This is not the same as saying they are three different Gods. They were three different expressions or manifestations of the same divine nature. To put it in more philosophical terms, the divine persons subsist as specific expressions or modes of being God (determinations), circumspect and defined by their relationship to one another, while the relationship preserves the unity of the divine substance.[4] This divine substance they share is what makes them God.

The distinctions come not in terms of their divinity, but in terms of their work and relationship to us and to one another. In his writings, Tertullian often used illustrations that compared the Trinity to the sun (Father), ray of sunshine (Son), and the warmth of the sun (Spirit). The three were distinct experiences of the same reality. They were also different in terms of their function, just as the spoken word is different from the

---

[3]Note Rene Brauns's argument regarding Tertullian usage in *Deus Christianorum,* 175–76.

[4]I develop this argument further in my dissertation, *Infinity in Finitude,* 34–36.

word of reason that exists within us, as expressed in another of Tertullian's illustrations (1959, 134–150).

The Greek Church

However, while this way of understanding the doctrine of the Trinity has prevailed, it did not resolve all the problems. Tertullian's Latin terms did not quite translate to the Greek-speaking churches in the East with the same level of clarity. The term "substance" translates directly into the Greek as "*hypostasis,*" *hypo* (under) and *stasis* (standing), but is closer in its meaning and use to the Greek "*ousia*" or essence. The Greek use of *hypostasis,* although etymologically meaning the same as *ousia,* came to be used in a way that was closer in meaning to Tertullian's use of person (Rusch 1980, 16). At the same time, another Greek word, *prosopon* ("face"), is the literal translation of person into the Greek. Why this confusing vocabulary lesson? Because it shows the difficulties theologians in the early church faced as they tried to understand the Trinity.

The Cappadocians and Nicaea

It took the Cappadocians and the Council of Nicaea to defeat the Arians and establish the most commonly accepted doctrine of the Trinity. The Cappadocians included Basil, his brother Gregory of Nyssa, and their friend Gregory Nazianzen, possibly with a little help from Basil and Gregory's sister, Macrina. They emphasized the relational nature of the Trinity. According to the Council, the three persons of the Trinity were different persons, but all three shared the same substance or essence. The answer laid in understanding that the distinctions came through their relationship with one another and to us, not in their underlying essence.

Later Controversies

Yet, even then, other controversies split the Christian church. These included the *filioque* (and the Son) controversy regarding whether the Spirit proceeded from the Father **and the Son** (*filioque*)–accepted in Rome and the West–or whether the Spirit proceeded from the Father **through the Son** as was accepted in what became the Eastern Orthodox Church.

Modern Options

The problems inherent in our attempts to understand the Trinity still persists, as people continue to try to comprehend this complex mystery. In recent years, our approach to the doctrine of the Trinity has changed from a starting point in divine unity–and I might add, its assumptions about God's nature–to a starting point grounded in our experience of the three persons.[5] Today, the language of static substances and essences means little

[5]See Stanley Grenz's assertion regarding this movement and his warning against the dangers of falling prey to tritheism in *The Social God and the Relational Self,* 50–51.

in a society driven by scientific research that speaks of quantum physics, subatomic particles, quartz, fields, energy, and superstrings. Quantum mechanics presents a world where particles exist in interrelated manners, interacting with one another even at great distances, and functioning both as a wave of energy and as a material particle. Such a worldview can provide many rich models and parallels for articulating a doctrine of the Trinity, but that is beyond the scope of this essay.

Similarly, terms like "person" now carry a variety of meanings, including psychological concepts far removed from the original intent of the framers of the doctrine. Even parental relationships mean something else in an age of cloning and alternative family structures. Today, Trinitarian language is turning to relational and dynamic models, social and economic paradigms, and scientific definitions of systems and organisms to make sense of this complex doctrine. We who live at the margins are also lending our own perspectives, while still incorporating some of the traditional and new approaches to understanding how God is for us.

Perspectives from the Margins

Ultimately, when we speak of the Trinity, we must speak of our experience of God from a human perspective. While we may speculate about the nature of God, the ontological or immanent Trinity, our only insight into God is through God's work in human history and in our salvation.[6] However, as human beings, we inhabit different contexts that may affect our perspective. To put it simply, one single, monolithic, human perspective does not exist. Our interests, our socioeconomic location, power issues, limitations, and other factors influence our perspectives. Hence, while we may agree on certain aspects of God's self-revelation in history, how we interpret God's saving work and God's self-communication will vary depending on our particular perspective.

But our limitations and unique perspectives are not a detriment to theology. Each of these perspectives has something unique to contribute to how we understand God. As we explore each perspective, our theology and our understanding of who God is and how God is for us becomes richer and fuller. For those of us living at the margins of society, who endure cultural, economic, or sociopolitical oppression in different ways, the perspectives often take on different shades from that of those in positions of power and dominance. The perspectives here are by no means an exhaustive list of perspectives from the margin. Yet each perspective

---

[6]LaCugna uses Rahner's axiom to establish the unity of the economic and immanent Trinity from the perspective of God's economy of salvation. But whether we argue that the two must be identical or not, the key to both Rahner and LaCugna's arguments are that we inevitably must start from how we as human beings experience God to try to understand the Trinity (1991, 211–25).

provides a unique insight into the doctrine of the Trinity and into our understanding of God.

The Trinity as Community

Living in community is central to many of us who live at the margins of society. Although often rejected from the dominant structures of their broader communities, ethnic and racial groups at the margins draw strength from their immediate communities and families. Because of the rejection they experience in society at large, the sense of belonging felt in their *barrios*, ghettos, neighborhoods, faith communities, and families offer an oasis from their marginalization and a place for renewal. By understanding the Trinity in terms of communal relationships, those living at the margins of society cannot only find parallels with their experience, but can discover a sense of belonging as part of God's community.

To speak of the Trinity in terms of community means we understand God as being relational in nature. In this sense, the Trinity discloses to us that God's very being is relational and communal in nature. Relational models of the Trinity seem to abound today, which might give us a false impression that this is a new perspective on the Trinity. However, understanding the Trinity and God in terms of relationships has been around for quite some time.

The relational nature of God is at the very core of the Doctrine of the Trinity. When we speak of the Father and Son, we are using analogical language that refers to God in terms of parental relationships. As the Cappadocians, such as Gregory of Nyssa, argued effectively, the terms we use for the Trinity reflect God's relational nature, preventing us from thinking of one without being forced to think of the other (Vol. V, Bk. I:14). Even when Augustine illustrates the Trinity in terms of lover (Father), beloved (Son), and love (Spirit), the nature of the illustration again is one based upon relationships (1997, 232). Today, the relational nature of the Trinity continues to appear in the works of Karl Barth, Eberhard Jüngel, and others who see God's nature as being relational by virtue of God being for us. Even the very possibility of God speaking to us, of God's word coming to us, reveals God as one who comes to us and exists in relationship with us (Jüngel 1983, 140–53, 285–86, 370).

Called to Be in Community

If the Trinity reveals to us a God who is relational and communal, then we can affirm several things about God and humanity. First, we can affirm that because God is relational in nature, we too must be in relationship and in community as created in God's image. Just as God seeks out others and enters into relationship with others, our calling as Christians is to develop new relationships and to enter into community with others, not merely with those who are the same, but also with those who are different. Only in this manner can we truly reflect the nature of the Trinity. We are called to exist in community with others. When we reject others from our community simply because they are different from us, as often happens, we also reject God's call for us to exist in community. This means we reject the image of God.

Affirming the Value of Relationships

Second, understanding the Trinity as relational affirms the value of communities and relationships, countering trends toward isolation, detachment, and self-sufficiency that seem to permeate dominant cultures, academic practices, and our present ethos. We often imagine God as self-sufficient, existing in isolation. Yet both the scriptures and the doctrine of the Trinity present us with a different way of seeing God as one who exists relationally. While sin breaks relationships, alienating us from God and from others, God seeks reconciliation and the restoration of relationship with us. As Trinity, God does not operate as a self-sufficient individual person. Each person of the Trinity does not function as a separate and discrete entity or divinity–something that would inevitably lead us to tritheism. Rather, God operates cooperatively and through relationships to bring forth our salvation. God is not God in isolation. God's divinity is grounded in the full dynamic of relationships and interrelationships that form the Trinity, making divinity a reality found in a dynamic cooperative relationship. This way of thinking about God is not just an intellectual exercise that helps us peer into the mysteries of God. The Trinity as a community also serves as a model for our own communities, both in society and in our faith, a model that we are called to follow.

Offering Hope

Third, for those of us who live at the margins of society, disenfranchised and rejected by dominant communities, seeing the Trinity in terms of community offers us a hope. Liberation theologians argue in favor of understanding God as one who stands in solidarity with the disenfranchised and rejected of society. Thus we are able to identify with God through Jesus, who, like us, lived in a marginal community and suffered rejection. Jesus, who was displaced by society, makes a place for us in God's communal life.[7] Hence, we find a greater community beyond our own immediate communities. There we are accepted, vested with value, and find our ultimate belonging as we are bonded to the triune God through Christ and through the communion of the Holy Spirit. Through this bonding, we can be called children of God. The rejection of the dominant community becomes circumspect and suspect by our initiation and acceptance into the community of God.

---

[7]See chapter 5 of my book, *Jesus Is My Uncle,* where I argue about Jesus as not finding a place outside of death and rejection, but also as the one who prepares a place for us.

The Trinity as Divine Immanence

Our participation in the life of God and our ability to understand the Trinity in terms of relationships and community allow us to understand the Trinity in a second way that is relevant for those of us living at the margins of society. Typically, theologians speak of the Trinity as "immanent" to argue that it is essential to God's being. However, there are other ways to speak of an "immanent" Trinity from our perspective in the world. According to Alfred North Whitehead, the doctrine of the Trinity was one of the greatest philosophical innovations offered by Christianity because it pointed to a mutual immanence of God in the world that was lacking in Platonic metaphysics (1933, 168–69).

Both in the particularity of the person of Jesus and in the presence of the Spirit, the doctrine of the Trinity seems to favor God's direct immanence in the world. Rather than understanding God as distant and removed from the world, the divine immanence revealed in the Trinity allows us to understand God as one who is near us, inhabiting our world and connected to our lives.

At times, philosophical arguments and misguided views of God's holiness have erected barriers between humanity and God. Our efforts to guard God's sanctity or to develop logical philosophical arguments of God as unmoved, unchanging, and perfect separate God from a world perceived to be somehow inferior to the spiritual reality of God. These efforts have led us to develop many problematic ways of understanding God and our relationship to the world through false dualisms and hierarchies that place the spiritual divine realm in contrast to the base material world of the created order. This split between the sacred and the profane, the spiritual and the material, often has led us to abuse the environment, exploit nature, and reject our physical embodied reality as human beings. Furthermore, at times, oppressors have used these hierarchies and dualisms to justify their subordination of women and minorities as being more tied to the less spiritual, material world.

Within U.S. marginalized groups, as well as in many other Two-Thirds World perspectives, the opposite is true. In our communities there are strong sacramental tendencies that tend to see the world as sacred and filled with divine presence. When we begin to understand the Trinity in terms of divine immanence, not just as the mutual immanence of the persons in each other as part of life of God, but as reflecting God's immanence in the world, our attitude changes. If God can indwell humanity, not only in the particularity of Jesus, but in the fullness of the Holy Spirit present in us as well as in all creation, the dualities and hierarchies that distance us from God and justify our exploitation of creation are shattered. The whole of creation becomes infused by God's Spirit, and the distance between God and creation collapses. The Trinity not only helps us see how we are interconnected with God and with one another, it also helps us see how all of creation is connected to us and to God.

The Trinity not only brings us into relationship with God, it brings God into relationship with creation, investing us and the world with sacredness by virtue of God's presence. God dwells in our midst and in the midst of all creation. Because we can no longer separate God from creation and from humanity, we can no longer justify our exploitation of either. This becomes an important element for those who exist at the margins of society and who are subject to oppression. The sacred nature of all creation forces us to reject our exploitation and rape of nature and of humanity. The immanence of God revealed in the Trinity not only bridges the distance between us and God, but it also invests all of us and all of creation with value, dignity, and sacredness.

The "Economic" Trinity

Typically, when we speak of the "economic" Trinity, we refer to the Trinity as understood in terms of God's saving work in relation to humanity, usually used in contrast to the traditional understanding of the "immanent" Trinity. However, there is another way to speak of the Trinity in terms of economy. In speaking of the Trinity in his book, *Mañana,* Justo L. González takes a different and more literal approach to the notion of the economic Trinity. According to González, the very same theologians who argued in favor of the Doctrine of the Trinity in the fourth century also argued against economic injustice. Citing such figures as Ambrose, Jerome, Basil, and Gregory Nazianzen, all advocates of Trinitarian doctrine and staunch critics of greed and economic injustice, González begins to make a correlation between economic justice and Trinitarian language (1990, 112–13).

González continues by citing Bishop Christopher Mwoleka in Tanzania. Defending socialism, Mwoleka makes the simple statement that rather than viewing the Trinity as a puzzle or mystery to be solved, we should take the Trinity as a model to imitate (113).[8] The Trinity helps us to see God not just as relational, but also as one who shares divinity and power with others. God's nature is to share. This, both González and Mwoleka contend, is what the Trinity is all about. It is about sharing.

God reveals to us how to live with one another and in God's image by calling us to engage in a life of sharing. The communal nature of the early church as exemplified in the Book of Acts also points us in this direction. What the Trinity reveals to us is a God who exists by sharing both power and divinity. If God does not hoard power, then neither should we hoard power. If God shares the very property of divinity and if the essence of the divine is in sharing with others, then should we not live in the same fashion? Obviously, this has a very significant impact on issues of economic justice.

Rather than being driven by greed and the maximization of capital, as is the case with our society today, God calls us, as Christians, to live by

---

[8]See also Anderson and Stransky, eds., *Mission Trends no. 3,* 151–52.

sharing with others. In such instances, economic injustice can never be tolerated. Taking this model seriously, even power must be shared, destroying all structures of dominance and oppression. God's sharing does not stop with any one characteristic. God is the God of life, but also the one who gives life. God is the God of love, but also the one who loves us. In a way, this view shows us how we are to live in community through sharing.

Trinity and Power

The Trinity also serves another important function. By its very design, the Trinity is iconoclastic in nature. Just as Gregory of Nyssa shows us that Trinitarian language prevents us from thinking of the Father without also thinking of the Son, it prevents us from fixating on one way of thinking about God. When we think of God as the infinite and transcendent creator, we must also think of God as a finite human being who lived among us and died on the cross. But then, we must also think of God as the Holy Spirit who is in us and indwells all of creation, binding all things together. Yet, God is also other, transcending all creation. As a result, the Trinity prevents us from settling upon only one way of understanding who God is, forcing us to recognize that no single perspective or way of thinking about God is sufficient by itself to express and contain our understanding of God.

This becomes important for all of us who live at the margins of society for several reasons. Those who hold the venues of power in society and dominate us, often would have us think that they alone possess the sole understanding or definition of God. Typically, these ways of talking and thinking about God tend to equate God with the structures of power and domination or to portray God in terms of the patterns of dominant culture. However, the Trinity, if taken seriously, counters these tendencies. No single culture, social group, or race has the inside track on God. By the same token, no single perspective can ever capture the totality of God. Only through sharing our different perspectives and engaging each other in dialogue, can we hope to enrich our understanding of God.

The iconoclastic nature of the Trinity means God destroys our beliefs and traditions. This has significant implications for our understanding of God and human power structures. Our power structures tend to hold claim to an identification of the dominant structure with the divine. Many centuries ago, this would have been exemplified by royalty who claimed a divine status, as was the case with the Caesars in Rome. Later, it would be exemplified by royals who claimed to be appointed by God. In our more recent history, it has been exemplified by nations claiming a divine mandate, such as the U.S. doctrine of Manifest Destiny in the nineteenth and twentieth centuries.

Today, while we definitely do not have a shortage of politicians and figures who claim a divine mandate, there are other ways that we fall prey to these tendencies. Often, we claim an alignment between the structures of domination and goodness. Other times, we claim to be combating evil. We create different forms of civil religion that associate our way of life and culture with Christianity. Yet, in all these ways, we lift our way of understanding God over others. In the end, we use our understanding of God to justify our repression, domination, and oppression of those who espouse different views. But we fail to see that this is ultimately just another veiled form of idolatry. The doctrine of the Trinity as iconoclastic calls our assumptions into question and forces us to contend with our idolatry.

The Trinity, in terms of sharing, relation, and as iconoclastic, forces us to steer away from simplistic hierarchical notions of power that place one structure or one person over others. Arianism sought to interpret divinity in terms of a hierarchy of power. But this was rejected as heretical. In its place we find a doctrine that is not hierarchical in nature. Each person of the Trinity participates in divinity fully. While preserving their distinct functions, they continually share in the power and nature of God. Our current structures of power, dominance, and oppression stand in direct opposition to our understanding of God as Trinity. Rather than power over (dominance), we need to reconfigure our ways of understanding both God and our own structures of power in terms of sharing–that is power with (empowerment).

Diversity and the Trinity

Finally, the Trinity helps us see God exemplified not as sameness and totality, but in diversity. We who live at the margins of society are constantly forced to conform and adapt to the structure and worldviews of others who have power over us. Our own values, cultural expressions, and contributions are negated, rejected, and dismissed. Even in theology, our contributions often are taken to be less valuable, less academic, and less significant than those made by dominant theological perspectives. However, the Trinity points us in a different direction. Rather than dismissing diversity and the values of their unique contributions to the whole, the Trinity helps us to see that in diversity we find God. To be made in God's image means that we are made diverse. Only through our sharing and relating with one another can we ever fully attain the image of God we were created to bear.

When we understand that God is love, the Trinity immediately makes sense. Love always exists in relationship with another. Love also continually shares and gives to others. Love does not hold one view over that of the other. Love celebrates diversity. The power of the doctrine of the Trinity is that it reveals to us God as love. In love, God creates. Because of God's love, God seeks to be reconciled with us. God comes to us because of love and binds us through love. At the heart of the doctrine of the Trinity is God's nature as love.

5

Church

STACEY M. FLOYD-THOMAS

The Church Here and Now: Critical Reflections

The Church is often referenced as an indecipherable entity because there is no such thing as "the Church" *per se* but rather individual churches. When the Church is conceptualized as a whole or collective, this definition more than likely is constituted from majority cultural experiences and normative understandings. While this may be the usual practice in popular and academic discourses, such an assumption is true only when one makes an almost exclusive identification of the "church of the majority" as the subject of any discourse about *the Church* (capital C).[1] Implicit in this assumption is the belief that the lives and faith communities of marginalized persons are only quaint diversions but never the central substance of a description of the Church.

[1]For the purposes of this essay, when the phraseology "the Church" is used, it is intended to reflect the body of Christians who live according to the manifestation of God's will. In other instances, when the lower case is used ("the church"), it is merely referring to the mundane notion of religious believers who identify as Christians without regard to their Christian living *per se.* "The church of the majority" references those who use the religious authority of this institution to further a social agenda that runs counter to the expressed will of God as illustrated in the life of Christ.

It is important to repudiate this fallacy because this very orientation fosters the cultural captivity of the Church and leads it away from its prophetic role in human history.[2] My contention is that viewing the practices and experiences of communities of faith of the disinherited as the normative exemplar of the Church provides a very different picture. As Black liberation theologian James Cone puts it, the prophetic role of the Church is to be "called into being by the power and love of God to share in his revolutionary activity for the liberation of [humankind]" (1993, 67). This is a picture that sees the Church as being both the refuge of the weak and the salvation of the strong in need of repentance. This is crucial to understanding American historical foundations and everyday realities within contemporary society.

This chapter presents an overview of the Church from the perspective of the marginalized as historical and theological agents who have imbued the revolutionary activity and prophetic role of the Church called by God. What follows is an analysis of the Church in America as an institution, its meaning and crucial moments in United States history, and its present-day development through paying particular attention to dynamics of marginalization and oppression.

The Etymology and Theology of the Phrase "the Church"

Etymology

The word *church* is derived etymologically from two Greek words–*kyriake*, "belonging to the Lord" and *ekklesia*, "assembly." Thus, when merging the meanings of these two words together in its literal sense, the phrase, "the Church" represents the identification of a people who are called together by God for the fulfillment of a divine purpose. This purpose has most often been scripturally identified in the tradition as *the Great Commission*:

> Go therefore and make disciples of all nations, baptizing them in the name of the Father and of the Son and of the Holy Spirit, and teaching them to obey everything that I have commanded you. And remember, I am with you always, to the end of the age. (Mt. 28:19–20)

The Missionary Dimension

This missionary dimension of the Church has been at the core of its self-identity from its New Testament origins. Implicit in this commission is the command to pattern the life of the Church and its members after that of Jesus of Nazareth. This bears great significance not only for the confessional component of Christian faith but also for the material reality of its existence. The gospels give extensive witness to the works of healing,

[2]See Niebuhr, *Christ and Culture.*

feeding, and nourishing the dispossessed as being central to the ministry of Jesus Christ. Because of this, the Church needs to account for this essential part of its identity based on the work of "making the wounded whole" (Thurman 1981, chapters 1 and 5).

Theologically speaking, the Church has operated according to three key functions:

1. preaching of the gospel (*kerygma*), that is to profess God's triumph over the wickedness of the world without fear or vacillation
2. service (*diakonia*), that is a level of praxis that insists that the Church take an active and fervent stance in defiance of societal condemnation and oppression of the "least of these"
3. Christian fellowship (*koinonia*) that identifies the Church as a community called by God

Taken together, these three functions of the Church portray a vision of the Church that roots its very life and identity in "bringing good news to the poor, release to the captives, recovery of sight to the blind, freeing the oppressed, and proclaiming the acceptable year of the Lord" (paraphrase of Lk. 4:18–19). In sum, the Church as a community called by God must embody and reflect the gospel that it is called to preach in the world in word and deed.

The Lack in Today's Church

The Church is supposed to be a unified, holistic institution committed to *kerygma*, *dianonia*, and *koinonia* that inspires Christians with a liberating gospel that coincides with its granting of solace as well as a sense of ultimate concern. Measured against this standard, the contemporary mainstream church, "the church of the majority," in America is woefully lacking.[3] Unlike the Church that took shape in the New Testament (namely the Matthean form of Christianity), the modern church in America is more representative of the social and cultural identity of the nation's racial and ethnic majority than it is of any sort of religious conviction or sensibility.[4] It is largely rife with denominational, ideological, and demographic schisms. It has not only been aligned with, but also complicit in, the domination of the weak and disadvantaged. Clearly this is not consistent with the best aspirations of its theology as a community gathered around the memory of the One who gave His life for the marginalized and the disinherited (Gutiérrez 1984, chapter 6).

---

[3]See Tillich, *Theology of Culture.*

[4]See Cone, *A Black Theology of Liberation;* according to New Testament scholar Gerd Theissen, the New Testament Church found in Matthew (also known as Matthaen Christianity) seeks to be the fulfillment of an ethic of "better righteousness"–one that exceeds the sociocultural traditions of the scribes and Pharisees–standing out from the homogenous Jewish culture and the pagan milieu (170).

To faithfully witness to the spirit of that One, the Church in its mission must interpret and understand the world from the perspective of individuals who might be deemed as "the least of these." Only when such a realization is made does the true meaning of the Church come more resolutely into view.[5]

The Church in America as a Paradox

For many African Americans, Latina/os, and women of all races, the experience of being a part of the church has been paradoxical. The church has been an institution that fosters and empowers as it simultaneously denigrates those outside of the majority. Thus, the church is inextricably bound to personal, spiritual, and political empowerment as well as disenfranchisement and marginalization. It is out of this peculiar tension that notions of what the church *is* and what it *can be* is formed.

On the one hand, the church at its best gives witness to the sustained relationship between oppressed people of the world and God, thereby actually becoming the Church. Herein, people who otherwise have been classified as "other" find that in the solidarity of Christ's crucifixion and death and their participation in the power of Christ's resurrection, they are made new creatures. As God glorifies the risen Christ, and in so doing vindicates the ministry of salvation for the disinherited as exemplified in Jesus of Nazareth, so also does God give assurance to the disinherited of every age that neither their lives nor their suffering will be in vain. With that assurance comes the promise that no power nor system nor person will ever be able to finally separate them from the love of God in Christ Jesus in whom is grounded their identity as persons and children of God (Rom. 8:38).

On the other hand, the church can serve as an oppressive force that may provide ideological justification for inegalitarian and hierarchical structures of power along the bases of race, gender, class, and sexuality. Although the Bible contains no narratives that seek to negate the full humanity of any person, postbiblical interpretations of specific biblical narratives seek to indoctrinate. Such interpretation sacralized racism, sexism, and classism, to name a few social ills, as predetermined and inalterable systems ordained by God.[6] These adopted interpretations called for the justification of enslavement, women's silence and submission, the eradication of indigenous belief systems that ran counter to European modernist sensibilities. These interpretations together have culminated in contemporary stereotypical aspersions about blackness

---

[5]See Moltmann, *The Church in the Power of the Spirit.*

[6]See Felder, *Stony the Road We Trod.*

as a curse (Gen. 9:18–27), femaleness as inferior (Gen. 3:16; Eph. 5:22),[7] and poverty as a mark of God's disfavor (Mt. 26:11).[8]

Three Critical Junctures of the Church

In the face of this paradox, marginalized people have reached for a spirit of liberation from the crucial meaning and potential life of the Church. In so doing they have created theologies of liberation and strategies of church-building in challenging their own oppression. In the following, we will examine the Church in three critical junctures:

1. the Church as invisible institution
2. the Church in the face of *kairos*
3. the Church as power of change, which maps a way for dismantling the paradox and reconciling the church of America back to the Church that God intended

Herein, the marginalized serve as critical agents of change. They exhibit the "revolutionary activity" that has liberated not only them but also has begun to take on a new prophetic role that can even help the "church of the majority" to move away from its past practices of colonialism and into the spirit of liberation.[9] What we will discover in these movements is not merely a prophetic challenge to the "church of the majority," but rather "the Church" itself being inhabited and embodied by the marginalized.

The Church as Invisible Institution

Although the United States has proclaimed itself to be historically founded upon Judeo-Christian principles, much of the nation's political, economic, and social schema operates in ways that directly obscure any link between the sacred and the secular. The lives of many Christians have been defined by marginalization, discrimination, and inequality. Despite the popular notion that the United States exists as "one nation under God," several oppressive structures–most notably racism, sexism, and class privilege–create seemingly impenetrable barriers within the "church of the majority." Having been denied the opportunity to engage in Christian fellowship on the basis of race, gender, and/or class, countless believers had to develop their own sites and means of Christian worship that are commonly ignored by their privileged white male counterparts. Borrowing the notion of the "invisible institution" from the African American experience, one begins to imagine how people who have been excluded from the formally recognized body of the Church (the enslaved, women, the poor, the terminally ill, prisoners, etc.) and even denied the label

[7]See Ruether, *Liberation Theology.*
[8]See Ray, *Do No Harm.*
[9]See Gutiérrez, *A Theology of Liberation.*

"Christian" must struggle to create a community of Christian faith that exists separate from the dominant society.

The Origin of the Invisible Church

For example, at the height of American slavery, enslaved Africans were prohibited from being baptized or participating in any Christian services throughout the South under fear of severe punishment and even death. Faced with such grave odds, growing numbers of enslaved Black preachers and congregations risked all to gather beyond the watchful gaze of slave masters and overseers to celebrate the life and teachings of Jesus in the "brush arbors."[10] While still in the throes of inhumane bondage, the enslaved held on to a faith that helped them transcend the wickedness, horror, and despair of this world as well as imbued them with the promise of liberation in the coming Kingdom of God.

African Americans have found great solace and strength in the gospel that formed the basis of the invisible institution. Even as African Americans made the long, traumatic transition from slavery to freedom, they sensed a great resonance between the enslavement of Blacks in the New World and the bondage endured by the Israelites in Pharaoh's Egypt. Moreover, the plight that Black Christians underwent in their walk with Christ could be likened to the fear and suffering the early Christians experienced in the New Testament. Nevertheless, in the midst of such ostensible oppression, the Church as "invisible institution" for Black Christians also offered dignity, strength, and liberation to the enslaved years before they had physical and legal freedom. In spite of the hatred, bigotry, and alienation that gave rise to the "invisible institution," enslaved people embraced the gospel's true intent and rejected interpretations stemming from the "church of the majority" that contradicted the genuine mission of the Church. The invisible institution engaged in praise, worship, prayer, preaching, and bearing witness in times and spaces beyond the controlling gaze of dominant society. By so doing they provided a means by which the oppressed and downtrodden could lay claim to a vision of the Church that would sustain them despite the adversity of this world.

The Legacy of the Invisible Church

The example of the invisible institution made in the "brush arbors" of slave plantations teaches a lesson to all other forms of the church. As long

[10]See Raboteau, *Slave Religion.* The term "brush arbors" has also been used interchangeably with the term "hush harbors" or "bush arbors." Here, as African American religious historian Laurie Maffly-Kipp, author of *African-American Religion in the Nineteenth Century* (Chapel Hill: National Humanities Center, Univ. of North Carolina, 2000) states in an online article, the invisible institution as "hush harbor" is "[p]art church, part psychological refuge, and part organizing point for occasional acts of outright rebellion...these meetings provided one of the few ways for enslaved African Americans to express and enact their hopes for a better future."

as the "church of the majority" stands alongside the wealthy and powerful to maintain the *status quo*, the poor and disadvantaged will always need an alternate forum in which the lives of the marginalized are reaffirmed and their faith is restored. Although it emerged out of the historical subversive actions of enslaved Africans, the invisible institution remains an accurate metaphor to describe many modern efforts to expand and redefine the meaning of the Church. Yet God still calls women, African Americans, Latina/os, and other marginalized groups within the Church today to continue such invisible efforts.

In this regard, invisibility today takes on two dimensions. In the first instance, whether by cultural conditioning or conscious choice, the "church of the majority" does not see the existence of women, African Americans, Latina/os, and other marginalized groups in church. In the second instance, the marginalized and their efforts toward the radical act of "Church-building" are acknowledged but are deemed as commodities for mass popular consumption (for example, sacred music of the Black church as entertainment) or as quaint ornaments and resources for edifying the "church of the majority" (such as women financially supporting the church). What is rendered invisible in both scenarios is the Spirit of the Church that is moving through these marginalized faith communities. This Spirit is moving in organizations like Black denominations, women's concealed gatherings, and the popular religiosity movement of Latina/o America to redeem the "church of the majority" from idolizing race, class, and gender and rescue it from its acts of apostasy.

The Church, now made evident in the experience and witness of marginalized persons and their faith communities, consists of the gathering of the faithful remnant into communities of sustenance and resistance. From the "hush harbors" of African Americans ensnared in the abomination of chattel slavery to the concealed gatherings of women in church pews, kitchens, and missions, a consistent witness goes out to the work of the Spirit in the face of institutional unfaithfulness. What these communities and gatherings demonstrate is the continual intervention of the Word as truth in the midst of oppressive ecclesial formations and scriptural interpretations.[11] Their witness is a continual reminder that the promise of Christ's constant presence is not a *carte blanche* authorization of any institutional church but rather a commitment to gathered communities who live in the power of righteousness and justice.

The Church in the Face of Kairos

America's colonial history is important in understanding *kairos* as a God-given moment of grace and opportunity for freedom that challenges

[11]See Schüssler Fiorenza, *But She Said;* and *Discipleship of Equals.*

humanity to take decisive action (McAfee Brown 1990, 3). The entry into the new world on the part of the European settlers was a *kairos* moment afforded to those who sought new opportunity or fled persecution from the "church of the majority" on European soil. However, during this moment, European colonial societies largely set out with a decisive action to enslave Africans and dispossess Native peoples from their land. They saw this as sanctioned by God, having no regard for the consequences that would ultimately ensue. Coupled with military force, the hegemony of Europeans in large part was underscored by religious justifications.

The Church and Enslaved and Indigenous People

Although the earliest European settlers used Christianity to legitimize these unjust systems of oppression, they had no intention of introducing Christianity to the Native peoples and enslaved Africans. Such a thought was generally deemed either futile or dangerous. On the one hand, attempts to convert Native people or Africans to Christianity were deemed sacrilegious. Europeans had to uphold the predominant belief that nonwhites were primitive, uncivilized brutes bereft of souls to maintain the legitimacy of their colonizing oppression.[12] By embracing such a pejorative, racist outlook, the Europeans and their descendants in the Americas sought to enact policies with religious zeal. These ultimately resulted in an absolute campaign of genocide, oppression, and exploitation that has continued for the last five centuries in the Western Hemisphere and elsewhere around the globe. On the other hand, other European Americans thought the spread of Christianity among the indigenous and enslaved populations of North America was dangerous. Members of these groups might get the notion that freedom (Gal. 5:1) and equality (Gal. 3:28) in Christ also included freedom from enslavement and from imperial domination.

Some Catholic missionaries chose to initiate contact with the Native peoples of North America during the Colonial era. But only with the rise of the Protestant Church–especially the Baptist and Methodist traditions–did a branch of the church regard the conversion of indigenous and enslaved people as a glimpse of salvation, not for themselves, but rather for the enslaved and indigenous populace. However, even these Protestants did not aim at the formation of an integrated community of witnesses.

This new American church arose in the wake of the Revolutionary War, after breaking free of the Church of England (Anglican Church) and resisting the possible resurgence of the Roman Catholic Church. It became inhabited by a cadre of rugged frontier preachers who fervently embraced evangelical doctrines and praxis rather than the strict and rigid air that

[12]See Raboteau, *Slave Religion.*

pervaded over many "high church" congregations in the more established areas of the eastern seaboard. Even with these fervent evangelists, the thought of Christianizing "slaves" or "natives" remained a volatile issue in the United States. A Christian gospel that espouses the liberty, equality, and dignity of all humans before God was basically at odds with the emerging political-economic order of the United States that was sustained by the horrific bondage of African people and the murderous conquest of Native territory. Such policies resulted in decimating the cultural legacy of both groups.[13] Even with the best of intentions, the Church that arose in the early days of the American Republic did not speak out against such an array of societal injustices in any systematic or uniform fashion. This silence resulted in the continued degradation and suffering for the men, women, and children who are the heirs of the enslaved and conquered groups.

Seeds of Church Renewal

Ironically, such a tragic encounter also bore the potential seeds for the renewal and resurgence of the Church in unprecedented ways. The worship practices along with the belief and ritual systems were introduced to sustain the status quo and further oppress people of color, women and the indigent alike. Such practices as reading the Bible text and singing sacred songs led to more than the "church of the majority" expected. Subversion and reinterpretation of these sacralized symbols and systems occurred. Through syncretic practices, historical and theological agency was enacted. Syncretism, the fusion of two or more beliefs, was the means through which the marginalized could build a new church, though unbeknownst to the oppressor, that would seek to liberate them from their oppression.

A Road to Reconciliation?

One might ask if there is any possible way to reconcile the "church of the majority" with those who are marginalized into a more unified body of Christ. Such a feat is possible, but it depends most squarely on having the majority come to terms with how they have betrayed God's will. The Spirit of *kairos* provides an opportunity for the "church of the majority" to repent from its acts of idolatry and apostasy. In both its visibility and its invisibility the Church–inhabited and embodied by the marginalized–offers itself as a mirror that reflects the distortion of the "church of the majority." In this reflection, the "church of the majority" can see a special opportunity in time, a *kairos* moment. In this moment God offers them an opportunity that demands a soul-searching response in action. *Kairos* is not *chronos*– "ordinary time," an everyday opportunity, nor a chance happening. *Kairos,* as theologian and ethicist Robert McAfee Brown notes, is "the time of

[13]See Butler, *Awash in a Sea of Faith.*

Jesus" wherein the divine can be experienced within humanity by God extending to humanity the choice of salvation (1 Jn. 1:6–10) (1990, 3).

The "church of the majority" at this moment appears to be in a state of cultural captivity. But in such moments God can step in to *chronos* (our time) and evokes a *kairotic* transformation (God's salvific time). In its pratices and allegiances, the "church of the majority" can now decide not to be identified as a cult of its particular society but rather as a community of witness to the crucified and risen Christ. Put another way, "the church of the majority" can undo what history has seemingly wrought by reconciling itself to a form of emancipatory historiography wherein wrongs can be made right through collective redemptive action (Cannon 1996, 81; Harrison 1983b, 249). The "church of the majority" may join those whom it had marginalized and become inhabitants of the Church. In so doing the "church of the majority" will find it no longer sits astride the steed with Saul but in solidarity with Stephen (Acts 7:54–8:3). That is, the church will no longer collude with the mores and values of the dominant political, economic and social power structure to the detriment of the will of God and marginalized peoples.

This *kairotic* moment in the context of the United States would bring the church to realize that from its very beginning the American church has only episodically expressed sympathy for the poor and downtrodden. This was done only when it was deemed advantageous. Instead, the church has opted to collaborate with mercenaries and conquerors for dominion of the New World. What should have been "the Church" was actually a community given to its own idolatry. The church was complicit in the exploitation, enslavement, and in some cases extermination of certain men, women, and children, particularly those of color, deemed inferior by the so-called civilized powers. The church faces this *kairotic* moment. If the "church of the majority" cannot seize this salvific moment and decisively act in accordance with the liberation of the gospel, it may well find itself suffering the repeated consequences of its idolatrous past.

The Church as Power for Change

The final and eschatological moment in the life of the Spirit in the Church is the Church's full realization of its calling to be advocate and nurturer for the dispossessed. This realization means, of course, the material well-being of the poor. It also invites the church to repent with the promise of salvation to those who have been beguiled into the temples of the "church of the majority." Far from being a simple vision of a church of "social action," what I am offering here is a vision of the Church in which the spiritual nourishment and material well-being of all of God's children are inextricably bound as the ends of the Church. In other words, the Church here is seen as the "spring of Living Water" for both the body and the soul at which the lion (the oppressor) and the lamb (the oppressed) can lie down in peace with each other and experience the glory of Lord (Isa. 11:6). It is in this moment that a true religious revolution occurs within the Church because the tradition of social sin no longer appears relevant to present day experiences and practices.[14]

In our own day and time, we can envision the formation of churches that offer safe haven and solace to women of all backgrounds, African-Americans, Hispanics, Native Americans, Asian Americans, the working poor and underclass, gays and lesbians, the disabled, the elderly, the incarcerated and the untold scores of other people who have been left disaffected by the modern church. Whereas the Church once rendered such people invisible by marginalizing and persecuting them, the contemporary church in North America must now reckon with its past wrongdoing in order to achieve its higher purpose.

The extent of racism, sexism, classism, and other social ills present within "churches of the majority" and their social teachings has demanded that liberation theologians declare that the Christian church is not found where injustice exists. Thus if a church does not condemn the racist, sexist, and classist injustices that exist within society as "sin," its structure and practices have ceased to be related to the gospel. As many liberation theologians have stated, liberation takes place when preachers and congregations communicate God's love in the face of marginalization, understanding that God's plan places no one in the margins. The Church that is truly Christian does not accept suffering and oppressive systems. It preaches freedom, works for liberation, and represents the reality of the gospel. It does not merely hope for a better heaven; the truly Christian church strives to make a difference in the here and now.

[14]See McFague, *Metaphorical Theology*.

6

Anthropology

ANDREA SMITH

James Cone has argued that one of the fundamental distinctions between liberation theology and more mainstream theologies is that mainstream theologies concern themselves with the "nonbeliever" whereas liberation theology concerns itself with the "nonperson" (1984, 151). That is, liberation theology strives to concern itself with the anthropological concern of doing theology within a capitalist, racist, and sexist society in which some peoples (particularly poor people and people of color) have been deemed "nonpersons" undeserving of basic human rights. Rather than focus on "true propositions about God," Cone argues, liberation theology must focus on "concrete, oppressed human beings" (1986, 82–83). Furthermore, the focus is not on a universal humanity, but on those specifically oppressed by racism. "The basic mistake of our white opponents is their failure to see that God did not become a universal human being but an oppressed Jew, thereby disclosing to us that both human nature and divine nature are inseparable from oppression and liberation" (85). Or as Harold Recinos puts it: "Today, to be an adherent of Christ means enabling organized society to see the results of its own system of oppression in the barrio" (1996, 185).

Englebert Mveng further develops this framework with his concept "anthropological poverty," which signifies the "despoiling of human beings not only of what they have, but of everything that constitutes their being and essence–their identity, history, ethnic roots, language, culture, faith, creativity, dignity, pride, ambitions, right to speak" (1983, 220). Mveng's anthropological poverty includes racial, economic, and cultural analyses of poverty.

Not only has the West ravaged the economic resources from Africa, but it has ravaged its cultures as well. Furthermore, by identifying Black Africans as subhuman, the West has robbed them of their dignity and self-respect. This anthropological poverty is inclusive of political, racial, and economic pauperization, but also includes religiocultural poverty (220). The despoliation of cultural and community values makes socioeconomic revolution impossible. Both Cone's concept of the "nonperson" and Mveng's concept of "anthropological poverty" provide helpful reference points for analyzing the anthropological approaches of U.S. liberation theologians. This chapter cannot do justice in representing the vast number of U.S. liberation theologians, but will draw on a few from diverse backgrounds and approaches to illustrate some key issues in liberation theological anthropology.

Anthropological Poverty and The Politics of Remembrance

U.S. Black people have suffered severe forms of cultural impoverishment. Deprived by enslavement of their indigenous roots in Africa, most Black people have no knowledge of their original tribes, languages, or cultural practices. Through the trauma of slavery, they have developed a culture that draws upon African motifs. In formulating theologies, Black theologians attempt to draw upon the distinct cultural patterns of Black communities. Cone states: "For I contend that our rebellion against a European mentality should lead to a second step–namely, to an affirmation of our own cultural resources" (1983, 238). Consequently, Black and womanist theologians often draw from a variety of cultural resources–literature, spirituals/blues, and art–to counter the anthropological impoverishment of white theology.

Sources for Liberation Theologies

Many writers rely on literary sources and folk traditions. These include Delores Williams, Cheryl Gilkes, Dwight Hopkins, and Katie Cannon.[1] James Cone and Cheryl Kirk-Duggan do extended analysis of Black spirituals/blues as a source for theological reflection from Black liberation and womanist perspectives.[2] An interesting direction in this effort is Will

---

[1]See Cannon, *Katie's Canon;* Gilkes, "A Conscious Connection," in *Embracing the Spirit;* Williams, *Sisters in the Wilderness;* Hopkins, *Shoes That Fit Our Feet.*

[2]See Cone, *Spirituals and the Blues;* Kirk-Duggan, *Exorcising Evil.* For theologians utilizing cultural expressions of their communities for theological reflection, see Douglas, *The Black Christ;* and Mitchell, "Women at the Well," in *Embracing the Spirit,* 167–78.

Coleman's *Tribal Talk,* in which he attempts to situate his voice in conversation with his plethora of cultural sources rather than allow his voice to subsume these sources. His literary approach mirrors the cultural framework he is attempting to articulate.

> Indeed I have played many (compressed) rhetorical games along the way by juxtaposing my own voice within and around those of African storytellers (the griots), African American former slaves, Euro-American and African American cultural anthropologists, recorders, and editors who have likewise interpolated their voices into the give-and-take of history and fiction, fact and fancy, narrative and trope. This is what constitutes "poly-rhythmic" ways of "telling the story" of the African/American religious journey into the Americas. Many voices speaking at the same time, from different, even conflictive, perspectives, nevertheless also constitute a "beat" (2000, 193).

Critical Use of Sources

Some womanist theologians, however, have cautioned against an uncritical reclamation of culture, arguing all cultural practices must be assessed for their complicity in sexism and other oppressive practices. Williams, for instance, argues that it is important not to romanticize African cultural practices (1993, 193). She argues: "African sources will be of little value to African-American theologians if they are basically androcentric and female-exclusive" (153). Her words pose an important challenge: how do we develop theologians who reclaim cultures that have been erased and colonized, while at the same time, maintain a critical lens toward tradition, or at least toward how tradition is remembered, so that this remembrance does not reify sexism, homophobia, and other forms of oppression.

Unlike African Americans, Native Americans have access to many of their specific cultural practices. Even so, the cultures that remain have been severely "impoverished" by colonialism through the process of anthropological poverty. About sixty-five Indian languages are expected to disappear by 2010, and with them will go the cultures of which they are a part. Consequently, many Native Christian theologians, such as Steve Charleston, William Baldridge, George Tinker, and others have attempted to reinterpret the Bible and other Christian doctrines within indigenous frameworks.[3] As will be discussed in the next section, these attempts have,

---

[3]Charleston, "The Old Testament of Native America," in *Native and Christian,* 68–80; Tinker, "Spirituality, Native American Personhood, Sovereignty, and Solidarity," *Native and Christian,* 115–31; Baldridge, "Toward a Native American Theology," *American Baptist Quarterly,* 227–38; and Kidwell, et al., *A Native American Theology.*

in turn, been criticized by other Native scholars for simply enabling Christian imperialism. Tinker himself notes this tension when he states: "in the final analysis, however, the historical experience of colonization and conquest may continue to make any use of Jesus problematic for American Indian people" (1998, 17).

Although more indigenous people today are trying to reclaim their traditions, it is a very difficult process, given the extent to which Indians have been colonized by Western education and Christianity. Native activist Lakota Harden speaks to the difficulties of remembering tradition within the context of colonization:

> And so, in trying to piece together our history, and our stories, and our legends...because we're so Americanized now, we're so colonized now...it goes through the colonized filter, comes out changed. So how much of the tradition was really originally ours; how much of it was already Christian-influenced, already Calvary influenced, already dominant culture influenced...Because in my own process and learning about being a traditional woman–women didn't carry the pipe and women didn't...I really look at a lot of this, and question how much of that was really our culture, how much of it was because Christianity influenced to us to say women shouldn't do this, or shouldn't do that...Knowing the way women are now, how could we accept less? How could we let ourselves be ignored or degraded, or whatever.
>
> And I remember at our school, all us kids and everybody was preparing and we had a sweat lodge in our backyard. Our backyard was huge, the plains. And I remember the boys one of the boys, women can never carry the pipe. And now I realize that all comes from Christianity. Women never used to do this or that...And I remember feeling very devastated because I was very young then. I was trying to learn this. I was quite the drama queen and going to the trailer and my aunt was making bread or something. Auntie, this is what they're saying. She said, well you know, tradition, we talk about being traditional. What we're doing now is different. When we talk about trying to follow the traditions of say, our ancestors from 100 years ago, it's probably different from 300 years ago. If when the horses came and we had said, oh we don't ride the four-legged, they are our brother. We respect them; we don't ride them. Where would we be? Hey man, we found those horses and we became the best horse riders there ever were, and we were having good winters. So tradition is keeping those principles, the original principles about honoring life all around you. Walk in beauty is another interpretation. Respecting everything around you. Leave the place better than you found it. Those were the kind of traditions

> that we followed. But they change as we go along, as long as they stay in tune with that. So that's all, she told me that story.
>
> And in a few minutes, then I went back to a roomful of guys, and at that time part of picking up that pipe, you don't drink alcohol, you don't smoke marijuana, you don't take drugs, you don't fight with people, you don't abuse anyone. And I was really was trying to follow that because that's what my uncle taught me. So I went to the middle and I said I want everybody here who is following the tradition, who has given up the things I just named to stand here in the circle with me? I said until this circle is filled with men, when it's filled with men, I'll do something else. I'll learn how to make fry bread, but until then, there has to be someone standing here doing this, and if you're not going to do it, I will.[4]

Her words speak to how the sexism of Christianity influences how Native traditions are remembered. In addition, the notion that one can be a spiritual leader without changing one's behavior (by continuing to drink, do other drugs, etc.) is similarly Christian-influenced. This attitude reflects a Christian view of spirituality in which belief is more important than practice. Indigenous traditions, however, actually place a higher value on practice–and on practice throughout all of one's life. Thus, living one's life in a good way is central to Native spiritual traditions; it is not something one does only in ceremony. As Vine Deloria Jr. notes, Native religion is "a way of life rather than 'the proper exposition of doctrines'" (1977, 16).

Removing Humanity from the Theological Center

In addition, another important contribution Native theology makes to the project of theological anthropology is questioning the centering of humanity in theology. This is because indigenous worldviews do not privilege human (or "anthro") experience over the experience of other beings in creation. Terms that privilege humans–anthropology, humanism, etc.–often tend not to have much currency in indigenous circles. As Tinker states, "all in the circle are of equal value....A chief is not valued above the people; nor are two-legged valued above the animal nations, the birds, or even trees and rocks" (1994, 126). Consequently, Native theological anthropology questions its very conceptual framework. States Kidwell:

> Theological anthropology is concerned with defining the human person as a religious being. For Native Americans, the intimate relationship with the natural environment blurs the distinctions between human and non-human. Human beings are not the only people in the world...We must move beyond the Christian tradition of humans as unique creations of God to the idea that the world of persons is embracing (2001, 86).

---

[4]Lakota Harden, interview by author, Rapid City, S.D., 13 July 2001.

Resisting Cultural Assimilation

Because *mestizo* culture in United States has been suppressed, resisting cultural assimilation has also been a primary concern for Hispanic/Latino/a theology (Elizondo, 1983b, 53). Consequently, many theologians such as Elena Olazagasti-Segovia, Jeanette Rodriguez, Ana María Díaz-Stevens, and Orlando Espín focus on popular religiosity, art, and literature as theological sources.[5] Ana María Pineda further argues the importance of not only relying on written source, but on oral traditions of oppressed communities (1996, 104–16). Otto Maduro and Ada María Isasi-Díaz employ social science approaches to communicate with community members directly as a theological source (Maduro 1996, 151–66). For instance, Isasi-Díaz uses meta-ethnography as a way of including women at a grassroots level in the development of mujerista theology. She interviews Latinas from different communities in the United States about their lives and their spiritual practices and then draws from their interviews generative themes for mujerista theology.[6]

Virgilio Elizondo argues that Hispanic culture has "been able to blend harmoniously–without the elimination of either–the ancient religious traditions of the Americans with the traditions of western Christianity that started to arrive here in 1492" (1994, 63). Elizondo and many of the Latino/a theologians do not focus on learning indigenous languages or cultural practices and often depict indigenous practices as "ancient religious traditions of the Americas" rather than as contemporary cultures. This tendency has made Native scholars such as Ines Hernandez-Avila (Chicana-Nez Perce) suspicious of the claim that *Mestizaje* is not destructive of indigenous cultures, and has led her to call *Mestizaje* a "colonizing" discourse directed against indigenous people.[7] If *Mestizaje* is truly concerned with preserving "the ancient religious traditions of the Americans," then why, asks Hernandez-Avila, do so few mestizos know anything about indigenous cultures other than Aztec, Mayan, or Incan? Why is the language of *Mestizaje* Spanish or Portuguese rather than an indigenous or African language? Where are the efforts of mestizos to recover these languages and cultures in more than a general way? In *The Future is Mestizo*, Elizondo writes:

> As we came to know, appreciate, and make our own the mystically dynamic tradition and heritage of Spain, we could hold our heads up with great pride to be descendants of these noble pioneers of

[5]Olazagasti-Segovia, "Judith Ortiz Cover's *Silent Dancing*," 45–62; Díaz-Stevens, "In the Image and Likeness of God," 117–133; and Espín, "Popular Catholicism," 304–24, all three in *Hispanic/Latino Theology*.

[6]See Isasi-Díaz and Tarango, *Hispanic Women;* and Isasi-Díaz, *En La Lucha*.

[7]Ines Hernandez-Avila, "On Our Own Terms: Critical/Creative Representations by Native American Women," paper presented at the 1995 American Academy of Religion conference.

> the development of the human spirit, of the protection and purification of our Catholic faith, and of the great codes of international law. Being the children of Iberians and natives and discovering ourselves to be neither conqueror nor conquered, but the children of both, gave complete new meaning and direction to our present situation (1988, 43).

But what about indigenous people who are not "both conqueror or conquered" and who are still the targets of systematic genocide? Moreover, does claiming "with great pride" the colonizing spirit of Spain enable mestizos to stand in solidarity with indigenous people who refuse to be Catholic and who are still victims of the colonial spirit? If the future is Mestizo, will indigenous cultures find respect only if they choose to mix openly with the dominant cultures? These are difficult questions to answer, since he depicts Native cultures only as tributaries to Mestizo identity and fails to discuss their relationship to the indigenous peoples of today.

Oppressed as Oppressors?

Hispanic/Latino theologies raise a vexing "anthropological" question: Can the validation of one oppressed culture lead to the further impoverishment of another? The problem is especially apparent around issues of language. As Elizondo states, language is a primary site of oppression for Latinos in the United States "Because our past and our language have been denied by the dominant English-speaking culture of the United States, we have been made to feel as if we were an illegitimate people without a right to exist!" (55). To the indigenous people of South America, however, Spanish is the colonizer's language; Mestizo governments of the south have long attempted to destroy indigenous languages by forcing Natives to speak Spanish. At the same time, many indigenous people in North America internalize the anti-Spanish attitudes of the dominant culture and feel little or no solidarity with their indigenous brothers and sisters from the south. The slogan, "For indigenous people, there are no borders," seems to apply only to the First Nations of Canada; for the indigenous people of Latin America, the borders are often stronger than ever. Sadly, it was a Native person who spearheaded the proposition 187 campaign in California. It seems that an identity that is oppressed in one context may be the oppressor in another.

Attempting to do justice to these complexities, writers, such as Fernando Segovia, Yamina Apolinaris and Sandra Mangual-Rodriguez stress the importance of colonialism as a central point of analysis within Latino theology.[8] Theologizing from an actively colonized nation, Puerto Rico,

---

[8]See Segovia, "In the World but Not of It," 195–217; and Apolinaris and Mangual-Rodriguez, "Theologizing from a Puerto Rican Context," 218–39, both in *Hispanic/Latino Theology*.

affords Apolinaris and Mangual-Rodriguez in particular the opportunity to make linkages with similarly colonized indigenous peoples in the Americas within a contemporary context. Gloria Ines Loya further suggests that in addition to celebrating its "diversity," "Hispanics [must] really look into the darkness [sic] of *mestizaje*, the violence of the process of miscegenation characteristic of their life experiences....What is at stake here is not only what happened five hundred years ago, but also what is happening today: ongoing experiences of discrimination and domination" (1992, 129). Her pejorative use of the term *darkness* is not helpful for a dialogue between mestizos and their "darker" indigenous sisters. However, her attention to both the past and present violence involved in the contact between European and indigenous cultures provides an opportunity to address the conflicted relationship between indigenous people and mestizos. As oppressed cultures fight the legacy of anthropological pauperization, they must not presume that their efforts will always find support among other oppressed people. Certainly this issue requires further dialogue.

By centering the experiences and analyses of communities rather than abstract propositions of God in the theological enterprise, all of these projects counter anthropological poverty. In addition, these approaches have the further effect of potentially transforming the theological project from an individual project to a collective project. This focus recognizes that theology, most particularly a theology of liberation, cannot be done by one person, but must be done in community in order to inspire collective action.

In addition, these approaches can be helpful in reversing the ethnographic imperative whereby the scholar is supposed to study and analyze the community. Instead, these approaches suggest that rather than analyze our communities, we can actually learn from the analysis that comes from our communities.

However, Fumitaka Matsuoka warns liberation theologians against an overemphasis on cultural revalidation on the part of liberation theologians. He notes that the dominant culture is prepared to accommodate a little bit of "multiculturalism"–a pow wow here, a pipe ceremony there–as long as the structures of power are not fundamentally altered. Without a simultaneous strategy to address white supremacy and racism, Matsuoka argues, cultural revalidation essentially serves as an opiate of the masses–providing short-term comfort without challenging the status quo:

> The ultimate myth surrounding ethnicity, perhaps, is the belief that cultural symbols of the past can provide more than a comfortable illusion to shield us from present-day discontents. The central problems...have to do, ultimately, not with ethnic groupings or the distinctness of our cultural heritages as such, but with racism and its manifestations in American economic policy, social rule and class relations (1995, 93).

Anthropological Poverty and Christianity

Dianne Stewart critiques Black/Womanist theology for not significantly attempting to draw upon resources from Africa. Perhaps because specific African cultures have not been retained by African Americans, it has been more difficult to claim them as sources for theology. She states, "[Black] theological reflections have centered Christianity as the dominant religious tradition giving birth to liberative theological ideas and praxes in African American history...African North American religious traditions...have not been explored as normative sources for black theological construction."[9]

Pan-Africanist Approach

Her Pan-Africanist approach builds on the work of Josiah Young. Pan-Africanism is not necessarily related to specific tribal traditions, but is "a condensation of [African] values resistant to the oppressive power of Eurocentricism. These values were continuous with the cosmologies of the ancestors as they were emergent from essentially African worldviews" (1992, 11). Young's formulation seems to preclude learning the languages and traditions of specific African cultures. Yet Young also notes that Africa "is itself a treasure house of multiculturalism. The myriad languages and dialects, the many religions, and the several races are all emblematic of an astonishing diversity."[10]

This seems to imply a mandate to learn about the diversity, rather than to distill what is perceived to be the "essence" of African religions. Such Pan-Africanist approaches have the potential to radically challenge the centrality of Christian history in Black experience because they do not make the history and culture of Blacks since enslavement determinative of Black history in general. It also raises a critical question: Is resisting anthropological poverty fundamentally at odds within retaining a Christian tradition? (This question will be discussed further in the section on American Indian theology.)

Sylvester Johnson challenges Black theologians to consider their complicity in Christian imperialism by unquestioningly maintaining their allegiance to Christianity rather than African traditions. Cone, meanwhile, contends, that such an Africanist approach that de-centers Christianity may not resonate with Black communities mired in Christian tradition. Liberating Black theologies from Western paradigms run the danger, as Cone notes, of leaving behind Black communities as well.[11] Consequently, many Black/Womanist theologians remain squarely within the Christian tradition, despite their critiques of white Christianity. For instance, Delores Williams states: "I believe the black church is the heart of hope in the black

---

[9]Stewart, *The Evolution of African Religions in Jamaica,* 3.

[10]Josiah Ulysses Young III, "Can Christians be Pan-Africanists?" unpublished paper.

[11]Lecture, Union Theological Seminary, New York: 7 May 1996.

community's experience of oppression, survival struggle and its historic efforts toward complete liberation" (1993, 205). Williams draws a distinction between the Black church and African-American denominational churches, which she charges with a number of sins, including sexism, homophobia, classism, and a generally inadequate response to social and political ills of all kinds. Nevertheless, the locus of liberation is within a Christian church rather than within African traditions.

Hispanic/Latino/a Theologians

Similarly Hispanic/Latino/a theologians are clearly situated within Christian traditions. Because of the particular types of cultural blending and mixing with Latin American cultures, Roberto Goizueta notes that a simple dichotomy between Christianity and non-Christian African and indigenous traditions is particularly meaningless with this context (1996, 286). Because the streams of indigenous and African religiosity are often more visible in Latin American religiosity, theologians often highlight them more in their theological projects. As Jeanette Rodriguez states: "What would happen then if Christianity began to reclaim other cultural traditions–such as the Celtic, the African, and the Caribbean–that have been similarly eliminated? Perhaps then our brothers and sisters would no longer feel like aliens in the promised land" (1996, 133).

Native Theologians

Unlike many Black/Womanist and Latina/o theologians, Native theologians are often prepared to make radical breaks with Christianity. Native theologians note that most Indian nations, prior to colonization, were generally peaceful and egalitarian; 75 percent of tribes did not practice war (Jaimes and Halsey 1992, 315). Women were accorded high status, and violence against women, children, and elders were virtually nonexistent (Allen 1986, 5–7). Christianity has introduced abuse and internalized oppression into Indian communities. It is difficult, therefore, for any Indian concerned with liberation to argue in favor of Christianity's liberatory potential. Tinker states:

> Christianity has not established itself among Indian peoples with any great tenacity or vitality. To the contrary, there are growing numbers of Indian people today who are explicitly rejecting Christianity in favor of a return to their traditional ceremonial spirituality (1995, 123).

Because indigenous worldviews are not universalist, Native thinkers will not always say Christianity is universally wrong, but they are prepared to attack Christian hegemony. This is why Deloria challenges liberation theologians to move beyond their "singular dependence upon the Christian paradigm" (1989, 10). He raises the question if, in attempting to "save"

Christianity, liberation theology is essentially a colonial discourse disguised within the language of liberation. His contention is that liberation theology is grounded on a western European epistemological framework that is no less oppressive to Native communities than is mainstream theology. "Liberation theology," Deloria cynically argues, "was an absolute necessity if the establishment was going to continue to control the minds of minorities. If a person of a minority group had not invented it, the liberal establishment most certainly would have created it" (1999, 100).

According to Deloria, Native liberation must be grounded in indigenous epistemologies–epistemologies that are inconsistent with western epistemologies, of which liberation theology is a part. "If we are then to talk seriously about the necessity of liberation, we are talking about the destruction of the whole complex of Western theories of knowledge and the construction of a new and more comprehensive synthesis of human knowledge and experience" (106). The challenge brought forth by Native scholars/activists to other liberation theologians would be, even if we distinguish the "liberation" church from mainstream churches, can the black church, or any church for that matter, escape complicity in Christian imperialism? Deloria in particular raises the challenge that Christianity is necessarily a religion tied to imperialism. This is so because Christianity is a temporally based rather than a spatially based tradition. That means it is not tied to a particular land base, but can seek converts from any land base. Thus it will never be content to remain within a particular place or community. "Once religion becomes specific to a group, its nature also appears to change, being directed to the internal mechanics of the group, not to grandiose schemes of world conquest" (1973, 296–97). Hence, all Christian theology, even liberation theology, remains complicit in the missionization and genocide of Native peoples in the Americas.

Anthropology and the Body

An analysis of anthropology in liberation theology would be incomplete without a discussion of the body. That is, liberation theologians generally critique the "other-worldly" focus of dominant theologies. Such theologies often assure oppressed communities of justice in the hereafter with little interest in seeking justice in this world.

Divine Immanence and Sexuality

Many feminist theologians, such as Rita Nakashima Brock and Carter Heyward, stress the immanence of God within human relations, including sexual relationships. Brock contends that sexuality has generally been imaged within Christianity as a condition of sin and the sign of a fallen humanity. Instead, she argues, Eros is the power that connects the individual to relationships with humanity. "Erotic power is the power of our primal interrelatedness. Erotic power, as it creates and connects hearts, involves the whole person in relationships of self-awareness, vulnerability, openness, and caring."[12]

At the same time, Marcella Althaus-Reid critiques liberation theologians, even those who address sexuality and the body, for maintaining an "otherworldly" approach to the body that approaches sexuality, if at all, in the most sanitized fashion possible. For instance, while Brock contrasts what she calls a definition of Eros based on "male dominance" that focuses on lust, with a "feminist" definition that focuses on relationality, Althaus-Reid argues that "Lust and love, and lust and justice do come together." She invites theologians to discard "vanilla theology" and image the Virgin Mary as a "divine Drag Queen," Jesus as "faggot," and other "obscene propositions." She charges liberation theologians with "struggling to remain in their own sexual closets and in their own preferential beds...without sharing their sexual stories and even condemning them in their writings" (2001, 88).

The absence of body and sexuality, Althaus-Reid argues, has caused liberation theologians to present a romanticized, desexualized, and stereotyped picture of "the poor." She asks: where in liberation theological works who claim a preferential option for the poor do we hear about the "sweet transvestite who needs to prostitute himself in a nightclub to survive" (32). She argues the poor do not only care for food and their children, "we must care a lot about our orgasms too" (137). "If the theologian is committed to doing theology with the people," argues Althaus-Reid, "then the theologian must recognize that sometimes people do theology without underwear" (43).

Theologies of Disability

The issue of the body is particularly pertinent in theologies of disability. As Nancy Eiesland notes, disability is generally represented in biblical narratives and within Christianity as a state of sin, or at least as a condition that requires a "cure." By contrast, many disability rights activists challenge this notion of disability as a condition that necessarily requires a cure. Instead, the problem is not the person who has a disability, but the society that refuses to accommodate itself to the varied bodies that inhabit it. Nancy Eiesland states: "For persons with disabilities, the body is the center for political struggle. In challenging society's definition of our bodies as flawed, dangerous, and dependent, people with disabilities have...shifted focus from problem individuals to the social problem of the exclusion of people with disabilities as a group" (1994, 49–50). Consequently, "able-bodied" theologies are essentially anti-body theologies because they see the body

[12]See Brock, *Journeys by Heart,* 26; Heyward, *Touching Our Strength,* and Heyward, *Our Passion for Justice.*

with its limitations, abilities or disabilities, etc., as requiring divine intervention to be truly in the image of God.

> Related to the sin-disability conflation is the theme that physical disability is a travesty to the divine image and an inherent desecration of all things holy...Theological interpretations of the meaning of perfection have historically included physical flawlessness as a well as absolute freedom...According to such standards, people with disabilities lack perfection and embody unwholeness (72).

The Nonperson

In addition, theologians such as Elias Farajaje-Jones, Kelly Brown Douglas, and Renee Hill point to the importance of theologizing around the "nonpersons" within Black communities, and by extension, other communities of color, such as people with AIDS, lesbians, gay, bisexual, and transgendered peoples, and prisoners.[13] As Farajaje-Jones and Douglas argue, one of the techniques of white supremacy has been to image Black peoples as sexually perverse and hence deserving of subjugation.

Responding to False Imaging

The response to this technique of racism is that Black communities have often tried to depict themselves as sexually "pure" by marginalizing those in the community whose sexuality is seen as most suspect by the dominant culture. "It is clear then–from teenage sexuality, male-female relationships, sexism and heterosexism–that the lack of sexual discourse in the Black community has contributed to life-threatening and oppressive conditions for Black men and women. The time for a Black sexual revolution has come. The Black community can no longer allow White racist culture to deploy sexuality through its shrewd control over our sexual discourse" (Douglas 1997, 243). This example is illustrative of the larger trend of oppressed peoples creating nonpersons within their own communities.

The Cult of Black Heroic Genius

Victor Anderson contends that the tendency to theologize around those who are seen as more socially acceptable rather than around the nonpersons within oppressed communities is part of what he calls the "the cult of black heroic genius."

---

[13]See Kelly Brown Douglas's analysis of homophobia in the Black church, which centers around those marginalized for their sexuality, including people with AIDS and single mothers in "Daring to Speak," *Embracing the Spirit;* and *Sexuality and the Black Church.* See also Eugene, "How Can We Forget?" in *Embracing the Spirit,* 247–74; Farajaje-Jones, "Breaking Silence," *Black Theology;* Bill Smith, "Liberation as Risky Business," *Changing Conversations,* 207–23. For a treatment of prisoners, see Taylor, *The Executed God.*

> I use the word cult here to designate dispositions of devotion, loyalty, and admiration for racial categories and the essentialized principles that determine black identity. And racial genius refers to the exceptional, sometimes essentialized cultural qualities, that positively represents the racial group in the action of at least one of the group's members. Insofar as one member's actions are said to represent the genius of the group...that member also exhibits the heroic qualities of the race (1999, 13).

Turner sees the "cult of black heroic genius" as part of the project of "ontological blackness," which he claims marks most Black liberation and womanist theologies. "It makes race identity a totality that subordinates and orders internal differences among blacks, so that gender, social standing, and sexual orientations are secondary to racial identity" (85). It should be said, however, that this critique of Black liberation/womanist theology seems a bit reductionist, and his call for a theology that is capable of "transcending the blackness that whiteness created" seems impossible (and not necessarily desirable) in the racist society we currently live in (117).

Does God Side with the Oppressed?

Goizueta further explains that the concept of *Mestizaje* elucidates the fact that the world cannot be divided into oppressor versus oppressed in any simple way. "As mestizos, we know that our history and identity are tinged with the blood of rape and conquest; that the mixture of Europeans, Native American, and African cultures did not take place without much violence, perpetrated by some of our ancestors against other ancestors: we are the children of both rapist and *la chigada* (the raped woman)" (1996, 286–87).

This reality has led Frances Wood to question a common precept in liberation theology: that God sides with the oppressed. Such an approach, she argues, does not address the reality that there is not a simple dichotomy between oppressors and oppressed peoples. Rather, there are multiple axes of oppression; consequently those that are oppressed on one axis may well be oppressive on another. Consequently, she argues, it is more appropriate to say that God stands against oppression, rather than sides for the oppressed.[14]

Similarly, Rita Nakashima Brock contends that this notion that God sides with the oppressed has created a myth of innocence for oppressed communities. In order to have our issues about oppression heard, we are often forced to portray ourselves as innocent of acts of oppression. The complete aversion to discussing community problems in the presence of outsiders ultimately undermines the community's struggle by equating,

[14] Frances Wood, lecture, Woman-Church Gathering, Albuquerque, N. M., 1993.

albeit implicitly, oppression and innocence. Unless a community can prove itself unstained by vice, the reasoning goes, it can have no legitimate claim to the redress of its grievances.

> Moral high ground goes to innocent victims. There is danger, however, in this structure of morality and victims. If a victimized group can be proven to lack innocence, the implication is that the group no longer deserves justice. Any hint of moral ambiguity, or the possession of power and agency, throws a shadow across one's moral spotlight. Maintaining one's status as victim becomes crucial for being acknowledged and given credibility...
>
> This tendency to identify with innocent victims, and to avoid discussions of the moral ambiguities of life, continues to place responsibility for abuse on the victims of the system. Abuse is wrong not because victims are innocent, but because abuse, even by good people for a good cause, dehumanizes the abuser and abused. Hence, we need to focus not on innocence, but on what is wrong with abusive behavior (Brock 1996, 80–81).

Communities that have suffered from years of colonial and racist violence cannot reasonably be expected to have remained unscarred by the experience. Ironically, we often feel that the only way to publicly confirm our status as victims of such violence is to deny vociferously the effects of our victimization. In doing so, however, we not only burden ourselves with an unfair (not to mention impossible) standard of prelapsarian innocence, but we also set ourselves up for failure: knowledge of our problems cannot remain within our communities; inevitably, our shortcomings will be known. Consequently, charges Brock, we must argue that our oppressed must be addressed, regardless of the oppressive behavior or dysfunctionality that may exist within our communities.

Conclusion

Because liberation theology centers its concerns to the "nonperson" in U.S. society, it necessarily entails a strong engagement with oppressed communities as a central point of theological analysis. Consequently, the issues to be covered under theological anthropology in U.S. liberation theologies are diverse. This chapter does not pretend to cover all the relevant issues that U.S. liberation theologies consider. It hopes to give a starting point for considering how de-centering theology's concern from the "nonbeliever" to the "nonperson" and building theological projects that resist anthropological poverty can contribute to our collective analysis of oppression and resistance.

7

Scripture

Miguel A. De La Torre

According to the Bible, any child who disrespects his or her parents should be put to death. Specifically, Leviticus reads, "Anyone who curses their father and mother shall surely be executed (20:9)."[1] Now, as a parent of two pre-teenagers, I confess that at times I am very tempted to take this command literally. Yet I wonder, if we were to read in the newspapers that a father killed his son or daughter because they uttered a curse toward him, claiming the authority of scripture as his defense, would good churchgoing Christians rally to his support? If not, why? Why can't parents put their rebellious teenagers to death in accordance with the Bible?

[1]The reader should be aware that all scriptural quotes are the translation of the author from the original Hebrew or Greek. Additionally, we will assume that the early faith communities have accurately preserved the stories and traditions appearing in the biblical text. Usually, biblical scholars discuss the authenticity of authorship, as well as the accuracy of particular events, stories, or statements appearing in the text; however, such an analytical endeavor is beyond the scope of this chapter. Instead, my usage of scripture attempts to read the text from the perspective of the faith community. Such a reading is conducted from the marginalized spaces of society, attempting to understand and apply the biblical message to the reality of disenfranchisement. Finally, it should be noted that the contents of this chapter are a revision based on segments of my book *Reading the Bible from the Margins.*

The next verse (Lev. 20:10) calls for the death sentence for anyone who commits adultery. Just think of the impact this would have in depopulating our society! Additionally, Leviticus 24:16 makes the cursing of God's name a capital offense. While I personally shudder every time I hear people using the name of the Lord in vain, is their death a fit punishment for their transgression? Would anyone be willing to argue for the death sentence for those who constantly damn the name of God? Likewise, according to Exodus 31:14–15, anyone who works on the Sabbath must be killed.

As much as we do not want to admit it, we all read biblical texts selectively. Few, if any, would insist that these "peccadilloes" deserve death. Most of us simply choose to ignore or outright disobey inflicting the punishments associated with such passages. In effect, all who claim the authority of the Bible make a conscious or unconscious decision literally to follow some sections of the scriptures while following others symbolically. In fact, if we were to follow literally everything within the biblical text, we would probably end up in jail. For example, Psalm 137:9 provides a paradigm for treating enemies: "Blessed is the one who seizes and dashes your little ones against the stone." How can we reconcile the loving mercy of Christ with the vengeance of smashing the infants of our enemies against stones? We are forced with a choice. Either we take the Bible literally and commit crimes against humanity by obeying the psalmist, or we begin to question how we read and interpret certain sections of the Bible.

We can begin by realizing that some biblical verses have been misinterpreted, consciously or unconsciously, to protect the power and privilege of the dominant culture. Other verses seem to imply the sanctification of non-Christian actions like ethnic cleansing. How then can a Christian comply with the oppression of neighbors and continue to rely on the authority of scripture as the basis for Christian living? What type of morality can the faith community claim?

Bible as God's Revelation of God

The first point to be made concerning reading the Bible from the margins is that the biblical text is the witness of God's revelation to humanity, a book designed to point the reader to the Deity. But, is the Bible the fullest revelation of God to humanity? No, Jesus is the fullest revelation of God to humanity. The Bible bears witness to that revelation and, as such, becomes the basis of faith for the community of believers. Yet it is important to acknowledge that the Bible is written from within the social location of different writers. While this multitude of writers spanning centuries all proclaim the same revelation of God's love and mercy, a love and mercy that find their ultimate manifestation in the incarnation, these writers were born into and were greatly influenced by their social environments. Their writings assumed the normative oppressive structures of their times (polygamy, slavery, etc.), structures we clearly repudiate today. Does this invalidate the Bible? No! But it clearly places a greater responsibility on the reader so as to interpret the text in light of the life, death, and resurrection of Christ.

Anti-life Reading Is Anti-gospel

How then does the faith community read the Bible, still claiming authority for their lives, yet rejecting those passages that appear to call for death? Readers should always submit their interpretation to the Holy Spirit. They should always read the text within the marginalized body of faith and always remain cognizant of the basic purpose of the gospel. Jesus Christ, in the gospel of John said it best, "I came that they may have life, and have it abundantly (10:10)." Here lies the second point to be learned on how to read the Bible from the margins: if a biblical interpretation prevents life from being lived abundantly by a segment of the population, or worse, if it brings death, it is anti-gospel.

Interpretations of scripture cease to be biblically based when a reading of the Bible

1. ignores how minority groups are denied access to opportunities
2. rationalizes the riches of the center while disregarding the plight of the poor
3. vindicates the relegation of women to second-class status

Only those interpretations that empower all elements of humanity, offering abundant life in the here-now, as opposed to just the here-after, are biblically sound.

Jesus Christ and his life-giving mission become the lens by which the rest of the biblical text is interpreted. During the Sermon on the Mount, as found in Matthew 5–7, Jesus reinterpreted the Hebrew Scriptures to bring them in line with the gospel message, clearly telling his followers to reject those passages that bring subjugation or death to others. Specifically, Jesus said in Matthew: "You heard that it was said, 'An eye for an eye and a tooth for a tooth.' But I say to you, do not resist evil, but whoever strikes you on your right cheek, turn to him the other (5:38–39)." According to Jesus, his followers had to reject the biblical mandate of Exodus 21:24, which literally calls for "an eye for an eye and a tooth for a tooth." In short, Jesus called his disciples to renounce a segment of scripture!

These so-called laws of retaliation, known as the *lex tailionis*, were never intended to require vengeance, rather to restrict it. Yet Jesus does away with the whole concept of revenge by calling his followers to a higher standard in interpreting the Hebrew Bible. Instead, the disciple of Christ is required to express the unconditional love of God. The formerly accepted biblical interpretation that sanctioned limited retributive vengeance was replaced with a new interpretation that mirrored the life and mission of

Christ. In this same spirit, those who have historically suffered under the dominant culture's interpretations of the Bible question, as did Jesus, normative interpretations of the text and at times, the passages themselves, if the end results bring oppression and deny "life abundance."

How do we know if an interpretation or a passage is responsible for creating oppressive structures? By recognizing that at times, individuals have no choice but to choose among options that are all unsatisfactory. For example, most Christians agree that they should not lie. Nevertheless, Exodus 1:15–22 recounts the story of two midwives who were commanded by the pharaoh to kill all the male children born to the Israelites. The midwives, however, disobeyed the pharaoh because they "feared God." When questioned as to why they defied the pharaoh, they lied, stating that Hebrew women were more vigorous than Egyptian women and gave birth before the midwives were able to attend them. Even though they lied to the pharaoh, Exodus states, "And God dealt well with the midwives (1:20)."

If the Bible is read as a book of regulations that clearly determine right and wrong, then passages like this one in Exodus become difficult to understand. If lying is always wrong, how then can God bless these two women for lying? Here then is a third point; absolute truths derived from the Bible become somewhat problematic. Often, such absolutes become one of the privileges of those who are sheltered from the harshness of oppressive structures. Like the midwives, people who live under oppressive structures often find themselves in situations where decisions aren't easy or obvious and may even contradict supposed biblical principles. Many times the only choice available is the "lesser" evil. Yes, the midwives could have told the truth, but they would have been killed for disobeying the pharaoh. Someone else would have been found to carry out the pharaoh's wishes. Or they could have lied and continued to save as many Hebrew boys as possible. Both killing and lying are vices to be avoided. In this case, lying had the potential to save lives, and in the end Moses grew up to be used by God to liberate God's chosen people.

False Interpretations

When we read the biblical text, we read it from our social location. Unfortunately, if we are unaware of such a reading, we ignore how our interpretations justify lifestyles that are at times contradictory to the very essence of the gospel message. Historically, the Bible has been used to justify such acts as genocide, slavery, war, crusades, colonialism, economic plunder, and gender oppression. Bible verses were quoted, sermons preached from pulpits, and theses written in theological academic centers to justify barbaric acts that were labeled "Christian missionary zeal" or "righteous indignation." Millions have unjustly died and perished in the name of Jesus and by the hands of those who call themselves his followers.

How then, can we claim the authority of scripture when those who claim to be obedient to the biblical text have unleashed so much misery upon humanity in God's name? Here lies the fourth point in reading the Bible from the margins. While the faith community within marginalized racial and ethnic groups may claim that the biblical text is true and authoritative, they recognize that not all interpretations are true and authoritative. Biblical interpretations that justified crusades, inquisitions, colonialization, Manifest Destiny, and neoimperialism cannot be confused with what the text actually says, nor with its possible application to our lives today. Yet, we do this all the time. I'm sure you have heard well-meaning Christians make comments like the following: "The Bible says that the woman should submit to the man and take care of the duties of the household," "According to the Bible, God hates homosexuals," or "The Bible clearly calls for a separation of races." In these statements the interpretation of the speaker is given the same validity as the Bible, making the interpreter's words inerrant. I believe in the Bible, but not necessarily in how the Bible is interpreted by humans.

Reading from a Social Location

The fifth point to consider in how the biblical text is read from the margins is recognizing that we all approach the text from our specific social location. By social location, I refer to cultural experiences that influence a person's identity. Basically, being white in the United States is a vastly different experience than being black or Latino/a. These experiences define the meaning we give to the different symbols that exist in our lives, including whole texts or individual words that operate as a form of linguistic symbols. In other words, we are all born into a society that shapes and forms us. When we turn our attention to the biblical text as the source of our theological perspectives, we participate in a dialogue between the written word and the meanings our community teaches us to give to these words. We interpret the text the way we do because people whom we love and respect–our parents, ministers, friends, neighborhoods–have taught us from our earliest childhood how to interpret the Bible.

While I recognize that exceptions exist, generally speaking, if our family is Catholic, we are Catholics. If they are Baptist, so are we. In fact, if we were born in Saudi Arabia to Sunni Muslims, there is an excellent chance we would be bowing our knees to Allah. If we were born to a Buddhist family in China, we would now be seeking Nirvana. As much as we may want to deny it, our religious beliefs–and if we are Christians, our interpretation of the Bible–are mostly formed by social location, the family we are born into, and the community where we are raised.

But what happens when the community that bore and nurtured us has historically maintained biblical interpretations that cause one group to be oppressed? My Spanish forefathers theologically proved through the biblical text and philosophical reasoning that Amerindians were created to serve as natural slaves. The forefathers of those who are of European descent simply dismissed the humanity of Africans. Because Africans were believed to be recipients of Ham's curse,[2] they were conceived as being ordained by God to be slaves. Not surprising, they were seen as being three-fifths human, as spelled out in the U.S. Constitution. How would we, if born into this social location, rise above the interpretations our culture taught us?

All too often we approach the biblical text assuming that it only contains one meaning, specifically the meaning that existed in the mind of God and was revealed to the original person who verbalized this revelation to those who first heard or read the message. The task of the present-day reader of the Bible is to apply linguistic and historical tools to the text to arrive at the original meaning submerged in centuries of commentaries and church doctrines. By applying this methodology, the reader expects to be able to ascertain the original universal meaning, which remains applicable to all peoples in all times. In the reader's own mind, this interpretation, now elevated to truth, is objectively realized, devoid of any social or cultural influences.

But no biblical interpretation is ever developed in a social or cultural vacuum. Most interpretations are autobiographical! We ascertain the meaning of the text through the telling of our own stories, projecting onto the Bible how we define and interpret the biblical story in light of our own life experiences. Nevertheless, for a chapter about the biblical text (such as this one) to use the author's autobiographical information as a lens by which interpretations are formulated is considered at best inappropriate, at worst, unscholarly. Yet, all "official" interpretations reflect the social location of those with authority to make their personal interpretations the acceptable societal norm. Hence, to claim objectivity in biblical interpretations is to mask the subjectivity of the person, groups, or culture doing the interpreting. The interpretation of scripture can never occur apart from the identity of the one doing the interpreting.

Many of us have been taught to read the Bible through the eyes of those in power, specifically through the eyes of white, middle and upper-class males. When the Bible is read from the social location of those whom

---

[2]Genesis 9:20 was interpreted by the dominant European culture to justify slavery of Africans. According to this interpretation, Noah had three sons, one of whom was called Ham (the other two were Shem and Japheth). One day Noah, the first to plant the vine and create wine, became intoxicated and passed out nude in his tent. Although the text states that Ham gazed upon his father, it is believed that Ham committed some shameful act, either in deed or thought. When Noah became sober, he cursed Ham's son, Canaan. As a result, Canaan's skin turned dark and his hair became woolly; in other words, he became an African. Canaan and his descendants' punishment was to become his Caucasian brothers' slaves forever. Although the text never indicates the skin pigmentation of Noah or his sons, it is assumed that they were European, even though they very well could have been black.

society privileges, the risk exists that interpretations designed to protect their power and privilege are subconsciously or consciously constructed. Those who are the authority of society impose their views upon the text and confuse what *they* declare the Bible to say with what the text actually states. To counter this, autobiographical interpretations from the margins of society challenge the claim by the dominant culture that their interpretation of the text is objective and thus superior to any other reading.

Reading Autobiographically from the Margins

Reading the Bible from the margins of society is not an exercise that reveals interesting perspectives on how other cultures read and interpret biblical texts. To read the Bible from the margin is to grasp God in the midst of struggle and oppression. Hence, such a reading attempts to understand why God's people find themselves struggling for survival within a society that appears to be designed to privilege one group of people at the expense of others. The liberation theologian Gustavo Gutiérrez calls this process "a militant reading," one from the perspective of those dwelling on "the underside of history (1984, xi)."[3] The Bible becomes more than a text requiring scholarly analysis. It becomes a text of hope, a hope in a God whose essence is the liberation of all who are oppressed, all who subsist at the margins of society. Reading the Bible from the margins, by its very nature, challenges how the dominant culture has historically interpreted the text. The "marginal" interpretation automatically subverts how the text has normatively been read, highlighting the weaknesses of the dominant culture's interpretation, and showing how a privileged social location subconsciously informs and shapes their "objective" biblical views.

Liberating Oppressed and Oppressor

Hearing the biblical interpretations emanating from the margins of society challenges the subjective readings that justify the privilege of the dominant culture. This unmasking can lead to the dominant culture's own liberation from ignorance. Here lies the sixth point to consider: reading the Bible from the margins not only liberates those who are oppressed, but the oppressors as well. Reading the text through the eyes of the marginalized lets the authorities who dominate be liberated from their own hatreds and biases. They can be drawn closer to a more valid understanding of God and the Bible, as can also those whom they have considered to be their inferior racial, gender, or class Other who are also created in the image of the Deity. Reading the Bible from the margins is as crucial for the salvation of the dominant culture as it is for the liberation of the disenfranchised.

---

[3]For Gutiérrez, reading the text from the perspective of those residing in the underside of history reveals two implicit themes. The first is the universality of God's love. The second is God's preferential option for the poor.

Metaphoric versus Material Reading

A seventh point to observe is that reading the Bible to justify one's social location results in a spiritual or metaphoric reading of the biblical text rather then a material reading. A metaphoric reading is the process of interpreting the biblical text in such a way that its call for action becomes an intention or conviction of the heart rather than physical action to be undertaken. A material reading, on the other hand, attempts to introduce the reality of daily struggles into the Bible. Close attention is given to how the social location of the marginalized, both today and during biblical times, affects how the Bible should be understood.

For example, have you ever read a gospel parable only to think how unfair it was? Take Matthew 20:1–16. Jesus told the story of a vineyard owner who early in the morning sets out to hire laborers. He goes to the local gathering place where laborers usually wait to be hired, negotiates a fair day's wages (a *denarius*), and sends them to his fields. Several hours later, mid-morning, he comes across some individuals who have yet to be hired, so he employs them and sends them to his fields. At noon, he finds more unemployed laborers and sends them to his fields. This process is again repeated in the mid and late afternoon.

When the day ends and it is time to pay the workers, the vineyard owner reverses the order. He begins to pay those who were hired last and only worked a few hours. He pays them the same amount he originally agreed to pay those first hired. When it is time to pay those who worked the entire day, he pays the same amount of money as those who only worked a few hours. Some worked all day, some just a few hours, yet everyone got the same amount of money. Now is this fair? Is it any wonder that those who worked all day grumbled against the vineyard owner? Shouldn't workers be paid according to the amount of time they invested in the job?

To reconcile how fairness is defined based on our present capitalist economic system and how the biblical passage defines fairness, the Bible must be read metaphorically. Then the parable is understood as God providing the gift of salvation (the denarius) without regard to how much work is done by the individual, nor how long one has labored for God. All who come to God are given the same portion of grace regardless of when in their life journey they turned to God. While such a spiritual reading may provide additional insight, to read the text solely metaphorically while avoiding a material reading allows the reader to justify the injustices of the present economic system while ignoring the radical call of being a disciple of Jesus.

For those who are undocumented and accustomed to standing at designated street corners throughout major cities of this country waiting and hoping for a patron to stop and offer a job (off the books to avoid employment taxes), the fairness of this parable resonates. For those who are relegated to the ghettos and *barrios*, unemployed or limited to minimum wage service jobs, the fairness of this parable provides a vision for a just society based on the rule of God. How many of these migrant workers end up working all day only to be paid a fraction of their worth because they are undocumented? Or how many of these workers injure themselves at the job only to be dropped off at the closest hospital and left to fend for themselves? To read this parable from the margins, from the perspective of the poor, is to recognize that the vineyard owner, that is, the employer, has a responsibility toward the laborers, a responsibility that goes beyond what traditional capitalist thinking defines as just.

To read the text materially is to realize Jesus' awareness of the laborer's plight. Poverty is usually defined as a lack of resources, specifically money. Yet poverty's dysfunctions encompass

1. a higher likelihood of failed marriages;
2. a higher susceptibility to illness, disease, and sickness;
3. a greater likelihood of having children who will not complete high school;
4. a higher probability of having children who will have difficulties with law enforcement agencies;
5. a greater chance of being a victim of a crime; and a shorter life expectancy.

Poverty can never be defined simply as a lack of money; it is a debilitating lifestyle that robs its victim of dignity and personhood.

Jesus fully understood that poverty prevented those who were created in the image of God from participating in the abundant life he came to give. In his parable of the vineyard owner, Jesus attempted to teach economic justice so that all can have life abundantly. He recognized that it was not the laborers' fault that they failed to obtain employment for that day. They awoke in the early predawn, walked to the spot where potential employers came to find workers, and waited. Regardless of whether they were chosen to work, they still needed a denarius to meet their basic needs: food, shelter, and clothing.

As Justo González reminds us, to be chosen to work for only half a day and to be paid half a denarius was insufficient. Half a denarius meant that several family members would not eat that day. Only an uncaring and unmerciful heart will declare it just that these laborers leave without being able to meet their basic needs because, through no fault of their own, they were unable to find a job. The biblical teaching is that those who are economically privileged, like the vineyard owner, must remain responsible for those who are not (1996, 63–64).

As important as the metaphorical rendering of the parable of the vineyard owner may be, just as important–if not more so–is the material reading. For those living under an economic system that commodifies time, justice is defined as a set pay for a set number of hours worked. However, Jesus defined justice as insuring that each worker obtains a living wage, regardless of the hours worked, so that all can share in the abundant life. It did not matter how many hours a laborer worked. What mattered was that at the end of the day, she or he took home a living wage so that the entire family could survive for another day. It was the workers' responsibility to labor; it was the employer's responsibility that the employee left with enough. What does this say about our present system in which a person who works full time at the minimum hourly wage will earn several thousand dollars below what the U.S. government has determined to be the poverty level?

Reading with Those Who Suffer Death

The task of reading the Bible from the margins is complicated when misreading the text has often led to an enhancement of power and privilege. This task is further compounded when those in power believe that tampering with their interpretations is tantamount to tampering with the actual Word of God. Yet, if a biblical interpretation leads to the death of a segment of society, we can assume that such a reading is nonbiblical in the sense that it does not describe the will of God. If the message of Christ is one that brings abundant and eternal life, then any message that fosters death is a message from the anti-Christ. Hence the eighth point: to read the Bible from the margins is to read from the context of those who suffer death, literally and figuratively, because of the way society is constructed. Those with power and privilege are not cognizant of how their interpretations can foster the oppression of others. Hence liberating the Bible from these death-imposing interpretations requires a methodical reading of the scriptures through the eyes of the disenfranchised. In reading the text with marginalized eyes, the reader either claims a disenfranchised identity or commits to hearing the voices of those who are oppressed, diligently looking to the text from within a context of struggles to learn God's salvific will.

An Example of Marginalized Reading

Allow me to provide an example of what I mean. Let us say that we are pastors preparing a Sunday morning sermon. Our text is Exodus 20:8–10: "Remember to keep the Sabbath day holy. Six days you shall labor and do all your work. The seventh day is a Sabbath to Yahweh your God; you shall do no work that day." Most of us, without realizing it, approach the third commandment through the eyes of white middle-class America. This becomes obvious as we prepare the sermon. Every good sermon, of course, has three points, so we must come up with three points, three insights concerning the third commandment. We might choose these three: (1) Obeying the commandment is good for our spiritual life because it carves out a space in our busy schedule to study God's word and worship with the body of believers, demonstrating our willingness to be obedient. (2) Obeying the commandment is good for the health of our family because it carves out a space in our busy schedule to be with them at worship, share a Sunday meal with them, and catch up on what is going on in their lives. (3) Obeying the commandment is good for our physical health. It carves out a space in our busy schedule to allow the body and mind to rest from the grueling week of hard work. It refreshes us so that we do not burn out working like dogs, and it forces us to refocus on the important things in life, such as our relationship with God. While sermons on this passage will vary, the above outline is typical of what we might expect to hear in any given Sunday morning homily. Such a sermon would be soothing balm to the busy and overworked lives of most who are white middle and upper class.

Nevertheless, how would this same passage be preached from the underside of the U.S. economic system, read with the eyes of the marginalized? Justo González provides us with an excellent example. He recounts the sermon preached at a church composed mostly of very poor parishioners. The minister began by asking how many within the congregation worked six days last week? Five days? Four days? Few in the congregation were able to raise their hands to any of these questions. Then the preacher asked how many would have wanted to work six days last week but were unable to find employment. Almost every hand went up. To this response, the minister asked, "How, then, are we to obey the law of God that commands that we shall work six days, when we cannot even find work for a single day?" (1996, 59–60).

This interpretation subverts the dominant culture's interpretation that focuses solely on taking a day off. The poor teach those with middle and upper class privilege that God's third commandment is more than the capricious imposition of a Deity to choose one day in seven to do nothing. Rather, God establishes symmetry and balance in the created order. Working six days is counterbalanced with resting one. When we read this text from the position of economic privilege, we assume the privilege of being employed. We are blinded to the reality that segments of our society lack opportunities for gainful employment due to their race, ethnicity, gender, or class. By imposing upon the text our assumptions of class privilege, we are oblivious to the first part of the commandment, "Six days you shall labor."

Listening to the voices of the disenfranchised confronts us with our society's failure to keep this commandment. Our entire economic system is questioned. For our economy to work at top efficiency, an "acceptable" unemployment rate is required. In fact, when the unemployment rate drops too low, the stock market gets jittery and begins a downward turn. Why? Because corporate America needs a reserve army of underskilled and undereducated laborers to keep wages depressed. Full national employment means companies are paying too much to attract and retain employees, negatively affecting their profits. When we consider that those who are unemployed are disproportionately people from the margins, we realize that our economic system is geared to prevent certain segments of our population from keeping God's commandment, "Six days you shall labor." Reading the Bible from the margins, because it is a contextual reading, subverts traditional readings and seriously critiques the dominant culture.

Looking for the Marginalized in the Text

A ninth point to consider concerning reading the Bible from the margins is discovering the story of the marginalized within the text because the text is read from the depth of suffering and despair. When those who are disenfranchised suffer unbearable injustices, they develop an inexpressible feeling in the pit of their stomachs. The Korean community has a name for this pang. They call it *han*.[4] *Han* encompasses the feelings of resentment, helplessness, bitterness, sorrow, and revenge felt deep in the victim's gut. *Han* becomes the daily companion of the powerless, the voiceless, the marginalized. *Han*, however, is not restricted to the individual. When social injustices prevail throughout the whole community for several generations without an avenue of release or cleansing, a collective *han* (collective unconsciousness) develops. For many who are Asians, or of Asian descent, life in this country is a *han*-ridden experience. Yet, it is from the *han*–ridden margins that the dominant culture finds its salvation.

Jesus told the parable of the good Samaritan (Lk. 10:25–37) in response to a question from a promising lawyer, a member of the dominant culture. The lawyer asked what he must do to inherit eternal life, salvation. Jesus narrated the story of a man on his way to Jericho from Jerusalem. Suddenly, he finds himself in the hands of brigands. Beaten and robbed, he is left for dead. Shortly afterward, a priest traveling on the same road sees the wounded man but crosses the street to avoid him. Minutes later, another holy man from the dominant culture, a Levite, comes across the wounded man, but he, too, crosses the street and avoids him. Eventually, a member from the margins of society, a Samaritan, a person of color, sees the wounded man, has compassion, and ministers to him. He bandages his wounds by pouring oil and wine on them. Then the Samaritan carries the wounded man to a nearby inn and pays out of his pocket for the man to be looked after.

The Samaritan lived a life of *han*. Although the wounded man was a member of the dominant culture responsible for the Samaritan's oppression,

---

[4]A similar term exists among other Asian groups. For example, among the Chinese it is known as *hen* and connotes a more extreme passion for vengeance. Among Japanese, *kon* connotes grudge bearing and visible resentment. Vietnamese use the term *han,* defining it similarly to the Koreans.

the Samaritan was able to take pity because he had *han* inside himself. The ability to recognize *han* initiates a healing where the wounded are able to heal the wounds of others. One who suffers unbearable pain is able to understand and pour refreshing "oil and wine" on the others' wounds. Hence the importance of support groups, where people struggling with the same pain come together to help each other in the healing process. By picking the Samaritan outcast to be the catalyst for healing and salvation, instead of other members of the dominant culture, Jesus called the *han*-ridden communities located on the margins of society to be the agents of healing for a *han*-ridden world.[5] Those who are suffering *han* should not look to the priest and ministers for help, unless they, too, have experienced *han.*

The Correct Interpretation

Now, if a biblical text can be read and interpreted in several different ways, which interpretation is correct? The challenge faced by those who read the Bible from the margins is that the dominant culture has the power to shape and legitimize the religious discourse. The interpretations of the disenfranchised can easily be dismissed as interesting perspectives that may add some "color" to understanding the Bible, but in the minds of the dominant culture these interpretations are deemed lacking in scholastic rigor and without any universal relevance. Yet, violence is done to the biblical text when we reduce the interpretations that come from the margins into interesting perspectives among the multitude of possible perspectives, each equal in value and importance. Here then is a tenth point: reading the Bible from the social location of oppression does not call for the treatment of all biblical interpretations as equal, where the interpretation from the margins is but one competing perspective. Rather, an affirmation and an option are made for the interpretations of the disenfranchised taking priority over the interpretations of those who still benefit from societal structures of oppression.

At first glance, it may appear somewhat arrogant to claim the superiority of one interpretation over another. Why should the interpretations formed in the margins of society take precedence over the interpretations voiced by the dominant culture? Is it because the disenfranchised are holier? Smarter? Closer to God? No, of course not. The reason why an interpretational privilege exists for the disenfranchised is because such an interpretation is based on a concept known as the hermeneutical privilege of the oppressed. This term basically means that those who are disenfranchised are in a position to understand the biblical text better

[5]For a complete discussion of *han,* see Park, *Racial Conflict and Healing.*

because they know what it means to be a marginalized person attempting to survive within a social context designed to benefit others at their expense.

W. E. B. Du Bois, in his monumental book *The Souls of Black Folk,* introduces the reader to the concept of double-consciousness, a concept that describes the experience African Americans endure when they are pressured to forsake their self-consciousness. African Americans (and I would add all marginalized people) are forced to see themselves as the white world sees them. This leads to the disenfranchised defining themselves through the eyes of the dominant culture via common stereotypes imposed upon them (1996, 7). When they begin to read the biblical text, they look toward the dominant culture to set the standards by which the text is normatively read and interpreted. At times, these interpretations are responsible for the maintenance of very oppressive social structures that keep them at the margins of society.

Although Du Bois writes about double-consciousness, we can expand his work to include triple-consciousness or even quadruple-consciousness. If a black woman sees herself through the eyes of a white-dominated and male-dominated world, can her self-definition be understood as triple-consciousness? What if she is a black Latina woman? Does this constitute quadruple-consciousness? As a Latino male, I know what it is to be a victim of ethnic discrimination, but as a male, I also know what it means to be the benefactor of sexist structures. Likewise, because I have a lighter skin pigmentation and lack pronounced African or Amerindian features, I also benefit to some degree in a social structure that privileges those closest to the white ideal.

I am both victim and victimizer. Our culture's present structures of oppression go beyond a black-white dichotomy. Nevertheless, why then are the biblical interpretations of the disenfranchised so important in fully understanding the scriptures? It is because people of color know what it means to live in a Eurocentric society where their very survival requires them to learn how to navigate laws, customs, traditions, and idiosyncrasies designed to protect the power and privilege of the dominant culture. Although people of color know what it means to be marginalized within a Euro-American culture, those with power and privilege have no conception of what it means to belong to a disenfranchised group. In fact, most Euro-Americans can achieve success without having to know anything about or associate with people on the margins. The same cannot be said if the roles were reversed. Because those who are marginalized know how to exist in both their world and the world where they lack a voice, they can bring an expanded and raised consciousness to the reading of the Bible.

The Marginalized as First Hearers

As the disenfranchised read the Bible from the margins, that is, from their social location, their empowering interpretation unmasks and critiques oppressive structures. Reading the Bible from the margins implies that at times the Bible is read *to* the center. Often, in fact, the text is read from the social location of those who occupy the center of society, those with power and privilege. Hence, the Bible is read from the center toward the margins in order to teach those who are less fortunate what they must do to occupy privileged space. Yet, Jesus' audience was primarily the outcasts of society. This is why it is important to understand the message of Jesus from the perspective of the disenfranchised. Here lies our eleventh point: the marginalized of Jesus' time occupied the privileged position of being the first to hear and respond to the gospel. By making the disenfranchised recipients of the good news, Jesus added a political edge to his message.

Jesus used parables that resonated with the lives of the poor, the tax collectors, the prostitutes–in short, the marginalized. God's self-revelation to humanity does not occur from the centers of world power, but in the margins of society. It is not from the court of Pharaoh that God's laws are revealed to humanity, but from their slaves. Nor does the incarnation occur in the imperial palace of Caesar, or to the household of the high priest in Jerusalem. Rather, God is made flesh among the impure Galileans, impure because they were seen by the center as half-breeds, from a territory peopled by Arabs, Greeks, Asians, Phoenicians, Syrians, and Jews, a region where the unclean Gentiles outnumbered the Jews.

Jesus as Marginalized Human

It is always difficult for those at the center to listen to those who reside at the margins of society. The marginalized interpretation of God's movement in the world challenges what society has always taught to be normative. Yet Jesus was able and willing to learn from the margins of his times, and this is the twelfth and last point to consider. We sometimes forget that Jesus was human as well as divine. As a human, he had to learn how to overcome human frailties. As a child, Jesus had to learn how to walk, talk, and read. As an adult, he had to overcome the temptation of sin, specifically the human desire for fame and riches. Satan, according to Matthew 4:1–11, tempted Jesus with possessions (bread), privilege (jumping off the Temple and not being hurt because of who Christ is), and power (all the kingdoms of the earth). Although Jesus successfully rebuffed Satan while in the desert, it would be naive to assume that he was never again tempted. A careful reading of the scriptures shows how he had to learn not to fall into future temptations.

Another opportunity to be tempted by Satan came when Jesus refused to minister to a marginalized woman. Matthew 15:21–28 recounts the story of a Canaanite woman who came to Jesus so that her daughter could be healed. The Jews regarded Canaanites in very much the same way some Euro-Americans see people of color today. They were seen as an inferior people, no better than dogs. When the Canaanite woman appealed to Jesus for help, the Lord responded by saying, "I was sent only to the lost sheep of the house of Israel. It is not good to take the bread of the children and throw it to the dogs." How many times have people of the margins heard similar remarks from Euro-Americans? Jobs, educational opportunities, and social services are for "real" Americans. Instead of taking food away from the children of hard-working "Americans" to throw to the dogs, "they" should just go back to where they came from. Leticia Guardiola-Sáenz, interpreting the text from her social location, points out that this woman crosses the "border" not to worship her oppressor (Jesus), but to demand an equal place at the table of the Lord. She demands to be treated as an equal (1997, 69–81).

Now Jesus' response was typical for a person inculturated to believe in the superiority of his or her particular race. Jesus learned from his culture the superiority of Judaism and the inferiority of non-Jews. However, Jesus was willing to learn from a "woman of color" and thus avoided falling into the temptation of perpetuating racism. The woman responded by saying, "For even the dogs eat the crumbs that fall from the table of their masters." Her remark shocked Jesus into realizing that faith was not contingent on a person's ethnicity. In fact, Jesus had to admit that this was a woman of great faith.

Up to this point, the gospel message was only for the Jews. In fact, Jesus restricted the spreading of the good news to his own race. In Matthew 10:5, Jesus sent his twelve disciples on their first missionary venture. He clearly instructed them, "Do not turn your steps into other nations, nor into Samaritan cities, rather go to the lost sheep of the house of Israel." Yet five chapters later, from the Canaanite margins of Jesus' society came the challenge that the gospel would no longer be the exclusive property of one ethnic group and would instead become available for all who believe. Jesus learned something about his mission from this woman. By the end of his ministry when he gave the great commission, he commanded his followers to go out to all nations, not just the people of Israel. Now, if Jesus is willing to learn something from the margins of society, shouldn't his church be willing to do likewise?

8

Ethics

Moral Evolution: From Customary Societies to Atomistic Individuals

DARRYL M. TRIMIEW

A Historical Introduction

Like all other disciplines and ways of life, the practical moral inquiry, traditionally termed ethics, has been deeply impacted by the series of revolutionary changes brought about by modernity and, most recently, postmodernity. Traditionally, ethics were reflections on sets of practices instantiated in the customs and mores of particular societies and civilizations. Accordingly, various ethical systems were by no means identical. They were particular to their cultures, societies, politics, and religious systems. They were unique unto themselves creating self-containing, self-referencing worlds.

These ethical systems were grounded in their own understandings of obligation and responsibility. These understandings were common shared meanings particular to small homogenous communities.[1]

[1]For the term "shared meaning" see Michael Walzer's influential work, *Spheres of Justice*, 145.

Initially ethics were understood to be culturally and politically relative, that is to say, not binding on other societies. Each society was *sui generis* with limited knowledge of each other and no great compulsion to investigate, let alone convert, others. Some ethical systems did extend moral obligations to nonmembers who were sojourners in their land. Even then, morally speaking, sojourners were not regarded as equals to members.[2]

Community Ethics, Not Individual

Despite this inward-looking stance, some societies understood themselves as having ultimate truths and moral standards that they were expected, even under the terms of their own systems, to hold out as paradigms to others. Frequently, these systems were inseparably intertwined with religious views that supplied the ethos of the society as well as its worldview. Generally speaking, all of these systems saw as their primary moral agent not individuals in society, but the community itself; that is, the group.

As such, individuals were expected to carry out clearly defined roles in society. They were to exhibit standard superlative moral attributes or virtues and were to move toward some commonly shared destiny in some clearly defined conception of a good society.[3] Such systems emphasized membership. One root metaphor for such systems can be illustrated by the root metaphor of a corral. In this root metaphor, horses that are members of an organized group are within the corral. Other horses, not under any control and outside of the corral, constitute their own herd. The horses in the corral consider those outside as wild. These "outsiders" have their own separate memberships, but neither system is understood as being binding on the other. Sojourners–those who had "hopped the fence," so to speak–who shared the views of the corral members and who worked to achieve these ends were conditionally welcomed to share obligations. Over time, such foreigners could become members of the society.[4] In other words, they could come into the corral and stay. Or they were free to go, usually.

Complex Membership Notions

Most traditional societies did not have prohibitions against slavery. Therefore, they could and did, on occasion, contain people within their territorial boundaries who were neither citizens nor subjects, but rather property. Further complicating this picture were the widespread, complex notions of membership. Many societies were not classless, having also, in some cases, caste systems. In particular, mothers, daughters, and children

---

[2]Here I am referencing the Judaeo-Christian meganarrative that I claim as my own. Egalitarianism, as I point out to my students, is a very late historical development growing out of the Enlightenment.

[3]Aristotle's *Nichomachean Ethics* is a good description of such a society.

[4]The book of Ruth in the Bible depicts the life of such a sojourner in Israel.

were frequently understood to be subject to adult males within families and disqualified in general from holding authoritative positions. Accordingly, the customs that assigned social standing were stable, indeed, frequently inflexible. The moral justification for such societies was often ascribed to ancient myths or practices and was not subject to revision even by authoritative males. In such a world moral dilemmas were relatively limited as were moral obligations vis-à-vis nonmembers.[5]

The Rise of Imperialism

This moral stasis was upset by imperialistic societies, whether the imperialism was primarily political, moral, or religious. The creation of empires with ethnic and cultural diversity, complicated moral schemes by compelling and consolidating diverse and otherwise incompatible peoples. This process resulted in widespread moral diversity. The powerful ruling majorities usually responded to the problems of diversity by excluding minorities from policy formation as well as compelling them to contribute by bearing the most onerous burdens of the society.

In this world people were clearly bound to one another in nonegalitarian covenants of obligation and oppression. Eventually, the masses demanded, after many years of struggle, sometimes in revolutionary terms, the changing of arrangements so they could have greater opportunities to achieve flourishing conditions for themselves and their progeny. They demanded and fought for liberty. Indeed, liberty was considered essential to flourishing. In the New World this cry was often for the relinquishment of oppressive social control, a process that we now commonly call liberation.

People demanded the right to choose their destinies, their relationships, and their futures. These demands were made even by dominating colonials who were part of the ruling classes. Thus, for example, in America, even slaveholders such as Thomas Jefferson, fought for the recognition and implementation of "inalienable rights" for himself and other adult white males, owners of property in freehold. Compared to the ancient regime, this recognition of natural rights was revolutionary and over time became normative in the constitutions of many Western nations.

Universal Application

While these views were parochial in application and even in conceptualization, the concepts inherently had the potential for universal application.[6] The oppressed understood this potential and claimed it for

---

[5]Plato's seminal text, *The Republic,* is an attempt to justify this approach philosophically.

[6]Indeed, though actually parochial in application, these concepts were infrequently voiced in universal terms or given even divine sanction. Their extension to African Americans did not begin to be realized until after the Civil War.

themselves and subsequently established movements to fight for the extension of these rights. These liberation movements were diverse and vital and developed their own liberation ethics. Frequently, these ethics dealt with a number of different issues and situations, but had in common the demand for freedom.

Over time and with much bloodshed, various rights and equalities were ceded to the oppressed. However, this seemingly fortunate outcome coincided with a concomitant conceptual development. The Western claim for rights was made, taxonomically speaking, as a species of individual negative rights.[7] The moral agent's claim was for liberty for the individual from the constraints of several different groups–the state, religion, the family, and the economy. Further, this release was a granting of freedom from, or liberty from, rather than a freedom for or to any particular group, society, or way of life. People were, as H. L. A. Hart puts it, naturally free to "starve to death" (1955, 175–191). This world in transition had finally rejected notions of obligation and paternalism like noblesse oblige in favor of new and more egalitarian notions of social status. New notions of obligation and covenantal responsibility, however, have yet to be elaborated or established in widespread common practices.

Atomistic Freedom

The resulting condition of atomistic freedom was useful in protecting the individual from direct exploitation. But it had, ironically, the very negative effect of expelling the individual out of a bonded, covenanted obligated notion of a good society into a society of aggregated strangers.[8] In other words, corrals were dismantled. This moral progress was also moral regress. It created societies with protection of the individual from direct predation by the state and church and to some extent from capitalist exploiters. At the same time, covenanted corporate obligations to assist and provide for the unfortunate were almost completely eroded.

This newly created world of supposedly self-made men and women, capable of pulling themselves up by their own bootstraps to happiness, was as mythic as its predecessor in its conceptualization and realization.[9] This postmodern world is one in which huge groups of people live in abject poverty. Many of the most "fortunate" of the oppressed continue to be

---

[7]For a full description of this process, see my taxonomy of rights in my fuller statement on rights in *God Bless the Child That's Got Its Own,* 19–38.

[8]This atomism is, of course, somewhat overstated here as communities, families, and churches continued to exist and function. However, they now function for the good of the individual, rather than the individual functioning for the good of the community, family, or church. A certain undeniable rootlessness prevails. See Michael J. Sandel's influential article "The Encumbered Self," 569–77.

[9]For a full and convincing exposition of the mythic qualities of this new situation, see Roger G. Betsworth's enlightening text *Social Ethics.*

oppressed, not by foreign occupying armies but by exploitive domestic elites collaborating with transnational corporations.[10] Many of the least fortunate are economically, culturally, and politically expendable. They do not fit into any of the exploitative roles of the important people of their societies, and their very existence is constantly under scrutiny and challenge.[11]

What this brief evolution of moral society has attempted to explain is a sea of change and a paradigm shift in the world that presents problems for the twenty-first century. This means liberation movements of any kind must change in focus and terminology if they are to continue to make any kind of moral sense.

From Freedom to Flourishing

This new situation is unique and requires liberation theology/ethics to move beyond the demand for more liberty. People are already too free to starve to death and are freely and extensively doing so. Thus a liberation ethic for the future has to be centered on more than being free from oppression and other constraints. To a very large extent, liberation theology has to develop, in a much more systematic way, the development of a more just, sustainable, and participatory society.[12] This new emphasis is not really new. It has been addressed by a number of communities of resistance in a piecemeal fashion for decades.

Individual and Group Needs

Justice, sustainability, and participation are fuller, more complicated and useful concepts for the development of flourishing communities. With these concepts particular communities can more easily address their basic human needs. In recognizing their particular basic needs, they raise the possibility and necessity of recognizing the basic human needs of others. It is only with the satisfaction of one's own particular needs in relation to one's group and that of the group in relation to other groups that the possibility of the right relationships among individual and group and foreign groups can begin to be addressed. It is only with this coordinated relation of the needs and destinies of all people that the old notions of "corralled membership" can be properly dissolved. What duties I owe to my group, other groups, and myself help to explain and account for the rights I have–rights to exercise as well as rights to recognize and protect. Only with the

---

[10]José Miguez-Bonino's work has most informed my thinking on this subject. See *Towards a Christian Political Ethic.*

[11]For a full discussion on this point see Boff, *When Theology Listens to the Poor,* 38.

[12]The leader in this field is again my former professor, José Miguez-Bonino. See *Doing Theology in a Revolutionary Situation.*

recognition of this basic and universal connectedness can an ethic that is justifiable to individuals and groups be attempted, let alone realized.[13]

Three moral languages and systems are required for the adequate addressing of these issues and for the creation of a new revolutionary ethic that can be used to create a new moral world: these languages are that of human rights, basic human needs, and ethical responsibility.[14]

Human Rights and Flourishing

The development of human rights discourses and their instantiation in internationally binding documents forces all people to recognize certain duties–internal and external to their boundaries–that create a common moral playing field and an interconnected moral global village. Now one cannot do "in Rome as the Romans do" if doing so would be a violation of human rights. Human rights can become a point of contention, depending on how human rights are conceptualized with regard to their application, content, and function. Human rights function fairly well, conceptually speaking, in creating clear moral prescriptions that ban oppressive actions that elites have used to dominate historically. Human rights are notoriously ineffective in creating binding moral duties for governments and powerful groups and elites to share wealth, resources, and power while concomitantly protecting the economy, the environment, and democracy.[15] People are still free to starve to death while their neighbors stand idly by or worse, while they exploit them further. With great difficulty these problems are being addressed by modern basic human needs discourses.

Basic Human Needs and Flourishing

In a variety of ways, these discourses attempt to state a base material platform that all must acknowledge as necessary to be achieved by all human communities to enable human flourishing. However, the feasibility for the

---

[13]How and to what extent strangers should extend aid to others is problematic. Of this problem, Michael Walzer writes, "Groups of people ought to help necessitous strangers whom they somehow discover in the midst or on their path. But the limit on risks and costs in these cases is sharply drawn. I need not take the injured stranger into my home, except briefly, and I certainly need not care for him or even associate with him for the rest of my life." See *Spheres of Justice,* 33. Walzer is basically correct , yet he personalizes the scenario in a way that makes the extension of mutual aid seem supererogatory in nature. For liberation ethics to mean anything, it will have to function and on a systematic level at that, in a supererogatory fashion. Yet how this is to be arranged and agreed upon is very problematic.

[14]This new ethic is one that must use philosophical rather than theological terms. It must find terms accessible to all in the public arena so that it does not simply create a new corral of religious insiders and irreligious outsiders. Christian ethicists, like myself, must speak in these terms to many different partners. That we do so because of religious motives and by and for a religious power cannot figure deeply into the wider community conversations.

[15]When Leonardo Boff discusses positive duties such as preferential options for the poor, he also references out of necessity basic human needs categories, human rights, as well as divine rights and duties. See *When Theology Listens to the Poor,* 38ff.

creation of a society in which the necessities are provided for all founders. It founders not just on technological difficulties but also on the problem of determining the identity of duty bearers responsible for achieving these results. In other words, the necessity for devising and establishing a consensus theory on what material provisions and relationships provide substantially the provision and enjoyment of basic human needs is an inescapable and pressing concern.[16] In addition, a theory of ethical responsibilism must also be developed in which the terms of responsibility for addressing these problems can be explicated.

Ethical Responsibilism and Human Flourishing in a Just, Participatory, and Sustainable Society

The requirements of creating a just, sustainable, and participatory society address the concerns of liberation theology and ethics in the twenty-first century. In parts of the world in which oppression still prevails, where slavery or conditions close to slavery still persist, the oppressed will still emphasize liberty. In other places, such as the United States of America, conditions are markedly different. No one is politically enslaved. Oppression is more closely associated with poverty, discrimination, and lack of participation in the control of individual and group life, especially for many African Americans.

Differing Central Concerns

Under these conditions liberation is no longer the most central concern.[17] To demonstrate for and to demand freedom no longer has the morally evocative power that it once had. Yet oppression still needs to be overthrown, but this oppression is more accurately reflected in demands for participation in policy formation that leads to better housing, public education, fairness in the criminal justice system, the deconstruction of racism and sexism, and the instantiation of some form of democratic socialism.

At first glance, these concerns may look very different than the demands of Mexican revolutionaries from Chiapas, but they are not. The new liberation ethic is a Christian ethic that requires the meeting of basic human needs in the contexts in which people find themselves, without Christ, or a

---

[16]This is where Nancy Fraser's essay is so helpful. See "Talking About Needs," in *Ethics,* 291–313.

[17]William Julius Wilson's works *The Truly Disadvantaged* and *When Work Disappears* have focused our attention on the debate concerning what is the more demonic problem, racism or economic exploitation. This debate misses the more important recognition that Blacks, women, and others are free and oppressed. Liberation from enslavement is no longer the primary need.. The more pressing need is the elimination of disenfranchisement from primary processes of employment, social standing, and participation in public policy formation.

crust of bread or a place to lay their heads.[18] The enjoyment of these needs also requires the enforcement of basic human rights. The challenges of different oppressed peoples will vary according to the material, spiritual, and social conditions of their respective situations. But the need of all people to be able to participate in the creation, maintenance, and improvement of their societies is becoming clearer with every generation.

An Ethic of Participation and Solidarity

The most revolutionary liberation ethic is, accordingly, an ethic of participation and solidarity. In an ethic of participation and solidarity, all people are considered to be the children of God, and all are called to the same destiny of living in peace and harmony with one another. However, we are all called to do this in a sinful world in which violence is prevalent, scarcity abounds, and historical hatreds persist. This world, furthermore, has been globalized so that most of the levers of power are situated too far from the people. In such a sinful world, creating a cooperative human ethics of participation and solidarity is a monumental task. To do so requires us to recognize, empathize, and suffer for and with each other. We are all, in the final analysis, members of one family and, therefore, radically interconnected. We must recognize, accordingly, the interconnectedness of all these struggles. For liberation theology/ethics to be more than a futile whimsy, it must remain particular in a variety of manifestations–mujerista, womanist, liberationist, gay, and many others. Yet it must remain connected to other similar movements.[19] In today's global village, a concentration on only the struggle of one's particular group is no longer morally acceptable.[20] The oppression and nonsustainability of one's own society or in another society halfway around the world (where one has the ability to influence the outcomes there) are now strictly linked though problematic obligations. Morally speaking, the oppression of others also constitutes the oppression of local members. There is in this new understanding of moral obligation no justifiable boundary, no specific place beyond which people who are aware of these problems are free from the obligation to struggle, resist, sacrifice, and even to die. In short, there is only one large corral.[21] The refusal of various liberation movements to concern themselves with the fates of others is the self-issued death warrants of these moral movements.

---

[18]By Christian I mean here a public policy formation ethic furthered by Christians for the common good that is not based in and on the acceptance of particular and exclusive religious foundations.

[19]For a mujerista ethic see Isasi-Díaz, *Mujerista Theology*. For a womanist perspective see Cannon, *Black Womanist Ethics*. For a gay perspective see Heyward, "Heterosexism," in *Redefining Sexual Ethics*, 103–115.

[20]Actually it was never morally acceptable. What has become clearer is a recognition of the moral demands that interconnectedness demands.

[21]This is precisely the point that noted bioethicist Garrett Hardin misses in his classic root metaphor, the lifeboat. See "Living on a Lifeboat," *BioScience*, 561–69.

This new universalism is daunting, as it will require the cooperation of strangers, even strangers who may be competing for the very same scarce resources. Yet these barriers are not insurmountable, at least not conceptually speaking. Yet the tendency of liberationists to concern themselves with parochial interests cannot be underestimated. In this country alone, liberation ethicists show little interest in working together on projects of solidarity to overthrow common oppressions. How artificial boundaries that separate us can be deconstructed, as well as a unifying system of beliefs and action plans constructed, constitutes the greatest conceptual challenges to the liberation ethicist. It is to this task that we must remain diligently at work. The creation of such a construct is the first step in the creation of a new world.

9

Sin

ANDREW SUNG PARK

There are six things that God hates,
seven that are an abomination to God:
haughty eyes, a lying tongue,
and hands that shed innocent blood,
a heart that devises wicked plans,
feet that hurry to run to evil,
a lying witness who testifies falsely,
and one who sows discord in a family
—PROV. 6:16–19

Since the traditional doctrine of sin can be found in other books, we will treat the notion of sin as defined by feminist theology, womanist theology, Black theology, Hispanic American theology, native American theology, and Asian American theology.

Neoorthodoxy

In opposition to liberal theologians who underestimate the reality of sin, neoorthodox theologians stress the seriousness of sin. Reinhold Niebuhr stands out with his doctrine of sin, depicting "man as sinner." For him, since we have the freedom to choose this or that, we vacillate between choices. This vacillation produces anxiety. Anxiety per se is not sin, but the precondition of sin. To overcome the state of anxiety, we deny our finitude or limitedness that is the source of human sin by committing the sin of pride. Or, to avoid the anguish of anxiety, we escape into sensuality by giving up our freedom to choose. Drunkenness, drug abuse, and bodily glorification are the signs of sensuality. For Niebuhr, sin is "not necessary, but inescapable." In short, sin is primarily *pride* and secondly *sensuality*, and both of them are based on *self-love* (Niebuhr 1941, 178–240).

Feminists

In contrast to Niebuhr's notion of sin, Valerie Saiving declares women's sin to be different from men's. To her, most women do not face the same temptations as men to deny their own limitedness.

> The specifically feminine forms of sin–"feminine" not because they are confined to women or because women are incapable of sinning in other ways but because they are outgrowths of the basic feminine character structure–have a quality, which can never be encompassed by such terms as "pride" or "will-to-power." They are better suggested by such items as triviality, distractibility, and diffuseness; lack of an organizing center or focus; dependence on others for one's own self-definition; tolerance at the expense of standards of excellence; inability to respect the boundaries of privacy; sentimentality, gossipy sociability, and mistrust of reason–in short, underdevelopment or negation of the self (1979, 37).

Saiving refuses to accept the doctrine of universal sin interpreted by male theologians. Although both women and men are capable of sinning, the dilemma for women is the opposite of men's: women generally suffer from the rejection of the self and from a lack of self-identity rather than self-centeredness.

Rosemary Radford Ruether is one of the foremost exponents of feminist theology. For her, sin is primarily hierarchical dualism in relationship. "Sin always has a personal as well as a systemic side. But it is never just 'individual'; there is no evil that is not relational" (1983, 181). Such a sin of dualism undergirds the distorted relationships elevating one over the other between male and female, body and consciousness, Caucasians and non-Caucasians, the rich and the poor, heterosexuals and homosexuals, and human and nonhuman nature. The distortion of relationship takes place with oneself, neighbors, nature, and God. Even in the act of personal sins such as self-abuse, rape, assault, and murder, we find the systemic, historical, and social context of sin (181). Sexism emerges from distorted relationality and is "the underlying social foundation of the good-evil ideology" (160).

Black Liberation Theology

For James H. Cone, sin is a community concept. It is a condition of estrangement from the source of meaning and purpose and our being related to nonbeing. It denies the community (1998, 104).

The sin of white communities is different from that of black communities. For whites, sin is whiteness, the desire to play God in the realm of human affairs. Sin is the condition of setting apart ministers to compromise with slavery, the condition of communities that engenders lynching, and the safe venture of white theologians for theological enterprises. In short, racism is original sin.

The sin of blacks cannot be talked about by oppressors, but by blacks alone. For blacks, sin embodies the condition of estrangement from the source of one's authentic being, which makes blacks desire to be white. It is the loss of identity, saying yes to whites' absurd claims, letting whites define their existence, and being complacent with white solutions for the black problem. Sin for blacks continues in the form of reaffirming white values by letting whites define what is good and beautiful (106–09).

Womanist Theology

Womanist theologians reject feminists' presumption that both of them suffer from the same plight. Jacquelyn Grant, an architect of womanist theology, understands that black women are dubious of the feminist movement. Like their white male partners, white women have "as their primary goal the suppression, if not oppression, of the Black race and the advancement of the dominant culture" (1989, 201). Furthermore, she says, "Put succinctly, women of the dominant culture are perceived as the enemy" (201). For Grant, black women experience "their tri-dimensional experience of racism/sexism/classism" (209). Black women find common ground with other groups on suffering. With black men they share the pain of racism. With white women and Two-Thirds World women they share the burden of the sexism of the dominant male culture. With poor blacks and whites and other Two-Thirds World people, particularly women, they endure poverty together. Thus, speaking of Black women's tri-dimensional reality is not to speak of black women alone, but to advocate suffering people in the world (Grant 1998, 215–16). God is siding with those who are on the underside of humanity.

Delores Williams, in her book *Sisters in the Wilderness*, concretely sums up the threefold nature of African American women's tormented experience (racism, sexism, and classism) in the life of Hagar in Genesis. Exploited, abused, subjugated, and raped by masters and their spouses, African American women were forced to play surrogates for their masters' spouses–from being sexual partners for their masters to mammies to white children. Hagar as an Egyptian woman represents the plight of African American women, and her relationship with God provides a hope for their survival.

Hispanic American Mujerista Theology

Ada María Isasi-Díaz has developed *Mujerista* theology for Hispanic Americans, particularly for Hispanic American women. To her, alienation is sin, both personal and structural. It is "from God and from each other experienced by all in and through the oppressive societal categories and structures that cause and sustain oppression" (1998, 32). Alienation as the chief obstacle to the unfolding of solidarity affects the totality of the person and relationship with God, neighbors, and society. She believes alienation is a denial of God, quoting Gutiérrez's saying, "an atheist is someone who fails to practice justice toward the poor" (33). The poor and the oppressed are marginalized and exploited, suffering systemic violence and cultural imperialism. Some specific forms of oppression for them are sexism, racism/ethnic prejudice, and classism (33). These forms are not separated from but structured within a worldwide system of domination in which only a few elites rule over many. She points out that Hispanic feminists have been marginalized within the Anglo feminist community "because of our critique of its ethnic/racial prejudice and its lack of class analysis" (1993, 3). She wants her Anglo feminist sisters to hear the voices of their mujerista and other ethnic sisters.

Hispanic American Theology

In his essay "The Alienation of Alienation," Justo González treats the issue of alienation (2001a, 61–70). Questioning the treatment of the term *alienation,* González is critical of its exclusively psychological usage in church history. Such a psychologized term enhances the internalization and individualization of sin. Illustrating this with the examples of Pelagius and Augustine, he explains the individualization of sin in terms of the atomization of reality and the privatization of sin. Drawing upon Abelard and Anselm's theology, he further explores the meaning of the internalization of sin.

On the one hand, using Anselm's concept of sin, González points out that sin should be seen not only from the will and intention of the sinner, but also from the perspective of the sinned-against. On the other, against Anselm's idea of hierarchical authority and its consequential assumption of sin, González points to the subversive principle of the gospel concerning the concept of sin. Without denying the necessity of some measure of order, he rejects any authoritarian and hierarchical suppression in the process of the internalization of sin.

In opposition to the effort to fix the sin of internalization through psychotherapy, he suggests "the alienation of alienation." For him, the term *alienation* means not only becoming psychologically dysfunctional, but also turning into something alien from God and from ourselves. With his deep knowledge of Christian history, he discloses the abuse of the doctrine of sin for two thousand years. The church, he argues, has internalized and individualized the significance and breadth of its notion of sin. He suggests that we alienate the alienation of the doctrine of sin for the sake of the alienated. Unlike Hegel, who believed in reconciliation with alienation, he alienates the alienation of the doctrine of sin, contradicting Freudian psychoanalytic diagnoses of social wrongs. Contrasting with Marx, who wanted to remove religion altogether because of its role in generating alienation in a society, his notion of alienation can redeem our society by alienating the alienation of the traditional doctrine of sin.

Native American Theology

The idea of sin, particularly original sin, is at odds with Native American spirituality. Early missionaries have tried to translate the meaning of sin into Native American terms that convey the meaning of a mistake or being lost. They imply nonvolitional behavior. In the Creek language, sin means "to bother someone," indicating an intrusion into another person's will. For the Navajo, wrong acts are the result of not knowing what one is doing. The Choctaw words *aiashachi* and *aiyoshoba* mean "err at; to make a mistake at, sin about, or overlook" and "error, wandering; sin; place of sin" respectively (Kidwell, et al. 2001, 100–101).

There are several practical notions of sin among the nations of Native Americans:

- The power to control others' will

The idea of evil is associated with the will to control others through witchcraft–charms, incantations, and manipulation of objects. According to Black Elk, it is a kind of sickness (102).

- Individualism

While Indian societies respect the integrity of the individual, they refuse to subscribe to individualism. For the Lakota, "the worst thing that could be said of an individual was that he or she acted 'as if they had no relatives'" (106). Appropriate social relationships are essential to virtue. These relationships are extended to beings in the natural world and the spiritual world beyond the human world. They are cosmic in nature. Any violation of the connectedness of beings is sin.

- A failure to live up to one's responsibility

Sin from a perspective of Native Americans can be characterized as a failure to live up to one's responsibility, sometimes deliberately, but most of the times thoughtlessly and impulsively (110). It is a lack of responsibility to community. For instance, if one is attending a communal ceremony with inappropriate thoughts, his or her attitude may negate the effectiveness of the ceremony by obstructing the restoration of the relationships of community.

Native Americans do not have a vertical understanding of sin before God, but a horizontal notion of sin committed upon family members, friends, and communities. The sin of pride that is to be like God is not an issue for them because they relate themselves to God at a horizontal relationship. Irresponsibility to one's family and community is evil and sin (112).

Asian American Theology

Among Asian Americans, Rita Nakashima Brock has worked on the doctrine of sin from a feminist perspective. For her, sinfulness is neither an inevitable condition that arrives with birth nor a universal attribute that permeates all human beings, but "a symptom of the unavoidably relational nature of human existence through which we come to be damaged and damage others" (1988, 7). This concept of "sin as damage enhances responsibility and healing instead of miring us in blame and guilt" (7). Her presupposition is our "radical relational nature" that derives from our inability to face our own pain and be healed.

Our original grace arises from the ontological nature of our relational existence, which unavoidably results in the brokenness of our relational life. Thus, sin is the outcome of evil, "a sign of our brokenheartedness, of how damaged we are, not of how evil, willfully disobedient, and culpable we are" and in this sense, sin cannot be resolved in retribution, but in healing (7).

To Brock, the church has not treated the presence of evil seriously. She believes that Christians have not understood the depth of evil in our own patriarchal heart for all the discussion of racism, greed, alienation, pride, evil, and war. The church has had its proclivity to overlook the evils that attack the family, the heart of society–"evil such as child abuse, battering, rape, incest, or forced pregnancy and sterilization" (8). Patriarchy is one major factor of our damaged state, which has generated a doctrine of sin.

As an Asian American, I have grappled with the idea of sin and also its impact on its victims. By defining the Asian concept of *han* (the woundedness of the victim), I have tried to draw attention to the entanglement and mutual reinforcement of sin and *han.*[1] *Han* is a festering wound generated by unjust psychosomatic, social, political, economic, and cultural repression and oppression. Since sin is dynamically correlated with sinister traditions, customs, and systems, it can never be understood by itself. Sin can be grasped far better in light of *han.*

Sin causes *han,* and *han* procreates sin. Sin is of sinners; *han* is of the sinned-against. The sin of sinners may cause a chain reaction via the *han* of the sinned-against. Sometimes *han* reproduces sin. For instance, a baby

---

[1]*Minjung* theologians of Korea first talked about the concept of *han.* See The Commission on Theological Concerns, *Minjung Theology;* and Park, *The Wounded Heart of God.*

can inherit drug addiction and may commit related crimes such as selling drugs. We need to understand the sin or crime of drug dealing in light of the drug dealer's biological and home environments. Furthermore, sin and *han* collaborate to engender *han*. They reinforce each other and overlap in many tragic areas of life.

Sin is a paradigm of domination and has three levels: individual, collective, and structural. At the individual level, sin appears as controlling, selfishness, superiority complex, greed, lust, and exploitation. At the collective level, sin is the collective consciousness and unconsciousness of aggression such as the ethos of cultural hegemony, racial superiority complex, physical pride, exclusive ethnocentrism, and nationalism. At the structural level, sin is unjust and evil systems that perpetuate racism, sexism, exclusiveness, and monopolistic capitalism. From the perspective of the oppressed, monopolistic capitalism, racism, and sexism are the roots of structural *han*, while from the perspective of oppressors, these are the roots of structural sin.

Han has three levels: individual, collective, and structural. At its individual level, *han* is the will to avenge, the will to resign, bitterness, and helplessness; it is a reaction to individualistic oppression, which is often connected to collective and structural oppression. At its collective level, *han* is the collective consciousness and unconsciousness of victims such as the ethos of cultural inferiority complex, racial melancholy, racial resentment, the sense of physical inadequacy, and national shame. At its structural level, it is a chronic sense of helplessness and resignation before powerful monopolistic capitalism, pervasive racism, tenacious sexism, and oppressive classism.

Sin and *han* need to be understood in their vicious cycle and to be resolved in their connection; they look contorted in separation, and they can be identified in unity. Various types of sin are the outcome of unhealed *han*. Therefore, the church needs to care about the healing of its *han*-ridden parishioners and the redeeming of its sin-infected people in the drama of interplaying sin and *han*.

10

Spirituality

KAREN BAKER-FLETCHER

Introduction

We begin with the question, "What is spirituality?" Moreover, "What is liberation spirituality?" Miguel A. De la Torre and Edwin Aponte define spirituality as the religious symbols "that make sense of the world and provide a concrete point of contact with the Divine" (2001, 62). Spirituality is integral to life and to one's experience of life. It is the way one experiences and responds to divine love. Divine love is the very source and power of life. Peruvian liberation theologian Gustavo Gutiérrez, in *We Drink from Our Own Wells,* writes, "A spirituality is a walking in freedom according to the Spirit of love and life." He uses the image of a well to describe spirituality "like living water that springs up in the very depths of the experience of faith," quoting John 7:38. This "living water" refers to the gift of the Spirit that Jesus makes to his disciples" (37).

A Focus on Cultural Elements

Speaking from U.S. liberationist perspectives, Aponte and De La Torre focus on cultural elements within Latino/a Protestant popular religion to define spirituality. Spirituality is evident in a believing community that comes together to worship and praise God. In the Protestant *culto* or worship, as in the Catholic *misa* or mass, they write, a reaffirmation of community and identity occurs. Moreover, as Elizabeth Conde-Frazier and Justo González observe, Latino/a worship is a fiesta–a celebration. Such celebration of the goodness of God in the midst of the struggle for justice is a central element in liberation spirituality as a whole.

Insights form Ancient, Indigenous Religions

Not all theologies that advocate liberation are Christian, but the understanding of spirituality in liberation theology has emerged primarily from poor Christian communities of color. Therefore, liberation theologians tend to emphasize a spirituality that draws on the liberating activity of God in Christ through the power of the Holy Spirit. Yet, one may find references to spiritual wisdom and practices drawn from pre-colonial, indigenous ancient religions in liberation spirituality. In Mexican American spirituality, for example, some scholars note that Our Lady of Guadalupe is an experiential Spanish language renaming of the Indian Aztec goddess *Coatlaxopeuh,* a Nahuatl word meaning "crushes the serpent."[1]

For Mexican American liberation theologian Virgilio Elizondo, the Lady, in a 1532 apparition to Juan Diego, clearly identifies herself as the Virgin Mary in the story; yet there is a sense that as the mother of the indigenous peoples of Mexico and of all peoples she has always been there.[2] Womanist theologian Emilie Townes considers the Kongo cosmogram, a cross within a circle, in relation to African slaves from the Bas-Zaire region of West Africa as they encountered slavery in the New World (1995:22). Chung Hyun Kyung, who is originally from Korea, explores syncretism of Korean shamanist practices, Buddhism, and Christianity within Korean women's liberating spirituality.[3] In *Gaia and God,* Rosemary Radford Ruether examines an ecofeminist liberation theology, the relationship between God and the pre-Hellenistic Gaia, the living earth mother.

A Consensus View

Within the diversity of perspectives that make up "liberation spirituality," however, there is general consensus with Gutiérrez's understanding of "spirituality" as a sustaining, liberating reality that human

---

[1]According to the story, in 1531 a "Lady from Heaven" appeared to a poor Indian named Juan Diego at Tepeyac, a hill northwest of Mexico City, identifying herself to him as the Mother of the True God, "of all the people" of his land, and of humankind. The name "de Guadalupe" or "of Guadalupe" was the name given by the Lady in a subsequent apparition to Juan Diego's uncle, Juan Bernadino.

[2]See Elizondo, *Guadalupe;* and *Galilean Journey,* 11–13. Elizondo understands Guadalupe as the Virgin Mother, Mary, mother of Jesus, and as the mother of a new people, the *mestizaje* or mixed people of Mexico, who, after the *conquistadores,* are of Indian, Spanish, and sometimes African descent, though those of African descent are more often referred to as *mulatez.*

[3]Chung, *Struggle to be the Sun Again;* and "Following Naked Dancing" in *Inheriting Our Mothers' Gardens,* 67.

beings practice and experience in each moment as they work, pray, weep, rejoice, and create that which nurtures life out of scarce resources and abundant potential.

According to U.S. Puerto Rican liberation theologian Elizabeth Conde-Frazier, who writes from the perspective of Hispanic Protestant liberationist spirituality, "Christian spirituality":

> involves the response to and relationship with God, who is revealed in the Bible and especially in the person of Jesus Christ. Our relationship with God began at creation and was broken by sin. It can be restored through faith in Jesus. Some describe the journey of spirituality as a 'conformity of heart and life to the character of Jesus as Lord' (Rom 12:1-3). It is the presence and the power of the Holy Spirit working in the life of the believer that guides and guarantees our relationship with Christ (1997, 125).

Conde-Frazier describes Hispanic Protestant spirituality as "the expression of both contemplation and action" (130). It is both affective and cognitive, reasoning and experiential, thinking and feeling.

The Place of Testimony

It is visible through *testimonio,* an outward expression of one's faith through living out that faith and through sharing this lived faith verbally during worship in the form of spoken testimony. A similar practice is evident in much of traditional African American Christian spirituality as well. The purpose of testimony is to witness, to share one's experience of God's liberating response to the faith of believers in their everyday lives.

Priestly and Prophetic Elements

Hispanic spirituality has two dimensions: priestly and prophetic. The priestly aspects are cultic (evident in ritual) and contemplative; the prophetic aspects are found in pastoral practice, not simply among clergy, but more especially among women laity. Within this spirituality, the anger of protest along with compassion "fuels our mission of care" (143). Conde-Frazier observes Hispanic women's celebrative events such as bridal and baby showers, where women "express aspects of the otherwise taboo subjects of menstruation and sexuality." "It was a power in us," she writes. "Women dare to connect this power with the creative power of God. Salvation and creation are united in the meaning of the womb." Conde-Frazier introduces us to Doña Inez, a woman in her early seventies. She "spoke of a woman's body as a holy sanctuary of life and the Spirit of God," fleshing out "the biblical understanding of the worth of a woman" (139).

"The Holy Spirit," Conde-Frazier clarifies, "has been the one to lead us and empower us" while prayer "is the most important tool in connecting to the Spirit" (141). Quoting 1 Corinthians 2:10–11, "It is the Spirit who reveals these things to us, for it is the Spirit who truly comprehends what is truly God's," Conde-Frazier concludes. The Spirit transcends human experience and intimately connects it to the mind of God, building up communities in a faith that is filled with the *testimonio* of liberating praxis. In liberation theology spirituality is experienced and practiced in community. It is embodied, reasoned and practiced faith–*praxis.*

Spirituality, Praxis, and Experiencing the Spirit

For liberation theologians, spirituality is not an esoteric union with a wholly other, utterly transcendent, objective reality. Spirituality is experienced in every moment of life. It is a reality that individuals in community experience continuously in the here and now in their being and doing. Yet, to experience God, who is a spirit, relativizes the immediacy of human understanding, selfhood, and activity. For individuals in community, such experience generates glimpses into a reign or "kin-dom" of God that is yet and not yet, immanent and transcendent, present and yet to come (Isasi-Díaz 1996, 99–100).

Interlocking Forms of Oppression

There is a holistic impetus in liberation theologies, with increasing attention to interlocking forms of oppression.[4] The *praxis* orientation of liberation theologies presupposes that individuals and communities practice spirituality in every moment of existence, for good and for ill, in liberating ways and oppressive ways, in relation to every individual and community persons encounter and engage with, consciously and unconsciously. The question is not whether or not one can "become spiritual." Spirituality is embodied in the flesh-and-bones experience of human beings. The question is "*How will one act as an embodied spiritual being in community*?"

Praxis as a Core Theme

Praxis, the integration of theory and practice, thinking and doing, feeling and acting, head and heart is a core theme in liberation spirituality. Healthy spiritual praxis is liberating. Liberating praxis, however, is not possible without God, who is a spirit and the sustaining, liberating source of life. Liberating spirituality, a spirituality of experience and praxis, is made possible by a liberating God in whom all things are possible and a liberating faith that is "the substance of things hoped for, the evidence of things not seen," (Heb. 11:1, KJV). Liberation spirituality is not based in the way things have always been but in the full potential of life promised in what

---

[4]See The Combahee River Collective, "A Black Feminist Statement," in Kolmar and Bartkowski, *Feminist Theory,* 272. Black feminists coined the expression "interlocking systems of oppression," and the terminology is frequently employed by womanist theologians. The concept, if not the terminology, is evident in much of Hispanic/Latino/a liberation theology as well.

Cuban *mujerista* theologian Ada María Isasi-Díaz calls the kin-dom of God which is yet and not yet. For human beings, realizing the kin-dom of God is possible through a liberating spirituality of solidarity (love of neighbor), mutuality, *familia,* and *communidad* in the struggle *(la lucha)* for justice (1996, 99–100).[5]

Spirituality and Spirit

Spirituality is intelligent, feeling, and practical. It encompasses and pervades the whole of life. Spirituality most simply has to do with the spirit of a subject in relation to the pervasive and encompassing source of life, *Spirit* or God who is a *spirit.* Womanist theologians have drawn on Alice Walker's definition of "womanist," which emphasizes that a womanist, a black feminist or feminist of color, "*loves* the Spirit" (1983, xi-xii). For Walker "the Spirit" is not separate from creation. To speak of Spirit for Walker is to speak of life. For Walker a "womanist" is committed to "the healing and wholeness of entire communities, male and female." "Womanist" comes from the black folk expression "womanish," meaning grown up. In Walker's novel *The Color Purple* (1982) the sexually and physically abused Celie learns from blues singer Shug that God is not an old white man. Celie finds salvation in creation–first trees, then, air, then birds, then feels "being part of everything, not separate at all" (1982, 167).

"Creation" integrated with Spirit also means creativity. Celie finds economic freedom by making pants instead of cutting "Mister's" throat. Moreover, God celebrates the love relationship between Celie and Shug. Creation integrated with Spirit is imbued with love and invites loving response. Those connected to Spirit in creation find strength to free others and are committed to race, gender, sexual orientation, class, and ecological liberation.

Delores Williams employs Walker's definition of womanist to develop a womanist theology of survival and liberation. Her emphasis is on a spirituality of survival. She does not describe herself as a liberation theologian, because God does not always liberate. Yet, like most womanist theologians she includes the theme of liberating spirituality in her work, balancing it with the theme of survival and a praxis of resistance to oppression. For Williams "the spirit" empowers black women to survive oppression even when liberation is far off. Sometimes God provides quality of life and resources for survival, making a way out of no way. She builds on black women's response to the biblical story of Hagar who sat down with Ishmael to die from thirst in the desert when an angel appeared to reveal a hidden spring where none had existed before.

---

[5]Ada María Isasi-Díaz, engaging the work of Gustavo Gutiérrez, employs the term "kin-dom" rather than "kingdom" to emphasize the dynamic tensions between liberation and mutuality.

According to Williams, the God-content of womanist theology draws on a theology of "spirit" informed by political action and is represented by a diversity of voices.[6] Turning to African American worship, Williams observes that:

> Walker's mention of the black womanist's love of the spirit is a true reflection of the great respect Afro-American women have always shown for the presence and work of the spirit. In the black church, women (and men) often judge the effectiveness of the worship service not on the scholarly content of the sermon nor on the ritual nor on orderly process. Rather, worship has been effective if "the spirit was high," i.e., if the spirit was actively and obviously present in a balanced blend of prayer, of cadenced word (the sermon), and of syncopated music ministering to the pain of the people. The importance of this emphasis upon the spirit is that it allows Christian womanist theologians, in their use of the Bible, to identify and reflect upon those biblical stories in which poor oppressed women had a special encounter with divine emissaries of God, like the spirit (1989, 185–186).

This emphasis on experience of "the spirit" is not limited to worship service but is an integral part of political, economic, and social life. Womanist liberation theologian Jacquelyn Grant turns to black feminist Sojourner Truth as an example of a freedom fighter who knew how to listen to "the spirit" as the source of liberating power. A spirit she later identifies as Jesus appears to her in the hush arbor while she is praying about her situation as a slave and freedom. This spirit provides Sojourner Truth with wisdom and resources to free herself and her children and to become a leader in the abolitionist and feminist movements of the mid-nineteenth century. Similarly, in her discussion of black women freedom fighters, Williams highlights women empowered by the spirit.

Finally, Williams describes womanist spirituality as conflating Jesus/Christ/God under the term "spirit," noting that "Black women's stories attest to black women's belief in Jesus/Christ/God involved in their daily affairs and supporting them" (1993, 203). Spirit sustains survival and liberation efforts. Similarly, womanist ethicist Katie Cannon writes of African American spirituals, prayers, and storytelling as spiritual practices that generate agency for survival and liberation (1991, 86–89).

---

[6]See Baker-Fletcher and Baker-Fletcher, *My Sister, My Brother,* 25–42, 245, 257; Baker-Fletcher, *Sisters of Dust, Sisters of Spirit,* 109–16; and Williams, "Womanist Theology and Black Women's Voices," in *Weaving the Visions,* 185–86. Williams lowercases "spirit," perhaps to emphasize its pervasiveness in everyday life. In practice, African American women and men generally uppercase "Spirit" to distinguish the human spirit and evil spirits from the Spirit as God and Holy Spirit. Scripture and Sojourner Truth refer to God as "a spirit" but not as "spirit."

Womanist theo-ethicist Emilie Townes connects the centrality of the Spirit in black communities and churches with spiritual practice, writing that "Knowing the Spirit is to use both heart and head." Spirituality then requires knowledge of the Spirit. This knowledge emerges through reason and feeling. Moreover, Townes writes, "It is to lean into God's word as both salvation and challenge. It is to allow ourselves to experience and live out of the experience of being wrapped in God's love and peace" (1995, 143–44).

For Townes this love and peace are not separated from justice, but connected to it. That does not mean justice always appears as we want it when we want, but the heart that leans toward the justice of the Spirit finds enough peace and love to continue the struggle. Therefore, Townes writes about hope, love, and struggle, explaining that to know the Spirit is to "witness out of the hope we grow into with the Spirit. It is to love God with our minds through a rigorous and relentless pursuit of grasping, however imperfectly, God's unfolding revelation in our lives through our ever-expanding understanding of the nature of the universe. It is in our struggles to live into our witness that we find God waiting for us and also prodding us into wholeness..." (1995, 143). Spirituality is the struggle to know the Spirit.

Syncretistic Spirituality

Chung Hyun Kyung, in *Struggle to be the Sun Again,* writes about the distinctiveness of the spirituality of Asian women, who are often the poorest of the poor, the oppressed of the oppressed, or, in Korea, the *minjung* of the *minjung.* Chung, a feminist theologian from Korea, had two mothers, a birth mother–a surrogate–and the wealthier woman who raised her. Both mothers participated in a painful pact of secrecy until the wealthier mother died. Both mothers experienced *han,* the suffering and unresolved resentment of the *minjung.* Chung writes about their spirituality. Her mothers were syncretistic, meaning they mixed and matched all the spiritual resources they found around them "that were helpful and gave comfort to their hearts."

"I want to name my mothers' distinctive spirituality as 'survival-liberation-centered syncretism,'" she writes. "The heart of their spirituality was the life power that sustained and liberated them. 'Life-giving power' is the final criterion by which the validity of any religion is judged" (1991, 67).

Chung moves beyond the Christocentric emphasis of Gutiérrez's definition of liberation spirituality to a description of intentional syncretism. "Their center of spirituality was not Jesus, Buddha, Confucius, or any of the various fortune-tellers," she writes. Rather, "the real center for their spirituality was life itself," a conscious and unconscious selection of "the life-giving aspects of each religion" accompanied by rejection of "the death-giving ones" (66). Aware that orthodox Christians would find this mixing heretical, she counters that whether or not her mothers understood orthodoxy, they did know about "life-giving power," which for Chung is the test of truth in spirituality.

Liberation Spirituality and Creation

Until the 1990s, the rhetoric of mainstream ecologists, particularly of deep ecologists, appeared and sometimes was dismissive of emphases on human liberation. For liberation theologians, all life is sacred. If all life is sacred, then one cannot limit spiritual well-being either to human beings *or* to other creation. There is a direct economic and spiritual correlation between freedom of peoples and freedom of the planet. Liberation theologians observe that in a spirituality of oppression the earth and the poor, especially poor people of color, are each exploited.

Creation Stories and Intrinsic Value

Liberation spirituality draws on biblical, indigenous, and scientific creation stories that find intrinsic value in all creation, human and non-human, down to the smallest sub-atomic particle of energy that generates life and matter. Process theologian John Cobb's work with biologist Charles Birch in *The Liberation of Life* offers a metaphysical and scientific analysis of the integration of matter and spirit. The analysis has much in common with indigenous cosmologies that are *panentheistic*, finding God or Spirit intimately present in all that lives, animate and inanimate. The authors persuasively argue for the liberation of life, helpfully elucidating the integrative relationship between matter and energy. Missing from the volume, however, is race, class, and gender analysis. Cobb has since published several volumes that integrate global economic analysis with constructive work for a sustainable future.

The ecofeminist liberation writings of Rosemary Radford Ruether and Carol Adams, respectively, analyze the relationship between women's oppression and the oppression of the rest of the earth.[7] Adams's analysis finds connections between cruelty to animals and the economic oppression of the poor hired to slaughter them, while Ruether focuses on a revisioning of relationship to the planet earth or Gaia who experiences our creative and destructive acts. Ruether's feminist analysis *in New Woman, New Earth* was the first liberation theology to connect ecological oppression with oppression of the poor, women, and people of color.[8] Delores Williams

---

[7]See Ruether, *New Woman, New Earth; Gaia and God;* and *Women Healing Earth.*

[8]Leonardo Boff, a Brazilian liberationist ecotheologian, engages in similar research that is a helpful resource for U.S. liberation theologians interested in the impact of economic forces on indigenous understandings of being in community *with* creation. See *Cry of the Earth, Cry of the Poor.*

was the first womanist theologian to write on ecology and black women, offering a social-historical analysis of the "violation and exploitation of the land and of women's bodies." She observes assaults upon nature, the human spirit, and the divine spirit, describing the "defilement of nature's body and of black women's bodies" as sin (1994, 24–29).

Environmental Justice Movement

Beginning in the late 1970s, the grassroots environmental justice movement emerged to challenge the dumping of toxic wastes in poor neighborhoods of color. Environmental racism, the disproportionate placement of toxic waste sites and industry in communities of color, is a concern in the womanist writings of Emilie Townes and Karen Baker-Fletcher.[9] Townes includes environmental justice in a womanist spirituality that loves black bodies. Baker-Fletcher explores the meaning of what it means for human beings to be created from dust and spirit in a world in which embodied spirits of color and the earth are subject to exploitation and abuse.

As black liberation theologian James Cone observes:

> Many ecologists speak often of the need for humility and mutual dialogue. They tell us that we are all interrelated and interdependent, including human and otherkind...If white ecologists really believe that, why do most still live in segregated communities? Why are their essays and books about the endangered earth so monological–that is, a conversation of a dominant group talking to itself? Why is there so much talk of love, humility, interrelatedness, and interdependence, and yet so little of these values reflected in white people's dealings with people of color? (Baker-Fletcher 1998, 6)

Cone, like Townes and Baker-Fletcher, delineates the emergence of the environmental justice movement and the attention of African American churches to the problem of "environmental racism," a term coined by Benjamin Chavis Muhammed during the 1990s. Cone challenges ecologists and ecotheologians, including ecofeminists. "Blacks and other minorities are often asked why they are not involved in the mainstream ecological movement," Cone observes. "To white theologians and ethicists, I ask, why are you not involved in the dialogue on race?" Cone seeks "to urge us to deepen our conversation by linking the earth's crisis with the crisis in the human family" (6).

There is a tendency among middle-class ecofeminist and mainstream ecotheologians to enjoy the privilege of extensive international travel that

---

[9]See Emilie Townes, *In a Blaze of Glory;* and Karen Baker-Fletcher, *Sisters of Dust, Sisters of Spirit.*

informs their spirituality. Such a privilege enables them to have the luxury of providing a global analysis. In contrast, many within the U.S. environmental justice movement would find it a luxury to leave their own neighborhoods. This is the cause of a credibility gap between theologians in the academy and the grass roots from which liberation spirituality emerges.

Ecofeminist and mainstream ecotheologians tend to contend that the environmental justice movement does not go far enough in its analysis. While Rosemary Ruether concedes that ecofeminists need to do more research in the area of environmental justice and the fight against environmental racism in the United States, she maintains that the environmental justice movement must go further than an analysis of pollution and toxic waste. Likewise, Carolyn Merchant, who observes the agency of women as organizers in the environmental justice movement, concurs that the environmental justice movement "has a long way to go."[10]

The tensions between the environmental justice movement and the ecological movement must come to deeper resolution, however, if there is to be a truly global, holistic spirituality of liberation. Economic globalization from the modern period and beyond, as Ruether emphasizes, is a common denominator between ecological oppression of people of color in the United States and in Third World countries. The challenge to proponents of environmental justice is greater global economic analysis. However, the challenge to proponents of ecological-justice or "ecojustice" is to engage in greater "in-reach."[11] This would enable grassroots communities to share equally in global analyses, providing experiential understanding of commonalities and dissimilarities among the poor.

The U.S. poor live a life of paradox among the globally oppressed. What does it mean to struggle for economic, gender, cultural, racial, and ecological liberation within a First World nation? What are the farthest reaching goals of a spirituality of liberation when you are among the poor in an *empire*? A holistic spirituality of liberation recognizes that we cannot fight over the local versus the global. Liberation spirituality emerges from the grass roots whether in the United States or in the Third World. It always begins with particular experience and moves out toward the global to act

[10]Panel discussion with Karen Baker-Fletcher, Rosemary Radford Ruether, Carol Christ, John Cobb, Carol Robb, Hava Tirosh-Samuelson, and Carolyn Merchant, "Gaia and the Sacred: Religion, Science, and Ethics," Church Divinity School of the Pacific, Berkeley, California, 14 June 2003. See also Merchant, *Earthcare,* 66–70, 160; and *Radical Ecology,* 59, 164–167. The work of environmental sociologist Robert Bullard is frequently cited by liberation theologians who address environmental justice. See Bullard, *Dumping in Dixie;* and Bullard and Wright, *Confronting Environmental Racism.*

[11]The *environmental justice movement* to date has focused on toxic dumping in poor U.S. communities. The *ecological justice* or *ecojustice* movement to date is engaged in more global analysis of ecological crisis in relation to economic globalization.

in solidarity with another's particular experience. Only with the realization that the local and the global are within one another can there be holistic healing for the entire planet and its people. Commitment to mutuality is grounded in the grace of empathetic listening and action across differences in the experience of oppression as we struggle for liberation.

Conclusion

Liberation theologians have not agreed on one single definition of "spirituality." They do echo one common theme: authentic spirituality is sustaining and liberating, promoting survival and freedom in all realms of life. They have reached consensus that a diversity of forms of liberation and oppression are interconnected. The search for spiritual health and freedom in the areas of race, gender, and class are related to a multiplicity of liberation movements, the environment, sexual orientation, age, and the right to non-violence. The spirituality of liberation theologies features a diversity of approaches to religion and orthodoxy. Some authors are relatively orthodox while others intentionally are not.

Liberation theologians generally argue that authentic Christianity or the true spirituality of Jesus, is, according to Matthew 25, found in the spirituality of "the least of these." They witness a common emphasis on a spirituality that integrates liberating praxis and experience. For these theologians liberation is salvation. Healthy spirituality saves lives. It lives into God's kin-dom of love, life, and freedom. In the kin-dom of God, oppressors and oppressed become a new people.

Who are the oppressed and the oppressor? Oppression is sin, and the capacity to oppress is in every human being. As individuals in community live into the kin-dom, *all* are freed from external systems of oppression *and* from their own complicity in oppressive acts. What does that mean? It means that the white feminist who has been racist is freed from sexism and her own racism. The man of color who is liberated from systemic structures of racism is also liberated from his sexism. The feminist of color is freed not only from racism, sexism, and classism but from her own heterosexism. The wealthy gay white male is liberated not only from heterosexism but from his own classism. The traditional, nuclear middle-class family is awakened to new possibilities as a child overcomes anorexia, bulimia, gross materialism, or drug addiction to distinguish the American *dream* from the American *nightmare*, reality from illusion, false peace from true peace. The white corporate executive is freed from a success-centered spirituality that has left him or her internally impoverished.

Multiple, complex possibilities exist for how one might experience liberation spirituality in the kin-dom of God which is yet and not yet. Liberation theologians and grassroots communities who consistently consider the liberation of all creation–male and female, human and non-human–broaden understandings of interlocking systems of oppression to include genocide *and* ecocide, spiritually resisting anthropocentrism alongside racism, sexism, classism, heterosexism, ageism, ableism, and every form of injustice that besets humankind. Wherever the earth, the poor, and the rest of us are exploited, ill, and dying, we find profound sites of spiritual resistance and liberation. Christian liberation spirituality, grounded in the principle of solidarity with the oppressed, derived from New Testament understandings of love of God and neighbor, calls the entire earth into a relationship of mutuality and justice.

11

Eschatology

LUIS N. RIVERA-PAGAN

For I am about to create new heavens and a new earth...
(ISA. 65:17)

Then I saw a new heaven and a new earth...
(REV. 21: 1)

Dies irae, dies illa, solvet saeclum in favilla...
(LATIN MASS FOR THE DEAD)

The End of Time and the Time of the End

Neglect and Renewal

Eschatology has probably been the most neglected theme in post-Enlightenment theology. In their liturgies most churches regularly recite the last section of either the Apostolic Creed–"I believe in...the resurrection of the body and life everlasting"–or the Nicene-Constantinopolitan Creed–"We look for the resurrection of the dead, and the life of eternity to come." (Denzinger 1955, 7, 36). But most churches do not give much thoughtful consideration to the import of that profession of faith. It has frequently become a residual mythic image, part of the aesthetic museum of a nostalgic

Christendom, not an existential conviction. Even when considered a necessary doctrinal dimension of an orthodox understanding of the Christian faith, it seems to have lost the power to shape the believers' worldview or conduct. It is not absolutely discarded, but it is degraded from a grounding and fundamental conviction into a "mere idea," as the Spanish philosopher Ortega y Gasset would put it (1942).

The Western-educated Christian has been more impressed by Kant's "chiliastic vision" than by the Bible's apocalyptic imagery. For Kant "the hope that finally, after many revolutions of reform, nature's supreme objective...in which all of the human species' original capacities be developed–will at last be realized" (1985, 36, 38). The end of history, in this heroic vision, mutates into the endless development of human rationality and virtue (93–103), which will also lead toward perpetual peace among all nations (107–43).

Even Karl Barth, despite his revolt against liberal theology, accepted finitude and mortality as human destiny. In the final section of his treatise about time and history, included in his *Church Dogmatics*, he rejects any possible theological speculation about postmortem human existence:

> It also belongs to human nature, and is determined by God's good creation and to that extent right and good, that man's being in time should be finite and man himself mortal...In itself, therefore, it is not unnatural but natural for human life to run its course to this terminus ad quem, to ebb and fade, and therefore to have this forward limit. Man as such, therefore, has no beyond...[He] belongs to this world. He is thus finite and mortal. One day he will only have been, as once he was not....He does not hope for redemption from the this-sidedness, finitude and mortality of his existence (1960, 632f.).[1]

Despite the spate of sensationalist, fundamentalist, market-driven millennialist books published during the recent turn of the millennium, more general concern was generated, even in the churches, about the overrated threat of universal catastrophic computer failure and electronic breakdown (nicknamed Y2K) than about an eschatological divine intervention. A rather mediocre technological dystopia overshadowed the tepid apocalypticism of some millenarian sects (Weber 2001, 193–222).

Neither did the postmodernist disenchantment with grand utopias and narratives of human redemption provide any comfort zone for discourses about universal historical finalities. Endless multiplication of diversities and differences, not an eschatological unity and integration (*anakephalaiosis*) in

---

[1]The English version mistakenly renders German "seiner Existenz" as "mortality of His existence"; I have corrected it to "his existence."

a "plenitude (*pleroma*) of crucial time (*kairoi*)," seems to be the postmodernist utopia (Lyotard 1984).[2]

Eschatology was not totally forgotten: it was however left as a favorite theme for fundamentalist writers with a good eye for the market. If violence sells as much as sex, the ultimate and absolute violence of Armageddon could be quite a hit as the immensely popular apocalyptic best sellers novels of the evangelical writers Tim LaHaye and Jerry B. Jenkins have proved.[3] Academic theologians, however, generally regard with disdain those literary intrusions into the secret code of history's final destiny. Still, during the last years, the neglected theme of eschatology has begun to receive renewed attention in theological circles. From different quarters, the theological question is once more raised and pressed about, in particular, the eschatological nature of Christian existence and, in general, the possibility of an end of time and of a time of the end.[4]

Reasons for Apocalyptic Resurgence

It is always very difficult to describe the unexpected and surreptitious ways in which ideas lose or gain hold over human minds and hearts. It might, however, not be entirely wrong to speculate about the recent rebirth of apocalyptic interests. The tragic bankruptcy of human hopes and ideals during the past century, its immensely lethal and destructive wars, the breakdown of socialistic utopias, and the increase in global socioeconomic inequalities has contributed to the awakening of profound fears and hopes. Such an awakening traditionally leads toward a radical, religiously rooted, questioning of the conditions of human and historical existence. Many sensitive hearts and minds felt that the times at the end of the twentieth century were such as the great Irish poet, William Butler Yeats, described earlier in that same turbulent era:

> Things fall apart; the centre cannot hold
> The blood-dimmed tide is loosed, and everywhere
> The ceremony of innocence is drowned;
> The best lack all conviction, while the worst
> Are full of passionate intensity (Yeats 1972, 820).

[2]Eph. 1:10. On the history of the interpretation of *anakephalaiosis* as eschatological recapitulation of all things, see José Pedro Tosaus Abadía, *Cristo y el universo.*

[3]Between 1995 and 2003, LaHaye and Jenkins published eleven novels (*Left Behind, Tribulation Force, Nicolae, Soul Harvest, Apollyon, Assassins, The Indwelling, The Mark, Desecration, The Remnant,* and *Armageddon*) on the tribulations of the people "left behind" during the "last days," of Armageddon, the Antichrist, and divine judgment.

[4]See, for example: Moltmann, *The Coming of God;* Polkinghorne and Welker, eds., *The End of the World and the Ends of God;* Buckley and Jones, eds., *Theology and Eschatology;* and the dialogue among several important Catholic, Protestant, and Jewish German-writing theologians, Tiemo Rainer Peters and Claus Urban *Ende der Zeit?* See also, from the side of Latin American liberation theology, Libânio and Bingemer, *Escatologia Cristã,* and Pixley, *La resurrección de Jesús, el Cristo.*

Deeply felt fears and hopes, as the astute David Hume noted more than two centuries ago, are able to agitate hearts and spirits and to move minds to think the otherwise unthinkable.[5] Suddenly, at the end of the century so aptly named the "Age of Extremes" by Eric Hobsbawm,[6] two tendencies clashed. The first announces with glib satisfaction "the end of history," namely the eradication of political ideologies and social utopias;[7] the second, from the entrails of the subordinated subjects,[8] proclaims a new insurrection of human hopes for "another possible world."[9]

Prophecy and Eschatology: at the Margins of History

The Prophetic Call

Postexilic Hebrew prophetic literature begins to overcome the temporal frontiers of historical existence, in the sense at least of glimpsing a different future, in which the sorrows and pains produced by human violence and hatred disappear. "For I am about to create new heavens and a new earth" is the divine promise to the human cry of sorrow. A bold mythical image of peace and cosmic harmony shines through the divine promise: "The wolf and the lamb shall feed together, the lion shall eat straw like the ox; and the serpent [that old adversary!]–its food shall be dust! They shall not hurt or destroy" (Isa. 65:25).

The end of history is thus imagined as a promise, as a divine redeeming intervention that will put an end to the tragic sufferings that plague historical and human existence. Divine promise and human hope are the main defining marks of the early Hebrew prophetic eschatology. Its historical horizon is constituted by the brokenness and misery of the chosen nation, by the tragedy of Israelite history. This does not mean that history as temporal sequence will cease, but that the conditions of human existence will be drastically altered. "They shall not labor in vain, or bear children for calamity" (Isa. 65:23).

Eschatology as Reason for Fear

Certainly, there is a dark side to that promise lurking somewhere behind or below the promise. Eschatological harmony, in the prophetic literature, requires justice, interpersonal righteousness. The prophetic voice–Maintain justice, and do what is right, for soon my salvation will come… (Isa. 56:1)–intertwines justice with peace and redemption. This means, however, that the "day of Yahweh" is to be feared by those who fare extremely well in the unequal distribution of social resources, by those who are not looking forward to any drastic change in the way things are.

---

[5]See Hume, *The Natural History of Religion.*

[6]See Hobsbawm, *Age of Extremes.*

[7]See Fukuyama, *The End of History and the Last Man.*

[8]See Hinkelammert, *El grito del sujeto.*

[9]See Pixley et al., *Por un mundo otro.*

"Alas for the day! For the day of the LORD is near, and as destruction from the Almighty it comes" (Joel. 1:15). The prophetic proclamation of divine reckoning, a promise to the downtrodden and destitute, the wretched of the earth, as Franz Fanon called them, is also a horrifying threat to those who divide among themselves the spoils of power, for an avenging God is the LORD..."and the LORD will by no means clear the guilty" (Nah. 1:3). Oppressors and exploiters can only look upon the day of Yahweh with apprehension in their spirits: "Woe to him who builds his house by unrighteousness and his upper rooms by injustice"(Jer. 22:13). Promise and threat are therefore closely linked together in the prophetic eschatological pronouncements. The day of divine intervention will bring joy and gladness to the hearts of many, but also terror and panic to others. "Alas for you who desire the day of the LORD! Why do you want the day of the LORD? It is darkness, not light"(Amos 5:18).

Emphasis on Hope

The threat is the underside of the promise but does not overshadow or degrade it. The emphases lie upon hope, not despair, upon the mercy of God, not upon divine indignation. Historical existence is overturned, not annihilated. In the midst of oppression and misery, the downtrodden and destitute hope for a land of peace and righteousness, not for eternal emptiness, nor even for eternal beatitude. The people face immense destruction and tragedy–"How lonely sits the city that once was full of people!...She weeps bitterly in the night, with tears on her cheeks...Judah has gone into exile with suffering and hard servitude" (Lam. 1:1–3). Yet the hopeful expectation is not perpetual nirvanic blessedness, but the rehabilitation of meaningful historical existence: "They shall build houses and inhabit them; they shall plant vineyards and eat their fruit" (Isa. 65:21).

Prophetic literature, thus, begins to probe the limits of the conditions of historical existence and foregrounds the question about human hope in an utterly hopeless situation. "How could we sing the LORD's song in a foreign land?" (Ps. 137:4). This profound and painful lament echoes, one way or the other, through the whole corpus and canon of the Hebrew sacred scriptures.[10] Those sacred texts are the children of calamity and hope, of historical tragedy and divine promise.[11] The cry of the people to God achieves sublime poetry in its immense distress: "Cursed be the day on which I was born! The day when my mother bore me, let it not be blessed!...Why did I come forth from the womb to see toil and sorrow, and spend my days in shame?" (Jer. 20:14,18). It also attains aesthetic beauty

[10]See Smith-Christopher, *A Biblical Theology of Exile.*
[11]See de Wit, *En la dispersión el texto es patria.*

in its poetic hope in the mercy of God, the liberator: "Thus says the LORD...Do not fear...I will pour water on the thirsty land, and streams on the dry ground...They shall spring up like a green tamarisk, like willows by flowing streams" (Isa. 44:2–4).

Originating in the Margins

The poetic woes and hopes come both from the margins of history in two regards. First, in the sense that these laments and expectations proceed from a small, weak, marginal, and vulnerable people–Israel. It is still surprising to note how a rather insignificant geopolitical community was able to create and imagine the most influential and history-changing religious texts, symbols, and ideas. From the margins of international power springs a collections of texts (Torah, Prophets, Wisdom, apocalyptic writings) that has shaped much of human cult and culture.[12] But, second, they proceed from the margins of history in the sense that they put radically into question the finality (the end and the ends) of history. They possess the audacity to transgress the frontiers of the given and to imagine a radically different world.

History and Eschatology in Early Christianity

History as Christian Invention

In his classic and pathbreaking study, *Mythe de l'éternel retour (The Myth of the Eternal Return),* Mircea Eliade persuasively suggests the idea of a human history was an early Christian invention.[13] Its main building blocks can be traced in the two centuries of creative theological production between Irenaeus and Augustine. Both theologians view human historical existence as having a beginning (Creation), a defining center (Incarnation), and a consummation (Eschaton). History possesses a *telos,* in the double sense of conclusion and culmination. It is not, therefore, an endless and meaningless temporal sequence. It is marked by crucial divine events and interventions, *kairoi,* that confer upon it meaning and plenitude.

Thus, early Christian existence and thinking were eschatologically perceived, felt, and articulated. Temporal, earthly existence was considered provisional, a diasporic pilgrimage toward a more authentic mode of being. As an epistle of an otherwise unknown Christian writer asserts: "They [Christians] take part in everything as citizens and put up with everything as foreigners. Every foreign land is their home, and every home a foreign land."[14] Sin and death might rule upon the present order of being, what

---

[12]See Frye, *The Great Code,* xi: "The Bible had set up an imaginative framework–a mythological universe, as I call it–within which Western literature had operated down to the eighteenth century and is to a large extent still operating."

[13]See Eliade, *The Myth of the Eternal Return.*

[14]See "Epistle to Diognetus," in Quasten and Plumpe, *Ancient Christian Writers.*

the New Testament Johannine literature calls cosmos; but their hegemony is damned, and its days are counted. Individual life is ephemeral, indeed, but so is history in its entirety.

Opposing Perspectives on Temporal Existence

Curiously enough, this tension between history and eschatology entails radically different possible perspectives regarding the significance of temporal existence. One leads toward the devaluation of body and society: their provisionality implies their meaninglessness.[15] Mircea Eliade poignantly writes about the "terror of history" that arises from awareness of the irreversibility of time and the finite particularity of historical events (1954, 139–62). Another perspective, however, accentuates the importance of historical existence for the eternal personal fate. The end of history might thus be conceived as the redemption of history, not from history.

The eschatological tension, therefore, intrinsic to the Christian concept of history, might be conducive to very different ethical and political standpoints. History, flesh, and society might be perceived as the realm of death and sin, mortality and evil. As Kant so shrewdly describes in his essay about eschatology, from the shadows of eternal being, the earthly and historical world might be seen as a caravansary, a penitentiary, an insane asylum, or a cesspool (1985, 96). God's wrath and rage might be the main eschatological dimension emphasized. If the world is the kingdom of death and evil, the realm of human fallenness and cosmic brokenness, if, following the highly influential Platonic tradition, the body is the prison of the soul, or even its tomb (*sôma–sêma*),[16] dissolution of everything material and worldly appears to be the only possible escape from the pains and penalties of existence. This might be the key for the fascination that many have felt for the Gnostic redemption from history.

The Terrors of the End

Except that the end might entail even deeper terrors. Few pages written in the early twentieth century are equal in literary eloquence and intelligence, as well as in sheer horror and terror, as James Joyce's description of a priest's sermon about hell in *A Portrait of the Artist as a Young Man,* originally published in 1916.

> If men...persisted in their wickedness there remained for them an eternity of torment: hell...an abode of demons and lost souls...The fire of hell has this property that it preserves that which it burns and though it rages with incredible intensity it rages for ever...It is a fire which proceeds directly from the ire of God, working not of

---

[15]The classic study is Peter Brown, *The Body and Society.*

[16]Cf. Plato, *Phaedo,* 82 E; *Gorgias,* 493 A; *Cratylus,* 400 C.

> its own activity but as an instrument of divine vengeance...And through the several torments of the senses the immortal soul is tortured eternally in its very essence amid the leagues upon leagues of glowing fires kindled in the abyss by the offended majesty of the Omnipotent God and fanned into everlasting and ever increasing fury by the breath of the anger of the Godhead... Boundless extension of torment, incredible intensity of suffering, unceasing variety of torture–this is what the divine majesty, so outraged by sinners, demands, this is what the holiness of heaven, slighted and set aside for the lustful and low pleasures of the corrupt flesh, requires, this is what the blood of the innocent Lamb of God, shed for the redemption of sinners, trampled upon the vilest of the vile, insists upon (1962 edition, 119–31).

Lacking Joyce's exceptional literary brilliance and ironic style, this terrifying image of hell as eternal and unbearable punishment is part and parcel of a traditional perspective (*dies irae, dies illa...*) on Christian eschatology. In this view, the sins that impel a person, as an individual, to this perpetual and horrendous penalty are those of the flesh. "Sin...is a base consent to the promptings of our corrupt nature to the lowers instincts, to that which is gross and beastlike..." (127). And the divine answer is perennial unquenchable damnation and punishment. The end of time is the day of divine ire.

It should be noted, however, that in this tradition of divine indignation and punishment, sometimes a different emphasis is found. Bartolomé de Las Casas, despairing of his powerlessness to save the Native Americans from servitude and demise and aware of the proximity of his death, wrote a very peculiar testament. He envisages the divine judgment of the nations, at the end of time, as the day in which God will punish and destroy Spain for the injustices committed in the New World.

> God shall have to pour his fury and anger on Spain for these damnable, rotten, infamous deeds done so unjustly, so tyrannically, so barbarously...against those people. For the whole of Spain has shared in the blood-soaked riches, some a little, some a lot, but all shared in goods that were ill-gotten, wickedly taken with violence and genocide...(Las Casas 1995, 354).[17]

In this highly dramatic vision of the final day of judgment, the sins condemned and punished are social in nature: oppression, slavery, and genocide. The eschatological vision of universal day of judgment of the nations, articulated by Jesus in Matthew 25:31–46, is here reconstructed as

---

[17]On the theological development of Las Casas, it is hard to surpass the splendid book by Gutiérrez, *Las Casas.*

an event of divine retribution against colonial oppression, social injustice, and economic exploitation.

In his eschatological vision, Las Casas emphasizes divine retribution. That attitude surges from his bitter disappointment with his own nation. He had been convinced that Spain had a divinely assigned providential mission to expand the Christian gospel and that such a role was the main meaning and purpose of Christopher Columbus's expeditions and of the decrees of Pope Alexander VI granting Castile sovereignty over the encountered lands and peoples. He had, however, also reached the conclusion that by exploiting the Native Americans Spain had betrayed that divinely bestowed task. He then became the denouncer of his nation's misconduct and the announcer of the coming of God's rage. As the Old Testament prophets, from the margins of history–the sufferings and travails of the destitute Native Americans–he looks beyond the historical possibilities at hand and hopelessness mutates into hope in divine justice.

A letter to the Council of Indies, at the end of his long and tiring career, summarizes and culminates Las Casas's denunciations of five decades. It is brief, but its sharp condemning prophetic tone, which is the basis for his vision of divine eschatological judgment, can hardly be matched:

> 1.) All conquests are unjust and tyrannical; 2.) we have illegally usurped the kingdoms of the Indies; 3.) all encomiendas are bad per se; 4.) those who possess them and those who distribute them are in mortal sin; 5.) the king has no more right to justify the conquests and encomiendas than the Ottoman Turk to make war against Christians; 6.) all fortunes made in the Indies are iniquitous; 7.) if the guilty do not make restitution, they will not be saved; 8.) the Indian nations have the right, which will be theirs till doomsday, to make us just war and erase us from the face of the earth (1969, 282–83).[18]

Divine justice as the hope of the downtrodden and destitute of the world is the prevailing dimension of Las Casas's splendid eschatological vision. Utter despair would only lead toward absolute nihilism and cynicism. If the state and the church fail to hear the cry of the oppressed–as in fact they seem to be failing–the only possible hope lies in the margins of history–in the frontiers between history as the realm of human injustice and eternity, as the triumphant revelation of divine righteousness.[19]

---

[18]Reproduced as an appendix.

[19]Sometime before his death, Las Casas wrote a sharp letter to the Pope demanding his active intervention against the oppression of the Native Americans. It was unanswered. For an English translation of the letter, see Rivera-Pagán, *Essays From the Diaspora*.

Modern Eschatological Voices

During recent years, several theological voices have attempted to renew eschatological thinking and, simultaneously, overcome the individualistic and moralistic framework in which it has been frequently situated in the history of Christian theology and doctrine. Let me mention briefly some of these voices.

Jorge Pixley has described the several ways in which the biblical vision and concept of resurrection opens up new vistas of hope for the destitute and oppressed of the earth. Leaving aside the simplistic discussions about the historicity of Jesus' corporal reawakening from death, Pixley rediscovers the eschatological hope of liberation that serves as hermeneutical horizon for the New Testament faith in the resurrection and explores its favorable connotations for a liberating spirituality (1997, passim.).

Jürgen Moltmann emphasizes, in his latest writings on eschatology, that the idea of the justice of God requires the correlated belief in the social and historical regeneration of worldly injustices. God's eternal self-glorification conveys the hope that the struggle between justice and injustice is neither perpetual nor inscribed in an eternal nature of things. To wait in God means also to expect the final revelation of a kingdom of peace and justice promised in Isaiah and Revelation. There can be no divine righteousness without the regeneration of history and world.[20]

Miroslav Volf, on the other hand, foregrounds the idea, so marginal but never totally absent in the history of theology, of a universal *apokatastasis*, or reconciliation as an essential element of any reconfiguration of Christian eschatology.[21] Grace and reconciliation, not damnation and punishment, according to Volf, are the main characteristics of any eschatology grounded upon the doctrine of the Trinity as eternal community and solidarity in the being itself of God.[22]

Hope for the oppressed, liberating justice, and universal reconciliation are the distinctive signs of the new eschatology being forged by theologians who dare, in the face of the globalization of misery and injustice, dare to think the unthinkable: the coming of the kingdom of God.

---

[20]See, for example, Moltmann, "Is There Life After Death?," in *The End of the World and the Ends of God,* 238–55.

[21]*Apokatastasis,* or the universal redemption and reconciliation of all rational beings (the Devil not excluded) at the end of times, was a doctrine espoused by Origen. Traces of it can also be found in the writings of several Eastern theologians, such as Gregory of Nyssa, but it was severely rejected by Augustine. In Western Christianity it has thenceforth mainly been looked on as heterodox. It strongly emphasizes the ontological priority of divine grace and mercy over condemnation and punishment. See Breuning, "*apokatastasis*" in *Lexikon für Theologie und Kirche.*

[22]See his essays "Enter into Joy Sin, Death, and the Life of the World to Come," in *The End of the World and the Ends of God,* 256–78; and "The Final Reconciliation," *in Theology and Eschatology,* 89–111. Reconciliation is an important theme in Volf's theological corpus, developed in his text *Exclusion & Embrace.*

PART 2

CONTEXTUAL ESSAYS

12

Latin American Liberation Theology

PHILLIP BERRYMAN

On Sunday evening, April 26, 1998, as Bishop Juan Gerardi was pulling into his garage in Guatemala City, he was accosted and was bludgeoned to death with a piece of concrete. Two evenings before, he had presided at the cathedral during the formal presentation of a human rights report on violence in Guatemala over the previous three decades of repression. One of the report's findings was that 90 percent of the killings had been perpetrated by the Guatemalan military or the paramilitary groups that they had set up. The obvious motive for the killing was retaliation for the report.[1]

Bishop Gerardi and the team who prepared the report may or may not have seen their work as reflecting liberation theology, but it is unlikely that they would have undertaken the task without the influence of liberation theology, a pastoral and theological movement in the Latin American churches that began in the 1960s and that has been influential on theology

[1]In April 2002 the perpetrators, including members and ex-members of the army, were found guilty, but their conviction was overthrown on appeal.

around the world, including the United States. This essay describes that development and traces some of its major themes.

A New Approach to Theology

The Historical Prelude

One way to begin is to go back thirty years before the murder of Gerardi to the late 1960s. Catholics were considering the implications of Vatican Council II (1962–65), the meeting of bishops that ushered in a period of change (such as a shift from Latin to vernacular languages in worship) and turmoil in the church. The council had been largely led by European bishops and theologians. Its findings reflected the European experience, where the church had "lost" much of the working class and intellectuals in the nineteenth century. Many ordinary Europeans were atheists or agnostics; how could one even speak of God to people who seemed to feel no need for such a belief?

That was not the problem in Latin America, where few people were nonbelievers. The problem, some were arguing, was widespread poverty. What should the church be doing about poverty? What should the public role of the church be–if any–in countries where the vast majority of people were Catholics? Did preaching or teaching ("Blessed are the poor in spirit, for theirs is the kingdom of heaven") serve to justify unequal distribution of wealth and power? Did the times call for revolution? If so, could Christian participation in revolution be justified? In 1965 a prominent Colombian priest, Camilo Torres, had sought to form a broad political front to break the stranglehold of traditional political parties. Pressured by church authorities to leave the priesthood, he joined a guerrilla group and was killed in combat in 1966. Few agreed with his option, but he symbolized the importance of becoming committed and following through with one's convictions.

In many Latin American countries, groups of priests gathered and issued manifestos calling for reforms in church and society. For several years, Latin American theologians had been realizing that the theology that they had studied as universal Catholic theology was in fact the product of European history. They now saw that their continent had its own theological questions requiring their own answers.

The Influence of Gustavo Gutiérrez

In August 1968, a Peruvian theologian, Gustavo Gutiérrez, gave a talk titled "Toward a Theology of Liberation" to a group of priests and lay people in Chimbote, Peru. Like most of the other liberation theologians in Latin America, Gutiérrez did not teach in a university or seminary. His questions rose from the pastoral issues faced by people like his audience. Traditionally, Catholic theologians had assumed that theology was essentially a matter of presenting and explaining the truth already possessed by the church. In that talk, however, Gutiérrez proposed that action comes before thought, and hence, specifically, that pastoral action comes first. Theology should be a critical reflection on that action.

The questions for theologians come primarily from the situation faced by the church, and particularly by priests, sisters, and others doing the church's work. In former ages, the world might have been accepted as it was, but now human beings have a responsibility for "piloting" the ship of history. "The theology of liberation means establishing the relationship that exists between human emancipation–in the social, political and economic orders–and the kingdom of God" (1990, 62–76).

Gutiérrez reminded his audience of the traditional notion in which he and his audience had been raised: One was to save one's soul by avoiding sin for the sake of a reward in heaven. To it he opposed the emerging "holistic" notion of salvation. No sharp break exists between life on earth and life with God. Rather a continuum runs from very earthly things, such as satisfaction of subsistence needs and deliverance from oppression, to the ultimate goal of unity of all in God. Building a more just society on earth is thus closely linked with ultimate union with God.

Building a Just Society

How was such a society to be achieved? The conventional answer at the time was "development": less developed countries, such as those in Latin America, should follow the steps already taken by the more developed. Latin American social scientists were now challenging that assumption. The so-called "developing" countries, they said, were dominated by the already "developed" countries in an "international division of labor." This "division" assigned "developing" countries to export raw materials (oil, copper, coffee, bananas, beef, etc.) from their mines, fields, and labor, and to import industrial products from the developed countries. This order seemed to be controlled by the rich countries, especially the United States and its corporations. The problem was structural: as long as this arrangement remained in place, "developing" nations would never be able to "catch up" with the "advanced countries." They had to break free of the existing international system and build a new kind of society.

In fact, one country, Cuba, seemed to have done so with the 1959 revolution. This overthrew a dictatorship and established a revolutionary government. The new government was reorganizing the country around meeting the basic needs of all: food, employment, medical care, education. In the early 1960s guerrilla movements sprang up in many Latin American countries in imitation of Cuba. Most of them had been suppressed by the late 1960s, but the notion of "revolution"–a thorough reshaping of society starting by taking state power–was in the air.

The Bishops' Meeting

A month after Gutiérrez's talk, the Latin American Catholic bishops met in Medellin to consider how to apply Vatican II to Latin America. Aiding the bishops were a hundred theologians and other advisors, including Gutiérrez. The outline of their conclusions is itself significant. The first five topics were not "religious" but dealt with "human development" (justice, peace, family and demography, education, youth). The second set of issues was about pastoral issues, and the third was about how the church should be organized for its mission.

Similarly the starting point for each individual doctrine was not doctrine but issues facing Latin American society. Theological reflection followed and then considerations of how the church should act to deal with them. This was quite in line with what Gutiérrez had said in his talk: the church must adapt its action to serve the world rather than acting as though it had a timeless message. This practice of starting with an analysis of the situation in the nation, the city, or the neighborhood, reflecting on it theologically, and drawing pastoral conclusions became a hallmark of the liberation theology approach.

In one passage, the bishops presented what might be called liberation theology in a nutshell: just as God's people Israel felt "God's saving presence when he liberated them from oppression in Egypt" and led them through the sea toward the land of promise, today "we likewise feel" God's passing when "true development" takes place. True development means "passing from less human to more human conditions." "Less human conditions" are material want and selfishness, oppressive structures, the abuse of wealth and power, exploitation of workers. "More human conditions" means overcoming extreme poverty, broadening knowledge, acquiring culture, greater consideration for the dignity of others, cooperating for the common good, seeking peace, and ultimately the highest gifts of all faith, being united in the love of Christ, and being children of the "Father of all human beings."

Here a central event and theme of the scriptures–the exodus–is made a metaphor for the contemporary effort to reach development. God is said to be with his people in their effort to overcome oppression and to achieve a more human way of life. Again echoing Gutiérrez, the bishops see a continuity from very "earthly" things like hunger and oppression to the ultimate goal of life–union with God. God is present today in people's struggle for justice and a better life. A symbol like the exodus sheds light on the present, and the people's journey today toward a more human life gives biblical symbols a new meaning.

The Medellin Documents' Influence

Within weeks the Medellin documents were being widely read, discussed, and used as the basis for further theological reflection everywhere in Latin America. In its origins, Latin America liberation theology was quite Roman Catholic. Certainly, individual Protestant theologians and others were involved in the discussion and made significant contributions.[2] However, 90 percent or more of Latin Americans were Catholics (even though mass attendance on any given Sunday in a country might be 5 percent or even lower), whereas Protestants were perhaps 1 or 2 percent of the population. Because it had been part of the fabric of Latin American society since the sixteenth century, the Catholic church tended to have a public presence in society; for example, bishops could address the nation itself or its leaders. In fact, one of the concerns of the liberation theologians was that the church should use institutional weight in society not to buttress the status quo but on behalf of justice.

Starting from the Medellin period, many church people recognized that the Catholic church's resources and personnel were devoted disproportionately to the middle and upper classes. An obvious example was Catholic schools, which were located in the larger cities and which, because they charged tuition, excluded the poor. Recognizing this, many religious orders, particularly sisters, opted to devote more of their personnel to the poor in the countryside and in the swelling shantytowns of self-built housing around the cities. A first step was generally to go to live closer to the poor, often in poor neighborhoods. Sharing more closely in the ordinary life of the people, they sought to help people become organized to demand their rights and to form self-help groups and community organizations.

In the late 1960s, experimentation in Brazil, Panama, and elsewhere developed what were called "basic Christian communities." Typically, a priest or team of priests and sisters in a parish developed small communities meeting in people's homes for a discussion of scripture, prayer, community issues, and possibly the eucharist. The aim was for these to be lay-led. These communities set up a number of goals: pastoral outreach, development of lay leadership, and counteracting the inroads of Protestant churches, which had lay leadership and often met in small groups. It seemed to be a return to the practice of the "house churches" of the early Christians, many years before they were able to build churches. The "basic Christian community" model of pastoral work was a way to utilize liberation theology at the village or neighborhood level.

By the end of 1971 Gutiérrez had extended his ideas into a book, *A Theology of Liberation.* About this same time, Hugo Assmann (Brazil), Ignacio Ellacuria (El Salvador), Enrique Dussel, and José Miguez-Bonino (Argentina) produced book-length treatments of this new approach to

---

[2]Richard Schaull, a Presbyterian missionary in Colombia and Brazil, asked about the theological significance of revolution by the early 1960s. The Protestant ecumenical organization ISAL (Church and Society in Latin America) sponsored meetings and publications at which similar questions were raised in the mid-1960s.

theology. These early works tended to focus on the overall approach or method of liberation theology, rather than treating classical themes of theology.[3]

Conflict and Development

Political Revolution

In the 1970 election, Chilean voters, after six years of a Christian Democrat government (whose slogan was "Revolution in freedom)," gave a narrow margin of victory to a socialist coalition headed by Salvador Allende. That victory offered hope that perhaps revolutionary changes in society could be achieved through electoral means. The Allende government tried to speed up land reform and other social programs. However, forces in Chile and the Nixon government sought to sabotage the Allende government, and polarization increased. In September 1973, the military under Gen. Augusto Pinochet staged a coup: Allende was killed as the armed forces bombed and attacked the presidential palace. Even though there was no real armed opposition, troops rounded up thousands of people. At least three thousand were murdered, most in the first few weeks but others over the next fifteen years.

Chile was not alone. Brazil, the largest country in Latin America, had been under military rule since 1964. In the 1970s coups took place in Uruguay, Argentina, and elsewhere. By the mid-1970s, 60 percent or more of Latin Americans were under some form of military rule. Far from liberation, the situation seemed to be one of captivity. Many thousands of people were abducted, tortured, and killed. Very often they simply "disappeared," that is, family members were left with no trace of their loved ones. Only during the 1980s did the military regimes slowly return direct governance to civilians and electoral processes.

The focus then shifted to the small countries of Central America. In 1979 the longstanding dictatorship of the Somoza family was overthrown by a mass uprising led by the Sandinista National Liberation Front. Contrary to what had happened in Cuba twenty years previously, church people had been actively involved in the anti-Somoza struggle, and some were committed to the revolutionary process in the country (four cabinet-level positions were held by Catholic priests). A similar revolutionary movement in El Salvador seemed likely to take power, and another movement was having some success in Guatemala. Church people were also involved in both these movements.

---

[3]See Gutiérrez, *A Theology of Liberation;* and Miguez-Bonino, *Doing Theology in a Revolutionary Situation.* Also Assman, *Theology for a Nomad Church;* and Ellacuría, *Freedom Made Flesh.*

President Ronald Reagan, upon taking office in 1981, declared that these movements were Marxist and a threat to the United States. He made Central America a major focus of attention, supplying massive aid to the Salvadoran military and government, while the CIA assembled the remnants of Somoza's army as the core of guerrilla forces that began attacking civilians in Nicaragua. Thus the political context of the 1970–1990 period, when the major writings of the liberation theologians were published, was one of conflict, particularly from repressive governments, but also from opposition within the church (treated further on).

The Churches' Role

The churches were a major point of resistance to the abuses of military regimes. Priests, sisters, and pastors often helped people being hunted by the police or military to hide and escape from the country. They helped family members of those killed or "disappeared." When government polices produced widespread unemployment, parishes formed communal soup kitchens run by local volunteers. They provided information on human rights violations to international organizations. In many instances individual bishops and the national conference of bishops issued statements condemning human rights violations. This was especially important at a time when all other voices in society (congress, media, labor unions) were muzzled.

These actions made church people enemies in the eyes of the military and repressive governments. Under military rule, church people were often targeted for repression. In the late 1970s and early 1980s about a dozen priests were murdered in El Salvador and another dozen in Guatemala. Likewise, in 1980, in El Salvador Archbishop Romero was shot and killed. Three nuns and another American church worker were raped and killed by Salvadoran troops. In 1989 troops killed six Jesuits, including theologian Ignacio Ellacuria, their housekeeper and her daughter. Approximately 75,000 people were killed in El Salvador. Some of these died in combat, but the vast majority were civilians killed by official forces. Thus, the example of Bishop Gerardi, cited at the beginning of this chapter, was one in a long line of such instances. It should not be concluded, however, that widespread repression was continuous and universal. By the late 1970s the worst repression was over in Brazil and Argentina, for example, and some countries, such as Venezuela, did not have such episodes at all.

Publishing Liberation Theology

This general context must be kept in mind as the background for the writings of the theologians. After the initial "roadmaps" mentioned above, theologians began producing a rather large volume of work that soon numbered dozens and even hundreds of books. A good summation of that body of work is the collective work *Mysterium Liberationis Fundamental Concepts of Liberation Theology* (Ignacio Ellacuría and Jon Sobrino, eds.).[4]

The Church

Just as was true of Catholic theology elsewhere in the post-Vatican II years, much liberation theology dealt with the church, or what is traditionally called "ecclesiology." For example, theologians noted the temptation of the church to be concerned for its own institutional interests. By their presence, clergy seemed to bless (and certainly did not question) the disparity between plantation owners with thousands of acres of land and a rural population with small poor plots or, increasingly, with no land at all. Theologians stated that just as Jesus did not preach himself but the kingdom of God, the church should not seek its own aggrandizement or comfort but should point toward, and work toward, the reign of God, a reign of justice and community.

Evangelization, preaching good news, was said to be the church's mission. Theologians argued that it should be a "liberating evangelization." This meant that it should be good news not in general, but for the poor. Not only should it be addressed to the poor, but the poor themselves should also be its bearers; they should be empowered to play an active role in the church and in their communities.

Some theologians expressed the hope that "Basic Christian communities" were a new model of church. Parishes themselves could become networks of such small, local communities, led by laypeople. Perhaps in the future, the church discipline itself would change so that such laymen (feminism came later) could be ordained priests and so celebrate the eucharist. This new grassroots church could be Latin America's contribution to a renewal of the church, a "new way of being church" (Boff 1986).

Hot-button Issues Avoided

Latin American theologians generally avoided the typical hot-button issues in Catholicism in North America and Europe (birth control, abortion, ordination of women, sexual behavior, clerical celibacy). As a group they believed that they should avoid conflicts with local bishops and with the Vatican over such issues. Their reasoning was that in Latin America where Catholics were a majority and where the church willy-nilly had a public role, it was most important that the church's institutional weight be brought

---

[4]In 1981 the major theologians gathered and mapped out an ambitious project to cover all of theology from a liberation standpoint. The volumes would typically be co-written by two or more theologians and would cover not only issues thematically related to liberation but classical issues such as the Trinity. A dozen or so books were produced, but the project foundered.

to bear on behalf of the poor insofar as possible. At the height of the repression, when bishops were the only public voice to denounce human rights abuses, this may have made sense. Yet this option to ignore certain matters–abortion or the ordination of women–also suggests that most of the major theologians had not really internalized feminist theology let alone the feminist social critique more broadly considered.[5]

Poverty

We have already noted that starting in the 1960s, church personnel sought to go to the poor, even by living in a poor neighborhood. One of the Medellin documents was devoted to the "poverty of the church." In taking up the issue, Gutiérrez points out that for centuries poverty had been "spiritualized," as in "Blessed are the poor in spirit" (Mt. 5:3), in a way that could soothe the consciences of the privileged. Gutiérrez distinguished three interrelated meanings of poverty in the Bible. First, poverty in the sense of lacking enough to live a decent human life is an evil. In a second meaning of poverty–which does not annul the first–the Bible does see the poor as more open to God than the wealthy. Finally, says Gutiérrez, poverty can mean a commitment to the poor in solidarity. St. Paul says that Christ himself "became poor" in becoming human. Gutiérrez and other theologians sought to interpret the biblical sense of "poverty" in a way that did justice to the scripture and yet did not dull its prophetic edge. In the 1970s the "option for the poor" or "preferential option for the poor" became an ideal for the church as an institution and for church people.

The God Questions

Liberation theologians spent little or no time discussing classical questions of God, such as how to reconcile God's power and goodness with the presence of evil in the world, or how human beings can be free if everything that happens is willed by God. Their discussions of God tended to take as the starting point how ordinary Latin Americans conceived God and the questions they asked about God.[6] Theologians in Europe and North America have to struggle with making God believable in an atmosphere where many of their contemporaries, especially the more highly educated, are atheists or agnostics. That is not the case in Latin America, where the

---

[5]See Tamez, *Against Machismo.* Tamez interviewed the major male liberation theologians. All recognized the oppression of women, but in their major writings they devoted little or no attention to it. A possible exception is the Argentine layman Enrique Dussel who incorporated the "erotic" dimension (male-female attraction and bonding) into his works even in the 1960s. A few women were among the theologians in the Theology and Liberation series, but typically they were assigned to women's topics, e.g., Gebara and Bingemer, *Mary.*

[6]See Muñoz, *The God of Christians;* and Segundo, *Our Idea of God.*

overwhelming majority believe in God and consider themselves Catholics. Gutiérrez said that the issue for theology is not nonbelievers, but "nonpersons," whose situation robs them of minimum human dignity. In another context he said that the issue is "how to tell the poor that God loves them."

The problem then is not "whether God?" but "what kind of God?" Even though God is widely acknowledged and invoked, questions may be raised about whether God so conceived serves or hinders human emancipation. One scriptural motif is that of idolatry, says Pablo Richard. Money, power, and privilege–as idols–are severely criticized by the gospels. In a society in which a small number of people monopolize wealth whereas others barely survive, property can be a form of idolatry, that is, people are valuing the idol of their property over their fellow human beings who are in God's image. Likewise, the biblical God is a God of life. Whatever brings death to human beings cannot be of God. In struggling for a more just world, believers are battling idolatry and thereby assuring that God is more truly honored.

Christology

From the beginning christology (doctrine of Christ) has been a major concern of liberation theology.[7] Again, the starting point is the fact that Jesus is already present in Latin American culture, such as in annual Holy Week pageants that may depict Jesus making the way of the cross. That image might reinforce the notion that that is how the world is: if God's own Son is crucified, what can we expect?

The gospels present Jesus proclaiming "the Kingdom of God has come near" at the outset of his ministry. But how is the kingdom to be understood: as a realm outside this world? Latin American theologians noted that the reign of God in the prophets was the realization of justice for the poor. Jesus placed himself in that prophetic tradition when he said that he had been sent "to bring good news to the poor...proclaim release to the captives...sight to the blind, to let the oppressed go free" (Lk. 4:18). What the Kingdom or reign meant to Jesus, says Jon Sobrino, must be seen not only from his words but his action. "Preaching to the poor, forthrightly denouncing injustice and oppression, placing everything he has at the service of the approach of the kingdom, creating human solidarity from a point of departure in the poor, and staying faithful to that task even though the kingdom of God in its fullness did not come, and that kingdom 'at hand' seemed tragically far off in his death."

The experience of conflict in Latin America (such as killing priests and bishops) sensitized theologians to the elements of conflict and persecution

[7]See Boff, *Jesus Christ Liberator;* and Sobrino, *Christology at the Crossroads; Jesus in Latin America.*

in Jesus' own life. He was arrested and put to death by the civil and religious authorities. These elements are quite plain in the gospel, but were largely ignored over centuries when Jesus' death tended to be seen as a "sacrifice" in obedience to a foreordained plan of God, his Father. But before being a redemptive "ransom," or "sacrifice," Jesus' death was the death of a man who was faithful to his mission. Likewise, the resurrection was not simply a great "miracle" to show God's power. "Jesus' resurrection is presented as God's response to the unjust criminal action of human beings...it is the triumph...of God's justice and is thus transformed into good news, whose central content is that once and for all justice has triumphed over injustice, the victim over the executioner" (Sobrino 1987, 94; 1993, 185).

Much more could be said about this Latin American christology. It is quite different from the christology existing in Catholicism until Vatican II, which was largely about christological doctrine (Jesus Christ is "true God and true man"). Although that christology formally said that Jesus was man, there was little consideration of his life, and people could be left with the impression that Jesus was the Son of God "acting" as a man. Like other contemporary theologians, the Latin Americans have sought to recover the humanity of Jesus and to link his life and message to his death, and his death to his resurrection. Their own experience, particularly observing others give their lives, has heightened their sensitivity to certain themes: the poor, the reign of God, and the resurrection as the vindication of a Christlike life.[8]

Liberation theology was always a minority position in the Catholic church and in the Protestant churches as well. Within the Catholic church a backlash formed among the bishops in the early 1970s. These bishops were strengthened when Pope John Paul II, who had spent his life resisting communism in Poland, took office in 1978. On a visit to Nicaragua in 1983 he publicly reprimanded Ernesto Cardinal, the priest and poet who was minister of culture.[9] In 1984 the Vatican issued a strong criticism of liberation theology, accusing it of being Marxist and fomenting class struggle. The Brazilian theologian Leonardo Boff was silenced for a year.

These controversies cannot be dealt with in any detail here. Like other Latin American intellectuals at that time, the theologians generally thought that they should be in dialogue with Marxism and that Marxist analysis could offer "tools" for understanding society. They rejected the notion that they were fomenting "class struggle"; in sharply divided societies class conflict of some kind was a reality, regardless of what anyone thought

[8]Having received many death threats, Archbishop Romero of San Salvador said, "If they kill me, I will rise in the Salvadoran people."

[9]Far less noticed was the fact that in El Salvador, the pope called for "dialogue" (i.e., negotiations) at a time when the Salvadoran military and their U.S. sponsors rejected that idea, and in Guatemala he embraced Indians and implicitly denounced the army's mass slaughter of indigenous civilians.

about it. The question was how to deal with this reality in a Christian way. Many of the most conflictive issues were aired in preparation for the meeting of Latin American bishops at Puebla 1979 and in the long document they issued.[10]

Liberation Elusive

As suggested at the beginning, what drew attention to liberation theology was its apparent political implication. Latin America was assumed to be in the midst of a process of revolution in which the present model of society would be overturned and replaced by a new one. In the new one the present poor majority would be able to meet their basic needs. The theologians did not elaborate this vision in detail. Assuming that this was the direction history was taking, they sought to probe its theological meaning (for example, that the process from less human to more human conditions was an "exodus") and to reflect on the practice of the church and of Christians. They hoped this would make their response more adequate. The very vehemence of the violence against movements for change, including the murder of church people, seemed to validate liberation theology.

That possibility of revolutionary change came into question even in the 1980s as the military dictatorships gave way to elected civilian governments. The events of 1989–91 (fall of communism, and in Central America, the electoral defeat of the Sandinistas in Nicaragua and peace processes in El Salvador and Guatemala) made any alternative to market economies and electoral democracy seem highly unlikely. Left-wing parties, including some former guerrillas, could win some mayoral or congressional seats, but not enough power to change how society works. Social movements and NGOs (nongovernmental organizations) pressed for particular issues (land, human rights, labor rights, women, black and indigenous people, ecology), but even all added together they did not constitute sufficient force to create a new model of society. "Liberation," after all, is a metaphor, based on the freeing of slaves of on an exodus from a land of bondage to one of freedom. If, in fact, no alternative model is on the horizon, what does liberation mean?

Critics began to say that liberation theology was now irrelevant. The theologians replied that their basic commitment had never been to Marxism, and that since there were as many poor people as ever–perhaps more–liberation theology was as relevant as ever, even if the changes in the world might call for some rethinking. In the church, it became increasingly clear that the hopes of a generation of liberation theologians of a "new way of being church" based on the spread of "Christian base communities" would

[10]See Eagleson and Scharper, *Puebla and Beyond.*

not be realized. These small communities had always been a small minority and had depended on relatively large amounts of pastoral input from sisters and priests. That is, they had never become truly lay-led and had always been dependent on church personnel. In fact, one of the surprises of the 1990s was the realization that it was not liberation-inspired base communities but pentecostal churches that had become a mass movement. Protestants, who had been perhaps 2 percent or so of the population in 1960, had grown to the point of numbering 10 percent or more of the population in some countries. Given the low level of attendance at mass by Catholics (5 percent or fewer on any given Sunday), in some countries the number of "practicing" Protestants was on a par with that of Catholics. Liberation theologians and those engaged in liberation style pastoral work were inclined to dismiss pentecostal churches (and their Catholic cousin, the charismatic movement) as presenting a simplistic and alienating version of Christianity.[11]

In the 1990s, the concerns of Latin American theologians broadened. Writings by women theologians had appeared in the 1980s and expanded in the 1990s. Ivone Gebara (Brazil), Elsa Tamez (Costa Rica), and other theologians began to bring a distinctively female voice.

Culture and race were considered together, especially around the celebration of the five-hundred-year anniversary of the European "discovery" of the Americas in 1992. This topic was surrounded by controversy: was the "discovery" better seen as the conquest of the native peoples, in which the church was largely complicit? Had it remained complicit for five centuries of oppression, especially of indigenous and black people? These were the background issues when the bishops met in Santo Domingo, Dominican Republic (as previous meetings at Medellin and Puebla). Significantly, there is no mention of liberation theology, nor is the term liberation used in the Santo Domingo documents, although the bishops did express concerns about issues like debt burdens and rising inequality.

A central theme was "inculturation," a recognition that historically the Catholic church had imported European forms of language, liturgy, and mindsets. It was time once again to enter into dialogue with Latin American cultures and encourage new expressions of faith out of the people's own cultures. The bishops, under Vatican scrutiny, did not encourage experimentation, but theologians and others were exploring the issue.[12]

---

[11]Liberation theologians claimed that their method was to start with social reality and reflect theologically on it, yet they did not devote much attention to the phenomenon of the embrace of pentecostalism by a significant portion of the poor.

[12]See Hennelly, *Santo Domingo and Beyond;* and Irarrázabal, *Inculturation.*

Leonardo Boff pursued an interest in ecology and explored the connection between the "cry of the earth" and the "cry of the poor."[13]

There was no denying that the issues raised by the liberation theologians and their connection to grassroots practice of church people had brought valuable insights and inspired a whole generation of people in the church, which led to important developments in the Latin American churches. The centrality of the poor in scripture and in the church, the need to make an "option for the poor," the work of evangelization in villages and barrios, soup kitchens, defense of human rights, helping communities organize to promote their rights–all these were important developments in Latin American churches. The very violence that they had stirred up, including the 1998 murder of Bishop Gerardi, was a sign of liberation theology's effectiveness. But the liberation that had once been hoped for seemed more elusive than ever.

[13] See Boff, *Cry of the Earth, Cry of the Poor.*

13

African Americans

WILL COLEMAN

Demographics and Social Location

According to the March 2002 "Current Population" report of the U.S. Census Bureau, African Americans constitute approximately 13 percent (36 million) of the general population in the United States. Fifty-five percent of all African Americans live in the South, 18 percent in the Northeast, and Midwest, and 9 percent in the West. Over 52 percent live in "a central city within a metropolitan area." Only 13 percent live in non-metropolitan areas. Thirty-three percent are under the age of eighteen; 8 percent are sixty-five and older. In comparison to "non-Hispanic whites" (the official census terminology; neither Hispanics, Asians nor other ethnic groups are used in this comparison), the social location of African Americans maintains a status of larger family size, lower educational attainment, lower labor force participation and employment, a larger presence in service occupations than in managerial ones, lower incomes, and greater poverty. One major statistic not reflected in this census report is that concerning the incarceration of African Americans. On this note, African Americans also represent a larger percentage of the population. In fact, their presence in jails is extremely disproportionate in relation to that of the general population.

The plight of African Americans in the United States is rooted in deep historical and contemporary forces of oppression and neglect that are both external and internal to the African American community. Although some progress has been made in race relations, the United States remains a far cry from being a colorblind society. The purpose of this chapter is to explore the historical context out of which African American theology was created and present several contemporary thinkers who are contributing to its ongoing development.

Historical Context and Theological Creation

Despite the above statistical summation, African Americans have made profound contributions to the history of the United States in all of the arenas of public and private life. By far, their greatest influence has come through their cultural and religious creativity and their moral perseverance in the midst of seemingly insurmountable odds.

Historical Origins

Historically, persons of African descent entered the colonies of what would become the United States as chattel, property of English settlers and colonizers. Through a process of indigenous subjugation and economic exploitation, Native Americans were systematically eliminated and/or marginalized. At the same time, beginning in 1619, Africans were imported into the colonies to provide a cheap labor force for the emerging plantations. African slaves were acquired from various African nations via social, political, and economic relationships between European and African elites. They were removed from along the western coast and central interior of Africa and were distributed throughout northeastern South America, the Caribbean, and North America. This infamous trade in human cargo began in the sixteenth century and continued through the nineteenth century. It is important to note that the colonization of Africa through the exploitation of its human and natural resources began with slavery and continues today.

During the almost two and a half centuries of forced labor in the United States, without pay, African Americans created a spirituality and theology that sustained them throughout the brutalities of their enslavement. Initially, they were ignored by the so-called Christians who had enslaved them. Gradually, as their enslavers were convinced that the Eurocentric misrepresentation of Christianity (originally, like Judaism and Islam, it was a northeast African religion) would ensure better servitude from their property, some enslavers permitted their subjects to participate in an extremely limiting expression of plantation religion. Enslaved Africans were allowed to attend church with their enslavers, but not permitted to sit with them in the central part of the building. Instead, they were segregated away in some other part of the church structure. While attending church, it was the norm for them to be subjected to sermons that admonished them to obey their enslavers in order to minimize physical punishment here on earth and avoid eternal damnation in the afterlife.

The Rise of African American Theology

In response to the heretical plantation theology of Euro-Americans, many African Americans discovered and utilized strategies for creating their own theology. Drawing from the intellectual, moral, and spiritual resources they had brought with them from Africa, they combined their core beliefs and practices with their reinterpretations of the enslaver's messages. They also infused their daily experiences on the plantation into the shaping of a spirituality and theology that emerged from the "bush arbor" meetings. These clandestine gatherings were convened at night at the risk of severe beatings. Nevertheless, these enslaved African Americans persisted in seeking out opportunities to pray, sing, and share testimonies of how they believed God was intervening in their lives to bring about a better reality for themselves, their children, and their children's children *ad infinitum.*

In the bush arbor meetings African Americans took possession of the opportunity to transform plantation theology into a religion that would address their unique situation. Even though they used the same language system as their oppressors, they recoded the symbols and rituals to suit the faith that was emerging from within their own minds, bodies, and souls. This means they combined remnants of their African beliefs and practices with the biblical and liturgical stories of the Euro-American canon. Therefore, even though they might have worn the outer garments of the enslaver's religion, they covered themselves with the inner garments of a new religion that they themselves were creating. Along with this invention, they were engaging in theological reflection or discourse about ultimate reality in a language system (their own vernacular and idiom) that was relevant to them.

The Characteristics of African American Theology

What were some of the key characteristics of the spirituality and theology that African American slaves created?

1. A strong emphasis on the immanence of God in their midst
2. Prayer as a means of dialogue and struggle
3. A focus on the importance of the word or speech as transformative
4. Ecstatic mysticism as a vehicle for holistic healing
5. The "invitation to discipleship" as a call to participate in the work of God in their individual and corporate lives

First, African American slaves believed that God was not far removed from their immediate predicament. Indeed, their African sensibilities told them that this ultimate reality pervaded all of existence. Even though they would concede to a notion that their creator was beyond the human capacity to understand completely, they also knew that his/her presence was as close as the air they breathed. Therefore, when they gathered for worship they anticipated the influx of divine presence that would manifest itself in their midst at the appropriate time and place. Typically, this manifestation was presumed to occur whenever they gathered with the intent of "getting to know God" for themselves. Like their African foreparents, they would invoke this numinous power through prayer and song.

Second, when African American slaves prayed, they used this opportunity as a forum of thanksgiving, petition, and even protest. In thanksgiving, they expressed their appreciation for all of the blessings they had received, especially while enduring the hardships of their enslavement. They also approached "the throne of mercy" with their requests for relief from the burdens they bore and the fortitude to continue working and struggling toward a brighter future for themselves, their children, and their community. However, prayer was not limited to thanksgiving and petitions. It also included protest against the injustices they experienced at the hands of their enslavers. Like the psalmists of the Hebrew Scriptures, they would not hesitate to call God into accountability for the suffering they endured. Since they viewed themselves as living within a dialogical universe, they were not afraid to engage the supreme power to come to their assistance through both direct and indirect means.

Third, for the African American slave, the power of speech was paramount. In the African tradition, the *ase* or energy that pervades the universe, assumes special residence within the body and speech of particular individuals within a worshiping community. Through spirit possession, words of exhortation, and prophesy these individuals would inspire and motivate adherents of a faith community to "keep on keepin' on" through the storms and trials of life. Moreover, properly enunciated words of power could infuse everyone present with a sense of well-being despite present hardships and provide insight into how to participate in making "a way out of no way."

The fourth characteristic of African American spirituality and theology is possession. Not only is it related to the power of speech, but it is also a particular manifestation of spiritual presence within the body of the believer. During a period of prayer, exhortation, and song, one or more of the participants might experience an overwhelming force either entering or coming from within their bodies. They might temporarily lose conscious control of themselves as another power "takes over" what they feel, see, hear, and say. Often this phenomenon was coupled with some form of spiritual illumination that brought multidimensional healing and/or a sense of wholeness for the individual who is possessed and for others who are present.

Finally, the "invitation to discipleship" brought the community into a space where everyone, but especially those who are not yet members of the inner (initiatic) circle, was enjoined to commit themselves to discovering a better way of living out their lives once they returned to their more mundane existence. It should be added that the Eurocentric notion of separation between the so-called sacred and profane dimensions of life (including time and space) did not apply to the Afrocentric worldview.

Further reflection on creation of African American spirituality and theology reveals a genius that has been ignored in so-called traditional scholarship. Instead of ascribing to the preset dogmas and rubrics of confessional creeds and liturgical genuflections, African Americans were spontaneous and innovative. Even as they were attending churches along with their enslavers and listening to selected catechisms, songs, and sermons, they used their imaginations and own experiences as the basis for crafting theological "doctrines" and liturgical rituals that would correspond to the characteristics mentioned earlier. In so doing, they created a religion that was diametrically different from that of their enslavers. This liberative legacy continues today, even among conservative African American Christians.

Remnants of Folk Religion

Not all African Americans converted to Christianity. There has always been a remnant milieu of folk beliefs and practices such as hoodoo and voodoo that have informed African American cultural and spiritual expressions. Although these traditions have functioned alongside and outside of the Christian community, they have deeply influenced all aspects of African American life within the United States. One only has to think of the creation of the blues, jazz, and rap as examples of this cultural resonance. Thus, both Christian and non-Christian elements of African American culture have found their way, directly and indirectly, into African American theology. Contemporary African American theology cannot ignore all of "the ways of black folk" if it would be faithful to its historical legacy.

Representative Major Thinkers in Contemporary African American Theological Creation

One article cannot do justice to all the major contributors to the theological development of African Americans. Even though I have sought to highlight its earliest formulations during enslavement, African American theology's most prolific period, in terms of the emergence of a literary corpus, began during the 1960s and continues to increase each day. Therefore, in this section I will present several representative thinkers: Anthony B. Pinn, Cheryl A. Kirk-Duggan, Karen Baker-Fletcher, and Michael Eric Dyson. This selection is not intended to represent a "who's who" list. Rather it seeks to spotlight a category of African American religious thinkers who are both original in their own right and who, collectively, have produced a corpus of literature that demonstrates the variety that is present within contemporary African American theology. Even though these persons have Christian backgrounds, each has stretched themselves beyond the dogmatic confines of Protestant Christianity to incorporate non-Christian dimensions of African American life into their own intellectual works.

Anthony B. Pinn

Anthony B. Pinn identifies himself as a humanist. By this designation, he assumes no theological underpinnings for reflecting upon and coming to terms with either the plight or liberation of persons of African descent in the United States. Instead, he believes that one can interpret both of these on the basis of the realization (or lack thereof) of full human potential, here and now. At the same time, Pinn has researched and written extensively on "the variety of African American religious experience." In his book bearing the same title, he presents an engrossing survey of the rich diversity of religious life in the United States. It reveals manifestations of an ever-changing quest for religious authenticity. Through exhaustive interviews, travel, and research he gives an insider's view of Voodoo, Orisha devotion, Santeria, the Nation of Islam, and Black Humanism. In so doing, he brings into the foreground traditions that have been marginalized in most theological discussions. These practices include Caribbean-based religiosity, divination and healing, and black Muslim interpretations of the Koran and U.S. culture. Additionally, a smorgasbord of other African American movements is represented: church women's clubs, Pentecostalism, and private religious practices. These popular, non-Christian religious practices are rooted in African American past and are a foretaste of things to come.

On the basis of his research, Pinn argues for a rethinking of the "canon of black religion" and its related theological reflections. It can no longer assume sources, norms, and doctrines informed exclusively by Protestant Christian beliefs and practices. Instead, the contemporary African American theologian must become cognizant of the varied sources and influences that inform the imaginations of African Americans today.

Cheryl A. Kirk-Duggan

Cheryl A. Kirk-Duggan is a womanist ethicist and theologian, who has special interests in womanist theory, theodicy, African American spirituals, theomusicology and popular culture, the ethics of violence and religion, and the relationship between the Bible and culture. One example of these varied interests is her book, *Exorcising Evil: A Womanist Perspective on the Spirituals.* In this text, she probes what African American spirituals have to say about the action of God in the face of racial injustice and oppression. The context for this exploration begins with an interpretation of slavery and its offshoot–racism. According to her, spirituals are part and parcel of the soul of the African American soul. Born of the experience of enslavement, they represent creativity and affirmation of the presence of

God in the midst of the oppression of slavery and racial oppression. Their soul-reviving impulses were carried on through the civil rights movement via a language of power and survival as African Americans sang in celebration of their life force and belief in a God who sustained them in their suffering.

Kirk-Duggan's womanist analysis on the language of spirituals unveils a worldview in which men and women addressed themes such as a theology of justice and theodicy through story and music. Moreover, her historical and exegetical treatment of them reveal their ongoing appeal, both as inspirational music and as sources for contemporary theological reflection. This turn to slave songs represents an archaeological search for the roots of African American creativity under the duress of enslavement as another way of understanding how the imaginative and poetic urge gives rise to theological reflection within an oral tradition. Now, as then, one needs a keen sense of discernment to articulate how God is present within structures of alienation and marginalization.

Karen Baker-Fletcher

Karen Baker-Fletcher is a womanist theologian who turns her attention to constructing a theology of the land in *Sisters of Dust, Sisters of Spirit: Womanist Wordings on God and Creation.* Drawing inspiration from her own matriarchal heritage, she explores biblical and literary metaphors of dust and spirit to address the embodiment of God, Spirit, Christ, creation, and humans as these theological themes relate to justice-oriented spirituality of creation as a counter to issues such as environmental racism. While not embracing pantheism, she demonstrates a strong sensitivity to the presence of God in nature. In her own way, she reappropriates an African sensitivity toward the ubiquitous *ase* that is present everywhere, to be respected and honored.

Michael Eric Dyson

Cultural critic and Baptist minister Michael Eric Dyson has emerged as one of the premier public intellectuals of our times. Among his many acclaimed books, his more recent one, *Holler If You Hear Me: Searching for Tupac Shakur,* is an in-depth biographical analysis of an African American cultural icon. Dyson recognizes Shakur as someone who continues to become larger in death than he was in life. As a gangsta rap artist, his works continue to inspire and amaze both critics and admirers. As an enigmatic and controversial figure, Shakur aptly represents the existential angst and possibilities of an entire hip-hop culture. He embodied a wide range of paradoxical impulses.

On the one hand there is self-destructive behavior, moral ambiguity, iconoclasm toward acceptable mores, and male misogyny. On the other hand, religious and spiritual beliefs are also very real in rap culture. For some, Shakur himself has become a "ghetto saint" who represents an entire generation of marginalized African Americans. As a cult figure, he is like folk heroes of old: Stagolee and High John the Conqueror, who bucked the system through their extraordinary feats of daring. He also epitomizes the tragedy of African American male genius. And yet, he continues to live, like a messiah, whose return to the mike is expected at anytime.

Conclusion

If we revisit the five key characteristics of the spirituality and theology that African American slaves created in light of the above representative thinkers, we can discern traces of them within contemporary theological development. First, divine presence and/or optimum human potential are ubiquitous. There is no space or time that does not, in some way, represent a connection between the sacred and the profane. Even African American humanism cannot ignore the theistic and quasi-theistic sensibilities of most persons of African descent. The "varieties" of their religious expressions are a testimony to a belief in transcendent forces and powers that can be invoked to draw near.

Second, "prayer" is dialogical speech within a community of faith. It may assume both the form of adoration and protest. However, even in the midst of extreme anguish, African-descended people call upon numinous powers and use their imaginations to draw strength and encouragement from beyond their immediate capacities to effect change in their lives.

Third, the power of the word, from preaching to rapping, remains an effective mode of communication and speaks to the potential transformation today, just as it did in the past. Through spoken, printed, and lyrical words, African Americans continue to tell the story of anguish and hope.

Holistic healing, the byproduct of the fourth characteristic of African American spirituality, is more difficult to relate to the contemporary context. Nihilism seems to be more pervasive. But the spirit of liberation has not vanished. Instead, it assumes different forms in this postmodern context. The task of the theologian is to discern the movement of the spirit and reveal its presence to others.

Finally, the call to participate in the formation of a better world can still be heard between the lyrics of both so-sacred and so-secular songs. Moreover, the yearning to survive and prosper within a capitalistic and pluralistic society does not diminish the necessity of casting and vision that is larger than personal gratification.

Contemporary African American theologians have a tremendous challenge to face as they strive to remain relevant. Given the emerging spiritualities on the horizon within the African American community along with the complexity of society as a whole, it will not be easy to do so. Nevertheless, a great historical precedent has been set by their ancestors. If they follow their lead with a keen sensitivity toward what takes place beneath the surface, they will fulfill their role as diviners of true justice and liberation just as certainly as their intellectual, spiritual, and moral forebears did in their own context.

14

Hispanics

EDWIN DAVID APONTE

A Question of Context

The terms "Hispanics" or "Latinos and Latinas" describe groups in the United States that have engaged, appropriated, and developed the perspectives of liberation theology on their own terms and in their own particular North American contexts. For some people using "Hispanic" or "Latino/a" to refer to the same group is confusing and frustrating. There does not seem to be any established way to predict who will use which term when. Others use both terms interchangeably. Moreover, the mention of Latinas and Latinos or Hispanics immediately invokes numerous qualifications. On the one hand, Latinas and Latinos are connected with their varied roots whether they are recent arrivals from Latin America or trace their family's presence in North America over several generations, or even a few centuries. On the other hand, Hispanics do not come from one country, nor are they of one race in the usual everyday sense of race. In fact, the grouping of Latinos and Latinas in the United States is more the result of dominant understandings of race and ethnicity than roots in Latin America.

Although there are strong links with Latin America and the Caribbean that are continually replenished, U.S. Hispanics are distinct from their Latin

American counterparts. A chief reason for this is the perhaps obvious, but still important, factor of the differences in contexts. In a similar way theologically, Latino/a liberationist perspectives must be distinguished from those of Latin Americans. Hispanic liberation theologies are not an unchanged importation of Latin American liberation theology, although there are ongoing connections and conversations.

It cannot be said that all manifestations of Latino/a theologies in the United States understand themselves to be *expressions* of liberation theology at all. Some types of Hispanic theology intentionally distance themselves from liberation theologies. Likewise, not all theologies that mention an "option for the poor" or advocate the cause of the under-represented can be categorized as liberation theology. So then, a discussion about "Hispanics" or "Latinos/as" is not a simple task because of the questions of context regarding history, politics, economics, religion, and the movements of people. One way to access this complexity of terms, peoples, and the theologies that they represent is to better understand what "Latino/a" and "Hispanic" mean in the context of the United States.

Hispanic or Latino?

Several Groups under One Umbrella

Despite common societal understandings, being "Hispanic" in the United States is not simply a matter of being of Spanish descent or Spanish-speaking, as the literal definition of "Hispanic" primarily denotes. The usage of "Hispanics" or "Latinos/as" commonly indicates several groups placed under one demographic umbrella. However, under the one umbrella stand multifaceted issues of language, religion, generations, regional differences, history, and alternative self-understandings to consider. "Hispanic" or "Latino/a" are heuristic devices referring to the diverse groups of people of Iberian, other European, Native American, African American, and Asian descent and heritage living within the United States. Peoples of diverse backgrounds and histories are named "Hispanic" or "Latino" and "Latina" in the United States.

The U.S. Census Bureau, the official designator of race and ethnicity in the dominant society, seeks to count the country's population. In so doing it recognizes the diversity of this group. In the 2000 Census, persons had the following options to select:

- White
- Black, African American, or Negro
- American Indian or Alaska Native
- Asian Indian
- Chinese
- Filipino
- Japanese

- Korean
- Vietnamese
- Other Asian
- Native Hawaiian
- Guamanian or Chamorro
- Samoan
- Other Pacific Islander

For persons of Latin American or Caribbean descent the first set of options was just an initial step in a demographic winnowing process. A person additionally could select one of the above options and in addition, answer the following:

Is this person Spanish/Hispanic/Latino?

If a person answered "Yes" to the preceding question, further identification was requested using the following categories:

- Mexican, Mexican American, Chicano
- Puerto Rican
- Cuban
- Other Spanish/Hispanic/Latino

The U.S. Census Bureau recognizes some of the complexity involved in naming Hispanics. And yet, even this process did not get at all the possibilities of the group in question.

Hispanic Growth in the United States

Not only the diversity, but also the growth of the Hispanic population is confirmed by the U.S. Census Bureau information. In sheer numbers, Hispanics form the fastest growing so-called ethnic group in the United States. In March 2000, an estimated 32.8 million Hispanics lived in the United States representing approximately 12 percent of the U.S. population. Many observers believed that even this significant number was an undercount. However, the bare demographic data only begins to define who Latinas/Latinos really are and the cultural and religious impact they have in the United States. Their diversity means that a "typical" Hispanic does not exist.

Physically, many Latinos/as are recognized as "white" with straight blond hair and blue eyes, while others are dark-skinned with curly hair, and everything in between. Some have Native American features, while others have Asian features. Religiously Hispanics are Roman Catholics, historic mainline Protestants (Episcopal, Presbyterian, Lutheran, Methodist, etc.), Pentecostals, *evangélicos,* Jehovah's Witnesses, Mormons, devotees of the *Orichas* (African spirits), Jewish, Muslim, atheists, spiritualists, and followers of Native American religious traditions. Linguistically some speak only "pure" Spanish, others speak Spanglish, and others speak English, while a majority move easily among the three. Historically, some have recently arrived to this country, and others were here centuries before there was a United States of America.

Geographical Spread of Hispanics in the United States

Geographically, Latinos and Latinas in the Northeast are still primarily a Puerto Rican population, but not exclusively so. In St. Patrick's Cathedral in New York City, which still has a predominant Puerto Rican population, one can find a shrine to the Virgin of Guadalupe, who is central to the devotion and identity of the majority of Mexicans and Mexican Americans. Dominicans are numerous in the Northeast, particularly in the New York City area. This tragically came to the conscience of the nation with the crash of an airliner in New York shortly after the September 2001 attacks. The majority of the victims were Dominican passengers. Mexican and Cuban communities have existed in Pennsylvania since the nineteenth century, and Mexicans in the Upper Midwest from early in the twentieth century. Miami has Peruvians alongside of Cubans. In the Southwest, Mexican Americans (a diverse population themselves) comprise the majority of Hispanics, but this is changing rapidly as Puerto Ricans, Central Americans, and South Americans move into the region. One of the largest populations of Salvadorans outside Central America lives in Washington, D.C., with growing communities in Los Angeles and San Francisco and a burgeoning one in the Dallas-Forth Worth area. In Dallas, the national diversity mixes with the religious diversity as a *Changó botanica* (a type of shop of spiritual tools and folk remedies) sits near an *Iglesia de Cristo* (Church of Christ). Guatemalans reside in Florida and Texas, but a closer look reveals that many of these Guatemalans are Miskito (for whom Spanish is a second language). Those who are called "Hispanics" are already a multicultural people, *un pueblo de diversidad*, the heirs of many traditions, as a new identity and a new reality are built here in the United States. They are simultaneously "outsiders" and "insiders" on all sides. They live in an existential in-between space while interacting with the larger society.[1]

Terminology and Labels for Hispanics

Some within this diverse population group contest the idea that "Hispanic" was an invention of the U.S. government for Census Bureau purposes. They see U.S. racial politics of the 1960s and early 1970s as the prime mover behind the term. For these critics the label "Hispanic" has negative political and social implications as part of a larger effort of a specific racial classification of the population that is a basic principle of U.S. society. The term implies a connection with the Spanish language that all Hispanics do not have in common as well as being a term founded in European colonialism.

---

[1]For more on the diversity of Latino/a peoples and their cultural locations, see De La Torre and Aponte, *Introducing Latino/a Theologies,* 42–58.

Gender conscious "Latino/a," appeared as an alternative designation. Among some of Latin American heritage, the term "Latino/a" is the preferred self-designation because it is perceived to better describe the Latin American roots of the various communities. The terms "Latino" and "Latina" are seen as having emerged during the U.S. civil rights movement as a term of political and cultural affirmation. Strictly speaking, according to the advocates of the designation "Latino/a," not all Latinas and Latinos are Hispanic, in the sense that many people of Latin American or Caribbean heritage are not of European descent and speak Spanish only as a second language. Such is the case among indigenous groups in Central and South America. Hence, it is argued by many within the community that "Latino/a" is a more appropriate designation. Admittedly an issue with this term is its gendered rendering: it is cumbersome to always say "Latinos and Latinas." To simply say Latinos *or* Latinas denies the gender bias that either word could imply.

Advocates of the Latino/a option point to "Hispanic" as a politically incorrect reference reeking of European hegemony. Ironically, the geographic and cultural designation "Latin America" (from which Latino/a derives) appeared in the nineteenth century as a way to connect Spanish, Portuguese, and French America with the wider linguistic and cultural heritage of ancient Rome. So while the critique of the term "Hispanic" as a designation of the dominant society is compelling for some, the use of the term "Latino/a" also is problematic, at least historically. The "Latin" in "Latino" evokes the European, Spanish-Latin heritage at the expense of Native American, African, Asian, and non-Spanish European heritages of Latin American or Caribbean peoples. To complicate matters further, many in the United States reject "Latino/a" as too closely linked with radical left-wing politics in both the United States and Latin America. Some in New Mexico wish to affirm their Spanish heritage and call themselves *hispanos*. The compounded irony is that both terms used simultaneously as self-identifiers and imposed descriptions mask the complexity of a diverse cultural heritage of the very people they seek to describe. If the intent is to have a more descriptive term reflective of all the peoples involved, the search for an appropriate nomenclature without roots in oppression or exploitation is incomplete in the early twenty-first century. Although "Latino/a" seems to be gaining prominence, the question of "Hispanic or Latino/a" is unresolved.

Creation of an Ethnicity

The Immigration Origins

The Hispanic presence in the United States is not a recent monolithic phenomenon. Several factors shaped the ethnic formation of Hispanics or Latinos/as in the United States when compared to the large European immigrations of the nineteenth and twentieth centuries. The most notable difference can be seen in the circumstances surrounding entrance into the United States. The late nineteenth and early twentieth centuries were characterized by massive European immigration within short periods of time followed by a long period of cultural assimilation. In contrast, Hispanic immigration included the incorporation by the United States of the immense territory from Mexico along with its inhabitants in 1848. Following this was the U.S. acquisition of Puerto Rico in 1898 and political control over Cuba in the first few years of its life as a republic. These events produced migrations that were later supplemented by continuous immigration from other parts of Latin America. Such movements of people, often influenced by larger social and political forces, perpetually renew Latin American or Caribbean culture and language in the United States.

Another distinction between earlier European migrations and the continued influx of Hispanic peoples becomes clear from the perspective of U.S. racial categories. Irish, Germans, Jews, Italians, and other European migrations in subsequent generations were defined "white," whereas Hispanics of any generation are perceived to be "non-white" or "people of color" because they are seen as "mixed."[2] For this reason Latinos/as encounter some of the same treatment non-whites have historically experienced in the United States. Those factors set some of the social boundaries of U.S. Hispanic/Latina(o) ethnicity.

Cultural Influences

The creation of Hispanic/Latina(o) identity is influenced by Latin American or Caribbean factors as well. In very general terms several major cultural streams feed into the Latin American or Caribbean experience that impact the development of Hispanic/Latina(o) identity in the United States. The European stream consists largely of people from the Iberian Peninsula, although even this group is diverse. From ancient times various peoples and groups settled in what today is Spain and Portugal. The cultural diversity of centuries of different groups including the Moorish and Jewish presence helps create these two modern nations. Elements of this cultural mix settled in Latin America. Various groups from other parts of Europe, notably from mainland Italy, Corsica, and Germany in addition to Spain and Portugal settled in Latin America.

The second stream of culture affecting the present populations in Latin America and the United States is the African heritage brought to the Western Hemisphere through the injustice of slavery, which in some parts of the hemisphere continued late into the nineteenth century. This broad African diaspora within all of the Americas brought a wide distribution of peoples from different parts of Africa, mainly from West Africa. Not only were

---

[2]See for example Bodkin, *How Jews Became White Folks;* and Ignatiev, *How the Irish Became White.*

these people physically brought to the Americas, their West African cultures, traditions, and beliefs accompanied them. These beliefs have taken root, developed, and evolved into new entities through an ongoing cultural exchange.

Indigenous Native American cultures are the third stream in the Latin American or Caribbean confluence. Native Americans in Latin America suffered exploitation and genocide resulting from the European conquest. The indigenous Native American population, like the African, is characterized by numerous and distinct subgroups, each with its own history, culture, and in some cases surviving languages. In the current national groups of Latin America there is a different "mix" of these three streams depending on the historic presence of each in a given location.

A fourth stream, often overlooked, is the Asian presence in Latin America. Post-Colombian Asian arrival in Latin America can be dated to the sixteenth century, a product of the global empire of Spain. The growth of this movement began in earnest with the nineteenth century settlement of peoples from various parts of Asia, including laborers brought from China and the Indian subcontinent to Cuba, Puerto Rico, and other islands in the Caribbean, as well as Chinese in Peru, Chile, Panama, El Salvador, and Mexico. The modern Asian presence includes twentieth century migrations of Japanese and Koreans to different parts of South America such as Argentina, Bolivia, Peru and Brazil.[3] Given the diverse origins and complex histories involved, it is difficult to speak of Latin Americans as a homogenous group. And yet, all are incorporated into the Hispanic/ Latina(o) ethnic group in the United States.

Racial-Ethnic Identity and Domination

From both theological and sociological perspectives the "naming" or labeling of one group of people by another group can be viewed as an exercise in power and dominance. Naming can be both an exercise of the power of the dominant group and an effort to maintain de facto class distinctions between the groups. Such an exercise of power supports the dominant society's cultural and social constructions of reality as well as the cultural codes and symbols used to communicate and support those myths. So it can be said in this context naming is more than a descriptive identification and more than a disinterested, "objective" designation. Rather, naming is an attempt at molding, controlling, and relegating of one group's roles by another group. If this is so, then it is important to identify who names and what particular name is given.

Racial designations in the United States–such as Hispanic and Latino–are more descriptive of the social construction of the dominant society in

[3]See Cho, *Asians in Latin America;* Roth, *Brokered Homeland;* and Hirabayashi, et al., eds., *New World, New Lives.*

the United States than of a set of immutable characteristics (Farley and Allen 1989:2–6, 408–419). Omi and Winant describe a type of "racial etiquette" of interpretative codes and meanings that are at work in the everyday experiences of people in the United States There are unquestioned assumptions that "determine the 'presentation of self,' distinctions of status, and appropriate modes of conduct" (1986, 62). The power of the cultural code is displayed in the naming process.

Disguising the Nature of Social Classes

Part of the power of naming is that it disguises the nature of social classes that are present in U.S. society. Depending upon the nature and origin of a name, a false consciousness can be fostered in the people being named. That is to say, there is a concerted effort to tell people that they are something other than what they perceive themselves to be. One group's common-sense understandings of reality are supplanted by another's understandings.

This imposition can be made through coercion, deceit, or a combination of both. Individuals and groups subscribe to a definition constructed by someone else and thereby fall into the trap of domination, sometimes unawares. A people's cultural past is ignored or reinterpreted to accommodate the dominant cultural constructions (i.e., dominant cultural myth).

An aspect of the U.S. cultural constructions is the concept of the melting pot in which it is said that by the process of assimilation disparate groups amalgamate into a larger uniform entity in which all are equal and are treated impartially. Contrary to the usual explanation of this powerful social myth, the melting pot has not been proven to operate in this way. There is no single homogenized entity, but rather the constrained invention of two homogenized groups: one "white" and the other "black." Race and ethnicity are recognized in the United States only in specific predetermined categories. Any deviation from these categories results in a group's renaming and being given a new consciousness. The rich diversity of peoples in the United States is reinterpreted by the dominant society through the rubric of the color-line. As others have noted (admittedly with different groups in mind) there are and always have been some unmeltable ethnics in the United States.[4] In this context, unmeltable ethnics are not solely those of non-Anglo-Saxon European descent, but also many Latinos/as. The oppression of racial realities in the United States in which Hispanics are forced to one side of the color-line is both a context and a catalyst for the development of contextual Latino/a theologies of liberation.

---

[4]For example, see Novak, *Unmeltable Ethnics*.

Forced into Fixed Categories

W. E. B. DuBois wrote that the problem of the color-line, namely the problem of race, was the great problem of the twentieth century. Despite protestations to the contrary, the problem persists into the twenty-first century (1989, 10). Therefore, in deciding between "Hispanic" or "Latino/a," in one sense Latin Americans, Caribbeans, and people of Latin American descent are forced into the fixed categories of the U.S. problem of the color-line. The categories are "white" and "non-white," with the latter defined in terms of Blackness, whether or not African heritage actually is involved. Individuals and groups are socially positioned as members of the dominant white society–and are expected to assimilate to the profile–or they are assigned to a "colored" other.

The racial/ethnic-based labels of the dominant culture in the United States are problematic. They are neither truly descriptive nor do they positively add to a description of a people's ethnicity or culture. Instead these labels do violence to the people they purport to describe and perpetuate the prejudiced perceptions and actions of the dominant society. Reducing people to preconceived stereotyped traits and interchangeable generic categories erases their unique characteristics while limiting their contribution to society on the whole. Rather than dealing forthrightly with issues of self-understanding, socioeconomic class, and national origin, using racial/ethnic terms focuses on stereotyping. Ethnic stereotyping masks both distinctive cultural heritages and various types of oppression. The dominant process of naming ignores social-class and national-origin distinctions. In the United States race and ethnicity are not recognized as the conceptual abstractions they are. They are falsely seen as immutable conceptual terms, objectively available. "Hispanic" is not descriptive of a homogeneous people but ascriptive of the dominant society's preconceived notions of what is Hispanic.

Self-understandings

Prior to coming to the United States (or having the United States overtake them as in the case of Mexican Americans and Puerto Ricans), Latin Americans and Caribbeans understood themselves differently from the common Eurocentric understanding in dominant society. People of Latin American and Caribbean heritage living in the United States carried with them their own concepts of class divisions as experienced in their nations of origin. Upon arrival in the United States they perceived a class arrangement at work couched in racial/ethnic terms that resisted the addition of fresh concepts from Latin America and the Caribbean. Although the simplistic reduction to "whites" and "nonwhites" is inadequate to understand the racial, ethnic, class, and cultural understandings of Latin America and the Caribbean, there is a recognition of "the way things work" that compels them to deal with the power of the U.S. color-line.

A New People

Moreover, the cultural complexity does not end with the imposition of identity. A new people, by whatever name, is forming and constantly re-forming in the North American context. The Hispanic/Latina(o) reality is present and growing in the United States. Whether or not this reality is called "Hispanic" or "Latino/a" is a separate issue from the social reality of this developing, collective, pan-ethnic identity of people with Latin American and Caribbean roots living in the United States. The conditions of life in the United States, including imposed racial identities, help foster this growing sense of group identity. This becomes an additional and concurrent type of self-understanding and naming.

Among those, both native and foreign born, of Latin American and Caribbean descent in the United States a growing awareness is rising that a new ethnic group has emerged in the U.S. context. A flexible, contextual and contested shared ethnicity develops among different Latino/a groups in a location where there is recognition of common traits, needs, oppression, and solutions while acknowledging and affirming differences. Simultaneously, other self identifications are used. An ethnic solidarity has formed in the United States partly because this is how the game is played and partly through intermingling of the different groups of Latin American and Caribbean descent. Additionally, there is growing awareness of shared concerns.

Self-naming is a way that groups within the rubric Latino/a retain their own identity apart from the umbrella term. Some groups prefer to call themselves according to the country of their national origin. While acknowledging through self-naming the countries of origin that contribute to the Hispanic/Latina(o) population, simultaneously a "new people" is forming in the U.S. context from the diverse peoples of Latin America and Caribbean. The advocates of this perspective hold that a new ethnic experience has developed in North America through the coming together of different peoples from Latin America and the Caribbean.

Self-naming also is a way that expresses how groups perceive their present reality. Groups that aggressively identify themselves by terms such as Chicano/a, Mexican American, Puerto Rican, Cuban, Dominican, Salvadoran, Guatemalan, Chilean, etc., simultaneously appropriate pan-ethnic terms. It is not a matter one or the other, of national self-reference or pan-ethnic, but both.

The reality of something new and distinct from Latin America and the Caribbean is more easily seen in the imposed and created identities of the second and later generations, those persons of Latin American and Caribbean descent born and raised in the United States. These are persons of multiple cultural identities who move in and out of various contexts, speaking sometimes English, sometimes Spanish, or more often a combination of both producing a culture that is difficult to categorize. Although this may be elusive, the market sees this new reality and is making concerted efforts to address it. For example, radio stations employ English-speaking disc jockeys who sprinkle their talk with Spanish and play Tejano music. Bilingual cable stations like *mun2 televisión* (mun2 is a play on the Spanish "mundos", "worlds") target a younger audience with program fare in both English and Spanish.

Anglo-Saxon William Shakespeare asked the question: "What's in a name? That which we call a rose, By any other name would smell as sweet (*Romeo and Juliet* 2.1). In this context, "What's in a name?" reflects some of the complexity affecting how to name this diverse group who have so many connections. Because of the common usage and the myriad terms of self-designation, the terms "Hispanic" and "Latino" are used interchangeably by many as a compromise to address the actual use of terms in U.S. society. The terms may be the temporary preferred designation of some groups during this time of formation and development in the context of the U.S. color-line. The theological usefulness of a discussion concerning naming, domination, and the formation of identity lies in the possibility of viewing the reality of life in the United States from a different angle. Furthermore such a discussion helps in understanding the inchoate ways that dominant power is at work in U.S. American culture, as well as uncovering assumed cultural codes and myths.

15

Asian Americans

SEUNG AI YANG

Demographics

Asian Americans are the fastest growing racial group in the country when this is measured in terms of a percentage of their own population. The 2000 census reports about 12 million Asian Americans in the United States, which reflects a growth of 72 percent since 1990. The Asian American population is expected to double by 2010. Chinese, Filipino, Asian Indian, Vietnamese, Korean, and Japanese are the six largest groups. They account for 87.5 percent of Asian Americans. Smaller ethnic groups listed among Asian Americans in the census include Bangladeshi, Cambodian, Hmong, Indonesian, Laotian, Malaysian, Pakistani, Sri Lankan, Taiwanese, and Thai. The term "Asian Americans" generally refers to the U.S. population from East Asia, South Asia, and Southeast Asia since the U.S. Census Bureau includes the people from West Asia, also called the Middle East, in the white race category.

Immigration History and Social Location of Asian Americans

History of Asian Immigration

The first Asians to come to the United States were Filipinos. They settled in the 1760s in the swamps near New Orleans, Louisiana, then Spain's colony. They were descendants of the Manila galleon sailors who had settled in Mexico in the late sixteenth century. Chinese, however, are the first Asians to arrive in the United States in large number. By the 1840s, a sizeable number of Chinese people had been working on Hawaiian plantations. Starting in the 1850s, Chinese also came to the West Coast on the mainland to work in gold mines and later to help build the railroads. Japanese and Filipinos soon followed Chinese, and in smaller numbers, Koreans and Asian Indians as well.

Legal Discrimination against Asians

From the beginning of their immigration Asians have suffered severe discrimination. Viewed as exotic, non-American people and as the "Yellow Peril" to white labor and to "white civilization," Asians suffered from state-supported discrimination until 1965. This included anti-Asian policies and laws across the federal, state, and local levels. Since the 1850s, a series of restrictive laws against Asians were enacted. In 1870, Congress passed a law that made Asian immigrants the only racial group barred from naturalization. In 1882, the Chinese Exclusion Act was passed. This suspended the immigration of Chinese laborers for 10 years, but this was later extended indefinitely, eventually being lifted only in 1943. The 1917 Immigration Act further limited Asian immigration, banning immigration from all countries in the Asia-Pacific Triangle except for the Philippines–a U.S. territory–and Japan. Japanese immigration, however, was subsequently limited by the 1924 Exclusionary Immigration Act, which literally halted new immigration from Asia.

During this period, Asians also suffered from other discriminatory laws at the state and local levels. These included segregation in public facilities including schools, heavy taxation, prohibition of land ownership, prohibition of intermarriage with whites, and so on. Asians were also constantly the target of bigotry and violence. The most visible incident in the country's history of discrimination against Asian Americans was probably the internment of Japanese Americans during World War II. In February 1942, President Roosevelt signed Executive Order 9066, which resulted in forcing 120,000 Japanese Americans to evacuate their homes with a notice of less than seven days. They had to move to the internment camps, where many remained for the duration of the war. After more than sixty years, the issues surrounding Japanese internment still remain emotional among Asian Americans.

Ongoing Prejudice against Asians

Since 1965, when the anti-Asian immigration restrictions were finally lifted, a new wave of immigrants began to arrive from many different countries of Asia. Many of these new immigrants were highly educated professionals as a result of the preference system for skilled workers. In the

1970s and early 1980s, the upheavals in Southeast Asia caused by the Vietnam War brought a large number of refugees to the United States. Even though discrimination on the basis of race is no longer legal in the United States, in reality Asian Americans experience discrimination through prejudice, systematic bias, bigotry, and violence.

Several underlying factors contribute to discrimination against Asian Americans. Some of these factors arise out of the tendency of the general public and the media to stereotype Asian Americans. As a group the Asian American community is extremely heterogeneous, comprised of many ethnicities, of new immigrants and of persons whose families have been here for generations, and of persons of all socioeconomic statuses. Most Americans have very little knowledge of the history and cultures of Asian Americans and very little awareness of the diversity among them. This ignorance leads people to lump together Asian Americans in a single group and to perceive them through stereotypes. Other factors that contribute to discrimination include the linguistic, cultural, and religious differences that exist between many Asian Americans, particularly recent immigrants, and the general public. These differences foster misunderstandings between Asian and non-Asian Americans, as well as among different Asian Americans themselves.

A widespread public perception sees all Asians in this country as foreigners representing a faraway place defined as strange, exotic, and un-American. A black-and- white view of race in the United States, in sharp contrast to the history of Americans and to the emerging future of the United States, contributes to this public perception of Asian Americans who are neither white nor black in their appearance. One of the most frequent questions Asian Americans–regardless for how many generations they have lived in the United States–confront in their everyday life is, "Where are you from?" When the person replies, for example, "I am from New Jersey," or "I am from Chicago," the questioner usually tries once more: "No, where are you really from?" Asian Americans who were born here also frequently get such comments as "You speak English very well. Where did you learn English?"

Another aspect that contributes to this public perception is the difference of the cultural and religious backgrounds between Asian Americans and non-Asian Americans. Asian Americans are affiliated with a range of religions including Confucianism, Buddhism, Hinduism, Zoroastrianism, Islam, Shinto, Sikhism, Jainism, Taoism, and tribal religions as well as Christianity. The unfamiliarity of most Americans with those non-Western religions of Asian Americans often generates anti-Asian hostility and violence.

If "Yellow Peril" was the foremost stereotype of Asian Americans in the past, they are stereotyped as "Model Minority" today more than anything. Even though the view of Asian Americans as hardworking, intelligent, and successful people might sound complimentary, this mythical stereotype has quite negative consequences. It diverts public attention from the reality of prejudice and even violence Asian Americans often confront in their jobs and in their quests for promotion, higher education, health care, and for other public services. For Asian Americans everyday life is full of bias and hardship. In fact, a Wall Street Journal survey in May 1991 found that most Americans do not believe that Asian Americans face racial bigotry. Some even contend that they are granted "too many special advantages."

In reality, lots of Asian Americans, especially recent immigrants, suffer from poverty and unemployment, due to limited English proficiency and cultural differences. The myth of "Model Minority" often contributes to the elimination of Asian Americans from affirmative action and other programs designed to help disadvantaged minorities. It disguises their lack of representation in the most significant national arenas and institutions. It also stimulates anti-Asian sentiment and violence among less successful whites and minorities. In sum, the social context of Asian Americans today is that they live in a more ambivalent situation than black or Hispanic Americans because they are praised as "model minority." They are viewed as a solution to racial and economic ills of American society while suffering from unfair and discriminatory treatment as forever strangers in the United States

Asian American Theological Responses to the Social Context

The painful experiences of Asian American communities throughout their 250 years of immigration history to the United States have generated unique liberation theologies among Asian American theologians. There are several major themes found in Asian American liberation theologies.

Forever Strangers on the Margin

The most dominant theme found in Asian American theologies perhaps is the marginality experience of Asian Americans as forever strangers. This everyday experience of Asian Americans as individual and group was most intensified when 120,000 Japanese Americans were interned in the concentration camps during the World War II. Even after living in this country for generations as U.S. citizens, many Japanese Americans were officially treated as foreigners and as a threat to the country.

The experience of being viewed as un-American, as forever foreigner, is extended even to a religious and spiritual realm. Having origin in a faraway land where Christianity is a minority religion, Asians in their new home, America, are considered not only un-American but also un-Christian. Many Asians in America try hard to assimilate themselves to the dominant culture, totally rejecting their ancestral cultures and traditions as stumbling blocks to their assimilation. This effort, however, often results in a more painful experience of multiple marginality. They not only remain viewed as un-American in America, but they are also suspected and treated as a strange person by their own community. Asian American liberation theologians relate this experience of multiple marginality to the concept of "*han*," which Korean liberation theologians identified as representing the wounded inner hearts of *minjung*. *Minjung* means ordinary people who are "oppressed, exploited, dominated, discriminated against, alienated and suppressed politically, economically, socially, culturally, and intellectually" (Chung 1989: 138–39).

The experience of multiple marginality of people has helped Asian American theologians challenge the dominant form of Western Christian theology that seems to underlie the marginalization of Asians. Indeed, Western theology has taught that the indigenous cultures and traditions of the homeland of Asians are inferior to the Christian culture and tradition of the West and that to become a true Christian one has to shun one's own traditional culture and religion. Asian American theologians, therefore, identified this Western theology as the source of oppression and marginalization of Asian Americans and promoted indigenization as the source for liberation. They realize that Christian theology has been prisoner to "the Latin captivity of the church." Thus, indigenization becomes a central theme to Asian American theology in seeking to liberate theology from western captivity.

Religious Pluralism

Another major theme found in Asian American liberation theologies is religious pluralism. Religious pluralism is quite a new concept in the Western world, where Christianity was considered for more than 1500 years as the only "true" religion. Most of the homelands of Asian Americans, in contrast, have been practicing religious pluralism as a natural way of living for thousands of years. Accepting one religion never meant the necessity to shun other religions, and no single soteriology may have an exclusive claim over and against others.

When religious pluralism is valued, one easily becomes a religious practitioner of eclectic mixture. For example, before Christianity was introduced in the eighteenth century, an ordinary Korean would lead everyday life strictly in accordance with the Confucian teachings and rituals, regularly visit a Buddhist temple to pray and worship Buddha, and occasionally invite a Shaman to perform exorcism when a family member was sick. Still today in Japan, where Christians are less than 1 percent of population, most people celebrate new birth and wedding in Shinto temples and a funeral in Buddhist temples. Many Asians remain affiliated with their homeland religious traditions after they immigrate to the United States, whereas many other Asians come here as Christians or become Christians after arrival especially in an effort to assimilate to the dominant culture.

Since traditional Western Christian theology supports the exclusive claim that Christianity is the only true religion and that Jesus Christ is the single source for salvation, Christianity becomes a major source of oppression for Asian Americans for whom religious pluralism is their root. Traditional Western Christian theology would deny the very root of Asian Americans. In this context, therefore, Asian American liberation theologians challenge the exclusive claim of Christianity and promote interfaith or multifaith understandings of theology. In line with their homeland liberation theologians, Asian American liberation theologians formulate a Christian theology on the basis of their traditional cultures and religious ideas. For example, they understand Christian doctrine such as the Trinity or Jesus as Savior in terms of Hindu theology or Buddhist soteriology. They read the Bible in the light of Asian sacred scriptures as an invaluable wisdom source for Christian theology. They interpret the moral teachings and spiritual practices of Christianity in light of ethical and spiritual practices of Asian religions.

Story Theology

"Story theology" is another major theme found in Asian American liberation theologies. Asian American liberation theologians challenge the traditional Western theology as overly rationalistic and lacking imagination. They promote the value of using stories not only of the Bible but also of the oppressed people in constructing theology. Asian Americans, for whom stories are an integral part of their traditions, have much to say about their experiences of marginality, sojourning, suffering, and rejoicing. Asian American liberation theologians emphasize the importance of theological listening to those stories of their people, which is only possible when listening with imagination. This imagination as the power of perception and intuition enables theologians to compassionately listen to and reflect on the stories of the underside of history and reach the truth beneath the surface of things. According to Asian American liberation theologians, therefore, this imagination, which they also call "the third eye," inspires theology of head to include the heart.

For Asian American liberation theologians, not only their people's experiences and stories but also their own life experiences and stories become important factors in undertaking theology. Hence, several Asian Americans promote "autobiographical theology" as liberation theology. They believe that although not all autobiography is theology, Asian American liberation theology is autobiography since their understanding of Christianity has been shaped by their life experience and story as Asians living in the United States.

Major Thinkers in the Movement of Asian American Liberation Theology

Several major thinkers have contributed to constructing Asian American liberation theology. They may be divided into two groups according to their roles: the pioneers who began this movement in the 1970s and the next generation theologians who joined the movement in the 1980s or 1990s. Because of limited space, the pioneers will be given more attention.

The Pioneers

Jung Young Lee (1930–1996)

As a refugee from North Korea to South Korea, Lee came to the United States to study in 1955. Teaching at Drew University as professor of systematic theology until he died, he authored or edited about twenty books and fifty articles. His writing was devoted to understanding Christianity from his life experiences of marginality, as well as from the perspective of Asian cultures and traditions.[1] The concept of marginality as the major focus of his theology is perhaps best expressed in his book titled *Marginality: The Key to Multicultural Theology.* In this autobiographical approach to theology, naming racism as the fundamental determinant of marginalization in his life in the United States, Lee proposes a theology of new marginality.

According to Lee, Asian Americans are placed on the margins of both the Asian and American worlds. They live not only in the in-between world (neither Asian nor American) but also in the in-both world (both Asian and American). Lee argues that liberation of marginal people is possible only with liberation of central-group people from their exclusive thinking. Therefore, the people at the margin should build solidarity to make the change possible at the center, with the goal of living harmoniously in a genuinely pluralistic society. Only a new marginality overcomes the old marginality, since it will result in no centrality and thus no opportunity to oppress the marginal. This new marginality follows the paradigm of marginality of Jesus, who lived both in-between worlds and in-both worlds. This new marginality, then, is interested in love and service, not power. In this new paradigm of a theology of marginality, incarnation and creation are understood as internal and external forms of divine marginalization. The church becomes the new marginal people of God.

Choan-Seng Song (b. 1929)

Choan-Seng Song has been professor of theology and cultures at Pacific School of Religion and Graduate Theological Union in Berkeley, California,

[1]Most lists of important writings in Asian American liberation theology include Lee, *A Theology of Change; Embracing Change; Marginality; The Trinity in Asian Perspective;* and *Journeys at the Margin,* which he could not finish coediting because of his sudden death in 1996.

since 1985.[2] Born in Taiwan, his personal involvement in the political struggles of his homeland in relationship to China helped him understand the role of Jesus "from the bottom up" and become one of the most known advocates of story theology. Song has explained and practiced his method of story theology, which he also calls the Third-Eye theology, in his several writings. Perhaps one finds its most thorough application in his trilogy on Jesus, *The Cross in the Lotus World* published in 1990, 1993, and 1994, with cross as the symbol of Christianity and lotus of Buddhism and Asia. According to Song, through God's telling of Jesus' story, Asian Christians find the cross and God's reign in their own world shaped by the cultural ethos of religions other than Christianity. Song believes that the story of Jesus and the story of the reign of God is reflected in the stories of Asians: their myths, legends, and real life stories. To understand this intimate relationship between the two sets of stories, the only thing a theologian needs is a theological mind and imagination, the third eye. This enables the theologian to see God and God's activity in the stories of Asians and to see the sufferings of Asians in the story of Jesus.

Kosuke Koyama (b. 1929)

Born in Japan, Koyama taught in Asia and New Zealand before he came to Union Theological Seminary in New York in 1980, where he taught as the John D. Rockefeller Jr. Professor of Ecumenical Studies until he retired in 1996. A prolific writer, his most distinctive contribution to liberation theology is found in his efforts to indigenize the Christian faith into a "theology from below."[3] Living in Japan during World War II helped Koyama understand that living the Christian faith meant constant struggle against demonic forces that claim to destroy in the name of the Christian God. His experience as a missionary in Thailand in 1960–1968 helped him to "rediscover Asia" and to be conscious of living between the East and the West and to promote dialogue.[4] His well-known book *Waterbuffalo Theology* describes how he was forced to find new ways of expressing Christian faith to make contact with Thai people in their everyday life and explains the necessity for indigenization of Christian theology.[5] In *Mount Fuji and Mount Sinai*, he discusses his spiritual journey as a Japanese Christian

---

[2]Especially influential are his trilogy on Jesus, *The Cross in the Lotus World; Tell Us Our Names; Theology from the Womb of Asia; Third-Eye Theology*, revised edition 1990; *The Believing Heart;* and "Five Stages Toward Christian Theology in the Multicultural World" in *Journeys at the Margin*, 1–22.

[3]Koyama is the author of more than a dozen books, including his three-volume work titled *On Christian Life*, which is available only in Japanese, as well as one hundred articles.

[4]See also Morse, *Kosuke Koyama*, which identifies the theology of Koyama as theology of encounter.

[5]First published in 1974 by Orbis Press, this book was expanded and revised as the twenty-fifth anniversary edition in 1999.

and explores the interaction of two very strong cultures and religions, Christianity and Buddhism.[6] In doing so, Koyama brings together the biblical tradition with the historical, existential, religious, and cultural experiences of Asians. His theology is, as in the case of many other Asian American liberation theologians, story-oriented and autobiographical.

Roy Sano (b. 1931)

Born of immigrant parents from Japan, Sano was interned with his family in the Poston Relocation Center during World War II. Currently professor of United Methodist studies at the Pacific School of Religion, Sano's major contribution to Asian American liberation theology is found in his leadership roles. He was the founder and director of the Pacific and Asian Center for Theology and Strategies in the 1970s. The Center aimed at developing Asian American theology and building church involvement in civil and human rights movements. Especially important work is his resource material on Asian American liberation theology titled *The Theologies of Asian Americans and Pacific Peoples: A Reader*, which he compiled and distributed in 1976.[7] This "reader" looks very much like one of today's "readers" used for a course in colleges and graduate schools. Its handwritten page numbers, ring-binding, and different typefaces for each article reveals the urgency and necessity Sano felt for this work at that time as a pioneer in this field. The collection includes 50 writings by some 40 authors who have felt the emergence of ethnic consciousness and the issues of oppression, covering diverse themes from autobiographical theology to story theology, indigenization or inter-faith theology, and women's issues. All of these still remain major themes among Asian American liberation theologians.[8]

Raimundo Panikkar (b. 1918)

Born in Spain to a Spanish Catholic mother and Indian Hindu father, Panikkar is professor emeritus in religious studies at University of California at Santa Barbara. As a philosopher of religion who has published more than 30 books in several different languages, his contribution to Asian American liberation theology is perhaps most explicitly found in his well-known book *The Intrareligious Dialogue* (1999). Panikkar says that he finds himself a Hindu and a Buddhist without ever having ceased to be a Christian. He argues that it is not necessary for Christians to believe that all truth is exhausted by Christ and that the New Testament statement of Jesus as the Son of God does not mean that the Son of God is always and only the historical person Jesus of Nazareth. He holds that while the two

[6] Koyama, *Mount Fuji and Mount Sinai.*

[7] Unfortunately, an earlier reader he compiled in 1973, titled *Amerasian Theology of Liberation,* is no longer available.

[8] See Sano's preface in *The Theologies of Asian Americans and Pacific Peoples.*

rivers, Jordan and Tiber, respectively symbolizing Jewish and Christian dominated the past, now is the time that the two rivers flow into Ganges, which symbolizes Asian. The time is ripe for plunging into the Ganges, adopting a pluralistic attitude, and being liberated from one-dimensional supernaturalism and dialectical materialism.

The Next Generation

Most of the Asian American liberation theologians who belong to the next generation are already established scholars and prolific writers who rather recently began to publish in this field.

Kwok Pui-lan

Kwok Pui-lan, a native of Hong Kong, is William F. Cole Professor of Christian Theology and Spirituality at Episcopal Divinity School, Cambridge, Massachusetts. Kwok has published extensively in Asian feminist theology, biblical hermeneutics, and postcolonial criticism. Especially important in the field of Asian American Liberation theology are her books, *Chinese Women and Christianity, 1860–1927; Discovering the Bible in the Non-Biblical World*, and *Introducing Asian Feminist Theology.* Kwok emphasizes the uniqueness of Asia in the Third World with its long hermeneutical tradition of ancient scriptures. Kwok proposes a "dialogical model of biblical interpretation" and multifaith hermeneutics. The Bible should be seen not as a normative canon but as a "talking book" inviting polyphonic theological discourses and ongoing dialogues. "Plurality and multiplicity were an integral part of Asian culture, language, and religion long before the rise of postmodernism in the West. We have to avoid superimposing a European framework on the development of Asian hermeneutics, which must remain rooted in its own specific cultural context" (1995, 39).

Rita Nakashima Brock

Rita Nakashima Brock, a Japanese American feminist theologian, is currently a visiting scholar at the Starr King School for the Ministry in Berkeley, California. Previously, she taught religion, philosophy, and women's studies in several institutions. Most recently she held the endowed chair at Hamline University in St. Paul, Minnesota, and was the director of the Mary Ingraham Bunting Institute in Cambridge. Among her extensively published works, her contribution to Asian American feminist liberation theology is most explicitly revealed in her co-authored book, *Proverbs of Ashes.*[9] In this provocative, autobiographical theology, Brock rejects the

[9]Brock and Parker, *Proverbs of Ashes.* Another helpful writing is Brock and Thistlethwaite, *Casting Stones.*

traditional image of redemptive suffering and proposes a new paradigm of theology that presents love and presence as the source for saving power.

Andrew Sung Park

Andrew Sung Park, a native of North Korea, is currently professor of theology at United Theological Seminary, Dayton, Ohio. His major contributions to Asian American liberation theology are found in his comparison of the Korean concept of *han* and the Christian concept of sin and in his presentation of a theology of transmutation. Park argues that the transmutation of mutual enhancement is possible when ethnic groups cooperate in overcoming social sins and social *han*, while deepening their own cultural heritages, and thus bringing forth unity and celebrating the gifts of diversity.[10]

Peter C. Phan

Peter C. Phan is Warren-Blanding Professor of Religion and Culture at the Catholic University of America. In his essay of autobiographical theology titled "Betwixt and Between: Doing Theology with Memory and Imagination," he names "the three pillars upon which an authentically Asian theology must be built" as "liberation, inculturation, and interreligious dialogue."[11] This is a conclusion he drew on the basis of his life journey. He experienced himself being betwixt and between his Vietnamese roots and the culture in power, such as Western education and Latin Church. These constantly removed him from his cultural roots.

Chung Hyun Kyung

Chung Hyun Kyung, a Korean American Minjung theologian and ecofeminist, is professor of ecumenics at Union Theological Seminary in New York. Her childhood experience of not being allowed to participate in the family ancestral worship due to her gender helped her understand Korean women's unique *han* and construct a Korean feminist liberation theology.[12] A very creative and passionate theologian, her theology would be perhaps best represented by her opening address at the 1991 World Council of Churches assembly in Canberra, Australia, which shocked many conservative Christians. Accompanied by a traditional dance that she performed with indigenous Australian and Korean dancers, Chung invoked

[10]"A Theology of Transmutation," in *Journeys at the Margin,* 152–66. For his in-depth study on the concept of *han*, see his book *The Wounded Heart of God.* His book *Racial Conflict and Healing* received a Gustavus Meyers Award as an outstanding book on human rights in North American in 1997.

[11]Phan, "Betwixt and Between" in *Journeys at the Margin,* 132. See also his systematic exposition of diverse forms of liberation theologies in "A Common Journey, Different Paths, the Same Destination" in *A Dream Unfinished,* 129–51. Especially helpful is his comparison of the liberation theologies between Latin America and Asia.

[12]The best known among her writings is her book *Struggle to be the Sun.*

the Holy Spirit through the spirits of the oppressed throughout history, including women burnt in the witch hunts and the victims of Christian colonial genocide. She concluded her address by invoking *Kwan In*, a female bodhisattva (an enlightened being in Buddhism who voluntarily remains in the world until all beings are saved).

Anselm Kyungsuk Min

Anselm Kyungsuk Min was born in Korea, when the country was under Japanese domination. He is professor of theology at Claremont Graduate University. As a Korean American theologian, Min argues that Korean-American theology must create a synthesis. As such, theology must address the theological status of the Western tradition that has become an organic part of Korean Christianity, the indigenous Korean tradition, theological implications of the needs and experiences of Korean communities in the United States, and the solidarity with other ethnic groups and their theologies. Min argues, however, that it is time for ethnic theologies to move forward from regional theology to a concretely universal theology, proposing a new paradigm of theology called "solidarity of Others." This should enable the liberation of each particular group by global solidarity of others.[13]

Conclusion

Many emerging scholars in the field cannot be dealt with here. Especially promising in the near future is the contribution by Asian American biblical scholars, who have recently begun to present new biblical hermeneutical models integrating current, dominant biblical scholarship with the wisdom of Asian scriptures and Asian American experiences. For some of those scholars, the readers may refer to the double volume of journal *Semeia* (volumes 90–91) published in 2002.

As a relatively new voice, Asian American liberation theologians' contribution is already immense. With their focus on multiple marginality, story theology, and multifaith hermeneutics, they have opened up a new paradigm in doing theology and understanding Christian identity. However, in comparison with other U.S. liberation theologies such as black theology or Latino/a theology, the works of Asian American theologians are still more or less invisible and their publication sporadic. The time seems to be ripe for the Asian American theologians to vigorously present their scholarship more widely.

---

[13]Min introduces this new paradigm of theology in his autobiographical theology essay "From Autobiography to Fellowship of Others" in *Journeys at the Margin*, 135–60. He also published several articles on this topic and especially helpful to the readers are "Solidarities of Others in the Body of Christ," *Toronto Journal of Theology* 14 (1998), 239–54 and "Dialectical Pluralism and Solidarity of Others," *Journal of the American Academy of Religion* 65 (1997), 587–604.

16

Black Theology

Dwight N. Hopkins

Introduction

Definition

Black theology is a self-reflexive discipline questioning the intellectual consistency and practical accountability of African American people to the faith that they seek to believe in and practice. Methodologically, theological reflection is a second step. It presupposes the reality of black people in churches and community organizations involving themselves in advancing the particular affirming encounter between African Americans and God and reconstructing individual and systemic brokenness and woundedness. Black theology arises out of this ongoing dynamic and challenges people of faith to pause and think critically about whether what they are believing in and witnessing to is what they profess as their ultimate hope and final vision for all of humanity. Specifically, black theology investigates notions of racial and cultural identity in relation to faith.

Sources of Black Theology

The particularity of African American sources, out of which emerges black theology, determines the "black" dimension of this form of liberation theology. The claim is that people of African descent have undergone and continue to encounter rather clearly defined (if not certain unique) racial experiences revealed in a myriad of arenas.

Laying a Genealogical Foundation

The first source of black theology, therefore, hinges on laying a genealogical foundation from Africa, especially the African west coast from which the majority of black Americans originate. Black theologians today differ on the extent of African influences on current day U.S.A. black citizens. The theological gamut ranges from Afrocentrists (i.e., scholars hoping to replace Europe with Africa as the center of black faith, thought, and ethics and positioning people of African descent as subjects and not objects of history) to those who remain open to possible universal lessons from European and European American theologians (i.e., relying on black history and culture while incorporating thought systems from Europe). The common denominator among advocates is the recognition that black folk are, to whatever degree, an African people, hence the 1990s' increased popularity of the name "African American." In addition, all would agree that the African influence dictates a theological world view of "I am because of the community's well-being," thereby fostering a corporate sense of blackness that unifies all of African descent.

Underscoring Slave Trade and Bondage

The second source is likewise foundational, an underscoring of the (European Christian) slave trade in Africans and the 1619 to 1865 era of (white Christian) bondage of blacks in North America. Obviously, these momentous events likewise tie Africans and black Americans in connections that can never be broken. Yet the key to the slavery period, as a primal source for black theology of liberation, is its giving birth to a novel human creation called African Americans or black Americans.

Prior to slavery, black folk did not exist. In this sense, slavery is a primordial marker for the intricate origins and formative intimacies of today's black people of faith. How were these new people born? And how did they maintain perpetual faith in the midst of one of human history's most brutal religious persecutions and intense exploitations of working people's labor power? Black theologians, in general terms, investigate this crucial period. In so doing, they discern that African Americans co-labored with God to forge themselves out of memories of African sacredness, a reinterpretation of slave master theology (that is, "slaves, obey your masters" became "God is the highest authority"), and an accumulated common-sense folk wisdom surmised from daily survival. In a word, slavery indicates the coalescing of black people's race, culture, and faith identities.

Struggle for Full Humanity

A sense of a common heritage of struggle for the full humanity of black people underscores the third source. This suggests that a black theology of liberation takes seriously the power of God's grace of freedom reigning in and outside of Christianity and in and outside of churches. Wherever African Americans, especially poor and working-class folk, strive to be full human beings by asserting freely the racial, cultural aspects of their total lives, black theology perceives God being with them. Hence black theology draws on various and varied rich and creative paradigms:

1. Marcus Garvey and his six-million black membership Universal Negro Improvement Association
2. The kaleidoscopic cultural contributions of African Americans including the Harlem Renaissance, the 1960s black arts movement, musical expressions, material cultural forms, dance, sports, humor, and other types
3. The Nation of Islam (Malcolm X as the prime example)
4. The National Association for the Advancement of Colored People, radically organizing to alter the U.S. system
5. The press and workers' movements
6. The cyclical resurgence of Pan Africanism
7. Intellectual and academic contributions
8. Much more

The plumb line of struggle, hope, liberation, and eventual freedom forged by Yahweh in the Hebrew Scriptures and that laid by Jesus in the Christian scripture is complemented by the omnipresence of God's power for black humanity to be free wherever African Americans find themselves.

A Holistic Notion of Gender

The fourth source of black theology of liberation is that of appreciating a healthy and holistic notion of gender. One possibility is to develop a black theology by relying mainly on African American women's sources, such as fiction, single leaders, or institutionalized movements. Immediately, Harriet Tubman, Fannie Lou Hamer, the women's club movement, women's roles in the Student Nonviolent Coordinating Committee and the Black Panther Party, Zora Neale Hurston, black female slave labor, and ethnographic field work among today's working-class Christian women come to mind. Another avenue could be a dialogical encounter with current women's voices, heeding their critiques and offering constructive criticism, thereby forging a common stance. A third way might entail helping to provide equal opportunity of access and recognition; here, wherever black theology appears, womanist theology is cited and promoted. And fourth, black men could reconceptualize a new, progressive heterosexual and homosexual (from their respective sexual orientations) male gender. A turn in this latter direction more likely assures recognition of male structural power and the necessity of alleviating the oppression of women by equalizing systemic gender power asymmetry.

The Bible as Fundamental Source

Yet one ascertains the fundamental source of a black theology in the centrality of the Bible for African American life. The power of Christian scriptures, for this theology, resides in an accepted thread of liberation permeating both the Hebrew and Christian parts of the text. The exodus of slaves from bondage to freedom obviously becomes an overarching hermeneutical reference frame. Consequently, the incarnation of Jesus accompanied by his proclamation to bring a new reality for the oppressed seals the cornerstone norm of liberation for black theology. Enslaved Africans and African Americans in North America viewed their predicament and resulting hope as parallel if not identical to that of the Hebrew slaves.

In spite of white Christians tearing them from their African homeland and ritualizing a theologically justified slavery via homily, catechism, and lessons, enslaved black workers maintained hope in the many "miraculous" stories of Hebrew captivity and deliverance. This inchoate reading and production of a black theology feeds into current black theological developments. So too does a belief in Jesus as the ultimate freedom and healing for the materially poor and ill. Freedom defines the very being of Jesus, and Jesus offers freedom for people dwelling in structural poverty and for other working people.

Christian Churches

Moreover, and closely related to the Bible, Christian churches become prime sites for relating to, leading, and sorting out a black theology of liberation. The black church endures as the oldest institution created by and owned by African Americans. It stands as one of the clearest examples of black power. Furthermore and more important than this sociological, political, and economic fact is black theology's vocation from the spirit of liberation to practice liberation. Clearly institutionally, the black church is obligated by faith imperatives to act out a prophetic role in North American society and, indeed, the world. Biblical warrants of justice coupled with the black church's primary location wherever African Americans cluster (whether the inner city or the suburbs) suggest theological instructions and social location for black theology.

Origin

New York Times *Black Power Statement*

It is no accident that the leadership of the African American church's prophetic vectors (drawing on the Bible) and urban locations (existing in the heart of black America) gave rise to the contemporary black theology of liberation. On July 31, 1966, northern African American clergy published their "black power" statement in the *New York Times* newspaper. In it they spoke to the leaders of the nation, white church members, black citizens, and the media. Most significantly, they corroborated the recent cry for black power enunciated by younger members of the faltering civil rights movement. And these pastors articulated persuasively that the challenge was to recognize how white men had inordinate power with no conscience, and Negroes suffered from too much conscience without power.

This one document signifies the commencement of contemporary black theology. Yet, like all irreversible turns in history, this theological affirmation of black power was preceded by major proliferations in the concrete struggles for African American freedom. In a word, black theology burst onto the national and international scenes out of racial and cultural movements.

The Demand for Black Power

In June 1966, the Student Nonviolent Coordinating Committee (SNCC), represented by Stokely Carmichael, broke with the nonviolence by-any-means-necessary mantra of Martin Luther King Jr. Carmichael and King, during the Meredith March Against Fear, headed the procession through the backwoods of Mississippi. On June 16, at a preappointed place in Greenwood, Mississippi, Carmichael, without King's knowledge, launched into a chant demanding black power. The crowd of civil rights workers and rural blacks responded in Carmichael's favor.

Because of the coverage by local, national, and international press, the militant call for black power was the shout heard around the world. The demand for black power spread like wildfire because it reflected the preexisting, deeply held sentiments of the majority of poor and working-class blacks as well as of a significant sector of middle- and upper-income African Americans. Black power symbolized in the public theater what the overwhelming majority of blacks had been thinking and saying to themselves behind closed doors. That is, every white ethnic group had used group power and the force of their financial, political, economic, and racial power to advance their group interests. Indeed, from a black power perspective, white people as a whole, regardless of ethnic origin, coalesced as a solid racial block when it came to rallying against black folk and for white collective interests. In this sense, the black power program was an American phenomenon.

Moreover, black power argued against what it perceived as the spurious claims of the white community, that there were certain objective and normative means for achieving the civil and human rights for African Americans. On the contrary, the black power advocates stated that the key question remained as to who had the power to define and enforce definitions. For them, whites had used their power to define what was objective and normative for the liberation of poor and working-class blacks.

The young organizers of SNCC asserted the socially and culturally determined, and time-bound nature of all truth claims and objective positions. For them, the decisive question was the possession or lack of possession of power. It was in reaction to the power issue that white Americans recoiled and struck out in very emotional and deadly ways. As long as Negroes in the civil rights movement accepted the framework posited by whites with authority, then Negroes were good Americans. However, when Negroes transformed themselves, independent of white definition, into black men and women and challenged the prerogative of naming, the monopolization of ownership of resources, and the redistribution of power, African Americans then became un-American.

Reaction to Black Power

The immediate reaction to black power was overwhelming condemnation by most white ministers. Still, such a reaction was not the first indication of the expendability of black rights in America. This visceral negative stance followed the increased waning of white liberal support for civil rights. This loss of support could be seen in many ways:

- President Lyndon B. Johnson's reversal of the War on Poverty
- the ritual of summer urban rebellions or riots–beginning at least as early as 1964
- the impatience of northern inner-city blacks with the fruitless results of the southern civil rights movements
- the stepped-up attacks of right wing Christian groups (such as the KKK)
- and the national white intransigence openly displayed and signified by Chicago Mayor Richard Daley's defeat of King's northern civil rights campaign in 1966

Likewise, theological schools, seminaries, and divinity schools in America reflected the conservative and growing liberal backlash of white churches. White academics, school administrators, and boards of trustees of these institutions represented a form of apartheid. Promoted as universal theological pedagogical curricula, in fact, these schools could have been particularly deemed "European" or "European American" graduate schools of religious higher education. Even the few black seminaries maintained European-focused syllabi and graduation requirements.

In 1966, the number of tenured African Americans with Ph.D. degrees on the faculty of accredited theological schools probably could have been counted on one hand. If an African American was invited to campus, it was usually to offer an invocation, a closing prayer, a sermon, or to speak on what was really happening to angry Negroes outside the walls of the school. But the teaching arm, the administrative staffs, and the trustee groups remained white. Like discourse in the broader civic realm, institutional theological knowledge was heavily laden with white interests and the force to define truth. It, too, was about the monopoly of white power.

Founding Generation

James H. Cone

The ad hoc National Committee of Negro Churchmen, the signatories of the July 31, 1966, black power statement, announced that African Americans had the right to think theologically and that all God-talk inherently advanced notions of racial power. In March 1969, James H. Cone's *Black Theology and Black Power* was an inaugural book published on liberation theology. Using the lens of the African American experience, he argued that the core message of the Bible paradigmatically expressed by Jesus the Christ was liberation of the materially poor. Consequently, ecclesial formations, educational venues, and civic society were called by God to focus on the liberation of the least in society: the brokenhearted, the wounded, working people, the outcast, the marginalized, the oppressed, and those surviving in structural poverty.

Based on biblical theological criteria, Cone claimed white churches and most African American churches had failed their vocational assignments regarding their faith and their witness. This text offered the first sustained theological argument relating to issues of liberation, racial cultural identity, and a new material kingdom on earth in the interests of society's majority. Due to this pioneering work along with his subsequent publications, Cone is generally cited, nationally and internationally, as the father of contemporary black theology of liberation.

Albert Cleage

Yet despite filling the need for a coherent and persuasive theological articulation, Cone ushered in a sharp and pointed debate among the small first generation of black theologians. Now that the God-talk had been opened, diverse and multiple African American voices began to speak, not only against the provincial positions and discriminatory control of North American education by whites with power, but also in critique of Cone's line of argument. Albert Cleage offered a reinterpretation of the biblical witness from a black perspective. He cited the Bible as a drama played out between a literal phenotypical black Jesus and the occupying white, colonial presence from Rome (Europe).

Jesus became a black-skinned zealot whose sole goal was to wage a national liberation struggle, by any means necessary, to free the oppressed black nation of Israel from the white European colonizers. Cone had stated that Jesus was black because the business of the messiah was to be where the oppressed were fighting for liberation. Jesus' being is liberation. The black poor organize for liberation. Thus to enter and dwell among that community, Jesus had to be black. In contrast, Cleage stated that regardless of Jesus' vocation and Jesus' social location, Jesus was black not simply due to a theological rationale, but due to his natural biological skin color. There never was a white Jesus; and, therefore, to portray him as such a color in pictures and other iconography is blasphemy and the work of the antichrist. Moreover, the challenge to the African American church is to become the hub of the earthly revolution for nation building. It's nation time. And the leadership for the community hinged on an African American ecclesiology.

J. Deotis Roberts

J. Deotis Roberts approached black theology of liberation from a more pastoral position. He decried Cone's view as too strident. Hence, Roberts extended the peace offering of reconciliation to the white oppressor. In fact, he attempted to hold in equal tension liberation and reconciliation. For him, not only should an aggressive campaign for black rights be launched against white political systems (for Jesus' mandate and mission are liberation), but simultaneously a hand of reconciliation goes out to the white supremacist.

The liberation-reconciliation dynamic, in addition, held implications for christology. Roberts believed that black folk had the right to image Jesus as black primarily for psychological medicinal reasons. Because African Americans had drunk so deeply from the well of self-hatred (that is, in the depth chambers of their black hearts, African Americans really do want to be white people), they required a profound and radical healing of self-love resulting in liberation. So, they required a Jesus Christ imaged as biologically black for mental health rehabilitation and emotional restabilization. At the same time, according to Roberts, whites had the right to imagine and depict a white Jesus Christ. But, continuing, true reconciliation would result when both parties worshiped a colorless Christ.

Cecil Cone

Cecil Cone elaborated an entirely different trajectory in black theology. His unique stance begins with a description of profound theological crisis in black theology. This academic discipline suffered from too much reliance on the secular existentialism and politics of the black power movement (i.e., James H. Cone) and total mesmerization by white thinking systems (i.e., J. Deotis Roberts).

An authentic black theology, for Cecil Cone, draws from its primordial undercurrent the all-powerful African Almighty Sovereign God. When Africans and African Americans were enslaved in North America, they maintained their African sacred worldview and spiritual configurations and simply adopted Christian forms. If any thing, black folk converted Christianity into sacred Africanity. Today's black theology, consequently, should issue from an Africanized Christianity different from white religion and the rebellious substance of black power.

Gayraud S. Wilmore

In a similar vein, Gayraud S. Wilmore challenged James Cone's limited, for Wilmore, presentation of the African American religious experience. For Wilmore, prior to black theology, one has to peel back layers and discover the more all-encompassing notion of black religious thought. Black religious thought anchors itself in any manifestation in African history, and today that expresses the ultimate vision and practical struggle for liberation. Wilmore pushes theologians beyond Christian proclamation, theological categories, and ecclesial formations. Wherever black folk (i.e., poor people, or illiterate people, or the masses) initiate efforts for freedom, one discerns the sacred reality of black religious thought out of which surfaces black theology. Black religious thought reflects on the liberative folk impulse that has powered every struggle of African people in North America.

Charles H. Long

Proceeding beyond Wilmore, Charles H. Long opts for an entirely different deconstructive-reconstructive enterprise. He feels that both Christianity and theology are imperialistic discourses that embody, in a highly overdetermined manner, hegemonic linguistic power. In other words, one who adopts their language usage and language categories has already acquiesced in a process whose very nature is to oppress people of color or Third World people. Prior to the arrival of Christianity and its justificatory arm (i.e., theology), Long asserts, there already existed very interesting and informative religious practices among indigenous communities.

Thus, Christianity and its God-talk are by definition imperialistic; they are automatically over-against-others phenomena. So when one selects Christianity, one chooses voluntarily to be oppressed by the linguistic structures of the oppressors. James H. Cone employs both Christianity and theology and, thereby, his project suffers from the imitative game of mirroring white religious structures and systems of thinking. For Long, Cone's black theology is not black enough; it merely paints black existing white structures, which also shows the lack of doing black theology strictly from African American sources. Long, on the contrary, presents orientation to the ultimate as religious. Hence whenever blacks pursue the ultimate, especially in non-Christian forms (for instance, jazz singers or black public spokespeople or other such sources), one experiences the conditions of possibility for particularized black, sacred linguistic and thought structures.

Later Generations

Jacquelyn Grant

Since 1979 and 1980, other generations of black theologians have emerged. Jacquelyn Grant's 1979 article "Black Theology and the Black

Woman" heralded the eventual naming of African American women's religious experience as womanist theology and ethics. In her pioneering essay, Grant untangles the inconsistent internal logic of black theology as adjudicated by its own norm. If black theology is one of the initiators of liberation theology, based on the liberation of the oppressed, then how can it be authentic God-talk when the oppressed of the oppressed in the African American church and community are made imperceptible in or assumed to be represented by black male experiences?

Restated, black women are at best invisible in black theology and are at worst intentionally exploited by African American men. Womanist theology and ethics, the progeny of an incipient black feminist theology, situates itself differently from (white) feminist theology–a discourse partially disabled by white supremacy–and (male) black theology–a discourse partially reeking of patriarchal hegemony. More affirmatively, womanist theology and ethics explore positive black women's sources in relation to God's siding with African American women. It highlights the multidimensionality and positionality of black women in church and society.

Delores S. Williams

Perhaps the first book arguing for a reconfiguration of black theology is Delores S. Williams's *Sisters in the Wilderness.* Williams investigates thoroughly the biblical character of the African slave woman Hagar with her son Ishmael and their encounter with God. Instead of discerning liberation as the dominant theme within this divine response to the human conundrum, Williams uncovers a bi-focus theological dynamic: survival and quality of life. Similarly, God meets African American women in their dire predicaments and aids them in their daily survival. And God co-labors with black women to forge a quality of life appropriate to their situation and their heritage. Emblematic of God's relation to black women, the divine does not offer liberation to the African slave woman, Hagar. Obviously Williams's novel paradigm shift challenges by reformulation the substantive concerns of black theology.

Furthermore, Williams poses new theological perspectives on black theology's doctrine of christology. In some respects, the jugular vein of black theology has been Jesus Christ, the liberator divinity, with the centerpiece punctuated by the cross and resurrection. The faith assent and rational claim has been the following. Satan, with evil forces from his kingdom, attempted to do away with Jesus the liberator. Yet the countermove in the crucifixion connotes Jesus' struggle against and defeat of oppression. His subsequent rising on Easter portrays the final triumph and ascension into a new society. In radical contrast, Williams asserts that there is nothing salvific and liberative in the cross event. This wicked moment in Jesus' life literally shows the evil that men do against a Jesus whose power comes not from the crucifixion but through his ministerial vision of life when he walked this earth. Daily survival and a quality of life, therefore, accompany liberation. Womanists, by sustaining their integrated identities of gender, race, and class, carefully and critically compiled fundamental queries for the entire black (male) theological project.

Edward P. Wimberly and Anne Streaty Wimberly

The second generation of male black theologians, likewise, have forged common yet separate trails from the 1960s founding generation. Since its inception in 1970, the Society for the Study of Black Religion remains the premier organization for debates and developments. Pastoral theology has become a promising pathway left uncharted by the forefathers of the discipline but now progresses in various directions. Black pastoral theology combines the liberation accent with attention to personal salvation and emotional and spiritual healing.

In their groundbreaking text, *Liberation & Human Wholeness*, Edward P. Wimberly and Anne Streaty Wimberly deploy hermeneutic inquiry and sensitivity to postmodern constructs in a comprehensive investigation of autobiographies and interviews of formerly enslaved African Americans. The latter conjured images during religious conversion that intimated human wholeness and a relationality inclusive of minds, bodies, the environment, social institutions, other people, and, fundamentally, deep connections to the Christian God. What the slave heritage bequeaths to today's African Americans and, indeed, all Christians is the holistic reality of God's liberating activity: from personal guilt and sin, from political-economic-social-material oppression, from inner psychological turmoil, and from cultural debasement.

James H. Harris

A senior pastor of a black church, James H. Harris (*Pastoral Theology*) explicitly depicts his pastoral theology as liberation theology. For him, authentic evangelical ministry yields concrete transformation and liberation. Consequently, the African American church has to extend itself beyond one-by-one soul saving in Christ and assume its ecclesiological vocation to forge social change and liberation. According to this normative criterion, the black church has been slacking in what Jesus has called it to be, preach, and do.

As the institutional manifestation of the gospel message of freedom from injustice and oppression, a major task of the black church hinges on pursuing the end of racial discrimination and realizing equality. Christian freedom, regardless of color, in the final analysis means we are all unencumbered by the spiritual and material things of this world that turn us into what God has not created us to be.

Lee H. Butler Jr.

Lee H. Butler Jr.'s *A Loving Home* confronts us with the necessity of unifying spirituality and sexuality in our bodies as a precursor to healed and recreated relationships in the corporate body. Situating his argument within the African American experiences, he provides novel angles on liberation as transformation to freedom and power and on healing as the cornerstone for renewed relationships. Butler works with a complex set of notions of two-ness, the metaphor of home, the substratum of African spirituality as communality, the Hagar biblical story on complicated family structure, the omnipresence of men and women classifying one another as evil, and a positive project indicating the unity of spirituality and sexuality in a salutary connection among the self, God, and the other.

Noel Leo Erskine

Black theology has persistently perceived itself in solidarity with its "distant cousins" in Africa and with liberation movements and theologies in the Third World (i.e., Africa, Asia, the Caribbean, Latin America, and the Pacific Islands). This projection continues with the second generation. Noel Leo Erskine (*Decolonizing Theology*) resources U.S.A. black theology, Third World liberation theologians, and, with special insight, Jamaican-Caribbean social and religious evolutions.

Dwight N. Hopkins

Black Theology USA and South Africa by Dwight N. Hopkins analyzes sixteen black theologians, eight from each country. It discovers distinct differences overshadowed by more commonalities, especially in the theological areas of the culture of politics and the politics of culture. This interpenetrating dialectic is defined by historical-contemporary, theological, normative, and common resource parallels detected in both black theologies. Therefore, this shared dialectic of culture and politics, elucidated by four parallels, serves as the condition for the possibility of unifying USA and South African theologies.

Hopkins's *Down, Up, and Over*, constructs theology from enslaved African and African American religious experiences. Religious formations of race in Protestantism and American culture contextualize the contemporary Spirit of liberation among black folk. Black religion today can be understood better with historicity. That is to say, seeking religious freedom, Europeans brought their form of white supremacist Christianity, and enslaved Africans brought their traditional religions to the so-called New World. Eventually, black folk developed faith in a Spirit of liberation expressed as God (the Spirit for us), Jesus (the Spirit with us), and human purpose (the Spirit in us). Concomitantly, this liberation spirit moved blacks to recreate their formerly enslaved self on the levels of language, political economy, racial cultural identity, and daily rituals. The Spirit of liberation ultimately calls forth a *metanoia*: the birth of a new spiritual-emotional-psychological human being and the construction of a new common wealth of collective ownership/stewardship of all of God's wealth on earth.

George C. L. Cummings

George C. L. Cummings's *A Common Journey* entertains a similar methodological inquiry. For North American theologians, liberation manifests primarily on religio-cultural terms, whereas Latin Americans stress a socioeconomic significance. Both can undergo a common journey by jointly focusing more on the textures of the poor's situation, allowing this condition to evangelize the church, deeply filling out the contours of a social analysis, and linking more tightly the liberating work of the Holy Spirit to our understanding of Jesus Christ.

Josiah Ulysses Young III

Josiah Ulysses Young III in *A Pan-African Theology* explores a global theology for people of African descent. His effort seeks insight from nineteenth-century black ancestors, the state of the black American underclass and African peasantry, African traditional and black religions, and black music. From these sources, he extrapolates that the providence of God (historically incarnated in the ancestors) is directly intertwined with the practicalities of liberation for the present-day African diaspora.

Cain Hope Felder

African American biblical scholars of the second generation of black theology have offered well-argued judgments and scholarly documented assessments disrupting the dominant exegesis and accepted hermeneutics of the Hebrew and Christian scriptures. *Troubling Biblical Waters*, by Cain Hope Felder, substantiates the claim of the pervasive presence of African people in the entire Bible. Furthermore, his book reveals scriptural areas denoting the interaction between class consciousness and freedom. Such interaction, most pointedly, culminates in a biblical commission for justice.

Most dominant biblical scholarship either ignores or denies that such a charge exists, according to Felder. Following a reinvestigation of race and class in the Bible, Felder takes on the instances of family. Biblical pictures display family statuses in a much wider realm than contemporary beliefs and practices. The biblical text, in fact, supports black women's ordination, portrays family life that denies the normality of the nuclear family, and calls on the human family to link peacemaking inextricably to justice.

Felder's edited *Stony The Road We Trod* presses further along these lines by dismantling the Eurocentric politics of biblical analysis and interpretation. A group of eleven black Bible scholars portrays and proves how biblical studies in formal schools of education and in churches certify the biased nature of European and European American cultures. In contrast, as a theoretical and practical antidote, *Stony The Road* reintroduces the ancient biblical world view of racial and ethnic diversity.

The most authoritative black biblical scholarship to date, this collaborative writing submits new insights on specific African American methods of scriptural interpretations and the particular biblical and extrabiblical sources (such as African American sermons, work songs, and even mottos) modifying hermeneutical and exegetical warrants. The unique acumen in black women's hearing and reading the Bible also finds a prominent role in this groundbreaking text. In addition, the book deepens some trajectories clarifying race and ancient black Africa in the Bible, even crystallizing how ancient blacks were perceived by the Hebrews and other peer groups as objects of hope, wealth, and wisdom.

Brian K. Blount

In *Then the Whisper Put on Flesh,* Brian K. Blount continues a fresh, new voice in African American biblical discourse. He creatively combines black Christianity, biblical ethics, and New Testament cultural interpretations. He provides an entry point for the non-oppressed to read the Christian scriptures through the circumstances and conditions of the oppressed, mainly by drawing heavily on black folks' ethical engagement with the sacred text during U.S.A. slavery. Blount methodologically underscores the ways culture and context impact one's read of the text, and he deduces convincingly that liberation exists as a decisive thematic unity for each of the writers in the New Testament.

Theodore Walker Jr.

African American ethicists, likewise, have written diverse interrogations of their discipline. Theodore Walker Jr.'s *Empower the People* amalgamates African American political philosophers, sociologists, psychologists, musicologists, homileticians, black and womanist theologies, and ethicists into a black power manifesto of liberation struggle. More accurately, for Walker, not liberal government or philanthropy, but black church power is obligated to tackle fundamental negativities and proffer hope-inspiring possibilities for the African American community.

The ethical agenda includes, but is not exhausted by, drugs, crimes, premarital sex, black families, economics, education, music, black male-female connections, dance, African American church leadership, and governmental policy. In sum, Walker asserts a black theological social ethics (for the church) appropriated from, what he terms, black power philosophy or black theology.

Garth Kasimu Baker-Fletcher

Garth Kasimu Baker-Fletcher in *Xodus* moves a liberation ethics into a radical reconstruction of the African American male self–a self suffering from low self-esteem, low self-respect, and self-image crises with which the black church has failed to come to terms. *Xodus* conjures up a psycho-social space colored by an inclusive, nonsexist, liberationist partnership with womanists, and a reassessment of myths of black bodies. Xodus's new reality, in the lineage of Malcolm X, urges black men to pursue defiant confrontation with white supremacy, whereas Martin Luther King Jr.'s dream urges the realization of a multicultural society grounded on God's justice and unconditional love for all human beings. Xodus space, ultimately, is cosmological and ecological since all of creation emerges from the earth's dust that, for Baker-Fletcher, in West Africa attests to revelation and the divine. Along the journey to Xodus male space, the African American ecclesial formations need to transform into Xodus black church that speaks holistically to the entire African American people, especially to poor women and young people.

James H. Evans Jr.

Systematic and constructive theology rounds out this overarching survey of theological disciplines among second generation (male) black theologians. James H. Evans Jr.'s *We Have Been Believers* reinterprets the major doctrines of the Christian church–revelation/liberation to eschatology–from the standpoint of black faith and freedom. His systematic oeuvre draws on the Bible, biblical commentary, first generation black theologians, African religious scholarship, pivotal black thinkers (e.g., W. E. B. Du Bois, Zora Neale Hurston, and Howard Thurman), white feminist writings, narrative theology, and seminal European thinkers (e.g., Karl Barth and Paul Tillich).

Will Coleman

Tribal Talk by Will Coleman focuses this frontier consideration: must black theology simply be Christian? *Tribal Talk* urges inter- and intragenerational black theological expansion so that all interlocutors of liberational black religiosity can talk among the tribe called the African diaspora. Coleman proves his case somewhat chronologically.

Commencing with West African narrative cosmology (the departure point for most Africans), one enters African traditional faith beliefs and folklore. These lay a basis for African survival after slavery's Middle Passage to the "New World." Initially, enslaved blacks (Coleman attends to slave narratives of the Carolinas due to their location for continually receiving new boats of Africans) created hoodoo, a mixture of African survivals and African American religious novelty. Next, enslaved blacks nurtured their own folkloric spirituality, non-Christian spirituality, and then a reappropriated Holy Ghost pneumatology.

Finally, *Tribal Talk* examines critically the consistent manifestation of a black Christianity lodged in African American churches. Arguing against

Christian orthodox dogmatics and recognizing the multivocality of black life, Coleman advocates a plurality of African American narratives (West African, non-Christian, and Christian) for the decisive method of defining black theology.

Victor Anderson

Yet not all in the second generation of black theologians have readily concurred with the black, liberation, and Christian presuppositions. Victor Anderson in *Beyond Ontological Blackness* wonders if blackness (in black theology) is merely, and tragically so, an invention of whiteness. Moving us beyond the black heroic genius cult, Anderson grapples with and defends a nonessentialist notion of black identity, one better suited for naming and thereby freeing the multiple intracommunal identities among African Americans.

Anthony B. Pinn

Anthony B. Pinn's *Why Lord?* ponders why God has not ended (and, indeed, has perhaps approved of) black suffering. Pinn states that there is nothing redemptive in black people's suffering. Hence his alternative is to deny the existence of God and opt for a liberating, in his well-documented text, strong humanism–the catalyst needed for blacks to fight harder for their freedom.

David Emmanuel Goatley

Pursuing the theodicy doctrine from Jesus' crucifixion suffering and enslaved blacks' oppression, *Were You There* by David Emmanuel Goatley asks those who remain within the Christian camp to undergo a self-test about the efficacy of their God. He concludes that God, paradoxically, liberates the oppressed even in instances of God's hiddenness.

Mark L. Chapman

With Mark L. Chapman's text *Christianity On Trial* the concern is not so much the idea of suffering and a just God, but the entire endeavor of Christianity itself. What does it mean for blacks to embrace a faith proselytized by white supremacist Christians? Does Christianity engender black liberation or oppression? From his study of major African American religious figures pre- and post-black power (1966), he surmises that the survival and prophetic texture of black Christianity hinges on ongoing, trenchant critiques of white racist Christianity and on an unrelenting critique internal to the black church.

Admittedly, black theology writings have been predominantly Protestant. But this fact alone would obscure some of the more intellectually creative works hailing from black Roman Catholic theologians and womanists. African American members of the Roman Catholic Church endure a triple jeopardy. They undergo marginalization within black theology, in the African American community, and in the Catholic Church. Yet, their voice has been ever-present in the scholarly terrain of contemporary black theological advancements.

Lawrence Lucas

Lawrence Lucas published his *Black Priest White Church* in 1970 and rendered an autobiographical statement, from his childhood days until his priesthood, on his journey in the Roman Catholic Church in New York City. A recurrent theme, from his vantage, is the rigid white supremacy of his church. In addition to structural, ecclesial racial injustice, Lucas cites the Roman Church's failure to accent the black poor and the existential dilemma that others wrestle with: is it possible to be black and Roman Catholic?

Despite the searing pain and straightforward anger, he maintains hope; or else African Americans will desert the Church. In a sense, to avoid such a hemorrhaging, all books since Lucas's have sought to resolve the black and Roman Catholic knotty problem.

Other Black Catholic Contributions

Cyprian Davis's 1990 *The History of Black Catholics in the United States* offers a definitive testimony on the presence and contributions of African American Roman Catholics to the United States. Indeed, he documents that the first group of Africans in the future U.S.A. were Roman Catholics who spoke Spanish, thus preceding the 1619 Jamestown, Virginia, arrival of 20 Africans brought in bondage to that English-speaking colony. The black Roman Catholics were under Spain's jurisdiction in 1565 in the colony of St. Augustine in northern Florida.

The 1995 publication of Diana L. Hayes's *Hagar's Daughters* provides the first Roman Catholic monograph interpreting womanist thought. Furthermore, Jamie T. Phelps edits *Black And Catholic,* the first book that brings together African American scholars writing on a black Catholic reevaluation of theology, biblical studies, ethics, history, religious pedagogy, and method and context. The final essay, by M. Shawn Copeland, outlines foundational marks required for a Roman Catholic black theology.

Scaffolding for an authentically black and truly Roman Catholic theology consists of

1. grounding in the black American religious experience and religious consciousness
2. affirming all dimensions of black being
3. comprehending God's word in black culture
4. confronting shortcomings in black religious experiences
5. apprehending and implementing today the tasks of Jesus' time

6. fostering interdisciplinarity
7. integrating the aesthetic with ideational precision

A year later, Joseph A. Brown wrote *To Stand on the Rock*, again ruminating over the "authentically black, truly Catholic" way of life. Brown summons what he terms as the Black Catholic Church to recognize its coming of age in several respects. African American religious leadership must be trained and educated in the black cultural milieu, one characterized by the specificity of African American healing and transformation. Accompanying the cultural imperative is the obligation for leadership to receive economic support from the black Catholic community. African American priests and bishops, therefore, must perceive themselves as caretakers of the spirituality and cultural components of black people.

Resultantly, a dynamic unfolds. Leadership arises from the community, feels obligated to its point of origin, is accountable to the people, and approved by black Catholics. Brown ends with two additional counsels: an invitation for the laity to assume more leadership by institutionalizing itself within the black Catholic Church and a plea for more unity among African American liturgists.

Diana L. Hayes and Cyprian Davis have amassed the most recent collection of articles crucial to the emerging black Roman Catholic theology–*Taking Down Our Harps.* Hayes's essay declares that black faith is the real Christianity. Therefore, the entire Roman Catholic Church is mandated to become ontologically black in its innermost being because Jesus dwells amidst the oppressed black Americans.

Jamie T. Phelps's contribution proposes a reformed mission work to black Americans. Such mission work would manifest rigorous church self-critique on the nature of its commitment to inclusivity, focused energy on psychological healing and on viewing of the full humanity of African Americans, and intense intra-Church spiritual growth.

Continuing her constructive method in black Catholic theology, M. Shawn Copeland's piece opts for a sober utilization of the method of correlation (i.e., the Christian gospel responds, though not in a naive fashion, to queries from today's human culture) linked closely to critique (i.e., of texts and traditions), retrieval (i.e., of marginalized blacks and black Catholic histories), scientific social analysis (i.e., social theories), and construction (i.e., advancing the particularities of a black Catholic theology).

Future Agenda

The next phase of black theology necessitates heightened theoretical work based on the following practices. If liberation, in all of its variegated, multiple, ambiguous, and pluriform definitions, continues as a central internal criterion, then the rebuked and silenced segments in the discipline, the black family and church, and the larger African American community demand a scholarly hearing. More particularly, explorations into the young gay and lesbian voices in black theology portend pioneering work that could open up further the cognitive vistas for the academy and human living. Renee L. Hill and Horace Griffin have launched that scholarly expedition.

Similarly, black theology should take more affirming steps to cooperate closer with womanists. The collaborative writing of Karen and Garth Kasimu Baker-Fletcher models one encouraging paradigm. Interdisciplinary and multidisciplinary methodologies remain in order, connected to interaction with diverse departments within the university and other guilds. Black theology has always transcended provincial knowledge restrictions. However, historical memory of the discipline informs us that epistemology and academic inquiry come from civic conversations outside of the gates of institutionalized higher education. Thus religious studies and theology unite in their object of study (i.e. African Americans and global human interactions) and in their service beyond the formally-educated elites. So black theology's tradition embraces a profound sense that education serves the community beyond the "Ivory Tower."

In this regard, how does black theology form partnerships with faith organizations, community groups, and local governmental initiatives? How does it speak to the national media? What value resides in interfaith projects centered on justice work? Who are the poor? How does one clarify the need for both material transformation and emotional healing among those marginalized and without voices? And what does black theology have to say about the poor and ecology?

Finally, in this age of adverse globalization, black theology needs to mount an international network of black theologians, and solidarity with common interlocutors from Africa, Asia, the Caribbean, Latin America, and the Pacific Islands, most notably in the Ecumenical Association of Third World Theologians. Through the particularity of the African American experience and a conscious reaching out beyond that social location, perhaps the contours of a new human being and new society will surface in our midst.

17

Latino/a Theology

JUSTO L. GONZÁLEZ

Hispanic or Latino theology has exploded in the last twenty-five years. Virgilio Elizondo's *Galilean Journey* was published in 1983. *Apuntes,* the first journal on Hispanic theology, began its publication in 1980.[1] Orlando Costas published *Christ outside the Gate* in 1982. In the intervening two decades, thousands of articles and over a hundred books have been published in the field of Latino/a theology. To summarize or even outline all of this material within the scope of a few pages is an impossible task.[2] Therefore, rather than attempting a summary, or even a listing of the major authors and their views, what I propose to do in this essay is, first, to highlight some of the threads that run through most Hispanic theology, and then to mention some of the venues and structures within which such theology is being developed and promoted.

---

[1] *Apuntes: Reflexiones teológicas desde el margen hispano.* Published quarterly by the Mexican American Program, Perkins School of Theology, Southern Methodist University, Dallas.

[2] For a general overview of Latino/a theology, with a Catholic emphasis but including a number of Protestant authors, see Fernández, *La Cosecha.* A Protestant attempt to systematize Latino/a theology is Rodríguez and Martell-Otero, *Teología en Conjunto;* a Catholic counterpart: Espín and Díaz, *From the Heart of Our People.*

Identity: A Common Thread

Arguably, one of the central issues for Latino/a theology is the matter of identity. This may be seen at many levels and in sundry contexts. The very names we give ourselves, and the debate about them, are an indication of the significance of this issue. Until a few decades ago, the name "Hispanic" (actually, "hispano") was used as a means of self-identification only by some, mostly in New Mexico, who prided themselves in being descendants of those who owned the land before the United States took it over from Mexico. In some cases, it was used by this sort of "older aristocracy" to distinguish itself from the more recently arrived "mexicanos."

Then the U.S. Census began employing it as a catchall name for the varied and rapidly growing groups of immigrants from Spanish-speaking Latin America. At that time what could be called a "pan-Hispanic" consciousness was beginning to develop in the United States, and therefore, Mexican Americans, Puerto Ricans, Cuban Americans and others began using the term "Hispanic" as a common denominator to bring the various groups together. Still, two main reasons always fostered misgivings about that name. First, many preferred (and still prefer) to describe themselves with reference to their country of origin (Mexican American, Cuban American, etc.). They see Hispanic as a name imposed from the outside, mostly by the U.S. Census and by others who felt the need to classify us. Second, Hispanic inappropriately stresses the Spanish elements in our culture and genes, to the detriment of the African and Amerindian elements.

Thus the terms "Latino" and "Latina" came to the foreground as an alternative to "Hispanic." This has at least two advantages. It is not a name imposed by the U.S. government, but rather one chosen by ourselves. It stresses our connection with Latin America. For these reasons, it has become more common in more recent decades and is favored by many to the exclusion of "Hispanic."

On the other hand, this name also has problems. At one time it was employed in some sections of the country, particularly in New York and its surroundings, by the more recent immigrants from Latin America to distinguish themselves from "Newyoricans" whose Spanish, according to those more recent immigrants, was not "up to par." Thus, some still prefer not to use a name that reflects situations in which the Latin American immigrant was privileged over the native Puerto Rican or Mexican American–a situation that still holds in many contexts, including the higher echelons of theological education.[3]

[3]Until very recently, almost all Latino/a professors in the various fields of religion and theology were foreign born. This situation has improved markedly in the late 1990s and the first years of the twenty-first century thanks to the work of the Hispanic Theological Initiative, to be discussed below.

Then, if one goes back into the history of the very name "Latin America," one finds that this, too, was an imposition from outside. When the French were vying with the British for the hegemony over the recently independent countries of the Western Hemisphere, they sought to justify their insertion into the continent on the grounds that it was "Latin," just as the French were. Thus, the name "América Latina" is not originally Spanish or Portuguese, but is a translation of the French claim that our continent was "l'Amérique latine." At any rate, if it is true that we are not as connected with Spain as the title "Hispanic" would seem to imply, it is also true that we have even less connection with the ancient Italian *Latium*!

All of this was made clear when the Academy of Catholic Hispanic Theologians in the United States (ACHTUS) began making plans for the publication of an academic journal. After much consultation and debate, it was decided to give the new publication the somewhat cumbersome title of *Journal of Hispanic/Latino Theology*. This "solution" has become quite common among Hispanic/Latino/a theologians, so that most of us now tend to use the two terms interchangeably, speaking sometimes of "Hispanic" and sometimes of "Latino" issues and perspectives, and often deciding which to use on the basis of style and aesthetics. Thus, for instance, "Hispanic" is more gender-inclusive than "Latino." Therefore it is easier to say "Hispanics" than "Latinos and Latinas," "Latino/as," or the unpronounceable and typographically odd "Latin@s." On the other hand, when one wishes to refer to the theological work of Hispanic women, it is more convenient to say "Latina theology."

Identity: Undefined Edges

The matter of naming is only a symptom of wider issues of identity. Who is included under the heading of "Hispanic" or "Latino/a"? What is it that makes one a Latino or Latina? These questions are posed at many levels and in many contexts. A few examples should suffice to show the complexity of the issue.

When we have a gathering of Hispanic theologians in the United States or a discussion of U.S. Latino/a theology, does this include Puerto Ricans on the Island? Clearly, the issue of Latino identity here is connected with the unresolved issues of Puerto Rican identity and the political status of the island; but these issues of Puerto Rican identity must be taken into account by any group or movement dealing with "U.S. Hispanic" theology. In more recent times people of Brazilian origin in the United States have experienced a growing consciousness of exclusion. Brazil is part of Latin America or, as the area is sometimes also called, Iberoamérica. But they are not part of Spanish America. They certainly are "Latinos" and "Latinas," but they are not "Hispanic." What about those of us who were born in Latin America? When do we become "U.S. Hispanic"? (My wife says that she has witnessed my own transformation from a Latin American resident to a U.S. Hispanic.

Whatever that may mean, the focus of my attention and activities has certainly changed in the last thirty years. But still when I travel and speak in Latin America, I feel that I am traveling and speaking among my own people.)

This issue of our connection with Latin America and with the United States, and of the context or contexts within which we function, appears repeatedly in Latino theological discourse. One example may be the question of how Latinas characterize their theology. While some, following the lead of Ada María Isasi-Díaz, speak of their work as "mujerista theology," others prefer to speak of "Latina (or Hispanic) feminist theology." While there are many issues in this debate, one issue is the context vis-à-vis which a theologian defines her work. Isasi-Díaz uses the term "mujerista" to distinguish her work from U.S. and North Atlantic feminist theology, which is not always sufficiently aware of issues of class, race, and culture. On the other hand, María Pilar Aquino and others prefer the term "feminista" because, among other reasons, it establishes bridges with the work of sisters and brothers in Latin America working on similar issues (1998, 89–101).

This may also provide a good example of the manner in which the matter of the language chosen for communication impinges on issues of identity and naming. "Latina theology" is not the same as "teología latina." In English, "Latina" clearly means theology done by Latinas. In Spanish, the seemingly equivalent phrase simply means theology for a Latino/a perspective and says nothing about the gender of those doing the theology. (In Spanish, "teología" is always grammatically feminine, no matter who the theologian is. Thus, for instance, theology done by males would still be "teología masculina," and never "teología masculino.") Thus, when a Latina theologian chooses to write in one or another language, she is also making implicit decisions as to how to refer to her work and how it will be identified.

Identity: *Mestizaje* as Tension at the Core

The foregoing shows that the issue of identity is crucial for Hispanic theology because the edges of what we mean by "Hispanic" or by "Latino" are not well defined. Yet, the issue of identity appears not only at the edges of our reality, but also at its very core. Hispanic theology is, to a very large extent, theology done from a perspective of unresolved and unresolvable issues of identity.

Identity is at the heart of what may well be considered the birthplace of Hispanic theology in the United States, Virgilio Elizondo's work on *mestizaje*. Although he had worked on this subject before, Elizondo made this theme popular among Latinos and Latinas through his foundational book, *Galilean Journey: The Mexican-American Promise.* Significantly, to understand the Mexican American experience, Elizondo draws on the manner in which Mexico has dealt with issues of its own identity. The Mexican Revolution brought with it new appreciation for the Native element in Mexican culture and traditions. Therefore it resulted in much work on Mexican identity as it stems from the two main streams converging in it, the Native and the European. Particularly in the work of José Vasconcelos, the notion had been put forward, of the birth of a new race–what Vasconcelos calls "la raza cósmica"–out of the mixture and tensions between the two races that had clashed and fused as a result of the Spanish conquest. While in traditional Mexico, the *mestizo* (the "half-breed") was looked at with contempt by the Spanish and with hatred by the Indian, postrevolutionary Mexico began proudly defining itself as a mestizo country. Elizondo then picks up on this notion of the mestizo and applies it, in a sort of second stage of a dialectic of mestizaje, to the duality of existence and identity of the Mexican American.

In a divided society, the mestizo belongs to neither of the two poles of identity, and to both. In traditional Mexico, a mestizo was neither Spanish nor Indian, and both Spanish and Indian. Mestizos were seen as a lower caste by purebred Spaniards and their descendants, and as traitors and half foreigners, as collaborators with the exploiters, by the Indian population. Among the Spanish, mestizos were considered Indians or nearly such. Among Indians, they were considered Spanish or nearly such. Thus, there is no locus of identity for the mestizo. Identity resides in a fluid in-betweenness, in a "neither this nor that" that is also a "both this and that." Yet this very in-betweenness makes the mestizo a threat to the neatly established order of a divided society.

Mestizaje is feared by established groups because it is perceived as a threat to the barriers of separation that consolidate self-identity and security. It is perceived as a threat to the security of human belonging–that is, to the inherited cultural identity that clearly defines who I am to myself and to the world.

> A *mestizo* group represents a particularly serious threat to its two parent cultures. The *mestizo* does not fit conveniently into the analysis categories used by either parent group. The *mestizo* may understand them far better than they understand him or her...It is threatening to be in the presence of someone who knows us better than we know ourselves (Elizondo 2000, 18).

Using this paradigm, Elizondo argues that Mexican Americans experience another stage of mestizaje. In Texas, Mexican Americans are told that they are Mexicans. But if they travel to Mexico, they are considered "gringos." They are both Texans and Mexicans, and at the same time, they are neither.

Elizondo then compares this with the experience of being a Galilean Jew in the time of Jesus. This produces a highly stimulating reading of the gospel stories in which Jesus and his disciples are like *mestizos* vis-à-vis Judean Jews, who consider them less Jewish, and also vis-à-vis Gentiles, who consider them Jews.

Identity: *Mestizaje* and Hispanic Protestantism

One could even argue that there is now in the Latino Protestant community a further experience of *mestizaje*. In many ways, Hispanic Protestants stand in a situation of *mestizaje* vis-à-vis their Roman Catholic Hispanic sisters and brothers on the one hand, and their Protestant Anglo brothers and sisters on the other. The experience is poignantly told by David Maldonado:

> We were also accused of turning our backs on our Mexican-American community and culture. Because we were not Catholic, we were not truly Mejicanos, people said. The prevalent idea at that time was that to be Mexican-American was to be Catholic. The Protestant faith was defined as the religion of the Anglos (2001, 107).

To make matters worse, Maldonado and his family did not belong to an Anglo Protestant church. They belonged to Iglesia Metodista La Trinidad. He was a fourth generation Protestant. But still, he was a Mexican American, not an Anglo, Protestant. His *mejicano* peers believed that he was not really *mejicano*, because he was a Protestant. And his Protestant Anglo peers–whom he did not meet until he was twelve years old–felt that he was not one of them, because he was a "Mexican"–or rather, as they would say pejoratively, a "Meskin" (132). Although things have changed somewhat, and now few Catholic leaders would openly claim that to be Hispanic one has to be Catholic, a similar message is still communicated in countless, subtler ways. Significantly, when a group of Latinos/as met under Maldonado's leadership to discuss the meaning of being a Hispanic Protestant, the issue of identity soon became the common thread for our discussion.[4]

Thus, if the birth of Mexican identity took place in the painful experience of *mestizaje* between Spanish and Native, and Mexican Americans in general experience *mestizaje* as they stand between Mexican and American identities, Protestant Hispanics often experience a further *mestizaje* between their Hispanic and their Protestant identities.

Identity: Other Paradigms

The paradigm of *mestizaje*, originally proposed by Elizondo as applicable to the Mexican American experience, has been taken by other Latino/a theologians as a way to understand their own situation.[5] Among some of Caribbean origin, *mulatez*–the experience of the *mulato*, who is

---

[4]See Maldonado, *Protestantes/Protestants.*

[5]It may be significant to note that at the same time Elizondo was working on his Galilean model, Orlando Costas was thinking along similar lines, apparently without mutual contact. See Costas, "Evangelism from the Periphery: A Galilean Model," *Apuntes* 2, no. 4 (1982) 53–59; and "Evangelism from the Periphery: The Universality of Galilee," *Apuntes* 2, no. 3 (1982) 75–84.

both black and white, and neither black nor white–has begun to play a similar role (López-Sierra 1999, 84–95).

Another paradigm common among Latino/a theologians is that of exile. For a number of us, the process leading to our becoming U.S. Hispanics began through an experience of exile. Some of us were political exiles, others "economic" exiles who had to leave our countries of origin for economic reasons, and most of us a combination of both. Whatever the case may be, that process has led to a situation in which former exiles know that return is no longer a viable expectation, and yet they remain at least partially foreigners in their new lands. Thus the exilic experience, like that of *mestizaje*, involves a double presence and at the same time a double alienation. Both lands are our land, and neither is really our land. In some cases, Latinos and Latinas who have been born in the United States, and for whom therefore the experience of exile would seem to be alien, do however resonate with an image that expresses the many ways in which they are made to feel like aliens in their country of birth.

A further image commonly found in Latino/a theology is that of marginality. Significantly, already in 1980 the subtitle of the Journal *Apuntes* was *Reflexiones teológicas desde el margen hispano*–Theological reflections from the Hispanic margin. The initial editorial for that journal further explained its title partly as follows:

> ["Apuntes"] means jottings, notes, or marginal glosses. That is partly how we see ourselves. We do not deceive ourselves into believing that we are at the very heart of the theological enterprise. That enterprise reflects the structures of the society around it, and Hispanics are not by and large in the decision-making centers of that society. Hence the subtitle of our journal, "Reflections from the Hispanic margin." We intend for the theology aired in this journal to be a marginal gloss to the dominant forms of Christian theology (González 1980, 3)

Issues of identity, however, are never that simple. The very notion of marginality is more complex than it would seem to be at first sight. To say that we are marginal would imply that we are living in a monocentric world, when in fact we are living in a polycentric world and a polycentric church.[6] If there are many centers, there are many margins, and centers and margins overlap depending on the criteria one uses. Thus, the metaphor of marginality, like *mestizaje*, *mulatez*, and *exile*, while clarifying the issues of identity that lie at the core of Latino/a theology, also points to their profound complexity.

---

[6]A matter discussed more fully in my *Mapas para la historia futura,* 17–18, and in my *The Changing Shape of Church History*, 7–79.

A Common Theme: Rereading Bible and Theology

Significantly, however, these constant and unresolved issues of identity have not kept Hispanic theology from moving forward. On this score, some of us like to quote an old fable in which two hares are being pursued by dogs. One says "Hurry, the hounds are coming." The other responds, "They are not hounds; they are dogs." Then they get into a heated argument; and while they discuss who is pursuing them, the dogs/hounds arrive and kill them! Matters of semantics, while important, must not stop us from the urgent tasks before us. While we discuss and may even brood over issues of identity, this is not the entire content of Latino/a theology. On the contrary, a common thread in all Latino/a theologies is the need, from our own perspectives and experiences of *mestizaje*, exile, marginality, and so on, to reread the tradition that we have received, both in biblical interpretation and in the entire field of religion and theology.

Hispanic theology is thus not limited to issues that others would consider obviously "Hispanic"–issues such as immigration, culture, worship forms, etc. On the contrary, Hispanic theology deals with the entire corpus of theology, being very much aware that the manner in which that corpus has been produced, transmitted, and interpreted bears the mark of structures that generally exclude or at least marginalize us. This means that every point of theology, doctrine, and biblical interpretation is open to reinspection and rereading. It also means that Latino/a theology seeks to make a contribution to theology at large and to the entire church, and not just to its own community or its own particular brand of theology. Thus, the inaugural editorial in *Apuntes* quoted above continues:

> But the word "apuntes" also means aimings. And that indicates that we do not intend simply to doodle at the margins of the theological enterprise. We are taking a bead on the very heart of theology, hoping–even against hope–that our comments on and from the margin will help the Church at large to rediscover some forgotten dimensions of the biblical message. While still at the margin, and from the perspective of our Hispanic experience, we shall take a new look at Scripture, and at the entire theological enterprise. And we are convinced that this new look will be valuable, not only to us, but also to the Church as a whole (González 1980, 3–4).

Some years ago, I proposed just such a reexamination of the entire field of Christian doctrine and theology and explored what this might mean for some of the central doctrines of Christian tradition. I called the chapter on biblical hermeneutics "Reading the Bible in Spanish" (1990, 75–87). While I was gratified by the way in which that book was received, what has most surprised me is that the most quoted line in the entire book is the title of that chapter. It seems that the notion of "rereading," "reinterpreting," or "reinventing" resonated with what many Latinos and Latinas feel is their current task in theology.

Along such lines of a rereading of all theology, Roberto Goizueta, while agreeing with the move from orthodoxy to orthopraxis that has characterized much of this rereading, calls for a further correction. Part of what he suggests is placing aesthetics once again at the center of theological reflection:

> If the notion of praxis as social transformation suffers from the ambiguity inherent in the modern conflation of praxis and poiesis, what other categories might we look to in order to address this ambiguity?...The understanding of human action as essentially aesthetic is an important part of the intellectual heritage of U.S. Hispanics and Latin Americans (1995, 89).

That this is central for Latino theology is exemplified and developed with groundbreaking originality by Alejandro García-Rivera in *The Community of the Beautiful: A Theological Aesthetics.*

A general rereading of theology was also proposed when a group of Catholic theologians, gathering at the annual sessions of ACHTUS, decided that the time had come to begin the process of "reinventing dogmatics" by doing theology "latinamente." The beginning of this process, which involves both a Latino methodology and a Latino content, is reported in a volume edited by its initiators, Orlando O. Espín and Miguel H. Díaz.[7] Meanwhile, Ismael García has provided us with a rereading of Christian Ethics: *Dignidad: Ethics through Hispanic Eyes*,[8] and Luis G. Pedraja has attempted something similar with christology.[9] In church history, such rereading may be found among Catholics in the work of Moisés Sandoval,[10] Antonio M. Stevens Arroyo,[11] and, more recently, Timothy Matovina and Gerald E. Poyo.[12] The same is true among Protestants in the work of the now-defunct Academia para la Historia de la Iglesia Latina (APHILA),[13] and of a number of younger scholars such as Daisy L. Machado, Paul Barton, Edwin Aponte,

---

[7]See *From the Heart of Our People.*

[8]It is significant that García's book concludes with a section on "Rethinking the Marks of the Church," 170–72.

[9]*Jesus Is My Uncle.* As further corroboration of the importance of the theme of rethinking or rereading. Pedraja begins his book with a section on "Reading Theology in Spanish," 16–22.

[10]See *On the move.*

[11]See *Prophets Denied Honor.*

[12]See *¡Presente!.*

[13]See Rodríguez-Díaz and Cortés-Fuentes, *Hidden Stories.* Shortly after the publication of this book, APHILA merged into AETH, which is discussed later in this essay. While AETH still has an "interest group" on history, this group is not as active as APHILA once was.

and Miguel A. De La Torre.[14] A similar trend is also noticeable in the more practical fields of the theological curriculum, such as homiletics.[15]

The matter of biblical hermeneutics has been discussed amply and repeatedly by Latino/a scholars, who have also produced a significant number of commentaries, Bible studies, and other such materials, both for scholars and for common use in the churches.[16] While much of this work has been done by Protestants,[17] Roman Catholics such as Fernando Segovia, María Pilar Aquino, Jean Pierre Ruiz, and Francisco Lozada have produced important works on biblical studies and on hermeneutics.[18]

Bringing the Margins to the Center

In the field of systematic theology proper, or dogmatics, one of the most significant trends in Hispanic theology has been placing the people themselves at the center of theological reflection, not just as an audience for such reflection, but as a source and partner in it. Such is the work, for instance, of Orlando O. Espín, *The Faith of the People: Theological Reflections on Popular Catholicism.*

One of the most significant contributions of Hispanic, and particularly Latina theology, is its emphasis on *lo cotidiano*–the everyday–as an important element in theological reflection. María Pilar Aquino has repeatedly stressed this point, so often forgotten by more traditional theologians.[19]

Along these lines, it is significant that Ada María Isasi-Díaz's first book, published in 1988 jointly with Yolanda Tarango, is based on a series of conversations with Latinas in everyday life.[20] This has been a constant note in much of Isasi-Díaz's continuing work. In a later book, she explains the foundations of this methodology:

> There are four reasons why the voices of Latinas are presented in *mujerista* theology as unmediated as possible. First, there is the richness of the understandings and experiences Latinas have shared...Second, the materials presented here...fill a vacuum...We have had little opportunity to speak and much less to be heard. Third, there is a need to listen to Latinas to understand how and

[14]See Daisy Machado, "The Writing of Religious History" in *Hispanic Christianity within Mainline Protestant Traditions,* 83–86; De la Torre and Aponte, *Latino/a Theologies;* Barton's first book is forthcoming.

[15]See the forthcoming Jiménez and González, *Púlpito.*

[16]See the excellent summary by Segovia, "Reading the Bible as Hispanic Americans," *The New Interpreter's Bible,* 167–73. See also his fuller contribution, *Decolonizing Biblical Studies.* At a more popular level, see my own *Santa Biblia.*

[17]On this as well as on other subjects, consult Barton and Maldonado Jr., *Hispanic Christianity within Mainline Protestant Traditions.*

[18]Consult the annual bibliographies published in the *Journal of Hispanic/Latino Theology.*

[19]See Aquino, "Theological Method in U.S. Latino/a Theology" in *From the Heart of Our People,* 38–39; and Isasi-Díaz, *Mujerista Theology,* 66–73.

[20]See *Hispanic Women.*

why religion is a central vivifying element of Latino culture....Finally, *mujerista* theology wishes to respect variations among Latinas' religious moods, motivations, and practices, and such variations can only be appreciated by listening to what the women themselves have to say (1993, 86–87).

The significance of this emphasis on *lo cotidiano* as a subject and as a source for theology must be emphasized, for it goes beyond the obvious. Indeed, much of traditional theology has been preoccupied with "history" in contrast with "nature." Thus it has ignored the obvious point. Those who make history, as well as those who write theology, can only do so because countless numbers of people stand behind them. These people take care of *lo cotidiano*–they grow and harvest crops, cook meals, do laundry. These important people are mostly women and minorities in practically every society.

Sometimes the margin is brought to the center. This is accomplieshed by looking at the manner in which people who do not traditionally move in academic circles and who are seldom heard in academic discussions on liturgy actually worship and express their faith. In *Caminemos con Jesús*, quoted above, Roberto Goizueta has taken the devotional experiences and practices around Holy Week in San Antonio as a point of departure for very profound and creative theological reflection. C. Gilbert Romero has also taken the devotional practices of Hispanic Catholics as a source for his theological reflections.[21] On the Pentecostal side, a similar emphasis may be seen in Eldin Villafañe's work.[22]

Venues for Latino/a Theological Conversation

On the basis of what has just been said, it is obvious that the main locus of Latino/a theological conversation is the community itself, the local church, the *bautizos*, *cumpleaños*, *quinceañeras*, *novenas*, and many other occasions on which the people gather and express their struggles, hopes, and faith. This has been going on for generations, and Hispanic theologians very properly give credit to the *abuelitas*–the grandmothers–through whom much of this wisdom has been preserved, transformed, and transmitted.

There are, however, a number of places where more formal conversation takes place–hopefully always in the context of the wider community itself. A number of these places should be listed here, for many of them are scarcely known–or not known at all–by the theological community at large. These places are significant resources for those wishing to learn more about the content and practice of Hispanic theologies.

---

[21]See *Hispanic Devotional Piety*.
[22]See *The Liberating Spirit*.

Among Roman Catholics–and a few Protestants who have been invited as honorary members–the Academy of Catholic Hispanic Theologians in the United States (ACHTUS) has played an important role.[23] Originally conceived as a gathering of "theologians" in the strict sense of the word–that is, systematicians–in more recent years it has expanded its dialogue to include other scholars in the field of theology and religion. Its membership is highly qualified academically, and its constitution sets guidelines that guarantee that it remains so. It meets annually and has been the venue in which many a future theological project has first been discussed. ACTHUS publishes the *Journal of Hispanic/Latino Theology*, a scholarly quarterly.

Among Protestants, the Asociación para la Educación Teológica Hispana (AETH) plays a similar role, although AETH has always been open to Catholic membership and has significant Catholic participation in a number of its projects–particularly publication projects.[24] Its bylaws have been designed to allow membership to any who are engaged in theological reflection and teaching, regardless of academic standing or qualifications. Its assembly gathers biannually, but it also sponsors other meetings, some on a regional basis and some organized around a common discipline or issue.

The journal *Apuntes: Reflexiones desde el margen hispano* has been published by the Mexican American Program at Perkins School of Theology since 1980 and is the longest-running Hispanic journal of theology.[25] Not quite as academically oriented as the *Journal of Hispanic/Latino Theology*, it has been the place where many a chapter of a future book has first been published.

The Hispanic Summer Program (HSP) is a joint venture, sponsored by thirty-nine seminaries and universities, to provide Latino/a students of theology with an intensive experience in theological studies, with Hispanic peers and professors, and with worship and other opportunities that reflect their own cultural and religious backgrounds.[26] It is now in its sixteenth year of operation. It also offers, in conjunction with each summer session, a seminar for non-Latino faculty in its sponsoring institutions, "Through Hispanic Eyes."

The Hispanic Theological Initiative (HTI) is a mentoring and networking program that also grants fellowship support, all with the goal

[23]As an organization of a limited number of scholars, ACHTUS has no ongoing office. Its current president is Dr. Francisco Lozada, at Incarnate Word College in San Antonio. See www.jhlt.org/achtus.

[24]The offices of AETH are located on the campus of Austin Presbyterian Theological Seminary, 100 E. 27th Street, Austin, TX 78705. AETH@austinseminary.edu.

[25]Mexican American Program, Perkins School of Theology, Southern Methodist University, Dallas, TX 75275. Its current editor is Dr. Luis G. Pedraja.

[26]The offices of the HSP are housed at the Lutheran School of Theology in Chicago: 1100 East 55th Street, Chicago, IL 60615–5199.

of increasing the number of Latinas and Latinos qualified to teach in seminaries and university departments of religion.[27] It has significantly increased the number of Hispanics enrolled in Ph.D. programs, and very significantly decreased the attrition rate among them. One of its many venues is the series of "Latinas in Theology" gatherings, which fosters networking and theological reflection among Latinas.

All of these venues, and many others at regional and denominational levels, are places where intense theological dialogue is taking place. In such places the issues of identity discussed above are always present, but they are not allowed to obscure the urgent theological tasks before us. One task of particular urgency is that of listening to the silenced voices in our own communities and of seeking to translate what they say into a language the church at large, and theologians in particular, can understand. Fortunately, the number of those who are at least willing to listen seems to be growing, as the publication of this very book seems to indicate.

Emerging Issues

As Latino/a theology moves into the twenty-first century, it may well be dominated by what one could call issues of relationships. Some of these are matters of inner relationships, such as the particular contributions of various subgroups within the Latino community, how they differ, and how they may enrich each other. Another set of issues of "inner" relationships have to do with the manner in which various theological traditions within the Hispanic/Latino Christian community have affected one another. For instance, how does the Roman Catholic tradition that stands at the root of Latino culture impact and enrich Protestant Hispanic Christianity? How does Latino Pentecostalism impact and enrich Latino Roman Catholicism?

Others are matters of outer relationships. Among these, one that has already received some attention, but will need much more work, is the connection between Latino/a theologies in the United States and Latin American theologies. While in the last two decades of the twentieth century it seemed important for Latina/o theologies in the United States to carve their own space, the need is now growing to strengthen the dialogue with the theological work taking place in Latin America.

Another task facing Latina/o theologians in the twenty-first century is affirming the contribution of their work to the theological enterprise of the whole church. At one time it was necessary to create our own space, to legitimate our own particular experiences and perspectives. However, Hispanic theology does not have the vocation to be a province or a footnote to "regular" theology. The task before the coming generations will therefore be to develop ways to retain and affirm their own Latino/a particularity,

[27] 12 Library Place, Princeton, NJ 08540. See www.htiprogram.org.

not just as a matter of identity and self-affirmation, but also as a contribution to theology of the whole.

Finally, Latina/o theology will have to delve more deeply into its own non-Christian roots, how they have shaped Latino Christianity, and what they may have to contribute to theology as a whole. This includes the Native American as well as the African and Islamic roots of Hispanic/ Latino religiosity.

18

Asian American Theology

FUMITAKA MATSUOKA

A search for an alternative religious paradigm rooted in the lived faith experiences of Asian Americans sets the context in which Asian American theology is currently being done. To be sure, the impact of the dominant North Atlantic religious, theological, and cultural orientations cannot be minimized for Asian Americans' construction of theology. Asian American theology is part and parcel of a larger historical context in which theological traditions have been built and nurtured. At the same time, multivalent religious, cultural, and ethnic/racial orientations of Asian American faith communities are shaping their distinct theologies. The significance of institution-building is important for the shaping of Asian American theology. Two equally important issues that inform Asian American theology are the diasporic experiences and the impact of historical injuries. Finally, we will pay attention to theology being a collective memory as well as an agent of Asian American communities for their identity-seeking and constructive work in an increasingly fluid and conflict-filled world.

Asian American Theology and Institution-building

What does it mean to engage in theological studies as Asian Americans? An answer to what seems to be this simple question reveals often hidden, yet powerful, assumptions about doing theology. The question leads us to consider the derivative questions of who does theology, for whom theology is done, and for what purpose it is done. For many centuries theological learning consisted of theological reflection on the history of dogma. At the time of the Reformation, Protestants revised theological learning, grounding it first and foremost in the Bible, which was used to critique and reinterpret "the tradition." From the base of biblical studies, students learned dogmatics and the history of doctrine "with an eye toward the vindication of the Protestant movement against Roman Catholic claims" (Wood 1985, 2).

The Theological Education System and Its Roots

The fourfold organization of theological learning (biblical, dogmatic/systematic, historical, and practical) has dominated theological studies from early Protestant time into our day. Biblical and historical studies were significantly transformed by the rise and dominance of critical historical methodologies. As these new "scientific" methodologies became prominent, they helped to transform the universities (particularly German universities) into research universities. The theological disciplines of biblical studies, history, and theology were invited into the universities, but a condition of their participation was "to face the challenges posed by modern secular studies." The separation of "scientific" from "practical" in the German research universities was replicated in the structure of American universities. The pastoral or practical study was viewed as "an application of knowledge rather than a scientific producer of knowledge" (Wood 1985, 5–7).

Edward Farley, David Kelsey, Peter Hodgson, and others challenged the most fundamental issues and basic assumptions behind the present structure of theological education, which they judged to be seriously flawed. Farley in *Theologia: The Fragmentation and Unity of Theological Education* sees theology as the Christian community's response to issues, both inside and outside of the church, demanding reflection and action. He seeks to address and find a remedy for the fragmentation of theological education into a cluster of unrelated disciplines and rootless practical skills. He argues that theological education consists in the formation of a disposition or aptitude, which he called a *habitus*, a "sepiential and personal knowledge."

Charles Wood defines theology as critical inquiry into the validity of Christian witness (Wood 1985, 5–7). Kelsey, in *To Understand God Truly*, notes the tension between the nonutilitarian aim of theological learning (to understand God truly) with the focus on leadership training as the unifying aim of many theological schools. For Hodgson, in *God's Wisdom*, theological learning is also a form of *paideia* or cultivation of wisdom as the understanding of God.

New Ways to Cast the Issues

In the 1980s, the women of the Mudflower Collective and other underrepresented people devised different ways of casting the issues of theological studies. They began to raise fundamental questions of theological education: who teaches what to whom (Heyward 1985). It took Francis Schüssler Fiorenza, in "Theological and Religious Studies," to open up the conversation about the purpose of theological education. He argues that theological learning is entailing critical reflection on and reconstruction of Christian identity.

Paul Knitter, in "Beyond a Mono-religious Theological Education," along with Schüssler Fiorenza addressed how issues of social justice and injustice can play a key role in theological studies, particularly in providing the initial common ground for conversations with other religious communities. Knitter stressed that conversation cannot proceed unless those from dominant positions are actively committed to the freedom of their conversation partners. He was also an early advocate for the interfaith sensitivity to theological education.

The Asian American Role

Asian American theology emerged within the stream of this historical conversation about the question of what it means to engage in theology and theological education. Asian American theological educators and leaders of faith communities have been active participants in this conversation. Retired Bishop Roy Sano of the United Methodist Church is one of the powerful representatives of the initial Asian American theological movement that began in the 1970s. Bishop Sano insisted that theology must be engaged in Asian American faith communities by taking seriously their distinct cultural and religious heritages and the history of injustices done to them. The Pacific and Asian American Center for Theology and Strategies (PACTS) in Berkeley, California, under the direction of Bishop Sano, became the locus of the initial theological conversations among Asian American theologians and leaders of faith communities.

In the meantime, within both the fields of university-based religious studies and theological education, the attentions are increasingly given to the social, cultural, religious, and cosmological locations of those Asian American scholars who are engaged in the study of faith. One thing is clear: it is no longer possible to engage in the study of faith in isolation, whether within the traditionally understood context of "religious studies" or "theological education." A study of faith has become increasingly relational, self-critical, and inevitably political in nature. This is particularly true for Asian Americans and those who are underrepresented in the field of theology.

Not only has the content of the study of faith become more relational, self-reflective, and political, "Asian American" study of faith (religion and theology) has inevitably taken on a political and controversial tone in academia. We hear such questions as: what does it mean as an Asian American to engage in the study of religion and theology in a white institution? What are we doing with Asian American study of religion to help the Asian American and Pacific Islanders' communities? What else is an Asian American qualified to teach at a white school? These questions are posed in relation to such comments Asian Americans hear in academia as: We need more diversity. How nice for Asian American students to have something related to their culture and for white students to learn something about it. These questions and comments reflect a highly politicized reality of studying faith as an Asian American.

Given this climate of theological studies today, Asian American theology is really about institution-building both within and outside the Asian American community and about this particular underrepresented group's struggle for its right to interpret the reality it shares with the majority through the institutions it creates or infiltrates. To be sure, the matter of identity-building for Asian Americans is quite different from that for African Americans and other persecuted minority groups who have faced similar challenges. But institution-building, both within and outside the Asian American community, is a serious challenge that awaits our response as those who engage in the study of religion and theology.

Emerging Theological Themes in Asian American Theology

Commenting in the *Amerasia Journal* on the issues raised by scholars of Asian American religious and theological studies, Rudy V. Busto of University of California at Santa Barbara stated: "As scholars concerned not only with the salvaging of Asian American religious histories, but also with responsible constructive work for Asian American communities, it is imperative that we frame our analyses in conjunction with the very communities that determine and define Asian American religious identities" (1996, 190). What, then, are representative theological themes that emerge out of Asian American faith communities?

Diasporic Existence

One of the determinative factors for Asian American theology is the diasporic character of Asian American communities. Theologically speaking, to be in diaspora is to be in the state of dislocation and dispossession. Paradigmatically and morally speaking, to an Asian in North American diaspora means not to be at home in one's home. An alternative perspective that counters the dominant notion about community-building has been emerging in a certain segment of the Asian diasporic communities in the United States for some time. It is a perspective that reconstructs the often-neglected Christian tradition of the Holy Saturday (Easter Saturday) within the Asian American community of diaspora. This theological tradition echoes a particular life perspective represented in literary works of Asian American writers from Carlos Bulosan's *America Is in the Heart* to Ruthanne Lum McCunn's *Thousand Pieces of Gold*. This perspective defines relationship-building out of exclusion, displacement, the sense of tragedy, and mobility born not out of the luxury of freedom but of necessity.

Displacements are irreversible in our world today. Our bewildered, numbed, despairing society lacks way of thinking and ways of speaking that can give us remedial access to the crisis, that can (1) go deep into the crisis and so avoid *denial*, and (2) imagine past the crisis, and so avoid *despair* by abdicating silence. We are experiencing an emerging state of dislocation worldwide. In the ambiguous and amorphous state of Asian American identities–or what Lisa Lowe calls a "hybrid, multiple, and fluid" state–some Asian American literary writers have been reexamining the assumptions and implications, often hidden beneath our discourse, of the traditional culturally, ethnically, linguistically, and politically based identity (Lowe 1991, 24–44). They are exploring an alternate way of articulating our identity and meaning that speaks to the changing societal scene without falling into either denial or despair. The Christian theology of the "Holy Saturday" provides a window into this discussion in the current worldwide state of dislocation with a juxtaposed similar faith perspective.

The dominant Christian culture of the optimistic "Easter" faith bears a large measure of responsibility for the dominant "frontier" form of political religion prevalent in the United States. September 11 charged our societal climate. Now an impulse to achieve justice through the exertion of extravagant freedom and unmitigated mobility in the form of military power corresponds with this brand of the Christian faith with its idea of history. Our society has been founded on the principle of free, responsible human activity. What made "America" was not a new vision of humanity only, but a new idea of history. As Reinhold Niebuhr wrote, "The dominant note in modern culture is not so much confidence in reason as faith in history." The conception of a redemptive history informs the most diverse forms of modern culture (1949, 3).

However, another Christian culture lurks today. Its texture is exilic. It sees our history through another kind of mobility, usually associated with subjugation, coercion, impossibility of fulfillment for self or community. It is the theological motif of Israel's exile in the Old Testament and the realism of the cross in the New Testament. The central motif of faith according to this reading of reality is not emancipatory freedom but rootage, not the pursuit of happiness but belonging, not separation from community but location within it, not limitless opportunity but life amidst pain in the generation of promise about what can be.

This alternate Christian culture echoes the perspective of Bulosan, McCunn, and other Asian American writers to an extent. They have a keen awareness of mobility as a historical given rather than a private frustration or temporary setback. The central learning from history in this reading of life is that grasping for home leads to homelessness and risking homelessness yields the gift of home but in an unanticipated fashion. Immobility is not the negation of freedom but a realization of it. The mainstream and exilic Christian cultures intersect at the point of political interpretations currently taking place in society, the exilic in a danger of being overshadowed by the dominant discourse in the heat of the patriotic rhetoric.

The task of the theologian is to interpret the world and the life of a people in the light of a transcendent reference. The movement of God's triune history from Good Friday until Easter Sunday calls us into solidarity with the least of our neighbors and into similarity with the alien and different. Nurtured through this reconciliation is an affirmation in God's final reign of peace and justice over violence and unrighteousness–concrete, visible signs of which can and must be fashioned within our social ordering today. The boundary point, that presence-in-absence both divine and human, that significant zero and pregnant vacuum, so dense and tangible in its insubstantiality, serves both to conjoin and to separate the Friday cross and the Sunday garden. It prevents at once both rank despair and cheap triumphalism, both the nonoccurrence and the premature arrival of a resurrection sequel to the crucifixion.

"Where sin increased, grace abounded all the more." The story of the cross and grave tells of a contradiction between God and the world, a conflict in which evil triumphs over good, death extinguishes life, and the creatures annihilate their Maker. But the contradiction is not absolute, nor is the conflict finally resolved in favor of negation. For there flourishes even more grace beyond the great magnitude of evil, and a divine fertility beyond the barrenness of the demonic. A final and decisive Yes to the creatures, powerful, living, and redemptive, promises them freedom and fullness within the expansive embrace of God's own history and life. To this triumphal Easter Yes, which never cancels but does transcend God's judgmental No to the world on the cross and the world's destructive No to God in the grave, ecclesiology must clearly correspond.

To live the Easter Saturday story is to acknowledge and cherish, as the precondition of our self-fulfillment, the limitations, postponements, and terminations that belong to creaturehood. Indeed, it is to let oneself be taught to be a moral creature by the immortal Maker's own self-emptying accommodation to one's condition and one's death. Only through such awesome, humble grace may we learn to be at peace with ourselves and embrace the truth of who we really are.

Central to the good news in the Christian three-day story is its demonstration that death does not have the last word upon human destiny, that God sets limits to death and to death's power to oppress and limit life. But that this Sunday victory over death comes only through a Sabbath when life has been snuffed out by death is confirmation that the God who limits death also uses death to limit life.

For Easter Saturday is precisely a day of waiting, a hiatus and a barrier that prevents a knowing, onward rush to victory and joy by interjecting a painful pause, empty of hope and filled instead with death and grief, with memories of failure and betrayal, of abandonment and anguish. Across this motionless, unhurried time between yesterday and tomorrow, this lifeless time that faith has named as "descent to hell," God's own self is suspended upon Holy Saturday. Here in horrid captivity to time's protracted sluggishness, the Father and the Son–separated by the sin of our rebellion against limits–must await reunion through the Spirit at humanity's own place. Through participation in the patience of God's Spirit we learn the gift of waiting that restores us to ourselves from the destructive urgency of our desires and aspirations, and slows the tempo of our intemperance.

The God exposed to impotence and needfulness on Calvary is one whose very Godness, as Trinitarian community, consists of reciprocity and mutual reliance. God is dependence rendered infinite, unable to be Father without the Son, or Son without Father, just as the Spirit, neither self-generating nor self-regarding, proceeds from the Father of the Son as necessary source and finds its raison d'etre in the glorifying of them both. Such a reading of faith has not been very popular in Western theology. Asian American theology reclaims and transmutes this age-old faith tradition into an enriched and yet unexplored realm.

Historical Injuries

In the diasporic character of Asian American experiences, a powerful life-shaping factor is the impact of historical injuries inflicted upon them. The effects of historical injuries a larger society has imposed on Asian Americans provide a particular "angle of vision" about life. Life is here seen as a locus of "holy insecurity." For Asian Americans, their experiences on the North American continent have produced memories of events and incidents that now serve as the seed bed of their common narratives, the stuff that makes their communities "home."

Memory is a function of maintaining current values. History is a tale told to illustrate a presently operative philosophy of life. In exploring the way memory preserves and creates the past, the central question the individual as well as the community asks is: "How did we come to be as we presently are?" Several associated categories yield a fruitful investigation to respond to this question: What wounds or hurts do we resent having suffered? What gifts were we given for which we are grateful? Who were our important figures and models? What were the crucial decisions for which we were responsible? These questions focus attention not only on the remembered facts that constitute the raw material of autobiography but on the way in which memory functions to justify present attitudes, such as resentment or gratitude.

In *All Rivers Run to the Sea*, Elie Wiesel reminds us, "Memory is a passion no less powerful or pervasive than love...What does it mean to remember? It is to live in more than one world, to prevent the past from fading and to call upon the future to illuminate it. It is to revive fragments of existence, to rescue lost beings, to cast harsh light on faces and events, to drive back the sands that cover the surface of things, to combat oblivion and to reject death." Indeed, Asian Americans have suffered from countless injuries imposed upon them. These range from the Chinese Exclusion Act of the late nineteenth century (1882) to the internment of Japanese Americans during World War II, and to the more recent plight of Indochinese Americans both in their previous homelands and now in the United States. These experiences no doubt impact the ways Asian Americans understand life. The memories of these experiences are indeed "a passion no less powerful or pervasive than love." Particularly noteworthy is the experiences of Khmer Americans whose voices are seldom heard in Asian American theology.

"The tragedy of Cambodia has not yet run its course, nor will it for generations. Millions have died, a culture has vanished," writes Yathay Pin (Ebihara et al 1994, 1). Besides the loss of life, knowledge, and material things, there is also the sense of a loss of order in Khmer culture and a Buddhist era. Equally profound is the absence of a language that can express Khmer Americans' experiences. The horror of the Killing Fields simply defies any existing language to describe what happened. A period of silence often lasts a considerable time, judging from the experiences of the Holocaust victims during and after World War II.

A primary challenge to the traditional Khmer religions in the United States is to explain the events that have occurred in Cambodia in the past three to four decades, especially finding explanations for the years when the country was ruled by the Khmer Rouge. For Khmer Buddhists, the causes of extraordinary events are attributed to human actions when the events cannot be explained by any other means. When extraordinary events occur, however, the very essence of a social group's otherworldly explanation becomes problematic. So while Khmer have for centuries utilized Karmic theory to explain unusual or threatening events, the Democratic Kampuchea years were of such extraordinary horrors that usual explanations for the extraordinary did not always suffice. Some Khmers had turned away from Buddhism in anger and despair, saying that Buddhism was to blame for what had happened to their beloved Cambodia. "Perhaps the Christian God, working through the church groups trying to help them, was a better choice...The few who became Christians for the most part did so because they were searching for answers to unthinkable questions" (Ebihara et al. 1994, 1).

To further compound the matter, Khmer Americans are faced with an inability on the part of other Americans to empathize with their horrendous experiences. This puts them in an isolated place in American society. Ever so gradually, however, Khmer Americans are attempting to express their tragic experiences, worldviews, and beliefs through various means. They must do so to establish the identity of each person and of the community we belong to as well as our deeply held values and worldviews. These all are shaped by an ability to find a particular path of life in our often traumatic, painful, confusing, and sometimes unexpected discoveries of joy in decisive historical events and forces that swirl around us. Through prayers and storytelling, pains are eased. This places our lives within what we believe to be an ultimate context. By the easing of pain the will of the divine is revealed. In this way a person is able to live in harmony with the powers of the over-world that exerts a mysterious and powerful influence on our experiences.

Literary works emerging out of the Cambodian Diaspora in North America are few and far between. Besides the land, the society's knowledge, history, culture, and even commonly-held core values were almost destroyed. The reformulation of their identities in the new land is still a matter of speculation. The civil war and revolution of the 1970s left almost two million Khmer dead and a half million more scattered into exile in foreign countries. Given this painful situation, some voices are gradually beginning to emerge.

At this time in history, the voices of the exiles are likely to be "screened voices" and not necessarily the voices of individuals who speak for themselves. *Cambodian Culture Since 1975: Homeland and Exile* represents such "screened voices." The work attempts "to combine two perspectives: to provide some of the larger context by viewing the Khmer as people affected by national and international events, and at the same time to focus on the level of individuals and the process whereby they make decisions" (Ebihara et al., 87).

For the 150,000 Khmer who have come to the United States since the late 1970s, the Pol Pot era and the experience of concentration camp life, flight, refugee camps, and resettlement in a new land are virtually inexplicable. Traditional religious beliefs and worldviews, particularly Buddhism, are no longer sufficient for Khmers in America to understand the question of the brutality of the Khmer Rouge. "How could three million people have had bad karma at the same time?" The central core of Buddhist teachings is thus being repudiated in the experiences of the Khmer. "As refugees, Khmer in the United States face a new world; the realignment of all that has been, is, should be, and will be...lead Khmer to the conclusion that their past is unique and that explanation for their past is virtually impossible" (87). This is the context in which the Khmer literature is beginning to be formed. "Constant themes in modern novels both inside Cambodia and abroad are the misfortunes and tenor of the Pol Pot regime and the tragedy of life" (87).

While the emergence of literature among the Khmer in the United States is still in its infancy, some Khmer are beginning to use traditional Cambodian stories to cope with the inexplicable. Though written in France, *Phka Chhouk Kampuchea* (*Lotus Flower of Cambodia*) by Ing Kien gives us a glimpse of the possible themes and issues that are beginning to emerge in the U.S. Khmer communities. There are a few works of literature emerging out of the "killing fields" experiences of Khmer–for instance, Usha Welartna, *Beyond the Killing Fields: Voices of Nine Cambodian Survivors in America.*

Lotus Flower of Cambodia is a story about a young woman, Kolap, whose life is full of deception, ordeal, grief, and the loss of her family members at the hands of Khmer Rouge. She arrives in France alone with the aid of Catholic Relief. There she meets her former fiancee, Vidya, who is by then married to a woman named Ma Yan. Vidya offers Kolap a room in his home with the consent of Ma Yan. The relationship between Vidya and Kolap is a complicated one. Vidya treated their previous relationship as a thing of the past, whereas Kolap still struggles with the past relationship with Vidya. Sensing the complications, Ma Yan leaves Vidya and takes refuge in a Catholic church where Kolap meets Ma Yan by accident. Ma Yan consents to return home to the seriously ill Vidya. Eventually, Kolap accepts the reality of Vidya's marriage to Ma Yan and remains a friend to both.

The story revolves around several key themes. These include the destruction of the past life; an emergence of a new sense of community that is, nevertheless, affected by the events of the past; the role of Christianity and the questions about Buddhist teachings and values; and the shape of new identity as Cambodians in a new land. Particularly persistent in the story is the formation of a new Cambodian community in exile and its accompanying value and identity transformation for Khmer. Religious values and practices play a prominent role.

Community-building efforts in a new land are interwoven with an alternate belief system, Christianity. This newly found faith is appropriate for some Khmer Americans that hold it in affection because it is associated with those who have provided them with a new chance for life. Having coincided with the erosion of the credibility of Buddhism in the aftermath of the civil war, Christianity, or more precisely Christians who assisted Khmer in rebuilding life, has become a force powerful enough to mediate their efforts toward community-building around it.

At the same time, other forces are at work in the emergence of Khmer communities in diaspora. In the U.S., Khmer refugees needed to cope with social, economic, and cultural adjustments. Religious and traditional ceremonies, attended predominantly by the older generations of Khmer, are held in various Khmer communities. These ritual practices provide certain emotional, psychological, and cultural relief from depression, isolation, and homesickness. These ritual practices may eventually find their way into Khmer literature just as they play a prominent role in Ing Kien's work.

The tragedy of life inflicted by the Pol Pot regime is a necessary theme in Khmer literature. But the development of alternate explanations for the framing of their lives in the post-Pol Pot era is not adequate. Khmer in diaspora within U.S. society continue to ask a range of questions that challenge them in this new land with a set of new relationships with people around them. These are questions they would never have thought to ask before their lives made a radical turn. The future of Khmer literature in the United States will likely pursue these new and yet old questions and sets the foundation of the emerging theological voices.

Theology as An Agent of Collective Memory and Identity Formation

Asian American women theologians have been raising questions about identity amidst a complex set of issues of sexism and racism that underlies the social construction of what it means to be a woman in a white dominant society. They are indeed pioneers for grappling with the question of identity for their own generation but for generations to follow. Theologian Jung Ha Kim considers herself as "more churched than Christianized" (1999, 105). Her lived experiences in Christian faith community with people of multiple religious, historical, and social elements coming together constitutes her identity. In different ways, Asian American women theologians struggle to talk about faith amidst the "No Name Woman" syndrome, described by Maxine Hong Kingston in *The Woman Warrior*, that is, not having no name but also being ignored and treated as if they are not even present.

The literary field has proven to be a fertile ground for significant theological themes to emerge for Asian Americans. Real life has no beginnings or endings, no moments of intrinsic significance that form a framework of meaning around experience. Real life offers only days "tacked on to days without rhyme or reason, an interminable, monotonous addition," as Sartre would put it (1959, 56). Anything can really happen in real life. No universal reason sets limits to the possible and gives meaning to human history. In the face of pain, riddle, and perhaps absurdity of existence, the only option for the lucid individual is to create a reason or perhaps just questions for existing by writing a narrative, journal, poetry, or just plain telling a story. Only by choosing some project, however arbitrary, can the individual fill the present moment and avoid the absolute contingency and absurdity of existence.

Asian American writers such as Cambodian storytellers, others such as Joy Kogawa and Maxine Hong Kingston, have done just that. Each in a personal way affirms the unity of reality; yet sometimes questions about radical disruptions persist. The individual, the ethnicity, culture, and the cosmos present themselves in concentric circles of possible integrated meaning called life. Past, present, and future are bound together in a thematic continuation. These writers, each in their own way, take courage from their knowledge that they have roots in what had been and that their memories and deeds would be preserved in what would be. In effect, their works affirm that the reality of the individual is not reducible to the present moment of experience but belongs to a continuity of meaning that the flow of time could not erode even with its unspeakable pain and trauma. With such faith, they act with a sense of continuity and perspective; their spontaneity is tempered by memory and hope. The Christian theology of the "Holy Saturday" in its reimagined form provides a powerful tool in this discussion.

For Khmer Americans, the telling of their unspeakable pain is a way of justifying and sanctioning the values essential to building a community anew amidst the devastation of their total humanity. Joy Kogawa focuses on truth-telling in the face of the society-wide deception that attempts to erase the existence of her people. The works of Maxine Hong Kingston, spanning many decades and bringing together both the stories out of China and the reflective narratives of Chinese experiences in the United States, are efforts to come to terms with painful events as a prerequisite to "rerooting." What is needed is a reorientation to the paradoxical nature of life.

Their act of telling stories serves the diverse function of philosophy, theology, history, ethics, and healing, and even entertainment. It serves to locate the individual within the concentric circles of the cosmos, nature, community, and family. It provides a concrete account of what is expected of a person and what one may expect in that darkness that lies beyond the trauma of painful historical injuries, internment, unjust immigration policies, and the "Killing Fields." Each writer seems to have an article of faith in their acts of writing and telling these works, or at least a yearning for it. It is this yearning that the scale of Being be such that human beings could possibly grasp the meaning of the whole even in their often confusing, bewildering, ambiguous, and contradictory life.

Personality is not an epiphenomenon in an alien world of matter ruled by chance but is the key to the whole cosmos. Truth-telling, rerooting of one's identity, and community-building anew are not just their individual concerns but point to what their own people are all about, and eventually what a society's future will become. Each individual is a microcosm. In telling their own story, an individual has confidence that the concrete, dramatic, tear-filled images are not unrelated to the forces that make for the shape of the macrocosm. While their images and stories may reduce the proportions of reality to a scale that is manageable by the human spirit, their distortion serves the cause of truth. Kogawa, Kingston, and Khmer Americans are confident that their images, symbols, myths, and stories are the available means to grasp reality and are not merely illusions projected out of their isolated, subjective perspectives. America may remain ignorant of the names of the God or gods of these people and even the form of their religion. It may just be sufficient, at least for the moment, for the enrichment of life together if a wider America is willing to incline their attentive ears to these and other accounts told by the often-neglected people.

19

American Indian Traditions

TINK TINKER

Paddling a Canoe Upstream

I recall my second visit to the site of the 1864 Sand Creek Massacre, a trip to bury body part remains of two Natives who had died in that unprovoked surprise attack. Around midnight, several hours before the dawn ceremony, two of us walked out from the cottonwoods at the old village site in the hollow at the bend of the creek bed and ventured into the prairie a couple of hundred yards.

Sacred Experiences

As we stood under the light of the moon, we were quietly stunned by the sounds of a large and busy village coming from the cottonwoods. In the middle of this semi-arid Colorado ranchland, miles from the nearest town and more than a mile from the nearest house, we distinctly heard children playing, dogs barking, horses neighing, men singing around a drum, and people calling to each other. As we stood still and took it in, it reminded me of my first visit two years earlier, on the 125th anniversary of the Massacre.

Four of us had trekked to the site for a sunrise prayer ceremony to commemorate the murderous event and to remember those who died there.

The temperature was thirty degrees below freezing and a fresh four-inch snowfall coated the ground, similar to conditions reported for the day of the Reverend (Col.) Chivington's preemptive attack on the unsuspecting Cheyenne and Arapaho families that were just beginning to stir for the day.[1] Ours was the only car in the parking area in the early dawn darkness and the only tracks in the new snow as we began to walk through the icy cold.

By the time the sun had begun to rise above the horizon, we had walked beyond the cottonwoods out into the expanse of the prairie and had filled a *non-ni-on-ba* (a prayer pipe) and sung a ceremonial song to the pipe to ask for its help. Then as we each in turn took the pipe to speak our prayers, I noticed an Indian woman about sixty yards to the south, praying with her face to the sunrise. She was dressed in a black skirt or dress, wrapped in a red shawl, and had long black hair braided down her back. I watched her while we prayed until finally, as we smoked the pipe to finish our prayers, I looked up again and noticed that she was gone just as suddenly as she had appeared.

It took me nine years before I ventured to talk about that woman. I sat over coffee with Leonard Quiver, the person whose pipe we had prayed with that morning. Wanting to confirm what I had seen, I asked him about it. A rational, reasonable man not prone to exaggeration, he replied, "Yeah, I saw her." And then he went on to corroborate exactly what I had seen. "Yeah," he chuckled, "I went over and looked for footprints in the snow, just like you. No footprints; no other cars; no tire tracks. We were alone."

Experience and Politics as Theological Foundation

These two stories recall experiences, personal and communal, that have helped to shape my own understanding of the world. As is the case in other liberation theologies, but in a significantly different sense, any American Indian articulation of a theology will necessarily be constructed on the foundation of experience. Thus, I want to use these two narratives as the starting point for my own expression of an American Indian liberation theology. I choose this method not simply because the experiences happen

---

[1]No, the U.S. attack on Iraq was not the first of its kind. American Indians know this kind of immoral violence all too well. The best book on the Sand Creek Massacre (1864), as just one example of American violence, is still Hoig's *The Sand Creek Massacre.* For a fuller picture of the persistence of colonial violence in the Americas, see Churchill, *A Little Matter of Genocide;* or Stannard, *American Holocaust.* Churchill also has written an outstanding analysis of the failures of contemporary scholarly literature (since Hoig) about Sand Creek: "It Did Happen Here," in *Fantasies of the Master Race,* 19–26, where he argues that Hoig remains the most balanced and objective treatment of the travesty. In *A Little Matter of Genocide,* Churchill uses a Chivington quote (from instructions the evening before the attack, urging his men to kill Indian babies) as the title of an important chapter that traces the more general history of Euro-Western and explicitly Amer-European violence in North America: "Nits Make Lice: The Extermination of North American Indians, 1492–1992," 129–288.

to have been my personal experiences but rather because they capture something that runs deep in the experience of Indian communities both in terms of our awareness of our own history as recipients of injustice and violence and in terms of the experience of the sacred. As Indian liberation must, the stories combine spiritual experience and political sensibilities.

The classic liberation theologies have always been explicitly political. The liberation of oppressed and poor people must struggle with the role that political systems play in maintaining oppression. So too, American Indian perspectives on liberation must be nothing short of explicitly political. American Indians are the poorest of the poor in North America, consistently oppressed and suppressed politically, socially, psychologically, and economically with ramifications that manifest themselves in our physical and mental health and in our spiritual well-being as well.

Yet an American Indian liberation theology must necessarily have a different starting point than many of these other liberation theologies. Both the cultural particularities of American Indian communities (and indeed those of any indigenous community) and the particularities of Indian experiences of colonization and conquest mandate a different approach. Indeed, American Indians represent cultures and communities that predate the Euro-Western invasion of the Americas by thousands of generations. We were people who

- knew the spiritual side of all life
- had firm experiential connections with the Creator
- had well-developed ceremonies to help us maintain harmony and balance in the life of our communities and the world around us
- were communities of peace, most of whom did not even have words for war[2]

Thus any Indian liberation theology must take these ceremonies and spiritual traditions seriously. It must begin with the specifics of Indian cultures and cultural values.

---

[2]I realize this seems preposterous to those whose knowledge of Indian history is finely honed by Hollywood extravaganzas. Yet it is an important aspect of American Indian liberation that we Indians liberate ourselves from the self-serving colonizer histories of Indians, which are filled with fabricated myths and lies that seem solely intended to justify the conquest and validate the Amer-European occupation of the North American land base. See Jaimes and Halsey, "American Indian Women," in Jaimes, *The State of Native America,* 311–44; and also in the same volume, Holm, "Patriots and Pawns," 345–70. I am currently working on a chapter that will be titled: "War and Peace in Native North America," in which I will unpack some of the evidence that refutes the Hollywood portrayal, and even that of professional historians. On the use of lies and illegalities to secure the Amer-European theft of lands, see Ward Churchill, *Struggle for the Land.* On the American fabrication of legal pretexts (called "Federal Indian Law") see: Wilkins, *American Indian Sovereignty and the U.S. Supreme Court;* and Robert Williams, *The American Indian in Western Legal Thought.*

Jesus Is Not the Starting Point

The "classic" liberation theologies read in North America almost always begin with a radical interpretation of Jesus and the gospel. To be absolutely fair, they actually begin with the people–that is, with the "experience" of the poor and oppressed–and then move decidedly toward a people's liberating interpretation of the gospel.

For American Indians, to the contrary, the radical interpretation of Jesus would be an unproductive and even counterproductive starting point for a liberation theology. The first proclamation of Jesus among any Indian community came at the beginning of a colonial conquest that included the total displacing of centuries-old religious traditions and the replacing of those traditions with the imposition of a one-size-fits-all Euro-Western Jesus. Even the contemporary move to correct Jesus' ethnicity historically to some shade of Mediterranean brown helps little to obviate our historical experience of the way the missionary preaching about Jesus was used to destroy our cultures and legitimate the theft of our property (Tinker 1993).

Thus today, even embracing a radical Jesus and a radical interpretation of the gospel means validating to some degree the evil perpetrated against our ancestors by those who first brought Jesus to us and engaged in the colonization and conquest of our peoples and our lands. Moreover, to do so would also necessarily mean a continued disaffirmation of ourselves and the ancient spiritual traditions given to us by the sacred power that Christians call "god."

Aspects for A Native Liberation Theology

If Jesus is not to be our starting point, then we must look for another–a more unconventional and much more complex starting point for a Native liberation theology. Let me describe four aspects on which an American Indian liberation theology must build:

1. the tensions between Indian peoples and missionary Christianity
2. the peculiarities of Israelite history with regard to those tensions
3. the cultural abrasiveness of colonially imposed categories of cognition that derive from missionizing evangelism (past and present)
4. the renaissance of Indian traditional culture and ceremonial life as a source of revivification and uniquely Indian source of liberation

Tensions with Christianity

The tensions between Christianity and Indian peoples (including Christian Indians) derives first from those notions of Amer-European Christian triumphalism–Christian uniqueness; the proclaimed necessity of salvation according to the European missionary message; and the concomitant sense of Euro-Western and Amer-European superiority.

From a healthy Indian perspective, an Indian liberation theology must recognize the source of our bondage and thereby acknowledge a long and tension-filled relationship with Christianity as the religion of our colonizer and with its missionaries imposing themselves on our peoples. Today, all Indian people have been touched in some way by these missionary processes. Many have converted, some out of genuine desire to be like our White relatives; others out of some perceived necessity to placate the colonizer. For well over a hundred years there have been firmly established missionary outposts in every Indian reservation community, usually providing a variety of denominational choices.[3]

What must be acknowledged, however, is that the first Euro-Western missionary to set up shop on any reservation immediately functioned to divide the community against itself. For the first time, each person was forced to make a choice between participating in the life of the community (that is, particularly in the ceremonial and religious life of the community) and the newly introduced missionary church with its proclamation of salvation in Jesus alone. While this may have been a useful political function in terms of the conquest, it had devastating social consequences for which Indian people are still paying. Before long, other choices could be made among a variety of denominational mission churches.

This scenario works in a heavily individuated culture but was and is wholly destructive to the communitarian cultures of Native America. It becomes a cultural conquest, converting our communities to Euro-Western individualism and ripping our community structures asunder. Thus it must be explicitly said that in the missionary mandate, the absolute necessity for confessing Jesus as a means for accessing (individual) salvation meant the unequivocal disavowal of one's own culture in terms of its beliefs, experiences, ceremonies, community connectivity, and religious traditions.

Many traditional spiritual leaders on our reservations today are quick to affirm Jesus as a deeply spiritual person historically–one with continuing relevance and even continuing spiritual presence in our world. They would not, however, use language of "resurrected one" and, even less, "Lord"; and they are apt to denounce the historical and contemporary function of the church (that is, the churches) as key participants in the devastation of their own communities. This is to say that the problem is not Jesus but, rather, the particularity of the missionary preaching of Jesus. To this extent, missionaries worked through the institutional structures that promoted a

[3]The government-missionary alliance was established at the beginning of the U.S. republic in the form of federal funding allocated as a "Civilization Fund" for mission schools in the annual "Trade and Intercourse Acts." The alliance became more pronounced after 1869 when the Grant administration initiated "Peace Policy" which allocated control of reservation Indian agencies among the various mainline denominations. See chapter 5 in Tinker, *Missionary Conquest.*

singular brand of Christianity. Thus they were always a part of the genocide of Indian peoples in one way or another. Whether Indian people find liberation through accepting and adapting some version of Christianity or by rejecting it outright, these issues of religious conquest and religious colonialism must be acknowledged.

Exchanging Histories: Canaanites, Cowboys, and Indians[4]

In terms of constructing any "Christian" liberation theology for American Indians, one must reconcile the claims that two conflicting histories make on Indian peoples' lives. One of the curious oddities of Euro-Christianity relates to its canonical inclusion of the Hebrew Bible. This results in necessarily forcing all adherents to embrace a history that is not the natural or actual history of the persons or peoples who become adherents–unless they are "Jews for Jesus." That is, all converts and their succeeding generations are expected to embrace the history of one small, relatively insignificant Asian country, ancient Israel, as their own history. This entails investing their lives with meaning and identity rooted in the historical experiences of a people distant from their own both in terms of culture and time. This business of appropriating a foreign history as one's own means, in some regard (more for some than for others), the denial of one's own proper history. For American Indians it means, for instance, the denial of important aspects of our own history to affirm not only Israelite history but ultimately also Euro-Christian history, including Amer-Euro-Christian history. This is particularly evident, for instance, in any intellectual understanding of the history of Christian doctrine, which is inevitably a European history. We will return to this.

More significantly, for American Indians, affirming Israelite history means ultimately affirming precisely the historical narrative that has been used consistently by our Euro-Western colonizers to validate their own theft of our property and murder of our ancestors. As Robert Warrior has demonstrated, the Puritans' use of the Exodus narrative of Israel's escape from slavery and conquest of the land of Canaan empowered their colonial invasion of Indian lands and justified, in their minds, the murder of Indian people. Eventually, the same narrative gives birth to the religio-political doctrine of "manifest destiny" (and eventually the absurdity of the Monroe Doctrine) and all contemporary religious and political forms of American exceptionalism. As a narrative about escape from slavery, it has proven a powerful liberating story for African Americans. Yet for American Indians, Warrior reminds us forcefully, the conquest narrative is one in which we

---

[4]This subtitle is borrowed from Robert Warrior's 1989 essay: "Canaanites, Cowboys, and Indians: Deliverance, Conquest, and Liberation Theology Today," *Christianity and Crisis,* 261–65.

always discover ourselves to be the Canaanites, the conquered, and never the Israelites.[5]

The net result of this process is self-disavowal and even subtle forms of self-hatred on the part of American Indian peoples who are converted. It must lead the perceptive and sensitive observer to wonder whether any appropriation of the Euro-Christian gospel can be liberative for American Indians. It is curious that Christians are led logically to believe that "God," until the birth of Jesus, cared only for one small people on the face of the earth, leaving all others to ignorance, "sin", idolatry, self-destruction, and eternal damnation. For Indian peoples the message only becomes more difficult. It is conveyed through the clear inference that "God's" love (in the Jesus event) was denied Indian peoples until God, in God's graciousness, sent White people to kill us, lie to us, steal our land, and proclaim the saving gospel to us.

Imposition of the Colonizer's Categories of Cognition

Any Indian notion of liberation must attempt to break away from the way language is used so easily and comfortably by our colonizer. These categories are infused throughout the colonizer's language, from religious and theological categories to political ones to the simplest categories of everyday life–from Euro-Western individualism to images of the Sacred Other that the colonizer calls "god" with a capital G and then invests with particular anthropomorphic characteristics.

The problem is that missionary and government boarding schools have thoroughly inculcated colonial thinking in our minds over generations, making it more and more difficult for us to make the break. Even my own essay is only a beginning in this regard. I realize that it, too, is rooted too deeply in those Euro-Western cognitional categories.

The cover art on a recent book I coauthored can serve as a prime example of imposed categories of thought. The cover reproduces a famous American Indian painting done by Dick West many years prior. The portrait depicts Jesus as an Indian man praying in the garden of Gethsemane (Kidwell, et al. 2001). At a recent conference, a Mohawk critic, Chris Jocks, pointedly noticed that the image, even as it clearly depicts Jesus as an Indian, is still Euro-Western. This Jesus is kneeling in prayer with his hands reverently folded just like every other Euro-Western depiction of Jesus in

---

[5]Warrior's essay, "Canaanites, Cowboys, and Indians," has been reprinted at least twice: in *Voices from the Margins,* 287–95; and in *Native and Christian,* 93–100. One should note Norman K. Gottwald's groundbreaking work in his *Tribes of Yahweh,* in which he argues for a "peasant revolt" model–as opposed to the traditional (nineteenth century) model–of conquest underlying the Exodus/Judges materials. Yet for American Indians the narrative problems remain. Whatever the actual occurrence might have been, the historical uses of the conquest narrative have fueled the Euro-Western colonial projects and have served to justify their conquests–politically, militarily, religiously, theologically, morally, and even legally.

Gethsemane. This summons pious emotion for all Euro-Western peoples, but it represents a posture of prayer that is just as decidedly NOT Indian, even as it plays on Indian themes and tries to lend a sense of cultural comfort to Indian converts.[6] Kneeling and the folding of hands are not Indian postures of prayer any more than the bowing of the head. So when the missionary says, "Let us bow our heads and pray," Indians have to wonder what the biblical injunction is that demands the bowing of heads, kneeling, or the folding of hands. Indians must ask whether that has now become the only way to pray. Obviously, I am anxious to distance myself from the decision to use that painting for the cover of our book.

Categories of discourse run far deeper than postures of prayer, however, and affect thinking processes from the mundane to the explicitly theoretical. We only have space to point to a few examples here.

Individualism

We have already noted individualism, which, as is well known, explodes into Euro-Western critical consciousness with the beginnings of modernity, the Renaissance, and René Descartes. Luther seems to me to be another overlooked progenitor, with his teaching about individual salvation invested in the great Reformation doctrine of "justification by faith." In any event, teaching American Indians to value the private ownership of property as a means of inculcating individualism became a battle cry, repeated in speech after speech, for those American religious and political leaders who would "civilize" Indians in the late nineteenth century (Prucha 1973). We, whose cultural values are based on community, were explicitly taught to say "mine" instead of "ours" and "me" instead of "us."

Creedal Language

The traditional ecumenical creeds of Euro-Western Christianity are deeply rooted in the categories of late classical (Hellenistic) Greek philosophy, of Stoicism, and of middle Platonism. All Euro-Christian theology since has built implicitly or explicitly on these categorical distinctions. Christian seminaries still dutifully teach the complexity of early Christian debates dealing with the essence or substance of deity as if these Greek Christian decisions describe something that was actually real rather than a cultural metaphor for the real.

What does it mean that the father and the son are of the same substance rather than of a similar substance? To an American Indian the words can have little meaning at all within our cultural frames of reference unless we

---

[6]It makes no difference that the image was created by an Indian artist. The colonized are capable of, and to wit have been trained to, recreate colonial imagery as our own. Ngugi wa Thiong'o, like Fanon and Memmi before him, describes the process as the colonization of the indigenous mind itself; see *Decolonizing the Mind.*

purposefully distance ourselves from our own worlds and intentionally immerse ourselves in the substance of the world of the Euro-West. Spirit and substance are antithetical notions for Indian peoples; at least they are antithetical in the sense of a reciprocal dualism of spirit and matter. Wakonda, the sacred other, the primordial creative force, or god–whatever this thing is, Indians conceive of it as spirit or energy. This means, to talk about "god" as having "substance" is, for us, bizarre at best. Hence, to engage in Christian theology and Christian history once again requires that we engage in wholehearted denial of our own world of knowledge and experience to affirm the colonizer's (Greek/Hellenistic) understanding of the world.

Language of Fall and Redemption

Another aspect of missionary Christianity destined to be forever difficult for Indian people is the Euro-Western religious language of fall and redemption. Sin is the universal starting point in the Euro-Christian religious proclamation, with salvation in Jesus posited in some form as the answer to the problem of sin and fall.[7] This functions as an additional factor of stress in American Indian communities where people continue to suffer from the effects of conquest by European immigrants over the past five centuries. We live with the ongoing stigma of defeated peoples who have endured genocide; the intentional dismantling of cultural values; forced confinement on less desirable lands called "reservations;" intentionally nurtured dependency on the federal government; and conversion by missionaries who imposed a new culture on us as readily as they preached the gospel. All this has resulted in a current situation marked by a dreadful poverty and community distress not usually associated with the United States in the minds of the international community.

More to the point, its pervasive result is a depreciated level of self-esteem that all too readily internalizes any missionary preaching that intends first to convict people of their sin. Needless to say, this internalized self-depreciation is filtered through a lens of racial inferiority imposed by generations of conquest. White Christians see the inferiority of Indian peoples through one lens, while Indian peoples internalize this idea of racial inferiority through another lens. The end result is that for both groups, Indian "sinfulness" is seen as somehow connected to their racial/ethnic identity.

Unfortunately by the time the preacher gets to the "good news" of the gospel, people are so bogged down in their experience and internalization of brokenness and lack of self worth that too often they never quite hear

---

[7]See my argument in more detail in "The Integrity of Creation," *Ecumenical Review,* 527–36.

the proclamation of good news in any actualized, existential sense. Both in terms of intrinsic Native American values, then, and in terms of Native American sociological and psychological realities, a fall/redemption starting point is singularly unhelpful and even destructive. To the contrary, any Indian theoretical notion of the world and the role of human beings in it would begin with the creation of the whole as a gift, meaning a first article/creation starting point would form a natural bond with indigenous cultural roots. While the ecumenical creeds all include creation in a first article, they also commonly over-weight the second article, a tendency that has been exacerbated in modern Euro-Western ecclesial life.

Forced Adoption of Western Theology

If the convert is required to adopt Israelite history, on the one hand, it becomes an important part of the conversion experience for Indian people to adopt European history as well–at least, to a certain extent. If one is to become a "theologian" in my institution, it is expected that one will have studied the full history of European theological development, even if one intends to pursue an indigenous theology. In other words, it is not enough to know indigenous theology, but one must be at least well-enough versed to put it into the framework of nineteenth and twentieth-century European thinkers, from Schleirmacher and Hegel to Kierkegaard and Barth. In designing a course on "Western science and indigenous knowledge," I was chastised because I failed to include Whitehead in the discussion–not to mention other Western philosophers and theologians. In this way our own traditions are rejected out of hand as having any possible credibility as sources of knowledge (science) unless they can be measured against the presumed normativity of Euro-Western theology, science, and philosophy.

In this regard, Indian Christians–and other indigenous Christians–are destined to be forever "one down." This comes about because they are not native speakers of or educated in the technical languages of Christianity–Greek, Hebrew, German, Latin, Italian, etc. Neither are they as comfortably conversant in the cultural-linguistic concepts almost automatically presumed by Euro-Western Christians. Thus, Indian Christians must rely on "professional" interpretations of their Christian faith (i.e., Euro-Western interpretations) from the missionaries that the denominations have sent us. Even when we do learn Greek and Hebrew, we learn it from the same professional Euro-Western interpreters. Thus, we merely learn to mimic the colonizer who always knows more Greek and Hebrew than we seem to learn. If an Indian does become a scholar with intense language skills and resources, it always seems as if we lose that person to a deeply acculturated and possibly assimilated status within White church or White society. Then mimicry becomes even more enhanced. That is, in our mimicry, we always learn the technical language and concepts through those Euro-Western lenses of concepts like individualism.

Imposed Liberation Language

Even traditional liberation theologies' radical resistance language–like the "preferential option for the poor"–can become just another example of imposed language. This is a laudable and liberative notion within the Christian tradition, yet it does not immediately speak to Indian peoples as it speaks to so many others in the Third World or to those ethnic minorities in the United States. While the concept is attractive in one sense, for Indians it represents too neat a packaging of things in a traditional Christian language category. It sets priorities that are not ours. However well meaning, they remain priorities imposed by others.

Indian people are the poorest ethnic community in North America. Yet the language of "option for the poor" is nearly meaningless language for Indians. "The poor" as a category presumes a radically non-Indian world of social hierarchy, socioeconomic organization, and a social class structure. These are all foreign to traditional Indian communities. Furthermore, it implies a socialist (if not outright Marxist) analysis and proposed solution completely at odds with American Indian aspirations.

As I have argued in an earlier essay, Indian people want affirmation not as "persons" (Gutiérrez's language) or as individuals, but rather as national communities with discrete cultures, discrete languages, discrete value systems, and our own governments and territories (Tinker 1994, 119–32). To put it in straightforward language, Indian people do not aspire to be recognized in terms of class structure as workers, the proletariat, peasants, or even as ethnic minorities. We should add that "production," the Marxist category, is of little interest to Indians for whom the land is primary. Should the workers of the world finally unite and take control of the means of production, then Indian people will still be in the same bind they find themselves in today. The only change is that the means of production–and the control of Indian land–will shift from the upper (capitalist) class to a new class structure that must assimilate all cultures into itself and work to destroy Indian particularity and difference. The results will be no different than the imposition of the Christianity brought by the missionaries.

Rather, the Indian aspiration is to be recognized as peoples, as distinct communities living distinct cultures. Thus cultural autonomy becomes primary for any indigenous community rather than Euro-Western (Marxist) categories of class analysis. Indigenous peoples would certainly form a more or less united front of resistance against capitalism, Euro-Western notions of representative democracy, the forces of globalization, and Amer-European hegemony in general. They would never, however, create an indigenous rush to Marxist-style class analysis or political notions of socialism. The goal of every indigenous community is to be recognized as a community, as a cultural whole. We want an identity distinct from the colonial settler hordes who have surrounded us, murdered our ancestors, stolen our property, forced their education on our peoples, and made every attempt to deny us cultural continuity of language and community solidarity. Socialism provides no real solace for those who have suffered thus. Indeed, socialism intends the destruction of cultural autonomy just as much–even if for different reasons–as democratic capitalism.

For American Indians, the problem with this theological/ hermeneutic procedure is that it continues to presume the universality of the colonizer's religious foundations even as it radically reinterprets those foundations against the colonizer's self. In sum, while the claim for liberation can play on Christian and biblical themes, these are not *our* themes or *our* language. We will have to look elsewhere for freedom.

Liberating Renaissance of Indian Traditional Religious Structures

We are left yet with some choices. The liberation track I will argue for here affirms the old covenant promises that the creator has given Indian peoples. This style of liberation theology presumes that those promises are still good and appropriate for Indian peoples even if they dissolve into New Age pablum (that is, pabulum) when appropriated or misappropriated by our non-Native relatives. When my brother decided some years ago to bring the sun dance back to the Osage people, that was a clear liberative act with deep theological implications for the Osage Nation. The revival of the sun dance in so many plains and prairie Indian communities over the past twenty-five years is indicative of a larger movement among Indian peoples to reclaim the religious traditions and ceremonies denied us by the missionaries and even by federal policy and actual legal interdiction.

Nearly two decades ago, I suggested that Christian Indians (and colonial settler Christians) need to think of our traditional Indian cultures with their rich stories and powerful ceremonies as part of an "old testament" tradition. This tradition might become for Indian Christians the only appropriate foundation for affirming Jesus and expressing a Christian commitment.[8] Why adopt someone else's "testament" when we have had our own all along?

Ceremonial Revivification and New Age Colonialists

This suggests that the hundreds of traditional stories told and dozens of ceremonies observed in each of our different Indian cultures are indeed

---

[8]This idea was picked up by Steve Charleston (Choctaw), then on the faculty at Luther Theological Seminary in St. Paul. See his essay, "The Old Testament of Native America," in *Lift Every Voice,* 49–61. An African theologian, Kwame Bediako, *Christianity in Africa,* has made a similar argument in terms of "ancestor worship" serving as preparatory for the advent of Christianity in Africa. Kwasikwakye-Nuako, a Ghanaian scholar and former student of mine, has critiqued Bediako as not being bold enough, and implicitly his critique would apply to Charleston. Kwasikwakye-Nuako, "The Akan People, Ancestors and Christmas," 175–204. He writes, "Important as Bediako's arguments are, I regard his reflections to be triumphal; a characteristic of what I consider as bourgeois theology, in which Christianity remains the only true religion [to which] all others must succumb" (194).

more than mere pagan superstitions made up by human beings to satisfy the needs of communities at given points in time.[9] Rather, these traditions need to be respected as gifts from the creator, gifts given to the people to help them achieve balance and harmony in the world. We must not think of our traditions as somehow diametrically opposed in spirit and substance to the traditions of ancient Israel and Christianity. We think it is time to recognize something about this thing that our Christian relatives call "god." Their "god" has and historically has had multiple relationships in the world with huge varieties of peoples and cultures all over the world, even at that moment when the Jesus event was emerging in Palestine two millennia ago.

One possible Indian response, then, that would take Christian conversion and commitments seriously, would be to insist that we Indian people must be free to interpret the gospel for ourselves, even constructing an interpretation of Jesus on the "old" testament foundation of ancient tribal traditions. That, of course, is a difficult thing to achieve, given the deep roots of our colonization–physically, emotionally, intellectually, and spiritually. The controlling impetuses of every denomination are loath to allow Indians to move very far away from the denomination's central doctrinal focus in their own attempts to reinterpret.

We could argue that an interpretation of Galatians 5:1 gives Indian peoples the freedom "in Christ" to continue to practice their ancient and traditional ceremonies and rites. "For Christ has made you free" ought to allow for a great variety of religious experience and not merely cute liturgical inventions to "make" the gospel or worship "more relevant." We could ask missionaries and bishops alike: Exactly how free are Indian people to pray the way they want to or have done for generations?

Yet the internalization of colonialism in our personal and communal psyche, quite apart from denominations' continuing colonial control mechanisms, means that many Indian Christians are already so deeply inculcated in the act of disavowing their own traditions that they reject the very freedom that the gospel seems to preach. They have been taught that our own spiritual traditions and ceremonies are actually dangerous things to be avoided, that they can cause harm, that the spirits that are summoned can hurt people, that those who practice them will surely go to hell.

A corollary argument for the continuing validity of our traditions would allow Indians to choose another path. Especially since World War II, most Euro-Western and Amer-European Christians have finally begun to concede that God's promises (Old Testament) with the Jews must still be good, that God would not have summarily reneged on God's promise to them.

[9]The latter, of course, is only one of the traditional missionary arguments–the more liberal and generous argument. Others straightforwardly asserted that the stories and ceremonies derived directly from Satan and characterized them as elements of devil worship.

Otherwise, a logical problem would necessarily leave Christians with a sense of God's capriciousness that would allow them little faith in God's intention to keep the new promise in Jesus as the Christ. If God can renege on one promise, what makes us so sure that God will not change God's mind with regard to the new promise? In the same way, Indian people need to argue that creator's promises to each of our tribes, invested in our traditional stories and traditional ceremonies, are still valid and still a source of life and liberation for Indian peoples. We need to find the courage and strength to insist as whole communities that our traditional perspectives of and experiences of the Sacred are just as valid as the perspectives of the colonial Christianity imposed on our ancestors and enforced to this day by denominational mission dollars.

Thus, I want to argue that Indian people who are serious about liberation–about freedom and independence–must commit themselves to the renewal and revival of their tribal ceremonial life, bringing their ancient ceremonies back into the center of their community's political existence. More to the point, it may be important to live these traditions quite apart from any attempt to force them into some indigenous pattern of Christianity. Small groups within nearly every reservation community have made the move back to their ancient traditions, but seldom has this movement embraced the whole of a national community in such a way that the ceremonies have become once again the spiritual base for the political cohesiveness of an independent nation. To make this move may require a boldness that is able to say clearly that "Jesus" is not the answer for all Indians.

To say "Jesus is the answer" is to assume a Euro-Western question to begin with, to say nothing of the hegemony of the Amer-European denominational structures that direct mission activities on reservations. How can Jesus be the answer to the question of Indian genocide or, say, to the massacre of several hundred people at Sand Creek? How is Jesus the answer to the intentional destruction of our Indian cultures and languages–perpetrated by the missionaries first of all? More to the point, if we can successfully argue the continuing validity of god's promises to us in our traditional ceremonial prayer life, what is it that Jesus might offer our peoples in addition to the life promised in the regular completion of certain ceremonies? And what compromises must we Indians make in order to affirm Jesus as our own? Will we have to concede the intrinsic goodness of our colonial invaders and finally concede the historical thefts of our property?

While our traditional ceremonies do not address the trauma of Indian historical losses directly, they also were not participatory in causing those losses in the same way that Christianity and the missionaries were. After five hundred years of conquest and missionary imposition, it seems time for Indian communities to resuscitate their old, communal ways of relating to the Sacred, to find life for the peoples in those ceremonial ways and cultural values.

Thus, the ceremonies in which I participated at the Sand Creek massacre site are representative of a widespread revival of traditional Indian cultures and religious traditions. And the experiences I shared on those two occasions are also representative of the deep spiritual powers we know are an everyday part of our world. To buy into colonial Christianity means that Indians have to shut their ears to the chatter of spirits and close their eyes to the blessing presence of sacred energy like the woman spirit that came to us that day.

While the revivification of Indian tribal ceremonies must be seen as a source of healing and liberation for Indian peoples, these traditions must be understood within the parameters of tribal cultures and dare not be suddenly understood within the context of the colonizers' cultural traditions and values. Even as I write this essay, the cultural values inherent in ceremonial traditions such as the sun dance are shifting noticeably away from the *aged-old* communitarian values of "dancing for the people," to dancing "that the people might live." As more and more non-Indian relatives invade our ceremonies as the newest and hottest exotic playground, the values have shifted to address the needs and cultural values of these tourists. The sun dance is increasingly danced for the purpose of personal (individual) achievement, a new and exotic source of individual salvation and personal empowerment.

I would encourage our Amer-European relatives to find another way to find their own center of balance rather than invading our ceremonies and imposing their presence on Indian communities at moments of ceremonial intimacy. Indeed, there is unfinished business that deeply affects the spiritual well-being of our White relatives, business that cries out for attention today.

An Indian Challenge to our Amer-European Colonizer Relatives

For American Indians to deal constructively with contemporary realities, our struggle for liberation must go one step further. At our best, we understand that our liberation is not possible without the liberation of our White relatives who share this continent with us. We American Indians realize that our continued existence represents something of an embarrassment for White America since we serve as a constant reminder of America's history of violence. Yet the guilt will not simply evaporate with the final death of Indian people. We stand as a source of judgment over against the continued Amer-European occupancy of North America. We will always present Americans with a choice. Either confess and acknowledge that history and move beyond it in a constructive, healing way, or engage the addicts' device of denial and keep those memories deeply suppressed and repressed where they will continue to fester and disrupt all of American life and well-being.

An American Indian theology of liberation, then, will hold the colonizer to his and her own best spiritual and moral imperatives:

Thus, in the name of Jesus we call on all White Christians to

1. confess, that is, to acknowledge the American history of violence: violence as military genocide, as political genocide, as cultural genocide, and particularly as the spiritual genocide of missionary conquest;
2. cease and desist from any attempts to impose their beliefs on others. Especially we call on them to resist the temptation to attempt to convert tribal peoples from their ancient and god-given spiritual and religious traditions;
3. resist judgment of our religious and ceremonial traditions. The ways missionaries, government officials, professional academics, and Hollywood have interpreted these traditions are not the ways in which our ancestors actually lived them. Nor do they accord with our contemporary experience of our own world. Allow us to interpret our own traditions and cultures for ourselves–without judgmental second-guessing. After all, the vast majority of White interpretations of our religious traditions have been self-serving validations for Euro-Western and Amer-European conquest. Christianity is conceived as so much better than what Indian people believed that it must justify all the killing and stealing of American history;
4. reflect deeply and honestly on their own history and its contemporary manifestations in the form of mass consumption, commodification, the globalization of capital, and the establishment of a new world empire predicated on White American hegemony.

Challenges for Indian People

Even as I call on Amer-European (White) people to engage me and other Indian people in dialogue about the struggle for Indian freedom, I also want to end this essay by calling on Indian people to take their cultures and traditions seriously. If we want to be free and want our grandchildren to be free, then we need to do some things to secure a liberated future and to break away from the bondage we have experienced under the tutelage of Amer-European values, education, economics, and politics. We Indian peoples must realize several things:

1. Culture is lived by people; it is not something preserved in museums. Therefore, we Indian peoples must live the traditional cultural values of our peoples as faithfully as we can.
2. Our movement for liberation must be a spiritual movement as much as it is political. We must relearn that spirituality and politics are not separate but go together and need each other.
3. Our traditional spirituality and cultural values must become a real part of everything we do as Indian persons, as political action groups, as

nations participating in our ceremonies, and especially as Indian communities.

4. Liberation is freedom to practice, recover, restore, reinvent, etc., whatever tribal/indigenous practices and lifeways are enriching, healing, and life-sustaining.
5. Each one of us must strive to be personally in balance. We must live spiritually every day and every moment in balance within ourselves and with the people around us. We must live in harmony with the ceremonies we so affirm, in harmony with our tribal communities and their aspirations; and in balance with all our relations in this world. Those relations include our nonhuman relations–the two-leggeds, the four-leggeds, the winged, and all the living-moving-things, from rocks and trees to mountains and fish.
6. Affirmation of our own cultural values must accompany a commitment to live those values in the face of forces that insist on an increasingly globalized culture of commodification and consumption. We must, then, join our voices in solidarity with all those in the world today who are engaged in overt resistance against Amer-European hegemony and the globalization of capital.

These are the commitments to liberation we owe to the memory of those ancestors who gave so much in the colonial contest that resulted in the loss of our lands and the loss of so many lives during the last five hundred and ten years.

20

Feminist Theology

KAREN K. SEAT

The critical principle of feminist theology is the promotion of the full humanity of women. Whatever denies, diminishes, or distorts the full humanity of women is, therefore, appraised as not redemptive. Theologically speaking, whatever diminishes or denies the full humanity of women must be presumed not to reflect the divine or an authentic relation to the divine.

—ROSEMARY RADFORD RUETHER (1983, 18–19)

Feminist liberation theologians,[1] in solidarity with other liberation movements, seek to articulate a vision of God, scripture, and community that speaks to women's struggle for justice and redemption in a world where their full humanity is often denied. Feminist theology in the United States has developed as part of larger feminist movements, which have sought to change laws and cultural norms that have been oppressive to women. While some feminists in the United States focus primarily on gaining equality for women within the present socioeconomic system, liberationist feminists more radically challenge the system itself. They believe that existing systems

[1]While feminist thought is part of many religious traditions today (especially in the United States), this chapter will focus on Christian feminist theology.

of Western thought and life are inherently dependent upon unequal power distributions. In this vein, feminist liberation theologians call for the transformation of existing religious and social systems. Feminist liberation theologians envision a world that supports the well-being and dignity of all creation. Thus these theologians do not accept the terms of present institutions and ideologies, which are most often based on exploitation and hierarchy. They believe that to be committed to such a vision of justice is to be true to the redemptive call of the divine.

Historical Overview

Backdrop to Feminist Liberation Theology

In its laws and culture, the United States was founded as a patriarchal country. "Patriarchy" can be defined literally as the "rule of the fathers." A patriarchal society, by definition, is oriented toward a hierarchical distribution of power (e.g., men ruling over women). Such a society usually contains multiple power imbalances, including racial hierarchies and class hierarchies. This has certainly been the case in the United States. Throughout American history, white men of means have held most of the country's political and economic power. Supported by custom and law, men of means had the self-appointed right not only to determine the course of their own lives, but the lives of others, including white women and people of underprivileged classes, races, and ethnicities. The continuing effort to change the policies, ideologies, and customs supporting this rule of the privileged few has been long and hard. This has created a fundamental paradox in American history, for the predominant rhetoric of American society has been focused on ideas of individual freedoms and equality, while at the same time many Americans, especially those in positions of power, have passionately defended gender, race, and class hierarchies.

A primary reason Americans have so often defended patriarchy (and other hierarchies) is because traditional Christian worldviews seem to justify the maintenance of such inequalities. In the view of many American Christians, past and present, the Christian Bible mandates the rule of men in the home, church, and society as a whole. Any attempt to change patriarchy, therefore, has been seen as a challenge to the laws of God. Only as their understandings of God and the Bible have changed have Americans been able to think in new ways about gender.

Origins of Feminist Theology

The First Wave

Feminist theology had its origins in attempts to reconceptualize God and the Bible in ways that were supportive of gender equality. One of the earliest works of feminist theology in the United States was *The Woman's Bible* (1895), a project initiated by Elizabeth Cady Stanton. Stanton was one of the founders of "first wave" feminism in the U.S., which developed as a major organized movement in the nineteenth century. Its participants sought to change laws that defined women as the subordinates of men and to extend men's civil rights to include women as well, such as the right to vote (suffrage). Women and men involved in first wave feminism encountered seemingly endless roadblocks and hostility in their seventy-two-year struggle to gain women's suffrage (1848–1920).

After nearly fifty years in the struggle, Stanton was convinced that traditional understandings of Christianity had to change or women would never gain full equality in the United States. At that time, the general American public believed it was morally dangerous for women to have political and economic opportunities, because God's design was for women to be wives and mothers, living in joyful submission to men as their providers. With *The Woman's Bible*, edited by Stanton, numerous women theologians challenged the way biblical passages were used to justify women's subordination (thus *The Woman's Bible* was more of an examination of the Christian Bible than a "Bible" itself). However, such challenges to traditionally accepted approaches to scripture were too radical to be accepted in their time. Not only did the American public reject Stanton's theological project as a whole, but she was censured by her own women's suffrage organization.

Subsequently, American belief in the scriptural foundation of women's subordination went largely unchallenged well into the twentieth century. Even though American women finally gained the right to vote in 1920, their subordinate status did not change significantly, as women's participation in the economy, politics, religious organizations, and other central institutions of American society continued to be severely limited.

The Second Wave

The second-wave feminist movement arose in the 1960s as women began to organize once again to overcome the inequalities and obstacles they faced because of their gender. A number of second-wave feminists believed that Christianity was such a thoroughly sexist religion that it could only hinder women's liberation. Christianity certainly did not have a good track record. Even as the U.S. government was beginning to institute laws aimed at fostering more equality between women and men (such as the Equal Pay Act of 1963), many Christian organizations continued to openly advocate patriarchal values. Such organizations denounced the feminist movement. Feminists like Mary Daly called for women to develop new, post-Christian religious spaces, for she believed moving beyond Christianity was key if women were to move beyond patriarchy.[2]

---

[2]Mary Daly was a pioneer in developing feminist theology, beginning with her publication *The Church and the Second Sex,* in which she challenged the Christian community to purge itself of sexism. Later, she identified her perspective as "post-Christian", her case for rejecting Christianity can be seen in works such as *Gyn/ecology.*

A number of feminist theologians, however, believed Christianity was compatible with feminism and had the potential to be a positive force in the movement for women's liberation. These theologians, such as Elisabeth Schüssler Fiorenza, Rosemary Radford Ruether, Letty Russell, and Phyllis Trible were influential in transforming the way many American Christians thought about gender.[3] Feminist theologians made the case that it was against the will of God for women to be subordinated because of their gender, and they called on Christians to examine the Bible, theology, and religious organizations with this assumption.

The Continuing Situation

Even though a growing number of American Christians have developed a feminist consciousness since the second wave feminist movement of the 1960s and 1970s, much opposition to feminist theology and the feminist movement in general has continued within sectors of American Christianity. The rise of the religious right in the late twentieth century was in large part a response to the changing ideas of gender in American society. Since the 1970s, organizations such as the Moral Majority, the Christian Coalition, Concerned Women for America, and the Council on Biblical Manhood and Womanhood have devoted much energy to counteracting the feminist movement. This resistance is largely due to the fact that many Christians have continued to focus on biblical texts that seem to mandate women's subordinate status.

Thus, as it was for feminists in the nineteenth century, biblical studies and interpretation have been crucial for feminist theologians in the late twentieth and early twenty-first centuries. Feminist theologians have highlighted sources in scripture and Christian history that support full gender equality, asserting that patriarchal versions of Christianity have been perverted by the "sin of sexism." Based on in-depth investigations of biblical texts and human experience, feminist theologians have built a solid foundation for their belief in the divine message of liberation and equality.

Biblical Starting Points

The Bible is not a single book, but a collection of numerous documents, written in Hebrew and Greek over a period of many centuries and in various literary styles. It has been translated into English multiple times, because there is no consensus on how to translate the original, ancient languages and because the English language itself has changed over the course of history. A complex document, the Bible has been studied and interpreted in countless ways.

---

[3]Since the 1960s, feminist theology has become a vast field of inquiry with many contributors, too numerous to cover in this brief introduction.

In looking to the Bible for answers on gender, a problem immediately arises: the Bible contains contradictory messages about the value and status of women. Some biblical passages affirm patriarchy, even as others affirm the full equality of women and men. For example, the Old Testament begins with the pronouncement that both men and women are created in the image of God (Gen. 1:26–27). Yet, as Phyllis Trible states, there are "texts of terror" throughout the Old Testament, in which women's lives are presented as expendable, such as Hagar's abuse and rejection in Genesis 16:1–16 and 21:9–21, or the betrayal, rape and murder of an unnamed woman in Judges 19:1–30. Similar contradictions appear in the New Testament. The apostle Paul, for example, states that in the Christian faith, "there is no longer male and female; for all of you are one in Christ Jesus" (Gal. 3:28). Later, Paul (or someone writing in the name of Paul, as some biblical scholars believe) states that "women should be silent in the churches.... [they] should be subordinate, as the law also says" (1 Cor. 14:34).

So how does one arrive at a satisfactory interpretation of what the Bible has to say about women? Feminist theologians have generally applied the following principles to their biblical interpretation:

1. The life and message of Jesus provide the basic criteria by which the rest of the Bible (and the entire Christian tradition) can be evaluated.
2. The social and political impact of biblical interpretation on women (and others) must be taken seriously. If a particular biblical interpretation perpetuates social injustices, including social injustices against women, then it is not seen as an interpretation reflecting the "divine" (as indicated by Ruether's statement at the beginning of this chapter).
3. It is impossible to evaluate the Christian tradition or biblical texts from an objective or neutral standpoint. One either interprets scripture with a primary commitment to social justice, or one does not. Those who seek "objective" approaches to scripture are often confusing objectivity with their own unexamined worldviews.

Feminist Theology and Jesus

In the Christian Bible, four books known as the gospels (literally translated as the "good news") record the life and words of Jesus. The gospels were written in the years after Jesus' death. In viewing Jesus through the writings of these early Christians, feminist theologians have noted how consistently these texts portray Jesus as someone who treated women and men in radically egalitarian ways. The gospels contain numerous stories about women who were followers of Jesus, revealing that Jesus supported their decision to break with the patriarchal customs of the day to be a part of his movement. For example, in Luke 10:38–42 Jesus praises Mary for choosing to come and learn from him, even though she has left behind the "many tasks" expected of her. He proclaimed that she "has chosen the better part, which will not be taken away from her" (Lk. 10:42). In a culture where women were often seen as unclean, Jesus did not recoil from the touch of a woman with a twelve-year issue of blood; instead he commended her, stating that her faith had made her well (Mt. 9:20–22; Mk. 5:25–34; Lk. 8:43–48).

Jesus' unorthodox views of women seem to have forged an unusually committed group of female disciples. The women stayed with him during his crucifixion (Mt. 27:55–56; Mk. 15:40–41). The women found that he had been resurrected when they went to care for his body in the tomb (Mt. 28:1–10; Mk. 16:1–8; Lk. 24:1–10). The remarkable visibility of women in the gospels and Jesus' consistent acceptance of women–breaking with patriarchal traditions–illustrate the message of Galatians 3:28, that in the redeeming presence of Christ, gender differences are transcended.

Rosemary Radford Ruether views Jesus' egalitarian approach to women–as well as to the poor, the sick, outcasts, and other marginalized groups–as part of a "prophetic-liberating" tradition in the Bible. This tradition rejects "every elevation of one social group against others...every use of God to justify social domination and subjugation" (1983, 23). In light of Jesus' opposition to social hierarchies, all other biblical texts supporting human liberation can be seen as having more weight than biblical texts supporting social hierarchies. The Bible's prophetic-liberating tradition can be used to critique coexisting patriarchal texts within scripture. The Bible reveals both God's call for the full liberation of women and men, as well as the failure of God's people to fully perceive and follow this call.

Elisabeth Schüssler Fiorenza states that Jesus provided a model for how to engage in biblical interpretation itself, for "according to the Gospels [Jesus] realized freedom toward Scripture and tradition for the sake of human well-being and wholeness (cf. Mk. 2:27)" (1984, 13). Thus, to interpret scripture in accordance with Jesus' own example is to be primarily committed to human redemption, not "scriptural authority" over and above human liberation. Moreover, to say that the Bible has fixed "universal principles and timeless norms" is to limit the possibilities of the scriptures for communities of faith, both today and in the future (23). It is also to ignore the reality that the Bible has meant many different things to many different people throughout history. Instead, Fiorenza envisions the Bible as a "prototype" and a "resource" for people involved in struggles for liberation in particular historical circumstances. Since the Bible has been, in many different ways, both harmful and helpful to women (and men), it is up to those who are in specific movements for liberation to decide which biblical texts best speak to their particular circumstances (14).

Shifting the Focus from "Objective Truth" to Social Justice

Despite a strong prophetic-liberating message in the Bible, many church authorities throughout Christian history have favored the Bible's patriarchal texts. These texts have provided the basis for everything from excluding women from the priesthood to executing women accused of witchcraft.

Feminist theologians point out that Christians have often read scripture in ways that support their cultural assumptions and have confused this with "objectivity" and "truth." Why, for example, is 1 Corinthians 14:34 (cited above) so frequently highlighted to oppose women's leadership in the church, when it contradicts other biblical passages and larger biblical themes supporting full human equality? Could it be that the 1 Corinthians text more comfortably reflects the conventional values of patriarchal societies rather than challenging them?

Feminist theologians believe that the very texts used to support theological positions are themselves shaped by human perspectives embedded in language. For example, feminist theologians have shown that English translations of biblical texts have been influenced by the patriarchal biases of the translators, thereby predisposing future readers to unnecessarily sexist interpretations. Biblical scholar Phyllis Trible has made this point in her examination of the story of human creation in Genesis 2. One would assume by reading a translation of Genesis 2:7–22 that the story is about a man from whom a woman is created. This view has been influenced by the way translators understood the Hebrew word *'adam* to be referencing a male. However, Trible has shown that the Hebrew word *'adam* used in this passage is more likely a word for a gender-neutral figure–*'adam* can be read as "earth creature" (1978, 79–82, 94–105). If translated this way, Eve's creation in Genesis 2:22 is not about woman being created after man. It is about the origination of sexual differentiation; when Eve is created, the "earth creature" becomes male and female. Such a reading brings into question a traditionally held perspective that women's subordination to men is implied by the supposed secondary creation of woman in Genesis 2. Feminist theologians have raised similar challenges to numerous other biblical texts used to justify women's subjugation.

When one uncovers the worldviews embedded in biblical texts, translations, and interpretations, it becomes apparent that no "neutral" standpoint is possible. Biblical interpretation reflects the broad spectrum of human perspectives, including patriarchal and feminist views. When acknowledging the constraints of finite human perspectives, the emphasis can no longer be on "right" or "wrong" interpretations; instead the emphasis shifts to seeking an understanding that best reflects the character and spirit of the divine message.

Feminist theologians, like liberation theologians in general, are concerned with how Christianity has so often been interpreted and used in ways that have hurt people, all in the name of "truth." Feminist theologians find no compelling reason to approach the Christian tradition and scripture in any other way than to seek out the redemptive, liberating elements. Their goal is to understand and apply Christianity in ways that challenge, rather than support, the unequal power structures that characterize the world in which we live. They believe that to do otherwise would be against the spirit and message of Jesus.

Feminist Theological Ethics

With their liberationist reading of the Bible, feminist theologians call upon Christians to reshape their ethics–their values and actions–as if women really do count as full members of the body of Christ. This means that American Christians must radically alter their approaches to social issues both nationally and globally.

Liberation theologians, including feminist liberation theologians, believe American Christians have failed to adequately challenge local and global injustices because they have not developed an ethical framework that truly stands apart from the ideologies of America's ruling elite. U.S. economic practices and political policies that have had devastating effects on various populations within the United States and abroad have seemed justified to many Americans because of their uncritical acceptance of prevailing sexist, racist, and classist ideologies. Thus, not only must policies change, but the ideological foundations of these policies must also be dismantled for true social transformations to take place. Liberation theologians believe that Christians need to follow God's call and Jesus' example by actively working toward this revolutionary transformation.

Feminist liberation theologians support women in their various endeavors to survive in a capitalist, class- and race-stratified society. At the same time, they acknowledge that humans cannot achieve their full potential and live in dignity in an economy based on a gap between the rich and the poor and in an economy where private gain is valued over the well-being of the less privileged. Traditional Christian notions of charity and the so-called "Protestant work ethic" focused on the idea that "God helps those who help themselves." Such a focus fails to address adequately how debilitating the legacy of sexism and racism has been, especially in an economic system that values wealth over human community. Women have often borne the brunt of these economic realities, as they have been the primary caretakers of families, an effort not financially rewarded by the U.S. economic system. As a result of this and other liabilities related to sexism, women have generally been poorer than men and more dependent on government welfare or the financial support of others, such as their husbands. Such an economic arrangement has created situations in which women have been unable to easily escape situations of domestic violence or other oppressive contexts. Religious thought about reproduction, family, and gender roles must take into consideration these political and economic realities.

Many Americans today are worried about the breakdown of "family values." Numerous conservative Christians believe that this problem will be alleviated only when more Americans model their family life after the traditional ideal of the husband and father acting as the head of the family and breadwinner while the wife and mother devotes herself full-time to childcare and household duties. Christians who promote this vision often perceive the feminist movement to be a threat to the family. However, liberationist feminists are more likely to evaluate the "crisis of the family"–such as marital discord and often inadequate childcare–as a result of an accelerating capitalist system and continuing sexism, racism, and classism rather than as a result of women gaining more rights in society.

Feminist theologian and ethicist Beverly Wildung Harrison asserts that "[u]pward mobility in corporations and professions increasingly requires that family life be neglected." She continues to say that welfare "reform" has "targeted poor women and their children" when "the problem is a political-economic system that privileges the wealthy and obscures its own profoundly anti-democratic value system by victim-blaming" (1985, 105; 1999, x). In other words, today's economic system does not support family and community building, regardless of whether individuals focus their energies on waged labor or childcare (or on both, as is often the case). One reason feminists view conservative Christians' traditional family ideal to be inadequate is that it lacks an analysis of class dynamics. It obscures the reality that a family able to live securely on a single paycheck (rather than on a double income and/or extended community networks of support) has a rather elite, privileged social position not available to masses of Americans.

Harrison, further challenging conventional Christian approaches to contemporary social issues, writes that "[s]ince the capacity to produce income and to accumulate wealth...is the measure of personal worth in this society, anyone who does not participate in money-making will also be a priori a victim vulnerable to sexual oppression" (1985, 94). Thus, when certain Christian groups insist that a woman's God-ordained role is to stay at home as wife and mother, they are not adequately addressing the problem of women's exploitation in a capitalist society. Harrison states that "theories of women's 'special nature'...always mask the interest of those who, for whatever reason, wish to keep women 'in their place'...In the absence of a strong base of social, economic, and political power already developed by and for women themselves, there is no evidence that concern for the character and quality of women's lives will be given attention or priority" in a society where a privileged few benefit from their disempowerment (42–43).

Feminist liberation theologians have a different ideal for women and men than either the traditional family model or mere equality in the present political and economic structures. They envision a different world altogether, where the humanity of all is fully valued–not because such a vision is easily attained or even possible given our present understandings and realities, but because faith in the divine message and commitment to Jesus requires no less than this radical dream. Liberation in the current economic/political context is tenuous at best, for, in the words of Gloria Albrecht, "the pursuit of life, liberty, and happiness is destroying the very relationships upon which life, liberty, and happiness depend" (1995, 140).

Moreover, as the U.S. government and U.S.-based transnational corporations continue to restructure global dynamics to the benefit of the powerful, it is not possible for women in the United States to seek equality with privileged men without becoming complicit in the oppression of others. This moral dilemma has already become clear as upper and middle class, often white, American women have gained access to the structures that oppress others in the U.S. and globally. African American, Latina, Asian American, American Indian, and other minority women liberationists and theologians have made a particularly compelling case that those who strive to gain the rights and privileges of elite men are not in fact committed to a vision of justice.[4] bell hooks, an influential black feminist, makes the point succinctly when she states, "As long as [white women and black men] or any group defines liberation as gaining social equality with ruling class white men, they have a vested interest in the continued exploitation and oppression of others" (1984, 15).[5]

Minority Women's Liberation Theologies

Contemporary feminist theology has been profoundly influenced by minority women. The writings and activism of women who deal with multiple oppressions have challenged feminists to broaden their focus beyond gender to more fully examine the ways in which women are privileged or oppressed because of their race, class, and/or sexual orientation. As a result of minority women's influence, feminism today is

---

[4]There is no consensus on which terms to use for the social categories by which people are identified in the United States (such as race, ethnicity, sexual orientation, etc.). For example, the terms "African American," "Afro-American," or "Black"/"black" might be used by people who identify with any of these social categories. Among the indigenous peoples of the United States (and other countries in the Americas), some prefer the term "Native Americans" while others prefer "American Indians" when referring to themselves as a group; individuals, however, will usually identify with their specific Indian Nation (Apache, Lakota Sioux, Cherokee, etc.). Similarly, people in the United States with heritages in Spanish America often identify with the specific national/cultural origin of their ancestry (e.g., Mexico, Ecuador, Puerto Rico, Cuba, etc.). When referring to all people in the United States with heritages in Spanish America as a group, the terms "Latina/o" or "Hispanic" are most commonly used.

[5] bell hooks (who spells her name using all lowercase letters) identifies herself as a feminist rather than as a womanist, but her work is similar to that of womanists in her critiques of the racism of white feminist movements and the sexism of black liberation movements.

often called "third-wave" feminism, since it has largely moved beyond second-wave feminism's narrow focus on gender alone.

Rejecting Feminism

While many minority women have redefined the meaning of feminism to include their concerns, a number of women have rejected the term, because they have experienced the feminist movement, in Korean-American theologian Jung Ha Kim's words, as "someone else's movement" (e.g., a movement for middle class white women) (1997, 24). Therefore, for example, African American women theologians have widely used the term "womanist," and a number of Latina theologians have chosen to use the term "mujerista," instead of "feminist."

African American women theologians, in developing womanist theology, have emphasized that women are not a unified group and that women themselves are capable of being oppressors because of factors such as race and class privilege.[6] While womanists agree with feminists that sexism has shaped the lives of all women throughout American history, their experiences reveal that sexism affects women differently depending on their race and class. Womanists have challenged all liberation theologians to give more careful attention to the distinctive ways individual groups have been shaped by multiple social hierarchies, in order to avoid perpetuating oppressive practices and ideologies.

African American Women's Issues

While womanists support women in all social groups who seek to develop their own theologies and movements, womanist theologians are particularly committed to African American women's issues, which have been quite different from middle class white women's concerns. Katie Geneva Cannon, in *Black Womanist Ethics*, poignantly makes the point that African American women's experiences of sexism and patriarchy have been fundamentally linked to the realities of race and class when she states:

> The structure of the capitalist political economy in which Black people are commodities combined with patriarchal contempt for women has caused the Black woman to experience oppression that knows no ethical or physical bounds...Black women have never been granted the protective privileges that allow one to become immobilized by fear and rage. The Black woman's very life depends upon her being able to decipher the various sounds in the larger world, to hold in check the nightmare figures of terror,

[6]The growing number of influential womanist theologians today includes Karen Baker-Fletcher, Katie Geneva Cannon, Kelly Brown Douglas, Cheryl Townsend Gilkes, Jacquelyn Grant, Diana L. Hayes, Cheryl A. Kirk-Duggan, Marcia Y. Riggs, Cheryl J. Sanders, Emilie M. Townes, Renita J. Weems, Delores S. Williams, and others.

> to fight for basic freedoms against the sadistic law enforcement agencies in her community, to resist the temptation to capitulate to the demands of the status quo, to find meaning in the most despotic circumstances and to create something where nothing was before. (1988, 4, 125–26)

Throughout U.S. history, race, sex, and class oppression have been inexorably connected for African American women, because of the devastating economic ramifications of racism linked with sexism. Thus, reflecting the views of womanists in general, Jacquelyn Grant emphasizes in *White Women's Christ and Black Women's Jesus* that "Black women must do theology out of their tri-dimensional experience of racism/sexism/classism. To ignore any aspect of this experience is to deny the holistic and integrated reality of Black womanhood" (1989, 209).

While white feminists have often assumed that all women have a bond resulting from a shared experience of sexism, many African American women have found this assumption to be completely out of touch with their reality, as they and their foremothers frequently experienced white women as oppressors rather than "sisters." In shaping their own movement, African American women theologians "create[d] something where nothing was before," embracing Pulitzer Prize-winning author Alice Walker's term "womanist" to describe themselves.[7] Walker articulated a widely held perception among liberationist African American women by suggesting that "the experience of being a Black woman or a White woman is so different that another word is required to describe the liberative efforts of Black women" (Grant 1989, 204).

Liberating Elements

The writings of womanist theologians have brought to life the elements of Christian tradition, biblical texts, and African American heritages that are liberative for black women. Womanist theologians view these elements to be crucial for providing black women with the spiritual strength and courage to fight racism, sexism, and classism. Womanists, like other liberation theologians, see God's presence with the oppressed and the promise of universal human liberation as a central message in the story of Jesus. In her discussion of African Americans' Christian heritage, Jacquelyn Grant states that "Christian Black women in the past...identified with Jesus because they believed that Jesus identified with them. As Jesus was persecuted and made to suffer undeservedly, so were they" (212). Moreover,

[7]Alice Walker coined the term "womanist" in *In Search of Our Mothers' Gardens: Womanist Prose*. She defined a womanist as "[a] black feminist or feminist of color" (xi). She derived the term from black folk vernacular, in which the word "womanish" connoted "outrageous, audacious, courageous or *willful* behavior" (xi).

"Black women's affirmation of Jesus as God meant that White people were not God" (213), providing a point of resistance to white domination. Most importantly, just as Jesus' suffering and crucifixion was not the whole story, suffering is not the whole story for Black women. Grant states, "For as the Resurrection signified that there is more to life than the cross for Jesus Christ, for Black women it signifies that their tri-dimensional oppressive existence is not the end, but it merely represents the context in which a particular people struggle to experience hope and liberation" (217).

Womanist theologians and biblical scholars like Renita J. Weems and Delores S. Williams, examining biblical texts in light of Black women's experiences and histories, have illuminated how scripture speaks in particular ways to various social groups. For example, Weems's *Just a Sister Away: A Womanist Vision of Women's Relationships in the Bible* and Williams's *Sisters in the Wilderness: The Challenge of Womanist God-Talk* include explorations of the biblical story of Hagar, the slave of Abraham's wife Sarah and mother of Abraham's son Ishmael (Gen. 16:1–16; 21:9–21). Both authors find this text relevant and meaningful in light of black women's experiences.

Read even at its most basic level, Hagar's story is hauntingly analogous to Black women's stories throughout American history, for, as Williams states, "Hagar's predicament involved slavery, poverty, ethnicity, sexual and economic exploitation, surrogacy, rape, domestic violence, homelessness, motherhood, single-parenting and radical encounters with God" (1993, 4). Both Weems and Williams note that Hagar's relationship with Sarah reflects the historical relationship of black and white women in the United States. Sarah had the power and position to exploit Hagar, as well as the means to ruthlessly dispose of her when she no longer found her useful or pleasing. The story reveals the worst that has been possible in women's relationships, the opposite of what women need to build a movement for liberation. As Weems states, "we, like Hagar, are in need of a woman who will 'sister' us, not exploit us" (1988, 17).

Emphasizing that African American Christians often have been most interested in the Bible's portrayal of "God's response to…situations of pain and bondage," Williams particularly focuses on the parts of Hagar's story where God intervenes with her near-death experiences in the wilderness: "[W]hen Hagar and her child were finally cast out of the home of their oppressors and were not given proper resources for survival, God provided Hagar with a resource. God gave her new vision to see survival resources where she had seen none before" (1993, 4–5). Hagar's story provides a hope even more basic than that of liberation: it reveals that the miracle of survival is possible in the most desperate of circumstances. Williams states that like generations of black women in the past, black women today can take strength from Hagar's story, for:

> [Hagar] and Ishmael together, as family, model many black American families in which a lone woman/mother struggles to hold the family together in spite of the poverty to which ruling class economics consign it. Hagar, like many black women, goes into the wide world to make a living for herself and her child, with only God by her side. (33)

Womanist theology continues to develop in the present, as womanists engage with the evolving contexts of their communities. Although a disproportionately high number of African Americans continue to struggle with the most explicit legacies of American racism (such as extreme poverty), today there is in fact a widening gap between the rich and the poor among African Americans, reflective of a growing trend in the United States generally. Thus, the relationship between racism and classism becomes ever more complex. Womanists emphasize that it is important to maintain clarity about sex, race, and class dynamics, for though "they are interrelated," they "each have lives of their own" (Grant 1989, 221). Grant asserts,

> [W]e must explore more deeply the question of what Christ means in a society in which class distinctions are increasing. If Christ is among "the least" then who are they? Because our foreparents were essentially poor by virtue of their race, there was no real need for them to address classism as a separate reality. Today, in light of the emerging Black middle class we must ask what is the impact of class upon our lives and the lives of other poor Black and Third World women and men. (221)

Grant's point is that, like Euro-American women, African American women committed to liberation theology must continuously reexamine whether or not their actions are promoting justice for all, in an increasingly complex world.

Latina and Asian American Women's Issues

As womanist theology evolved into an established, recognized field by the 1990s, Latina and Asian American theologians, among others, challenged both Euro-Americans and African Americans to move beyond thinking about the United States solely in terms of "black and white." The United States is comprised of peoples with a vibrantly wide spectrum of heritages through which Americans are connected to cultures in every part of the world. As more women with non-European heritages contribute their voices and wisdom to the canon of Christian theology, Christian understandings of humanity and the divine become ever more rich and textured. María Pilar Aquino, Daisy L. Machado, and Jeanette Rodríguez have claimed a space and a voice for those in the U.S. who have frequently been invisible to the dominant culture. In their introduction to *A Reader in Latina Feminist Theology: Religion and Justice*, they state, "We want to express in our own words our plural ways of experiencing God and our plural ways of living our faith" (xiv). Increasingly, minority women are exploring the meaning of liberation theology in their own contexts and are revealing how their contexts are relevant to the larger goals of liberation theology. They insist on remaining true to the cultural specificity of the social groups for whom they speak. As Jung Ha Kim states in reference to her writings on Korean American women's Christian theology, "my attempt to disclose the self-understanding and complex realities of Korean American women in the church setting is based on my conscious efforts to adhere to the very ethos and the language they use in telling and retelling their stories" (1997, 24).

Ada María Isasi-Díaz resonates with the goals of womanist theologians in their commitment to African American women's liberation. Isasi-Díaz has been a particularly notable pioneer in developing a theology based on the experiences and perspectives of Hispanic women. She calls her work "*mujerista* theology." She states that *mujerista* theology "seeks to discover the [religious and social] themes that are important to Latinas, the ones they feel strongest about, the ones that motivate them.... Latinas' religious understandings...are part of the ongoing revelation of God, present in the midst of the community of faith and giving strength to Hispanic Women's struggle for liberation" (1993, 1, 132).

Like other liberation theologians, Isasi-Díaz is not only committed to a particular historical struggle for liberation–that of Latina women–but she also emphasizes that an important component of contextualized liberation theologies is to encourage all people to be more inclusive and holistic. Focusing on the concrete experiences of particular oppressed groups provides a vivid, less easily dismissed picture of the reality that "[t]o be poor and oppressed means 'to die of hunger, to be illiterate, to be exploited by others, not to know that you are being exploited, not to know you are a person'" (1996, 91). Specific contexts also reflect a larger reality, in which "sexism, racism/ethnic prejudice, classism.... are not self-contained realities but are interconnected parts of a worldwide system of domination in which the few oppress the many" (91). It is only with such clarity that those committed to justice may truly begin to work in solidarity with others, for "solidarity involves understanding and undoing the connections between different forms of oppression" (92). Solidarity is based on an awareness of "the commonality of interests that links humanity" (93), while simultaneously respecting human diversity.

Perspectives on the Future

African American, Latina, Asian American, and other minority women theologians make a strong case for acting on behalf of justice. They also make clear that women as well as men in the U.S. have actively made choices to benefit from and/or ignore issues such as racism, global poverty, ecological crises, and the United States' imperialist military might. It is impossible for all of the world's people to attain the lifestyle of privileged Americans, when such wealth is based on the exploitation of cheap labor within the U.S. and in the poverty-stricken countries where the majority of the world's people live.

In the final analysis, feminist, womanist, and mujerista theologians believe that the perpetuation of patriarchy and other forms of oppression is leading to disaster for all. Phyllis Trible writes that "feminism [does] not mean a narrow focus upon women, but rather a critique of culture in light of misogyny" (1978, 7). Thus she underscores the potential universal relevance of women's liberation movements, for misogyny signifies the presence of a larger system of destructive values. Misogyny can only exist within an ideological framework glorifying domination, violence, and alienation. Ruether, among others, has shown how the justifications for domination over women have also justified the domination and exploitation of the natural world. She states that traditionally, "the way...cultures have construed the idea of the male monotheistic God, and the relation of this God to the cosmos as its Creator, have reinforced symbolically the relations of domination of men over women, masters over slaves, and (male ruling-class) humans over animals and over the earth" (1992, 3).

This relationship between human beings in social hierarchies–and between human beings and the earth–has led to a present situation in which war, terrorism, and the destruction of the biosystem shape the world we live in. It is not possible to resolve one problem, such as sexism, without addressing the worldviews supporting oppression and destruction in general. In addressing the current ecological crisis, Ruether asserts that "a healed relation to the earth...demands a social reordering to bring about just and loving interrelationship between men and women, between races and nations, between groups presently stratified into social classes, manifest in great disparities of access to the means of life" (2–3).

Such an analysis of the ideological roots of global problems today reveals that language about God–theology–is profoundly political. Changing the view of God as a domineering power over and above the earth to that of a compassionate friend, spirit of wisdom, and seeker of justice calls human beings to model themselves after a different ideal. Sallie McFague, in *Models of God: Theology for an Ecological, Nuclear Age*, states that all language about God is more about our understanding of and relationship with God than a definition of God, since God is beyond definition. Thus, language about God as the "father" or "king" is metaphorical, representing certain experiences or perceptions of God–it does not define God in full. In understanding all language about God as metaphor, she suggests that there is no reason *not* to describe God as mother, lover, or friend

(1987, 31–40, 78–87). In fact, such metaphors may be helpful for our time, as they "project a different view of power, of how to bring about change, than the royal model. It is not the power of control through either domination or benevolence but the power of response and responsibility–the power of love in its various forms" (85). Such reimaginings of God are part of the process by which feminist theologians hope humanity can exchange "the culture of competitive alienation and domination for compassionate solidarity" (Ruether1992:201).

It leads to the liberationist vision of a just society. Such a society will witness equity

1. between men and women;
2. between human groups living within regions;
3. across human communities globally;
4. between the human species and all other members of the biotic community of which we are a part; and finally
5. between generations of living things, between the needs of those alive now and those who are to come. (258)

21

Lesbian and Gay Theologies

DANIEL T. SPENCER

Being gay is far more than just a matter of sexual behavior; it is rather a whole mode of being-in-the-world, an "existential standpoint" which colors all our perceptions of and interactions with the world and one which also stands over against established cultural and religious standards for gender roles and intimate human relationships. Such an all-encompassing givenness should also nourish and undergird our efforts at spirituality and theology.

—J. MICHAEL CLARK (1989, 1)

The divine presence is incarnate—embodied—in our relational selves. Our power in relation is being shaped in the matrix of each relational self who is true to herself as relational. The justice of God, alive in us insofar as we are true to ourselves, is reflected by the mutuality in our relationships with one another, which in turn enable us to sustain creatively the tensions in which the Sacred is at home among us. To know this deeply within ourselves is serenity.

—CARTER HEYWARD (1988, 33)

Origins of Lesbian and Gay Theologies

Lesbian and Gay theologies emerged in the United States in the 1960s and 1970s in the context of the emerging lesbian and gay civil rights and liberation movements. The civil rights movement in the 1950s and 1960s and the women's movement in the 1960s and 1970s provided the theoretical framework and activist energies and strategies. With this framework and these energies and strategies, many socially marginalized groups began to name for themselves their experiences of oppression within dominant U.S. society. They created movements of social change to transform what they experienced as oppressive realities. The women's movement and "free love" countercultural movements of the sixties and seventies in particular called into question long-standing beliefs about sexuality and gender, leading to the flourishing of a sexual liberation movement in which many lesbians and gay men formed the vanguard.

Religious activism and theological reflection within this context in turn laid the groundwork for a diverse and growing body of lesbian and gay–and more recently, transgendered and bisexual–theologies. The scholarly silence about homosexuality and Christianity was broken a generation earlier with the publication in 1955 of Derrick Sherwin Bailey's book *Homosexuality and the Western Christian Tradition*, which traced the development of anti-homosexual attitudes in the West from the biblical texts through the medieval period. A few years later, Robert Wood's *Christ and the Homosexual* became one of the first theological works to advocate the inclusion of homosexual persons within church and society.

Scholars, activists, priests, and pastors built on these early works and drew on their own experience within religious communities and churches to create theological writings that challenged the pervasive homophobic attitudes and practices in Christian churches and institutions. In the 1970s, Jesuit priest John McNeill's *The Church and the Homosexual* and Virginia Ramey Mollenkott and Letha Scanzoni's *Is the Homosexual My Neighbor?* drew on changing perspectives in psychology and the natural sciences to argue that homosexuality is as natural as heterosexuality. The problems many homosexual persons experienced were a result of society's and the churches' pervasive homophobia (fear and repression of same-sex feelings and practices) rather than their homosexual orientation itself. Together with biblical scholars Tom Horner, Robin Scroggs, and George R. Edwards, these authors also began to challenge the dominant biblical view that the Bible condemned homosexuality as unequivocally sinful and unnatural, against God's will.[1] John Boswell's landmark 1980 study, *Christianity, Social Tolerance, and Homosexuality,* took gay biblical, theological, and historical studies to a deeper level. He carefully studied the social context of biblical texts and their subsequent interpretation along with the implications for how these texts are used–or misused–in arguments about homosexuality today.

[1]See Horner, *Jonathan Loved David;* Scroggs, *The New Testament and Homosexuality;* and Edwards, *Gay/Lesbian Liberation.*

What characterized these early homosexual theological works is their apologetic stance. The authors addressed the pastoral, theological, biblical, and spiritual issues lesbian and gay Christians confronted as they came out within their churches and religious communities and the widespread efforts of the churches and religious authorities to continue to exclude homosexual persons from full acceptance in the Christian community. These authors argued that homosexual persons did not need to change to become heterosexual or remain celibate (as most Christian denominations demanded) to be either "normal" or accepted by God, and they sought to answer dominant and anti-gay biblical and theological arguments with alternative, gay-affirming perspectives.

Churches Affirming the Movement

Apologetic gay and lesbian theologies coincided with, and often grew out of, the rise of lesbian and gay-affirming caucuses within most of the mainline Protestant and Roman Catholic denominations. Dignity within the Roman Catholic Church, Lutherans Concerned within the Evangelical Lutheran Church in America, Affirmation within the United Methodist Church, the More Light movement in the Presbyterian Church (USA), and the Coalition for Lesbian and Gay Concerns within the United Church of Christ all advocated and worked for full inclusion of lesbian and gay Christians within their respective denominations. Lesbian and gay theologies of this period largely reflected these concerns and struggles in their efforts to provide biblical and theological grounding for the full inclusion of lesbian and gay people within the Christian church. As queer theologian Robert Goss notes, "Gay theology in the eighties centered on two issues: biblical texts that were used to justify homosexuality as sin and psychological issues of sexual orientation to deconstruct moral theologies based on natural law" (2002, 240).

These efforts continued to be thwarted in most denominations–and in some cases provoked a backlash such as in the 1986 Vatican prohibition of Dignity's meeting in Catholic churches. This led many lesbian and gay theologians and activists to move to a much more critical stance of Christian churches, theology, and tradition. No longer content to work for full inclusion in the churches, lesbian and gay scholars began to incorporate the frameworks of liberation and feminist theologies to argue that homophobia, heterosexism, and sexism lay at the very core of the Christian tradition. They contended that these evils needed to be rooted out and transformed if Christianity were to be faithful to the liberating message of the gospel. These authors argued that lesbians and gay men must stand on the authority of their own embodied experience to challenge external authorities of scripture, tradition, and psychology that were used to justify their exclusion and subordination in church and society.

At the same time, tensions were emerging within the lesbian and gay movement in the churches. Lesbian theologians such as Carter Heyward and Mary Hunt grounded their activism and theology within feminism. Hence they linked their critiques of homophobia and heterosexism with critiques of sexism to argue that patriarchal notions of gender and sexuality must be transformed for lesbian and gay people–as well as all women and other marginalized groups–to experience full liberation. Gay male theology, in contrast, largely overlooked issues of sexism, focusing instead on homophobic church practices, including the exclusion or expulsion of gay and lesbian clergy, the denial of ordination to openly gay and lesbian seminarians, and the refusal to bless same-sex unions.[2]

Moving Beyond Apologetics

Within this context, lesbian theologian Carter Heyward was among the first lgbt (lesbian, gay, bisexual, transgendered) theologians to move away from an apologetic framework to articulate an explicitly lesbian feminist theology of liberation. Her 1984 book, *Our Passion for Justice: Images of Power, Sexuality, and Liberation,* gathered together her writings and sermons from the previous decade where she had begun to develop her theological analysis and critique of relations of power along lines of sexuality and gender within church and society. Essays such as "Lesbianism and the Church," "Theological Explorations of Homosexuality," and "Sexuality, Love, and Justice," began the shift in lgbt theological discourse away from merely seeking full inclusion within Christianity to a profound critique of Christianity itself for the ways it is rooted in and reinforces patriarchy.

Heyward developed this theological analysis more fully in her 1989 book, *Touching Our Strength: The Erotic as Power and the Love of God.* She critiques the dualistic and heterosexist character of the Christian theological tradition, while also developing a constructive theological and moral alternative, grounded in reclaiming our embodied experiences of the erotic in relations of mutuality as a central experience of God. In introducing her book, she writes "In struggling to come to terms with the pervasiveness of evil in our life together...I have become increasingly interested in probing the character of that which is radically good in our common life: our power in mutual relation as the basis of our creative and liberating possibilities, literally the only basis of our hope for the world" (1989, 18). Building on

[2]For an example of some of the differences and dialogue around these differences between lesbian and gay male theologies, see Heyward, "Embodying the Connections," and Hunt, "Opposites Do Not Always Attract," in Clark and Stemmeler, eds., *Spirituality and Community,* 133–63. For a response to Heyward and Hunt, see Gorsline and Spencer, "Putting Our Bodies on the Line" in *The Journal of Men's Studies,* 291–309.

the groundbreaking work of the lesbian African American writer Audre Lorde, Heyward reclaims the erotic to articulate a sexual theology. This theology is rooted in embodied, mutual relationship that calls into question dualistic and patriarchal configurations of gender and sexuality that privilege male over female, heterosexual over homosexual, disembodied love as *agape* over embodied *eros*.

Also in 1989, J. Michael Clark's groundbreaking book, *A Place to Start: Toward an Unapologetic Gay Liberation Theology*, was published. Several features of Clark's book distinguish it from earlier gay male theologies. As the title suggests, Clark sought to break from an apologetic approach and explicitly incorporate a liberation theology framework that drew from the authority of gay male experience to articulate theology. Clark writes also from an explicitly pro-feminist gay male stance, learning from and in dialogue with feminist theologians such as Heyward and Rosemary Radford Ruether to name patriarchy as the primary social context and contradiction that leads to gay oppression. Finally, Clark writes within the context of the explosion of the AIDS pandemic as an openly gay man with AIDS who has seen his primary community devastated in recent years. Not only homophobia, but also "AIDS-phobia, structure the oppressive context against which gay men must struggle for liberation" (1989, 49).[3]

A Move to Academic Settings

Heyward's and Clark's publications also mark a tenuous shift in the context of lgbt theologies to an increasingly academic setting. Up to and through the 1980s, institutional hostility to openly lesbian and gay scholars largely prevented these scholars from either landing academic jobs or being able to write openly about lgbt themes. Increasingly, some graduate students and young faculty were writing about these issues, risking career possibilities to create and advance the much-needed theological discussion around lgbt concerns. In 1987 at the annual meeting of the American Academy of Religion in Boston, Michael Clark and Michael Stemmeler cofounded the Gay Men's Issues in Religion group. For many years this would provide the primary outlet for publications in gay theology as most work in this area continued to be rejected by mainstream presses.[4] During the same period, the Lesbian Feminist Issues group in the AAR began, illustrating the continued confluence between issues of lesbianism and feminism in religion.

[3]Clark addresses the theological issue of theodicy–evil and suffering–in the context of HIV/AIDS in many of his writings, and especially his book *Defying the Darkness*.

[4]In fact, many of these early works were either self-published or relied on small, non-mainstream presses such as Monument Press in Dallas. Lack of support from major publishers effectively prevented their wide circulation.

Features of Non-apologetic Theologies

What were some of the main features of these early non-apologetic lesbian and gay liberation theologies? All liberation theologies share several methodological assumptions and characteristics that, when analyzed, can shed light on the particular nature of each theology. Four main steps of the "hermeneutical circle" that frame theologies include the following:

1. the *starting point or context* of theology, which includes the social-historical context out of which theologies arise, the communities that produce these theologies, and the issues, questions, and contradictions these theologies seek to address
2. *social-historical analysis,* where we seek to get a clearer understanding of the social-historical dynamics that shape the contradictions theologians seek to address
3. *theological reflection,* where we name the sources and norms we reflect on to construct theology (traditionally these have included Christian scripture, tradition, and experience)
4. *action/response,* the praxis that both informs and flows from our theologies[5]

Using these categories, the starting point of lesbian and gay theologies is naming the contradictions lesbians and gay men experience between their lived, embodied experience as fully human persons and the teachings and practices of both church and society that deny this full humanity. Such denials claim that homosexuality is inferior to heterosexuality; is sick, perverse, immoral, or illegal; and is therefore to be repressed. Lgbt theologies thus explicitly develop a "hermeneutic of suspicion" with respect to dominant theologies, arguing that their heterosexist claims and practices reflect distorted and oppressive human values and assumptions rather than the experience of God or the divine. They name these contradictions variously as homophobia, heterosexism, sexism, erotophobia, and AIDS-phobia–whatever attitudes and practices that prevent lgbt people from experiencing our full humanity within church and society.

---

[5]Hermeneutics is the field or philosophy of interpretation. The hermeneutical circle is a method within liberation theologies that understands all theologies to be rooted in and rising from particular contexts, communities, and questions that then shape the kind of theology that is developed. For one of the earliest discussions of the hermeneutical circle within the methodology of liberation theology, see Segundo, *The Liberation of Theology,* 7–38. In the conduction of theological reflection, the theological assumption behind naming sources for theology is that God or the divine somehow is revealed through them. Hence traditional Christian theologies have claimed that God is revealed through the Bible, through the Christian tradition (such as in the creeds, teachings, and doctrines that have been developed and passed down), and through the ongoing experience of Christians in the church. *How* these sources are developed and interpreted is shaped largely by the *norms* we develop, which serve as filters. Liberation theologies, for example, explicitly use the norm of *liberation* through which to interpret these sources, arguing that God acts in the world in such a way to transform suffering and oppression into liberation.

From this initial stance, lgbt theologies analyze the roots of these contradictions, exploring how the patriarchal heritage and history of Christianity and Western culture have given rise to these attitudes and practices. This analytical step is critical for demonstrating that these beliefs, values, attitudes, and practices are not an inevitable part of our reality–"natural" or "God-given"–but rather they have been socially constructed, shaped by specific communities and historical contexts. These social and historical factors can be identified, named, and "deconstructed" in order to open up new, more human and liberating possibilities.[6]

Traditionally the Christian community has named the Bible and Christian tradition as two of the primary or authoritative sources for constructing Christian theology. Many lgbt theologies also include them, but now from an explicitly critical stance. These theologians no longer try to reconcile lgbt experiences with the Bible and tradition or to somehow fit ourselves in (the task of apologetic approaches). Instead, lgbt theologies name the third source–experience–as having primary authority. They draw on authority of the full humanity of lgbt persons and experience to *critique* the homophobic, heterosexist, and sexist dimensions of the Bible and tradition as *not* authoritative for theology. The authority of all sources is understood *relationally* rather than *externally* or directionally one-way. We engage scripture and tradition to discern *in what ways* they may reveal God, rather than assume that they are authoritative in and of themselves. Hence Gary David Comstock, in his *Gay Theology Without Apology,* uses the metaphor of "friend" to describe the norm through which he engages scripture. "Instead of making the Bible into a parental authority, I have begun to engage it as I would a friend–as one to whom I have made a commitment and in whom I have invested dearly, but with whom I insist on a mutual exchange of critique, encouragement, support, and challenge" (1993, 11).[7] Carter Heyward, in critiquing the assumed external authority of the Bible and tradition, writes, "No person, religion, tradition, profession, rule, or resource should be inherently authoritative for us. We should always ask this question: Does it help us realize more fundamentally our connectedness to one another and hence the shape of our own identities as persons-in-relation?" (1989, 74). Authority, then, is recognized in that which can be trusted to reveal ourselves and our humanity more fully.

Finally, as in all liberation theologies, lgbt theologies are praxis-based theologies, rooted in the ongoing interaction of action and reflection. The particular locations and struggles are varied: working with battered women

---

[6]Hence, as an example of this, Carter Heyward deconstructs the traditional Christian emphasis on *agape* as self-giving, self-sacrificing love as the superior or normative example of Christian love to reclaim *eros* and the *erotic* as "the power in right relation" to open up new possibilities of relating (1989, 3f). See also Gilson, *Eros Breaking Free.*

[7]For an example of a lesbian-feminist theology that uses friendship as the primary metaphor for knowing God, see Hunt, *Fierce Tenderness.*

and children to end abuse, activism around AIDS and HIV issues, organizing for same-sex partner benefits in institutions and society, confronting church denominations and religious communities on their exclusive and oppressive practices, and more. What each have in common is drawing on developing and transformed theological and theoretical understandings of sexuality, gender, justice, and liberation, informed by the experiences of diverse lgbt persons and our allies. These commonalties are used to confront the diverse array of contradictions and injustices we encounter in our settings. The goal is a profound and integrated personal and social transformation of individuals, institutions, society and the church.

An Explosion of Diverse Perspectives

The last fifteen years from the end of the 1980s have seen an explosion of diverse lgbt theological perspectives as writers and activists in diverse settings have developed liberationist and non-apologetic stances to address many issues and circumstances. With the emergence of womanist theology in the African American community, for example, lesbian womanists Reneé Hill and Irene Monroe have confronted the womanist community with the need to take seriously lesbianism, homophobia and heterosexism within the African-American community.[8] Elias Farajaje-Jones, a gay-identified bisexual African American theologian and activist, lifts up biphobia and transphobia and the experience of bisexual and transgendered persons as critical to theologizing both within and outside the African American community (1993, 139–159). Hill, Monroe, and Farajaje-Jones, together with some white lgbt theologians such as Robin Gorsline, insist on focusing on the multidimensional nature of oppression and privilege, foregrounding issues of race and class in developing lgbt theologies.

Similarly, emerging Latino/a theologies are beginning to break the silence around sexuality in general and homosexuality in particular within Latino/a communities. In their text, *Introducing Latino/a Theologies*, Miguel A. De La Torre and Edwin David Aponte note that Hispanic bias against lgbt persons differs from homophobia in the dominant U.S. culture. "Hispanics do not fear the homosexual; rather homosexuals are often held in contempt as men who choose not to prove their manhood."

Sexuality in Latin American cultures typically is constructed around the notion of *machismo*, where to be a man, a *macho*, implies both the domination and protection of those under you, specifically women. Machismo is a multidimensional construct that integrates sexism, heterosexism, racism, ethnocentrism, and classism. In addition to serving to justify the subordination of women, *machismo* also "transfers to the non-elite male Other effeminate characteristics, placing him in a feminine space

[8]See, for example, Hill, "Who Are We For Each Other?" in *Black Theology,* 345–51. See also Douglas, *Sexuality and the Black Church.*

for "easy mounting." Hence within male same-sex acts, only the man who occupies the "position" of the woman (i.e., is penetrated) is considered to be gay. Rather than calling into question the masculinity of the "dominant" male sexual actor, he is able to retain, if not enhance, his sense of machismo. Significantly, within this masculinized machismo, space for lesbian identity is absent, since there is no dominant male referent present. Rather than seeing lesbianism as a threat, it is largely ignored as outside of and irrelevant to the macho's construction of sexuality. Within Latino/a contexts, therefore, lgbt liberation requires the dismantling of machismo and is linked to the liberation of other groups oppressed within machismo, whether for reasons of gender, race, class, or ethnicity (2001, 158–59).

Other lgbt theologians have sought to develop gay theology within a broader ecological context, expanding the notion of right-relation to include our relatedness with the entire earth community. Michael Clark's 1993 *Beyond Our Ghettos: Gay Theology in Ecological Perspective* sought to synthesize insights from ecofeminism with gay male experience to develop a gay ecotheology that would move gay theology beyond the "gay ghetto" as its primary context, linking social justice for lgbt persons with ecological justice. My 1996 *Gay and Gaia: Ethics, Ecology, and the Erotic* similarly built on feminist work in reclaiming the erotic with process theological insights about ecology to articulate an ecojustice liberationist ethic of right-relation at all levels of our lives, from the most intimate (the erotic) to the planetary (ecological).

Moving in a different direction than many lgbt theologies that explicitly use a liberation theology framework, gay theologian Ronald E. Long has argued for taking a phenomenological approach to gay male sex to ground gay theology and ethics. Long disagrees with the pro-feminist approaches of gay theologians like Clark, Gorsline, and Spencer. Long insists that such approaches move too quickly away from what is distinctive to gay male experience–gay sex and the gay ghetto–and thus miss what is of deepest religious significance for gay men. Long argues that sex has multiple meanings. He seeks to decouple the link between sex and intimacy as the assumed acceptable or ethically superior sexual ethic. Instead, he explores the phenomenon of casual sex with multiple partners as a distinctive characteristic of gay male experience that can be revelatory and valued. "What I hope is that I have given an account [of gay male sex] which is sufficiently true…to establish a recognition of the validity that casual sex can have in the life of a gay man as a vehicle of his 'humanization'–a process which some of us recognize as the substance of spirituality" (1995, 69–111). Rather than address the injustices and exclusionary practices of church and society, Long locates his theology explicitly within the gay ghetto, developing a "ghetto theology" that focuses more on understanding and revealing meaning in gay male experience than developing critiques of either societal or gay male practices.

Working from the opposite perspective of Long's ghetto theology with its assumptions of a normative gay male experience is the development of queer theology. This is rooted in the rise of queer activism around AIDS/HIV issues in the 1980s and 1990s and in the violent reaction of the religious and political right. Queer theory and queer theology seek to blur and subvert fixed and rigid categories of gender and sexuality to open up transformative and transgressive possibilities in both interpersonal relationships and societal structures. Queer theologies started with the work of Elias Farajaje-Jones (discussed above) and the 1993 publication of Robert Goss's *Jesus Acted Up: A Gay and Lesbian Manifesto.* It continued up through the recent publication of Argentinian theologian Marcella Althaus-Reid's *Indecent Theology: Theological Perversions in Sex, Gender and Politics.* These queer theologies "proceed from critical analysis of the social context that forms our sexual and gender experiences and the web of interlocking oppressions and from our innovative and transgressive practices. Queer theology is an organic or community-based project that includes our diverse sexual contextualities, our particular social experiences of homo/bi/transphobic oppression and their connections to other forms of oppression, and our self-affirmations of sexual/gendered differences" (Goss 2002, 20). The recent collection of queer biblical studies in *Queer Commentary and the Hebrew Bible* demonstrates how this approach of "queering" the tradition has moved even into the biblical field.[9] The 2001 publication of Vanessa Sheridan's *Crossing Over: Liberating the Transgendered Christian* signals the arrival of transgendered liberation theologies.

In summary, from the initial apologetic stances of trying to fit lesbians and gay men into a homophobic and heterosexist church, lesbian, gay, bisexual, transgendered, and queer theologies have developed within a liberationist theological framework. They call radically into question the very theological assumptions about sexuality and gender that have undergirded the church's practices and theology. Reflecting the increasing diversity of the ecosocial locations where lgbt persons are found, and the diversity of issues lgbt persons continue to confront, lgbt liberation theologies continue to develop in dynamic and transformative ways in seeking more inclusive patterns of justice and relationship for all.

---

[9]See Ken Stone, ed., *Queer Commentary and the Hebrew Bible.*

22

Theology of the Poor

DEBORAH W. LITTLE

I cannot write *about* theology of the poor. But I can tell some stories about our poorest people in Boston and how they talk about God. I should say that my understanding of the "theology of the poor" is just mine, from my experiences and through my eyes and ears. I am not poor myself. I am a white middle-class woman who worked for nearly 30 years in publications and management. At midlife, I felt the tug to get out and meet folks on the park benches to see if there was anything I could offer and to learn about God from the people I feel Jesus sends us to. I wanted to learn about God, and to do my part in the world, to get closer to what Jesus is doing and saying.

I fell in love with the understanding of God and the church and Jesus and the work of the people described by liberation theology. What made the most sense was their idea that the Christian life is not an abstraction. I learned that the poor can lead us into the shadow and depth and revelation of God who is present in the nooks and crannies, where God is *desired* and *sought* out of necessity. Even a white middle-class Brand X woman could seek salvation by a quest into the God of the oppressed expressed by others, revealing my own poverty.

Of course, no one is "the poor" or "the homeless." Speaking of "the poor" is one way we either romanticize or stigmatize the majority of people on our planet–our neighbors–whom God clearly calls us to love not abstractly, but in a concrete way. It does not seem honest to generalize. "Do not put meaning on it," my spiritual director admonishes me when I'm tempted to "understand" something. Hence I'll tell you some stories.

My Experience in the Streets

At forty-five, I went to seminary and at fifty was ordained an Episcopal priest. The day after I was ordained, I put on a knapsack full of socks, string, a first-aid kit, meal and shelter lists, a prayer book, stole, healing oil, AA meeting lists, lip balm, and peanut butter and jelly sandwiches. I took to the streets. I still remember that first day. I stopped at the Café de Paris near the Ritz Hotel in Boston, bought two cups of coffee, and walked across the street to Boston Public Garden. I looked around for someone on a bench who "looked homeless." I spotted a man with a few paper bags, went over, and sat down. I had no idea what I should say. I handed him one of the cups of coffee. He took it, and looked at me. "So, how are you doing today?" he asked. In my first five minutes of "street ministry," I had learned who is ministering to whom.

A few weeks later, I asked Mary–who was sitting with all her things at her usual spot by a big church fountain–how she was doing. "I'm fine," she said. "God woke me up this morning." I never had that thought and certainly not after spending a night in a Back Bay alley. Jesus was right. Go to the poor to learn about God. Mary does not have an alarm clock, breakfast, a roof over her head, a job, a telephone call to make, or any of the protective layers that I am so anxious to offer her. But Mary has *God.* Here is a woman in so much pain she has not gone inside anywhere for anything in at least twenty years. But Mary's terrors do not derive from lack of intimacy with God.

One miserable night, I was leaving a meeting downtown. Some cookies and donuts were left over so I decided to go up to Boston Common to see if anyone was around and hungry. It was pouring rain. Here, I ran into Sam on one of the benches. He asked if we could pray. "God, I know you are up there," he began, "but down here, things are real bad. I cannot stop drinking. But tonight, I am not praying for myself. A few days ago, my friend Fred died right over there." He pointed to the fountain in front of him. "When I found him, his shoes were missing. His hat was gone. He always wore his hat. These streets have turned to hell. We need you, God. I have lived on these streets for years. I do not have any money, but I will beg money for my brother if he needs it and I do not have it. I wish I had known Fred was in trouble. We have got to watch out for each other. God, help us." Sam did not go to any seminary. He is not an outreach worker. But Sam loves his neighbor and is on speaking terms with God. Even drunk and soaked to the bone, Sam knows God and directs himself to justice and righteousness. He may have as much trouble as any of us acting out that love every day, but he is close to the heartbeat.

Doing Good Is a Hustle

One morning in the early months, I got "The Question" I had dreaded since my first day of street ministry. "Why are you talking to me?" Jack asked from his panhandling post in front of a fancy jewelry store. I stammered out something like, "Just trying to be helpful." Jack–I had yet to learn that he is smarter than I–leaned against the window full of gold watches and said to me in the kindest way, "Doing good is a hustle, too, you know." Jack asks questions and expects the truth. Doing good is a hustle unless we get honest, confess our contradictions, and take care of ourselves so we do not spill out all over the people we want to care for and learn from. Being with poor people transforms *us.* That's a major way God's work and desire happens on earth.

We associate a kind of listening with Jesus and view it as integral to his healing powers. I have observed and am the recipient of that kind of listening all day long. A man named Luke has been homeless for five years now, having lost his apartment and his job due to what he names "injustices." He will sit for hours listening to Tommy, or Dusty Don, or any of a number of homeless men and women whom many of us find hard to listen to for even ten minutes. On a freezing night, Alex will search the Common for people too drunk to find their own way to a shelter. He will tie them to himself with a long rope, and pull them down the street to a warm place. It is important not to sentimentalize homeless people, but many are unaccountably generous.

Ernie always wants me to pray for his pal Sam who is dying in the blankets next to his under one of the bridges. Tom, who panhandles in front of a downtown church, says he always prays for the people who, as he says, "look down on me." Roger and Bob, when I handed them blankets one snowy night, asked me whom they could pray for. Moses always tells me God is taking care of him. "I know I cannot take care of myself. I just hope I do not keep God so busy other people get forgotten."

A block from St. Paul's Cathedral, Dave sits on the sidewalk upon folded cardboard with a cup. It is his daylight routine and a ministry. Back a year or so ago, when I first met Dave, I asked him, stupidly, "Why don't you go to the free meals?" and then "Could I bring you something from the soup kitchen?" "I like *whole* chicken," he replied. It was not hard for me to picture the way chicken comes at the Cathedral soup kitchen. "I do not need much," he said, "but I like to choose what I eat. *And I can't stand in a line.*" With that sentence I understood that *none* of the "resources" I was so anxious to offer him would work. He was insisting on what he needed–to be a free man. So, I sat down with him on the sidewalk. "Could you tell me about God?" I asked. "Oh, I know God," he responded. "I pray all day long. Mostly, I pray for all these poor people" as he swept his hand the length of Tremont Street. "They all look so sad, so lost, so busy...They do not look like they know about Jesus. They do not know how much God loves them." I asked him to pray for *me.*

Learning about Ourselves

One of the gifts of our homeless community is how much they teach us about ourselves. Being with people in such pain and proximity to the holy is excruciating and elating all at once. I often describe what I do as looking at my character defects all day long. I see my persistent need to fix people, to do something, *anything,* to assume my agenda should be the other person's. I learned the hard way in early interactions and still today, that my ongoing spiritual struggle is simply to *be* with people, to learn from them, to offer a suggestion if asked. I am not to expect or judge "results." Jesus asks "only" that we give wholeheartedly.

Each of us has our own path. Why should I sell the white middle-class agenda, which creates its own miseries, to anyone? Such wisdom has come slowly to me, and I frequently forget it. Surely this is Jesus talking through the lives of the poor, calling us all to be simpler, to give without hope of return, not with disdain for people who make different choices, but to be openhearted and to love as God loves.

About a year and a half into my street ministry, on Christmas Eve, I decided to offer the Eucharist to people who spend the day in Boston's central train station. While I was reading the Christmas story, a gentleman spoke up. "My name is Joseph," he said through tears. "I wish I had been like this Joseph here," pointing to the text. "When my wife cheated on me, I hated her." I learned that evening about how immediate and concrete scripture is for people who have nothing between themselves and the good news. Joseph lives alone, just his bags, his meals, and God. Not to put meaning on that, but he is close enough to touch God. We have a lot to learn from him. Billy says, "I think every time I hear the Twenty-third Psalm the Holy Spirit is all around. And that is absolute proof to me that there is more than just people here–it is the Spirit, the living Spirit."

A few months after that train station service, I started a worship service outdoors in a public park, Boston Common. We have come together every Sunday since, where our gathering ranges between 100–150 people. We developed this service to offer church to people who cannot or will not come into buildings. Many homeless people have been frightened or shamed in churches. Others are concerned about their behavior or their dress or cannot stand enclosed places.

When non-homeless people began to hear about us and wanted to come, I was worried and protective. I did not want our folks to feel crowded or stared at or taken over. What I learned was that the homeless people were more ready than I to share our worship and their lives, thus welcoming the strangers from the suburbs. They speak of this as offering their "home" to others. They feel hopeful and want to connect with a world they have come to appreciate as hungry to learn from them.

A Native American started coming almost from the beginning, but not in our worship circle. Rather, he would sit on the steps of a church across the street. We would take him communion and a sandwich. He spoke very little. Once I asked who God is for him. Looking directly at me for the first time, with an incredulous look, he said, "Why, God is *every*where; God is in *every*thing! I know *God* is with me," as if to underscore the tragic obvious, that otherwise he is alone.

Beyond Personal Concerns

Surprisingly, our homeless people are not simply concerned about their own life-threatening circumstances, although of course, food and shelter are crucial. Frances, who many homeless folks call "Mama," is one of the most faithful Christians. She has a booming voice for hymn singing and for whatever else is on her mind. She arrived one Sunday as we were reflecting on the story of Jesus healing the blind man, dropped her bags in the center of our circle, put her hands on her hips, and threw her head back for maximum volume. "I've heard all this gospel talk before," Frances said. "When is lunch?" Then she began the most powerful soul deep version of the hymn "I am Standing on Holy Ground."

Over and over, I experience the presence of the raising up of God's simple desires in the words and actions of our poorest people. They seem to pray more, be more grateful, worry about each other more, be more honest, and be clearer about who God is than most of the privileged people I know. Their access to truth and grace and their willingness to share themselves sets the table for everyone else. I thought I would hear a lot of anger toward God, but that was not the case. Perhaps expectations of God that lead to resentments and disappointment are one more privilege of people who have enough to feel entitled to a "good life." Homeless people in America have always been blamed for their homelessness. What is true is that they do not fit into the usual molds of social success or control, as described by Kenneth Kusmer in *Down and Out*. Nor do they always fit the mold with their theology and understanding of church and God (2002, 8).

Theological Understandings

"I do not want to sound like I am off the wall, but the many times that I have invited God and Jesus to be here, He comes when He can. He does not come when I want Him to," Gary told me. "I notice Jesus more so because if you modernize the Bible it fits every one of us." Gary continued, "When I tell people my stories out on the streets, I try not to speak of the Bible, because I want my own credit. Jesus did his thing, and I do mine, and if they both seem to be the same, it's just one of those things."

Most people who live outside carry everything they own with them all day long. If they show you what they have in their bags, you will most often find a worn, obviously read, Bible. Our sisters and brothers who have nothing teach us who have everything about God, about life with Jesus, about church being a place where we tell the truth, break ourselves open, and allow ourselves to be held however well and badly humans do that. They teach us to claim our faith. Barbara stands in the middle of our circle singing "Amazing Grace" in that way only Barbara can, complete with tears running down her face. We who hear that want to run away. We have heard it before. We do not want pain, such pain, in the middle of our worship! Yet when she finishes, a woman from the suburbs who has everything her pain needs (medication, a psychiatrist, a church, a family, a home, education) will stand in the middle of that circle, and for the first time ever, tell us something she has been carrying alone about her own childhood. We all stand in awe and wonder in those moments.

One of our beloved, Alison, died on the grass of Common Cathedral. She was hugging her bottle, and she had our Common Cathedral cross around her neck. "Listen to me kid,"–it was Gary calling to console me–"We all have a name out here because of you. We are all fighting the same system. The system wins; it takes away. But God takes care."

We privileged people have everything to learn from the poor. How do we go about doing that? It is easy to say and hard to do, but we need to do what we can to step out of our safety zones physically, emotionally, and spiritually. José Comblin presses for what he calls "a true liberation" of theology. "Christian concepts of traditional theology have been distorted by the situation under Christendom." By "situation" he means domination, clericalism, and imperialism. "Everything has to be reexamined and reinterpreted–from the idea of God, to the theology of Christ, the church, grace and sin, the sacraments, and so forth" (1998, 213). We might ask: How can we step aside both to promote the freedom of our oppressed poor and to express and see God from their starting point? It is not enough to look at a theology of the poor from our usual social locations. The poor are free of the bonds and limitations of middle class understanding of theology because they are not included or beholden to it. Consequently, Jesus says it is much harder for the rich to enter the kingdom of God.

Vision Driving to Action

Liberation theology tells us it is not enough for Christians to mean well. Our theology must include the vision of the poor, and this must drive us to action. In *Remember the Poor,* Joerg Rieger leads us to ask how has theology been part of the sin of growing imbalance and poverty in the third and first worlds? "At the beginning of the twenty-first century, a time when we have all gotten used to the victory of capitalism, poverty levels and other indicators of imbalance and injustice are increasing not only in certain parts of the 'third world' but in the 'first world' as well. There is still much left to be done (and to be undone). Theology needs to grasp its own role in this context." Rieger insists that this not be a matter of curiosity or superficial inclusion, but that we be driven by urgent necessity to achieve collaboration (1998, 224).

This collaboration, I would argue, should not simply be between theologians, clergy, and others who package words. It needs to happen at the level of life lived. The poor are the majority and must be listened and attended to. As Rieger argues, "without encounters with the repressed human other who is different, encounters with the divine Other are unlikely" (229). The poor have an angle of vision that we who are others, need. If we are to take drawing closer to listen and learn from the poor seriously, we must, as Rieger says, participate "in God's work of liberation already going on in both church and world and thus creating new forms of solidarity of rich and poor, oppressors and oppressed, and self and other. Here theology is reshaped...The poor as teachers are able to expose hidden fault lines and to raise new questions that lead us beyond the current impasse" (222). What better vocation might we seek than our own particular response to Jesus' invitation, "Come and see."

23

Environmental Racism

STEVEN BOUMA-PREDIGER

Poor and Oppressed Unite: Overcoming Environmental Racism

In 1969, Hazel Johnson's husband died of lung cancer. Although he smoked, he was too young and smoked too little to blame cigarettes. Hazel suspected something else had caused her husband's premature death. More exactly, she suspected that industrial emissions around her home in the Altgeld Gardens public housing complex on the southeast side of Chicago contributed to her husband's early demise. And so Hazel began to gather air pollution data and talk to her neighbors. In 1982 after years of research and discussion, Hazel founded "People for Community Recovery," Chicago's first well-known minority community-organizing group devoted to environmental issues. This group has opposed numerous projects in their neighborhood, most notably hazardous waste incinerators, by arguing that environmental issues are matters of community health and social justice. These all go together hand-in-glove.[1]

Hazel has company, lots of company. The group she founded over twenty years ago is now only one of many such groups in the city of Chicago

[1]Some of this information was gathered from the *Chicago Tribune*, 29 June 1992.

and all over the United States' grassroots organizations of people of color dedicated to overcoming what is called environmental racism and its deadly effects. In 1978 the residents of Northwood Manor, a middle-class community in northeast Houston made up of over 80 percent African Americans, organized themselves into the Northeast Community Action Group to oppose a dump in their neighborhood. Along so-called "Cancer Alley"–the Mississippi River corridor south of Baton Rouge, Louisiana–mostly African Americans have banded together to fight hazardous waste facilities. In 1986 Hispanics in Albuquerque formed the Southwest Organizing Project to protest industrial pollution. In 1988 the Havasupi Indians who live in and around the Grand Canyon organized to resist plans for uranium mining on their lands. And the list goes on.

Indeed, the evidence of environmental racism, and of resistance to it by various groups, is not limited to the United States. It can be found worldwide. For example, Puerto Rico is one of the most heavily polluted places in the world, with groundwater contaminated by drug companies and oil refineries. The Marshall Islands and other islands in the Pacific have been devastated by nuclear weapons testing. In Central America the poor and racial minorities often bear the brunt of water pollution and garbage dumps.

The Historical Background

All of this, of course, is not really new. There is a history, a sad and sobering history, albeit one we usually don't learn in school. For example, in the 1930s hundreds of African Americans from the South were brought to the Gauley Bridge of West Virginia to dig the Hawks Nest tunnel. A project of the New Kanawha Power Company, a subsidiary of Union Carbide, this was the site of one of the worst occupational disasters in U.S. history. Over a two-year period "approximately 500 workers died and 1,500 were disabled from silicosis, a lung disease similar to Black Lung." As Charles Lee tells it, "Men literally dropped dead on their feet breathing air so thick with microscopic silica that they could not see more than a yard in front of them," and "those who came out for air were beaten back into the tunnel with ax handles." At congressional hearings after the fact, one contractor revealed that "I knew I was going to kill these niggers, but I didn't know it was going to be this soon." In Lee's words, "an undertaker was hired to bury dead workers in unmarked graves" and "agreed to perform this service for an extremely low rate because the company assured him that there would be a large number of deaths" (1990, 22).

The beginning of the end, according to some, came in September 1982. In Warren County, North Carolina, more than 500 residents, most of them African American, blocked the paths of trucks carrying toxic PCBs (polychlorinated biphenyls) to a new hazardous waste facility. Many of those protesters were arrested. Reminiscent of the many acts of civil disobedience during the civil rights era, this well-organized action was a protest against both social injustice and environmental degradation. What previously was seen by many as two separate issues now were joined at the hip.

Defining Environmental Racism

So what exactly is environmental racism? Among those taken into custody in the Warren County protest was Rev. Benjamin Chavis, then executive director of the United Church of Christ's Commission on Racial Justice. Chavis and Charles Lee, also of the UCC, published in 1987 the milestone report, "Toxic Waste and Race in the United States: A National Report on the Racial and Socio-Economic Characteristics of Communities Surrounding Hazardous Waste Sites." The study examined the locations of hazardous waste facilities and then, controlling for different variables, looked for positive correlations between the location of those sites and factors like class, sex, and race. The findings were striking:

1. Although socioeconomic status plays an important role in the location of commercial hazardous waste facilities, race is the leading factor.
2. Three out of the five largest commercial hazardous waste landfills in the United States are located in mostly Black or Hispanic communities.
3. Three out of five Black and Hispanic Americans live in communities with one or more uncontrolled toxic waste sites.
4. Cities with the large Black populations–such as St. Louis, Cleveland, Chicago, Atlanta, and Memphis–have the largest numbers of uncontrolled toxic waste sites.
5. About half of all Asian/Pacific Islanders and Native Americans live in communities with uncontrolled waste sites.[2]

The overarching conclusion of this groundbreaking study was that race is the best predictor in identifying communities most likely to be the location for toxic waste sites. Lee provides a succinct and clear summary: "The racial composition of a community is the single variable best able to explain the existence or non-existence of commercial hazardous waste facilities in that area. Racial minorities, primarily African-Americans and Hispanics, are strikingly overrepresented in communities with such facilities" (1990, 25).

A growing body of empirical evidence documents the existence of environmental racism. Positive correlations and, in many cases, causal links exist between the location of toxic waste sites and the residences of people of color. The one person who has probably done more than any other to

---

[2]This summary is taken from an interview with Charles Lee in the 1990 Panos Institute publication "We Speak for Ourselves: Social Justice, Race, and Environment," 9.

document these patterns of environmental racism is sociologist Robert Bullard.[3] Starting with a study in Houston in 1978, Bullard has studied many cities and sites. His conclusion is short and simple: "People of color (African Americans, Latino Americans, Asian Americans, and Native Americans) are disproportionately affected by industrial toxins, dirty air and drinking water, and the location of noxious facilities such as municipal landfills, incinerators, and hazardous-waste treatment, storage, and disposal facilities" (1993, 25). In sum, a disproportionate environmental burden is placed upon racial minorities. This reflects the ugly and intransigent reality of racism.

Hence Chavis, Lee, Bullard, and others use the term "environmental racism" to name this injustice. They insist that the issues of environmental degradation and racial inequity be linked.

These two forms of oppression are of a piece. Humans treated unjustly by virtue of race often suffer inordinately the negative effects of our exploitation of the earth. Poor and oppressed unite–an oppressed earth and humans oppressed because of their skin color. Put more positively, ecological harmony and racial justice are interdependent goals.

Other Examples of Environmental Injustice

Environmental racism is but one manifestation of environmental injustice. Ecological degradation, in other words, is linked not only to race but also to sex and class. For example, contemporary Christian feminist theologian Rosemary Radford Ruether argues that "we cannot criticize the hierarchy of male over female without ultimately criticizing and overcoming the hierarchy of human over nature" (1983, 73). Sexism, in other words, is integrally connected to anthropocentrism, and anthropocentrism contributes to ecological degradation.[4] Thus, those who work to overcome the domination of women must realize that the success of their struggle is dependent on the struggle to stop the exploitation of the earth. And ecology activists must realize that their work goes hand in hand with those fighting for greater equity for women. Like many ecofeminists, Ruether claims:

> Women must see that there can be no liberation for them and no solution to the ecological crisis within a society whose fundamental model of relationships continues to be one of domination. They must unite the demands of the women's movement with those of the ecological movement to envision a radical reshaping of the

---

[3]See, for example, his classic work *Dumping In Dixie;* see also the work of Bryant and Mohai, *Environmental Racism,* and also Bryant and Mohai, eds., *Race and the Incidence of Environmental Hazards.*

[4]For an informed and nuanced exposition of ecofeminism, see Warren, *Ecofeminist Philosophy,* especially chapter 2.

> basic socioeconomic relations and the underlying values of this society (1975, 204).

The chain of double domination–of women and the earth–must be broken by uniting the efforts of those who seek the liberation of each.

So also with regard to socioeconomic class, exploitation of the earth is more prevalent in communities of the poor. Indeed, some argue that any cost-benefit analysis, conducted according to conventional economic principles, would dictate that the costs of pollution, for example, ought to be borne by the poor. It would be hard to find a more glaring example of this reasoning than that of Lawrence Summers, then chief economist of the World Bank and now president of Harvard University. As quoted by Laura Westra, Summers argues:

> The measurement of the costs of health-impairing pollution depends on the foregone earnings from increased morbidity and mortality. From this point of view a given amount of health-impairing pollution should be done in the country with the lowest cost, which will be the country with the lowest wages. I think the economic logic behind dumping a load of toxic waste in the lowest-wage country is impeccable and we should face up to that (1995, xvi).

So we should put our pollution in the poor neighborhoods. It's more efficient. It makes sound economic sense. So argue the economists of business as usual. Racism, sexism, classism–such are a few of the faces of environmental injustice.

Seeking a Solution

If it is true that racism, sexism, classism, and the exploitation of the earth are connected, then the poor and oppressed must unite. The ecology movement and the various movements for human liberation, which have for too long been separate and at times antagonistic projects, must see themselves as allies in a common quest to dismantle the logic and practice of domination. There is, happily, growing recognition of this fact. For example, in 1993 the Sierra Club, an overwhelmingly white and upper middle class organization concerned almost exclusively with wilderness preservation, acknowledged that it must adopt ecojustice as one of its central goals (1993, 51ff).

This insistence that various forms of oppression are linked is commonly called the ecojustice argument, or of late the environmental justice argument. Coined in the early 1970s by the Board of National Ministries of the American Baptist Church, the term ecojustice was picked up by the Eco-Justice Project and Network at the Center for Religion, Ethics, and Social Policy at Cornell University and also by the National Council of Churches

(NCC). In 1985 the NCC formed the Eco-Justice Working Group (now the Economic and Environmental Justice Working Group) to systematically address this cluster of issues.[5] So there is a thirty-year history of commitment by some prophetic Christians to fight for both social justice and ecological integrity–indeed of seeing them as inextricable.

More recently the term environmental justice has come into more common use. The term is defined in a variety of ways. The Environmental Protection Agency (EPA) offers this comprehensive though ponderous definition:

> Environmental justice is the fair treatment and meaningful involvement of all people regardless of race, color, national origin, or income with respect to the development, implementation, and enforcement of environmental laws, regulations, and policies. Fair treatment means that no group of people, including racial, ethnic, or socioeconomic group, should bear a disproportionate share of the negative environmental consequences resulting from industrial, municipal, and commercial operations or the execution of federal, state, local, and tribal programs and policies. Meaningful involvement means that: (1) potentially affected community residents have an appropriate opportunity to participate in decisions about a proposed activity that will affect their environment and/or health; (2) the public's contribution can influence the regulatory agency's decision; (3) the concerns of all participants involved will be considered in the decision making process; and (4) the decision makers seek out and facilitate the involvement of those potentially affected.[6]

Simply stated, environmental justice is fair treatment, with regard to bearing the costs of environmental degradation, for all people and communities, regardless of race, class, or ethnicity.

What does all this have to do with Christian theology and ethics? As should be evident, everything. For if the core of the Christian gospel is about liberation from oppression and reconciliation not only with God but also with other people, ourselves, and the earth, and if the God of the Bible has compassion on everyone, then racism, sexism, classism, and the like have no place in the church and ultimately no place on earth. As St. Paul puts it so powerfully in Galatians 3:25–28:

> But now that faith has come, we are no longer subject to a disciplinarian, for in Christ Jesus you are all children of God

---

[5]Bakken, "The Eco-Justice Movement in Christian Theology: Patterns and Issues," *Theology and Public Policy*.

[6]EPA Web site at www.epa.gov/compliance/environmentaljustice/.

> through faith. As many of you as were baptized into Christ have clothed yourselves with Christ. There is no longer Jew or Greek, there is no longer slave or free, there is no longer male or female; for all of you are one in Christ Jesus.

Those who follow Jesus–that is, the church–must stand firmly against all forms of oppression and alienation–all that breaks God's shalom–for we are all part of the same body. We are wedded through faith to Christ and woven and knit to each other.

Many contemporary Christian theologian-ethicists could be cited in support of these claims. Among Latin American liberation theologians perhaps no one has been as staunch an advocate of ecojustice as Leonardo Boff. In his pathbreaking *Ecology and Liberation* he firmly argues that "social injustice leads to ecological injustice, and vice versa" (1993, 25). We need, therefore, to champion "ecologico-social democracy" in which we humans "advance beyond our anthropocentric viewpoint" by acknowledging that "every form of being, animate or inanimate, has a value as such" and by taking seriously the inescapable fact that "human history is inseparable from that of our environment" (85–88). Or as Boff puts it in his more recent *Cry of the Earth, Cry of the Poor,* we must "connect the cry of the oppressed with the cry of the Earth" for "the logic that exploits classes and subjects peoples to the interests of a few rich and powerful countries is the same as the logic that devastates the Earth and plunders its wealth, showing no solidarity with the rest of humankind and future generations" (1997, xi). The poor and oppressed must unite.

In sum, we need to understand in our hearts, as Thom White Wolf Fassett and his Native American friends so eloquently state, that "not only are the surviving Native people crying out for justice...but the Natural World people, the rest of creation, are pleading for mercy and justice from modern technological civilization." The plaintive cries for justice from oppressed people and exploited earth rise and join, like fingers from a burning fire. And we must remember, Fassett continues, that the roots of our society of death-dealing domination "do not grow in first-century Christian justice paradigms" because these roots "forsake the sanctity of creation and the nations of people who belong to it" (1996, 179). Authentic Christian discipleship, in contrast to our culture, provides another, more shalom-giving, life-affirming way. As Christians our passion for shalom should embrace all creatures–for their sake and for the sake of our human neighbors whose voices cry out for justice to roll down like waters and righteousness like an ever-flowing stream. May it be so.

24

Postcolonialism & Liberation

MUSA W. DUBE

Introduction

Postcolonialism is a framework that takes seriously the historical experience of imperialism, colonialism, anti-imperialism, and liberation movements that characterized the nineteenth and twentieth centuries. It is a framework that recognizes imperialism and colonialism of these centuries was not only vast and intense in its reach, but also that it did not end with the historical wars of liberation and independence won by the colonized. Rather, in many different ways, imperialism of different forms such as economical, ideological, military arrogance, and cultural continues today.

The postcolonial framework of analysis, therefore, employs many different methods and categories of analysis. These are used to investigate the methods and ideologies of domination employed by the colonizer, the response of the colonized, and the various methods the colonized employ to resist, collaborate, survive, fight back, and win their liberation–or survive under imperial domination. If anything, the postcolonial framework underlines the interconnectedness of the colonized and the colonizer. It highlights their overlapping histories, cultures, geographies, and economies pointing to our coexistence and the reality of our hybrid identities in the world. Excellent theoretical books and anthologies on postcolonialism include Edward Said, *Culture and Imperialism*; Elleke Bohemer's *Colonial and Postcolonial Literature*; and Bill Ashcroft et al., *The Postcolonial Studies Reader.*

Postcolonialism and Cultural Texts

Further, the postcolonial framework underlines that modern history of imperialism was not merely characterized by geographical, economical, and political contests for power. It involved equally the participation of cultural texts and the production and use of diverse genres of narratives. Some narratives rose from imperialized historical contexts, written by various colonizing agents in colonies. Some came from supporters of colonialism in the mother countries. Some narratives rose from resisting and collaborating colonized people at different stages and times of resistance.

Some narratives, however, were written in earlier times, way before modern imperialism, but they were used in the discourses of domination, collaboration, or resistance. A good example here is the Bible or Homer. These are undoubtedly ancient texts, but they provided the ideological base for modern imperialism, often being used to displace the cultures of the colonized. One must add that the colonized also seized these tool of the "masters" and made impressive efforts to dismantle imperialism by reading for decolonization and liberation. The participation of narratives of ancient times in modern imperialism has pushed the boundaries of postcolonialism further. This makes it legitimate to ask

1. how imperialism was constructed in ancient times
2. how its ideologies of domination have informed modern imperialism
3. how the dominated responded in ancient times
4. how these textual strategies have been seized and used in modern times

In biblical and theological studies, for example, postcolonialism can examine how theology participated in the domination and creation of colonies and how it produced an ideology that made it acceptable to subjugate certain nations and people. It can examine what kind of theologies of resistance rose from the anti-imperialist movement and the kind of strategies they employed. It can examine how gender oppression and resistance operate within the postcolonial historical space. It can examine how imperial domination, resistance, and hybridity work with class, race, ethnicity, and sexual orientation.

Postcolonialism also recognizes that the relationship between the colonizer and the colonized in imperial contexts was not only characterized by two opposing forces, but also had a space of interaction and exchange. Thus postcolonialism involves a great deal of exploring the concept of hybridity. It underlines the overlapping identities, histories, cultures, and geographies of the colonizer and the colonized. Hybridity is also explored as a space of resistance that undermines the ideological claims of the dominator as well as the often oppressive nativist discourses of the nationalism. An excellent text on this theoretical base of hybridity is Homi Bhabha's book *The Location of Culture.*

Postcolonialism consists not only in a framework that investigates the narratives, but also in the theories and methods of reading that have emerged from these diverse historical contexts. Postcolonialism investigates how theories and methods of reading participate in the ideologies of these histories and the sides they take. For example, it may scrutinize how theories of Marxism, feminism, postmodernism, and deconstruction operate within the postcolonial space of contest for power and struggle for justice. For biblical/theological/religious studies the application of the postcolonial perspective can take some of the following investigations:

1. How the comparative approach to religion or literature often functioned to endorse and legitimate the cultural/ideological assumption of the empire of the time, an assumption that the empire and its cultures were the best.
2. How methods of historical criticism in biblical studies and their insistence on reading from a neutral, scientific standpoint in fact subscribed to imperial ideology. Here it was assumed that we must all read in one universal way, a fact that suppressed voices from the margins, rejecting them as unrepresentative of standard scholarship.
3. How revolutionary western feminist methods of reading, read against patriarchy but still subscribed to imperial oppression by their failure to read for decolonization.
4. How methods and theologies of Two-Thirds World countries in fact sought to resist imperial domination by adopting different methods of reading or reasons for reading as compared to the Western scholarship.[1]
5. How theologies of migrant populations, who for historical and contemporary reasons have been forced to live in the metropolitan centers of the empire, continue to engage in a discourse of decolonization and liberation.
6. How white male exegesis subscribed to the colonial ideology of white supremacy by suppressing black presence in biblical texts.

Liberation and Postcolonialism

According to Joyce Ann Mercer, "liberation is the struggle for freedom from oppression as subjugated people become conscious of their situation and work to transform the conditions of their existence" (1995, 168). As Virginia Fabella points out, in theological studies the term "liberation" made its entry to the practice in the early 1970s through James Cone's

[1]While the phase "Third World" is commonly used, I have opted to use "Two-Thirds World" to underline that in fact, people of the South or the so-called developing nations constitute two thirds and not one third of the population.

book *A Black Theology of Liberation* in 1970 and Gustavo Gutiérrez's book *A Theology of Liberation* in 1973.[2] It was not by coincidence that this term entered at this particular time, for it was a historical moment in which many colonized nations sought to be liberated from their colonial masters. And hence, a theology of liberation notably rose from Two-Thirds World theologians. It is only fair to say liberation theology rose from a context of resisting both imperial oppression and deformation of people through exploitation, racism, and dispossession.

The term *postcolonial* is a newcomer in the theological/religious/biblical guild. It is a framework of analysis that comes to religious and theological studies from literature, where it has been used much longer. However, as the above points indicate, postcolonialism describes a practice that is much older both in literary and biblical/theological/religious studies. Postcolonialism is by far not new to the religious academic community and socially engaged faith communities. It can be seen in the mainstream academic guild, which is mainly Western and which originated within the time and the context of imperial domination as this guild participated in the discourse of domination–be it intentionally or through silence and omission. Postcolonialism can also be recognized so far as various Two-Thirds World theologies are shown to have overtly or covertly engaged the imperial domination in search for liberation. What is new is the systematic theoretical framework (and the number of different theories it employs) that provides for interpretation and understanding powers of domination and the many ways of resistance in search for a more just world.

Two-Thirds-World biblical/theological practices, in particular, openly engaged the empire in their studies. For example, African hermeneutics is captured in Emmanuel Martey's book, *African Theology: Inculturation and Liberation.* His is/was a comparative approach that, unlike the imperial approach, sought to show that African cultures are as good as biblical ones or even better. Black South African theology, best captured by Itumeleng Mosala's book, *Biblical Hermeneutics and Black Theology in South Africa,* sought to engage the ideology of racism, which was used to dominate and exploit the black majority. As Martey holds, "Liberation theology in Africa emerged primarily in response to white oppression and Western cultural imperialism. But it is also a response to oppression of Africans by Africans, including the oppression of women" (2000, 127).

Asian biblical readings and theology sought to show that far from the colonial Jesus, who was presented as above all religious figures, he is in fact among and with the many religious figures of other religions. Sugirtharajah's collections of Asian theological writers in the titles, *Asian Faces of Jesus* and

[2]Fabella, "Liberation" in Fabella and Sugirtharajah, eds., *Dictionary of Third World Theologies.*

Readings in Indian Christian Theology captures this dialogue of resistance and hybridity. Imperialism also employed a strategy of enslavement, using the Bible to legitimate its act, but readings of former slaves, such as African Americans, underline that God is a God of liberation. God is a God who sets them free from oppression. Vincent Wimbush's edited volume, *African Americans and The Bible: Sacred Texts and Social Textures* is good place to start.

Many native populations, who during modern imperialism were subjected to dispossession and annihilation in their own lands by colonizers who claimed to be God's chosen races insist on reading the Bible as Canaanites. Robert Allen Warrior's article, "Canaanites, Cowboys and Indians," best captures this approach. A larger scale work is represented by George "Tink" Tinker's book, *Missionary Conquest: The Gospel and Native American Genocide.* Contemporary immigrants and border dwellers find themselves in constant struggle with former colonizers, who continue to dominate and exploit them. This situation has also given rise to exciting theological/biblical readings. Leticia Guardiola-Saenz's article, "Border-crossing and Its Redemptive Power in John 7:53–8:11: A Cultural Reading of Jesus and the Accused," is of particular note.

In addition, Two-Thirds World women from many different contexts have explored the intersection of imperial, patriarchal, race, ethnic, and class oppression in an attempt to chart their own empowerment and to dream a better world. Their works are found in many volumes, but to list a few edited volumes, we have, Mercy Amba Oduyoye and Musimbi Kanyoro's *The Will to Arise: Women, Tradition, and the Church in Africa*; Elsa Tamez's *Through her Eyes: Women's Theology From Latin America*; and Virginia Fabella's *We Dare to Dream: Doing Theology as Asian Women.* One collection that combines all three voices is *With Passion and Compassion: Third World Women Doing Theology*, edited by Fabella and Oduyoye. Two-Thirds World women are and were often caught in the crossfire between the struggles against patriarchy with their Western feminist counterparts and the struggle against imperial domination with their fellow colonized men. While it could be expected that the struggles against patriarchy and imperialism would intersect and work together, the two, more often than not, functioned as parallels. The approach of Two-Thirds World women in the above volumes is particularly noted for taking both imperialism and patriarchy seriously as well as seeking ways of reading that can liberate women and men from all that oppresses them.

Of late many biblical/theological writings explicitly employ the framework of postcolonialism in their work. The works of Fernando F. Segovia and R.S. Sugirtharajah are notable here,[3] while for postcolonial feminist works Laura Donaldson, Kwok Pui-lan and my work are good

[3]See Segovia, *Decolonizing Biblical Studies;* and Sugirtharajah, *The Postcolonial Bible.*

examples.[4] One may ask, what is the difference, if any, between Two-Thirds World theologies of liberation and postcolonial approaches? They overlap in many different levels. I would define postcolonialism more as a servant of liberation. In my view, postcolonial works are not limited to those who employ the term explicitly. Rather, it includes those who highlight the empire's various strategies of domination and the various methods of resistance that arise from their overlapping identities and cultures. It includes those whose works resist the empire of various times and forms and actively seek to imagine and build a just world.

Postcolonialism's New Dimension

The postcolonial framework, however, does add a new dimension to our critical studies and search for liberation in several ways.

First, it forcefully brings the whole academic guild, First and Two-Thirds, to focus on the context of imperialism and how it informs their work. As Edward Said holds, "we are at a point in our work when we can no longer ignore empires and the imperial context in our studies" (1993, 6). He further underlines that "whether or not to look at the connections between cultural texts and imperialism is therefore to take a position in fact taken either to study the connections in order to criticize it and think of alternatives for it, or not to study it in order to let it stand" (68). Postcolonialism, therefore, underlines that we cannot ignore imperial ideology and its literary form in our critical studies, regardless of whether we live in the former colonized, colonizer, or settler colonies context. We cannot be neutral. Wherever we are located, we need to reexamine how our biblical and theological discourse works within the postcolonial framework. Whatever methods we use in our studies, we need to ask how they address or how they do not address and why they remain silent toward postcolonial realities of our world.

Second, the postcolonial framework also sharpens Two-Thirds World theoretical approaches by insisting on a self critical approach toward its own discourse of liberation and how it sometimes participates in oppressive ideologies. Hence strategies of resistance such as nationalism and nativism, while fully recognized for their contribution to the struggles against colonialism, are nonetheless subjected to critical scrutiny. In biblical studies and theology, readings of liberation are challenged to become more ideologically suspicious of their sources of theology and to be more critical of biblical texts than they have tended to be.

Third, Two-Thirds World women challenge the feminist and Two-Thirds world liberationist discourse to take both imperialism and patriarchy seriously in the search for justice.

---

[4]See Donaldson, *Semeia 75;* Kwok, *Discovering the Bible in the Non-Biblical World;* Donaldson and Kwok, *Postcolonialisms, Feminism and Religion;* and Dube, "Postcolonial Biblical Interpretations," in *Dictionary of Biblical Interpretation;* and *Postcolonial Feminist Interpretation.*

Fourth, postcolonialism helps the Two-Thirds World to have a more sharpened view toward ideologies of oppression and their textual forms and frameworks.

Fifth, postcolonialism highlights the continuation of international domination of some nations by others and the various models and ideologies that accompany such strategies. In so doing, postcolonialism offers critical awareness, hoping that ethical scholars and students would commit themselves to search actively for and work for justice in the world.

In sum, a postcolonial framework offers a better language for assessing/highlighting global oppression and the international search for justice. Liberation and postcolonialism are not opposites. Rather postcolonialism can be rightfully regarded as a servant of justice. Its major aim is to critically bring all of us to be aware of the international forces of oppression in our narratives, theories, and real world, hence, bring us to be committed to the struggle for the establishment of liberation and justice.

25

Epilogue

MIGUEL A. DE LA TORRE

Moving Beyond the Rhetoric of Blame

For the last five years, I have taught at a predominately white, conservative (both politically and religiously) West Michigan college rooted in the historical Christian tradition. Part of the reason I was hired was to expose the students to Christian perspectives they might otherwise never encounter. As mentioned earlier in the preface, this college, like so many throughout the United States and Canada, has historically taught a course titled "Introduction to Theology." To accomplish the task for which I was hired, I added a colon and the word "Liberation" immediately following the course title, hence to read "Introduction to Theology: Liberation."

Seldom in class do we ever review Eurocentric theologians. Rather the course concentrates on the basic concepts of Latin American liberation theology, feminist theology, Black theology, Latino/a theology, Asian American theology, Native American theology, and gay theology. For the most part, the students are engaged in expanding their understanding of Christianity from the perspectives of historically marginalized U.S. groups. Still, every so often, I run across a student who confuses the theological perspectives being voiced from the margins of society with a personal attack on his or her being or character. One such student in particular, angered by the disenfranchised voices being explored, responded by seldom attending classes and by handing in substandard work. I had little choice but to reflect his lack of engagement with the class objectives in the grading process. The student received a D minus.

The student, however, felt he deserved a higher grade. Perceiving a pedagogical moment, I made myself available to discuss why he earned the grade he received. At one point during our conversation, the student, looking at me straight in the eyes, said, "I cannot see how anyone can get a grade lower than a B in your class. After all, all these different groups are saying the same exact thing from their collective anger. They are the good; white people (specifically white males) are the bad. It's not hard to simply repeat this theme."

The student simply labeled the theological expressions generated from the periphery of power and privilege as angry voices. By labeling the theological perspectives of historically U.S. marginalized groups as "angry," these perspectives ceased, in his view, to be valid. Any insight into theological concepts was simply reduced to a subjective view shaped by a group's so-called collective anger, rather than the product of rigorous scholarship or reflection. As long as the diverse theological views of the marginalized can be lumped together and reduced to a product of collective anger, then their perspectives can easily be dismissed as unscholarly with little, or no, relevance to the overall discourse. Even though this student received a low grade, he maintained the power to label the Other, which in effect, gave him the power to terminate, silence, and/or control the overall theological discourse.

What this particular student failed to realize is that regardless of the Christianity expounded by the U.S. dominant culture, self-perpetuating mechanisms of oppression continue to normalize and legitimize how subjugation manifests itself in the overall customs, language, traditions, values, and laws of the United States. Our political systems, our policing authorities, our judicial institutions, and our military forces conspire to maintain a status quo designed to secure and protect the power and wealth of the privileged few at the expense of the disenfranchised many. In some cases, the Christianity advanced by those belonging to the dominant culture, like my student, appears to rationalize these present power structures, hence protecting and masking the political and economic interest of those whom the structures privilege, in effect, a Christianity driven by the self-interest of Euroamericans.

Through a critical social analysis, as employed by the multiple voices collected in this text, it is possible to uncover the connection between the Christianity that supports the present power arrangement and the political, economic, and cultural components of the mechanisms of oppression that protect their power and wealth.

All too often Christianity, as understood and practiced by the dominant culture, masks societal structures designed to protect the privilege of those with power, usually at the expense of their gendered, racial, and ethnic Others. Throughout this book, several leading scholars from within marginalized communities provided a liberating voice to combat such structures of oppression through their understanding of theological concepts. After reading this book, it should be clear that the marginalized groups examined face institutional racism, individual bigotry, and collective discrimination. Although this fact is undeniable, intrastructures of oppression also exist within these same groups–where the oppressed oppress themselves–and to ignore such structures simplifies theologies of liberation as did my student who challenged the grade he earned.

Edward Said coined the term "rhetoric of blame" to describe the activity of disenfranchised groups who attack the dominant culture for being white, privileged, and insensitive to structures of oppression. Such societal structures of oppression are very real in the lives of the marginalized, and I have no intention of minimizing the misery and distress such structures fosters. Still, to solely attack the United States for being complicit is not an alternative to blaming the victims for their predicament. Proscribing to one's own form of nativism accepts the consequences of North American racism, classism, and sexism by reinforcing subservience, even while reevaluating the ethos of marginalized groups. Regardless of any aggressive stance taken, such discourses become trapped within a defensive role (1993, 14, 96, 228–30). Faithfulness to any liberationist theological perspective requires a confession of how marginalized groups oppress their own Others.

U.S. marginalized groups wrestle not against "flesh and blood" (white men), "but against the rulers, against the authorities, against the world's rulers of this age of darkness."[1] Marginalized groups do not battle against white men; rather, they battle against the unfair privileges, the illegitimate interests, and the oppressive powers that contribute to the pretensions of white men and the countergospel version of Christianity that they form to justify their lifestyle. Still, in all honesty, there are some from the dominant culture, who in their own quest for justice, have cast their lots with the disenfranchised, sharing in solidarity their lives and their struggle for justice. Likewise, there are some from the marginalized group who through assimilation have cast their lots with the privileged and powerful, even though they still endure oppressive social structures. If history is any guide, any group, given the chance, has the potential to surmount societal structures and become the new oppressors. It just so happens that in the geographic location known as the United States, during this time in world history, the

[1]See Eph. 6:12: "Because we are not wrestling against flesh and blood, but against the rulers, against the authorities, against the world's rulers of this age of darkness, against the spiritual powers of evil in the heavenlies" (author's translation).

social structures are designed to benefit white Eurocentric men. Social activist César Chávez understood this. When striking farm workers, with and for whom he labored, were described as some sort of superhumans, Chávez retorted, "Cut that nonsense out, all right?...You take the poorest of these guys and give him that ranch over there, he could be just as much of a bastard as the guy sitting there right now" (Matthiessen 1969, 115). Chávez understood that the allure of power and privilege has a way of making bastards out of all of us.

Hence, as Cornel West warns, liberation can never simply be equated with the white American middle-class man (1982, 112). Although equal access to the socioeconomic resources of our society is desirable, the marginalized must stand vigilant of the danger of simply surmounting the present existing structures that cause oppression, and thus become the new oppressors. The primary praxis of any theology of liberation is, and must remain, the dismantling of social mechanisms that benefit one group at the expense of another, regardless if the group privileged is white, black, brown, yellow, red, male, female, gay, heterosexual, or any combination thereof. The hold of the dominant culture upon societal resources will not be effectively challenged until separate marginalized groups begin to accompany each other toward justice, understood here as the dismantling of oppressive structures.

Unfortunately, the overall liberationist discourse seldom explores inner or intrastructures of oppression (within and between marginalized groups) that are masked by the assumption that marginalized groups are not, nor can they be, oppressors because of their overall disenfranchised position. If traces of racism, classism, or sexism are to be found within disenfranchised groups, it is usually dismissed as a lingering influence of Euroamericans' social ill. Regardless of these assertions, among marginalized groups, specifically those who have learned to see themselves through the eyes of the dominant white Eurocentric culture, privilege is usually bestowed among those who are closest to the "white" ideal by both the dominant culture and the disenfranchised. This creates oppressive division within marginalized groups that only benefits and secures further the privileged space occupied by those of the dominant culture while fostering horizontal oppressive structures.

Hierarchical structures are constructed within marginalized groups ranked by how close one's skin pigmentation or economic status is to the "ideal" white. Those whose skin coloration is lighter then other marginalized groups, or those who have amassed sufficient financial resources, are assured greater success (relatively speaking) over against those who display more pronounced Amerindian, African, or Asian features and/or the poor. For some, operations to thin noses or reduce lip size have been performed to create a more European look. Others have participated in painful procedures to straighten hair or lighten skin coloration though bleaching.

Some have simply dyed their hair blond. Still others wishing to avoid such drastic actions nonetheless learned to dress, speak, and behave like white Euroamerican men, suppressing their own culture and heritage.

Within marginalized groups, those who are closest to the "white" ideal can take advantage of their "elevated" position to hold considerable power and prestige among the disenfranchised. Although existing under the eyes of the dominant culture, a system of domination within the domination of the marginalized is developed. Among the subjugated, a space is created generating some privileges (greater opportunities among the marginalized for employment and education) for the "whiter" members whose position becomes assured due to the overall system of white supremacy. In addition to these inner structures of oppression based on skin pigmentation, disenfranchised groups also maintain a repressive patriarchal hierarchy, as several writers in this book attested to. Women face sexism, relegated to subservient roles, regardless of which marginalized group they belong to. Also, gay men and lesbians are as ostracized among marginalized racial and ethnic groups as they are among the Eurocentric dominant culture.

Finally, this epilogue would not be complete if the obvious were not also stated. Even though collegiality exists among the so-called "leaders" of marginalized groups, that is intellectuals, politicians, and business executives, still, among the vast majority, racism and ethnic suspicion and distrust prevail. Although riots in Los Angeles (1992) and Miami (1980, 1983) stemmed from the overall black/white dichotomy fueled by white police brutality upon black citizens, a subtext also existed, revealing hostility among African Americans, Latino/as, and Koreans in Los Angeles[2] and African Americans and Cubans in Miami.[3] Tensions, leading at times to violence, between marginalized communities are real as are tensions within marginalized groups, usually along lines of nationality, specifically among the Latino/a (Cubans, Puerto Ricans, Mexicans, Central Americans, etc.) and Asian American communities (Chinese, Japanese, Koreans, Indonesians, etc.). No doubt, the dominant culture's own privilege remains secure as these different disenfranchised groups are pitted against one another to compete for the limited numbers of jobs, governmental services, and other forms of public support (such as small business loans).

For example, when the January 22, 2003, front page article of the *New York Times* proclaimed, "Hispanics Now Largest Minority, Census Shows," some Latino/as felt that they had finally come into their own, receiving long-overdue recognition. Yet an unspoken underlining message was being communicated to other marginalized groups, specifically African Americans. "Hispanics are now the top dog, so you are going to have to

[2]See Park, *Racial Conflict and Healing*, 29, 41–43.
[3]See my own work, *La Lucha for Cuba*, 59–62.

compete against them for resources." But as Justo González perceptively observed, justice can never be served by having marginalized groups compete with one another for the meager resources doled out. For example, within churches, seminaries, church agencies, and church colleges, a small portion of the budget, a few positions, and a couple of courses are reserved for minorities who are encouraged to fight amongst themselves for their small slice of the pie (1990, 36). These Christian institutions can now point at programs run, in spite of such limited resources, to herald their political correctness, all the while continuing institutionalized oppressive structures that secure the dominant culture's privilege. In effect, marginalized groups are prevented from working together to bring changes to these institutions.[4]

The good news is that the hope of redemption and salvation is held out for all oppressors, those of the dominant culture and those within marginalized groups, for they, who benefit from the current sociopolitical and economic structures, are themselves oppressed. While not to the extent of intellectual, physical, and material depravation felt in economically deprived areas, the oppressor still lacks the full humanity offered by Christ. To oppress another is to oppress oneself. Hegel's concept of "Lordship and Bondage," as found in his *The Phenomenology of Mind,* avers that the master (the oppressor) is also subjugated to the structures he or she creates to enslave the laborer. The master, hoping to define him–or herself through the recognition offered by the laborer, instead finds his or her own enslavement. For the very social structures created to deny the laborer's self identity also perverts the master's ability to accurately construct his own consciousness based upon how he defined his slave, his Other (1967, 238–40). Because an oppressive structure also prevents the master from obtaining an abundant life (specifically in the spiritual sense), those supposedly privileged by said structures are also in need of the gospel message of salvation and liberation. The task before those who are oppressed and those who are privileged by the present structures is not to reverse roles. It is not to share the role of privileged at the expense of some other group, but rather, to dismantle the very structures responsible for causing injustices along race, class, and gender lines regardless of the attitudes bound to those structures. Only then, can all within society, the marginalized as well as the privileged, achieve their full humanity. Only then can everyone become able to live the abundant life offered by Christ as per his promise, "I came that they may have life, and have it abundantly (Jn. 10:10)."

I did not change the D minus grade of the student who saw no difference among the different theologies of liberation. If the truth be known, I seldom

---

[4]See the first chapter of my book *Doing Christian Ethics from the Margins* for more information on how the present societal structures reinforce as normative the dominant culture's worldview, hence fostering competition, rather than cooperation, among marginalized groups. This, in turn, prevents any real challenge from forming against the unjust prevailing status quo.

ever change a student's grade. Still, in a way, this entire book was written for him and others like him, who see the marginalized as some angry monolithic group. If Paul's assertions in 1 Corinthians 1:27–28 are true,[5] and if God's way never changes (Mal. 3:3), then those who are marginalized in this country have a sacred responsibility toward the dominant culture, a calling to bring liberation and salvation. We can never become the new oppressors who would subjugate our present oppressors, but rather, as Paulo Freire reminds us, we are to be

> ...restorers of the humanity of both. This, then, is the great humanistic and historical task of the oppressed: to liberate themselves and their oppressors as well. The oppressors, who oppress, exploit, and rape by virtue of their power, cannot find in this power the strength to liberate either the oppressed or themselves (1994, 26).

It is the liberation found in Christ, understood as salvation from the powers of sin–both personal and communal–that becomes the good news that the multiple authors of this text hope to share with those accustomed to their power and privilege. We hold on to the hope that the societal structures responsible for so much of the dehumanizing misery faced by the marginalized can be dismantled once and for all! Such a task can only become doable when we participate in liberative praxis that moves us beyond the rhetoric of blame.

[5]"But God chose the foolish things of the world that the wise might be shamed; and God chose the weak things of the world so that God might shame the strong things; and God chose the lowborn and despised things of the world, and the things that are not, so that God can bring to nothing the things that are.

Bibliography

Abadìa, José Pedro Tosaus, *Cristo y el universo: estudio lingüístico y temático de Ef. 1, 10b, en Efesios y en la obra de Ireneo de Lyon*. Salamanca: Universidad Pontificia, 1995.

Adams, Carol J. *Neither Man Nor Beast: Feminism and the Defense of Animals.* New York: Continuum, 1995.

Albrecht, Gloria. *The Character of our Communities: Toward an Ethic of Liberation for the Church.* Nashville: Abingdon Press, 1995.

Allen, Paula Gunn. "Violence and the American Indian Woman." In *The Speaking Profits Us.* Seattle: Center for the Prevention of Sexual and Domestic Violence, 1986.

Althaus-Reid, Marcella. *Indecent Theology: Theological Perversions in Sex, Gender and Politics.* London and New York: Routledge, 2001.

Anderson, G.H., and T.F. Stransky, eds. *Mission Trends,* no. 3, *World Theologies.* New York: Paulist Press, 1976.

Anderson, Victor. *Beyond Ontological Blackness: An Essay on African American Religious and Cultural Criticism.* New York: Continuum, 1999.

Apolinaris, Yamina, and Sandra Mangual-Rodriguez. "Theologizing from a Puerto Rican Context." In *Hispanic/Latino Theology: Challenge and Promise,* edited by Ada María Isasi-Díaz and Fernando Segovia. Minneapolis: Fortress Press, 1996.

Aquino, María Pilar. "Latin American Feminist Theology." *Journal of Feminist Studies in Religion* 14, no. 1 (Spring 1998): 89–101.

______. "Theological Method in U.S. Latino/a Theology: Toward an Intercultural Theology for the Third Millennium." In *From the Heart of Our People: Latino/a Explorations in Catholic Systematic Theology,* edited by Orlando O. Espín and Miguel H. Díaz. Maryknoll, N.Y.: Orbis Books, 1999.

Aquino, María Pilar, Daisy L. Machado, and Jeanette Rodríguez, eds. *A Reader in Latina Feminist Theology: Religion and Justice.* Austin: Univ. of Texas Press, 2002.

Aristotle. *Nichomachean Ethics.* New York: Cambridge Univ. Press, 2000.

Ashcroft, Bill, Gareth Griffiths, and Helen Tiffin. *The Post-Colonial Studies Reader.* New York: Routledge, 1995.

Assman, Hugo. *Theology for a Nomad Church.* Translated by Paul Burns. Maryknoll, N.Y.: Orbis Books, 1976.

Augustine. "On the Trinity, 9.1.1." *The Nicene and Post-Nicene Fathers, First Series, Vol. 3.* Edited by Phillip Schaf. Albany, Ore.: Ages Software, 1997.

Bailey, Derrick Sherwin. *Homosexuality and the Western Christian Tradition.* London: Longmans, Green, 1955.

Baker-Fletcher, Garth Kasimu. *Xodus: An African American Male Journey.* Minneapolis: Fortress Press, 1996.

Baker-Fletcher, Karen. *Sisters of Dust, Sisters of Spirit: Womanist Wordings on God and Creation.* Minneapolis: Fortress Press, 1998.

Baker-Fletcher, Karen, and Garth Kasimu Baker-Fletcher. *My Sister, My Brother: Womanist and Xodus God-Talk.* Maryknoll, N.Y.: Orbis Books, 1997.

Bakken, Peter. "The Eco-Justice Movement in Christian Theology: Patterns and Issues." *Theology and Public Policy* 7, no. 1 (Summer 1995): 14–19.

Baldridge, William. "Toward a Native American Theology." *American Baptist Quarterly* (December 1989): 227–38.

Barth, Karl. *Church Dogmatics: The Doctrine of Creation, Vol. 3, Part 2.* Edited by G. W. Bromiley and T. F. Torrance. Edinburgh: T. & T. Clark, 1960.

Barton, Paul, and David Maldonado, Jr. *Hispanic Christianity within Mainline Protestant Traditions: A Bibliography.* Decatur, Ga.: AETH, 1998.

Bediako, Kwame. *Christianity in Africa: The Renewal of a Non-Western Religion.* Maryknoll, N.Y.: Orbis Books, 1995.

Berryman, Phillip. *Liberation Theology: Essential Facts About the Revolutionary Religious Movement in Latin America and Beyond.* New York: Pantheon, 1987.

______. *Religion in the Megacity: Catholic and Protestant Portraits from Latin America.* Maryknoll, N.Y.: Orbis Books, 1996.

Betsworth, Roger G. *Social Ethics: An Examination of American Moral Traditions.* Louisville: Westminster/John Knox Press, 1990.

Bhabha, Homi K. *The Location of Culture.* New York: Routledge, 1994.

Bingemer, María Clara. "Women in the Future of the Theology of Liberation." In *Feminist Theology from the Third World,* edited by Ursula King. Maryknoll, N.Y.: Orbis Books, 1994.

Birch, Charles, and John B. Cobb, Jr. *The Liberation of Life.* New York: Cambridge Univ. Press, 1981.

Blount, Brian K. *Then the Whisper Put on Flesh: New Testament Ethics in an African American Context.* Nashville: Abingdon Press, 2001.

Bodkin, Karen. *How Jews Became White Folks and What That Says About Race in America.* New Brunswick, N.J.: Rutgers Univ. Press, 1999.

Boehmer, Elleke. *Colonial and Postcolonial Literature: Migrant Metaphors.* New York: Oxford Univ. Press, 1995.

Boff, Leonardo. *Jesus Christ Liberator: A Critical Christology for Our Times.* Translated by Patrick Hughes. Maryknoll, N.Y.: Orbis Books, 1978.

______. *Church: Charism and Power–Liberation, Theology, and the Institutional Church.* Translated by John Dierksmeyer. New York: Crossroad, 1985.

______. *Ecclesiologenesis: The Base Communities Reinvent the Church.* Translated by Robert R. Barr. Maryknoll, N.Y.: Orbis Books, 1986.

______. *The Maternal Face of God: The Feminine and its Religious Expression.* Translated by Robert R. Barr and John W. Diercksmeier. San Francisco: Harper and Row, 1987.

______. *Trinity and Society.* Translated by Paul Burns. Maryknoll, N.Y.: Orbis Books, 1988a.

______. *When Theology Listens to the Poor.* Translated by Robert R. Barr. New York, Harper & Row 1988b.

______. *Ecology and Liberation: A New Paradigm.* Translated by John Cumming. Maryknoll, N.Y.: Orbis Books, 1995.

______. "Trinity." In *Systematic Theology: Perspectives from Liberation Theologies,* edited by Jon Sobrino and Ignacio Ellacuria. Maryknoll, N.Y.: Orbis Books, 1996.

______. *Cry of the Earth, Cry of the Poor.* Translated by Phillip Berryman. Maryknoll, N.Y.: Orbis Books, 1997.

Boswell, John. *Christianity, Social Tolerance, and Homosexuality: Gay People in Western Europe from the Beginning of the Christian Era to the Fourteenth Century.* Chicago: Univ. of Chicago Press, 1980.

Bounds, Elizabeth M., ed. *Welfare Policy: Feminist Critiques.* Cleveland: Pilgrim Press, 1999.

Brauns, Rene. *Deus Christianorum: Recherches sur le vocabulaire doctrinal de Tertullie,* 2d ed. Paris: Etudes Augustiniennes, 1977.

Breuning, Wilhelm. "Apokatastasis." In *Lexikon für Theologie und Kirche.* Freiburg: Herder, 1993.

Brock, Rita Nakashima. *Journeys by Heart: A Christology of Erotic Power.* New York: Crossroad, 1988.

______. "Ending Innocence and Nurturing Willfulness." In *Violence Against Women and Children: A Christian Theological Sourcebook,* edited by Carol Adams and Marie Fortune. New York: Continuum, 1995.

Brock, Rita Nakashima, and Rebecca Ann Parker. *Proverbs of Ashes: Violence, Redemptive Suffering, and the Search for What Saves Us.* Boston: Beacon Press, 2001.

Brock, Rita Nakashima, and Susan Brooks Thistlethwaite. *Casting Stones: Prostitution and Liberation in Asia and the United States.* Minneapolis: Fortress Press, 1996.

Brown, Joseph A. *To Stand on the Rock: Meditations on Black Catholic Identity.* Maryknoll, N.Y.: Orbis Books, 1998.

Brown, Peter. *The Body and Society: Men, Women and Sexual Renunciation in Early Christianity.* New York: Columbia Univ. Press, 1988.

Bryant, Bunyon, and Paul Mohai. *Environmental Racism: Issues and Dilemmas.* Ann Arbor: Univ. of Michigan, 1991.

______, eds. *Race and the Incidence of Environmental Hazards: A Time for Discourse.* Boulder, Colo.: Westview, 1992.

Buckley, James, and L. Gregory Jones, eds. *Theology and Eschatology At the Turn of the Millennium.* Oxford, U.K.: Blackwell Publishers, 2001.

Bullard, Robert. *Dumping In Dixie: Race, Class, and Environmental Quality.* Boulder, Colo.: Westview, 1990.

______. "Anatomy of Environmental Racism." In *Toxic Struggles: The Theory and Practice of Environmental Justice,* edited by Richard Hofrichter. Philadelphia: New Society, 1993.

Bullard, Robert, and Beverly Wright, eds. *Confronting Environmental Racism: Voices from the Grassroots.* Boston: South End Press, 1993.

Bulosan, Carlos. *America Is in the Heart: A Personal History.* Seattle & London: University of Washington Press, 1943, 1973.

Busto, Rudy V. "Critical Reflection on Asian American Religious Identity." *Amerasia Journal* 22, no. 1 (1996): 161–95.

Butler, Jon. *Awash in a Sea of Faith: Christianizing the American People.* Cambridge, Mass.: Harvard University Press, 1990.

Butler, Lee H., Jr. *A Loving Home: Caring for African American Marriage and Families.* Cleveland: Pilgrim Press, 2000.

Cannon, Katie Geneva. *Black Womanist Ethics.* Atlanta: Scholars Press, 1988.

______. "Surviving the Blight." In *Inheriting Our Mothers' Gardens: Feminist Theology in Third World Perspective,* edited by Letty Russell, Katie Cannon, Ada María Isasi Díaz, et al. Louisville: Westminster John Knox Press, 1991.

______. *Katie's Canon: Womanism and the Soul of the Black Community.* New York: Continuum, 1995.

______. "Emancipatory Historiography." In *Dictionary of Feminist Theologies,* edited by Letty M. Russell and J. Shannon Clarkson. Louisville: Westminster John Knox Press, 1996.

Chapman, Mark L. *Christianity On Trial: African-American Religious Thought Before and After Black Power.* Maryknoll, N.Y.: Orbis Books, 1996.

Charleston, Steve. "The Old Testament of Native America." In *Lift Every Voice: Constructing Christian Theologies from the Underside,* edited by Susan Brooks Thistlethwaite and Mary Potter Engel. San Francisco: Harper and Row, 1990.

Cho, Jane. *Asians in Latin America: A Partially Annotated Bibliography of Select Countries and People.* San Francisco: Bolerium Books, 2000.

Chung Hyun Kyung. "Han-pu-ri: Doing Theology from Korean Women's Perspective." In *We Dare to Dream: Doing Theology as Asian Women,* edited by Virginia Fabella and Sun Ai Lee Park. Hong Kong: Asian Women's Resource Center for Culture and Theology and the Asian Office of the Women's Commission of the Ecumenical Association of Third World Theologians, 1989.

______. *Struggle to be the Sun Again: Introducing Asian Women's Theology.* Maryknoll, N.Y.: Orbis Books, 1990.

______. "Following Naked Dancing and Long Dreaming." In *Inheriting Our Mothers' Gardens: Feminist Theology in Third World Perspective,* edited by Letty Russell, Katie Cannon, Ada María Isasi Díaz, et al. Louisville: Westminster John Knox Press, 1991.

Churchill, Ward. *Struggle for the Land.* Monroe, Maine: Common Courage Press, 1993.

______. *A Little Matter of Genocide: Holocaust and Denial in the Americas, 1492 to the Present.* San Francisco: City Lights Books, 1997.

______. *Fantasies of the Master Race: Literature, Cinema and the Colonization of American Indians,* 2d edition, revised. San Francisco: City Lights Books, 1998.

Clark, J. Michael. *A Place to Start: Toward an Unapologetic Gay Liberation Theology.* Dallas: Monument Press, 1989.

______. *Beyond Our Ghettos: Gay Theology in Ecological Perspective.* Cleveland: Pilgrim Press, 1993.

______. *Defying the Darkness: Gay Theology in the Shadows.* Cleveland: Pilgrim Press, 1997.

______. *Erotic Ecology: Field Guide to a Relational Ethic.* Asheville, N.C.: BMC Originals, 2002.

Cleage, Albert. *The Black Messiah.* New York: Sheed and Ward, 1968.

______. *Black Christian Nationalism: New Directions for the Black Church.* New York: William Morrow, 1972.

Cobb, John, and Charles Birch. *The Liberation of Life: From the Cell to the Community.* Cambridge, Mass.: Cambridge University Press, 1981.

Coleman, Will. *Tribal Talk: Black Theology, Hermeneutics, and African/American Ways of "Telling the Story."* University Park, Pa.: Pennsylvania State Univ. Press, 2000.

Comblin, José. "The Holy Spirit." In *Systematic Theology: Perspectives from Liberation Theologies,* edited by Jon Sobrino and Ignacio Ellacuria. Maryknoll, N.Y.: Orbis Books, 1996.

______. *Called for Freedom: The Changing Context of Liberation Theology.* Translated by Phillip Berryman. Maryknoll, N.Y.: Orbis Books, 1998.

Comstock, Gary David. *Gay Theology Without Apology.* Cleveland: Pilgrim Press, 1993.

Commission on Theological Concerns of the Christian Conference of Asia, ed. *Minjung Theology: People As the Subjects of History.* Maryknoll, N.Y.: Orbis Books, 1983.

Conde-Frazier, Elizabeth. "Hispanic Protestant Spirituality." In *Teología en Conjunto: A Collaborative Hispanic Protestant Theology,* edited by José David Rodríguez and Loida I. Martell-Otero. Louisville: Westminster John Knox Press, 1997.

Cone, Cecil Wayne. *The Identity Crisis in Black Theology.* Nashville: The African Methodist Episcopal Church, 1975.

Cone, James H. *Black Theology and Black Power.* Minneapolis: Seabury, 1969.
______. *A Black Theology of Liberation.* Maryknoll, N.Y.: Orbis Books, 1970, 1986, 1998.
______. *Spirituals and the Blues: An Interpretation.* San Francisco: Harper & Row, 1972, 1992.
______. "Reflections from the Perspective of U.S. Blacks: Black Theology and Third World Theology." In *Irruption of the Third World: Challenge to Theology,* edited by Virginia Fabella and Sergio Torres. Maryknoll, N.Y.: Orbis Books, 1983.
______. *For My People: Black Theology and the Black Church.* Maryknoll, N.Y.: Orbis Books, 1984.
______. *Martin & Malcolm & America: A Dream or a Nightmare?* Maryknoll, N.Y.: Orbis Books, 1991.
______. "The White Church and Black Power." In *Black Theology: A Documentary History, Vol. 1,* edited by James H. Cone and Gayraud S. Wilmore. Maryknoll, N.Y.: Orbis Books, 1993.
______. *God of the Oppressed,* rev. ed. Maryknoll, N.Y.: Orbis Books, 1997.
Congar, Yves. "Motherhood in God and the Femininity of the Holy Spirit." In *I Believe in the Holy Spirit.* New York: Seabury Press, 1983.
Costas, Orlando E. *Christ Outside the Gate: A New Place of Salvation.* Maryknoll, N.Y.: Orbis Books, 1982.
______. "Evangelism from the Periphery: The Universality of Galilee." *Apuntes* 2, no. 3 (1982): 75–84.
______. "Evangelism from the Periphery: A Galilean Model." *Apuntes* 2, no. 4 (1982): 53–59.
Cummings, George C. L. *A Common Journey: Black Theology (USA) and Latin American Liberation Theology.* Maryknoll, N.Y.: Orbis Books, 1993.
Daly, Mary. *The Church and the Second Sex.* New York: Harper & Row, 1968.
______. *Gyn/ecology: The Metaethics of Radical Feminism.* Boston: Beacon Press, 1978.
Davis, Cyprian. *The History of Black Catholics In the United States.* New York: Crossroad, 1990.
de las Casas, Bartolomé. "De regia potestate o derecho de autodeterminación." In *Corpus Hispanorum de Pace, Vol. VIII,* edited by Luciano Pereña, et al. Madrid: Consejo Superior de Investigaciones Científicas, 1969.
______. *Indian Freedom: The Cause of Bartolomé de las Casas, 1484–1566.* Translated by Francis Patrick Sullivan, S.J. Kansas City: Sheed & Ward, 1995.
De La Torre, Miguel A. *Reading the Bible from the Margins.* Maryknoll, N.Y.: Orbis Books, 2002.
______. *La Lucha for Cuba: Religion and Politics on the Streets of Miami.* Berkeley: Univ. of California Press, 2003.

______. *Doing Christian Ethics from the Margins.* Maryknoll, N.Y.: Orbis Books, 2004.

De La Torre, Miguel A., and Edwin David Aponte. *Introducing Latino/a Theologies.* Maryknoll, N.Y.: Orbis Books, 2001.

Deloria, Vine, Jr. *God Is Red: A Native View of Religion.* New York: North American Press, 1973.

______. "A Native American Perspective on Liberation." *Occasional Bulletin of Missionary Research* 1 (July 1977): 15–17.

______. "The Coming of the Spirit." *Voices from the Third World* 12 (June 1989): 14–25.

______. *For This Land: Writings on Religion in America.* New York: Routledge, 1999.

Denzinger, Henry. *The Sources of Catholic Dogma.* Fitzwilliam, N.H.: Loreto Publications, 1955.

de Wit, Hans. *En la dispersión el texto es patria.* San José, Costa Rica: Universidad Bíblica Latinoamericana, 2002.

Díaz-Stevens, Ana María. "In the Image and Likeness of God." In *Hispanic/Latino Theology: Challenge and Promise,* edited by Ada María Isasi-Díaz and Fernando Segovia. Minneapolis: Fortress Press, 1996.

Donaldson, Laura, ed. *Semeia 75: Postcolonialism and Scriptural Reading.* Atlanta: SBL, 1996.

Donaldson, Laura, and Kwok Pui-lan. *Postcolonialism, Feminism and Religious Discourse.* New York: Routledge, 2002.

Douglas, Kelly Brown."God Is as Christ Does." *The Journal of Religious Thought* 46, no.1 (Summer-Fall 1989): 7–16.

______. *The Black Christ.* Maryknoll, N.Y.: Orbis Books, 1994.

______. "Daring to Speak: Womanist Theology and Black Sexuality." In *Embracing the Spirit: Womanist Perspectives on Hope, Salvation, and Transformation,* edited by Emilie Townes. Maryknoll, N.Y.: Orbis Books, 1997.

______. *Sexuality and the Black Church: A Womanist Perspective.* Maryknoll, N.Y.: Orbis Books, 1999.

Dube, Musa W. "Postcolonial Biblical Interpretations." In *Dictionary of Biblical Interpretation, K-Z,* edited by John H. Hayes. Nashville: Abingdon Press, 1999.

______. *Postcolonial Feminist Interpretation of the Bible.* St. Louis: Chalice Press, 2000.

Du Bois, W. E. B. The *Souls of Black Folk.* New York: Bantam Books, 1989; Grand Rapids: Candace Press, 1996.

Dussel, Enrique. *History and the Theology of Liberation: A Latin American Perspective.* Maryknoll: N.Y.: Orbis Books, 1976.

Dyson, Michael Eric. *Holler If You Hear Me: Searching for Tupac Shakur.* New York: BasicCivitas Books, 2001.

Eagleson, John, and Philip Scharper, eds. *Puebla and Beyond: Documentation and Commentary.* Maryknoll, N.Y.: Orbis Books, 1979.

Earl, Riggins R., Jr. *Dark Salutations: Ritual, God, and Greetings in the African American Community.* Harrisburg, Pa.: Trinity Press International, 2001.

Ebihara, Mary M., Carol A. Mortland, and Judy Ledgerwood, eds. *Cambodian Culture Since 1975: Homeland and Exile.* Ithaca, N.Y. and London: Cornell University Press, 1994.

Edwards, George R. *Gay/Lesbian Liberation: A Biblical Perspective.* New York: Pilgrim Press, 1984.

Eiesland, Nancy. *The Disabled God: Toward a Liberatory Theology of Disability.* Nashville: Abingdon Press, 1994.

Eliade, Mircea. *The Myth of the Eternal Return.* New York: Pantheon Books, 1954.

Elizondo, Virgilio. "Toward an American-Hispanic Theology of Liberation in the U.S.A." In *Irruption of the Third World: Challenge to Theology,* edited by Virginia Fabella and Sergio Torres. Maryknoll, N.Y.: Orbis Books, 1983a.

______. *Galilean Journey: The Mexican-American Promise.* Maryknoll, N.Y.: Orbis Books, 1983b, 2000.

______. *The Future Is Mestizo: Life Where Cultures Meet.* Bloomington, Ind.: Meyer Stone Books, 1988.

______. "Popular Religions as Support of Identity." In *Spirituality of the Third World: A Cry for Life,* edited by K.C. Abraham and Bernadette Mbuy-Beya. Maryknoll, N.Y.: Orbis Books, 1994.

______. *Guadalupe: Mother of the New Creation.* New York: Orbis Books, 1997.

Ellacuría, Ignacio. *Freedom Made Flesh: The Mission of Christ and His Church.* Translated by Robert R. Barr. Maryknoll, N.Y.: Orbis Books, 1976.

Ellacuría, Ignacio S.J., and Jon Sobrino, S.J., eds. *Mysterium Liberationis: Fundamental Concepts of Liberation Theology.* Maryknoll, N.Y.: Orbis Books, 1993.

Epps, Archie, ed. *The Speeches of Malcolm X at Harvard.* New York: William Morrow, 1968.

Erikson, Millard J. *Christian Theology.* Grand Rapids: Baker Book House, 1985.

Erskine, Noel Leo. *Decolonizing Theology: A Caribbean Perspective.* Maryknoll, N.Y.: Orbis Books, 1981.

Espín, Orlando O. "Popular Catholicism." In *Hispanic/Latino Theology: Challenge and Promise,* edited by Ada María Isasi-Díaz and Fernando Segovia. Minneapolis: Fortress Press, 1996.

______. *The Faith of the People: Theological Reflections on Popular Catholicism.* Maryknoll, N.Y.: Orbis Books, 1997.

Espín, Orlando O., and Miguel H. Díaz, eds. *From the Heart of Our People: Latino/a Explorations in Catholic Systematic Theology.* Maryknoll, N.Y.: Orbis Books, 1999.

Eugene, Toinette. "How Can We Forget? An Ethics of Care for AIDS, the African American Family, and the Black Catholic Church." In *Embracing the Spirit: Womanist Perspectives on Hope, Salvation, and Transformation,* edited by Emilie Townes. Maryknoll, N.Y.: Orbis Books, 1997.

Evans, James H., Jr. *We Have Been Believers: An African-American Systematic Theology.* Minneapolis: Fortress Press, 1992.

Fabella, Virginia, and Sun Ai Lee Park. *We Dare to Dream: Doing Theology As Asian Women.* Maryknoll, N.Y.: Orbis Books, 1990.

Fabella, Virginia, and Mercy Amba Oduyoye, eds. *With Passion and Compassion: Third World Women Doing Theology.* Translated by Phillip Berryman. Maryknoll, N.Y.: Orbis Books, 1988.

Fabella, Virgnia, and R.S. Sugirtharajah, eds., *Dictionary of Third World Theologies.* Maryknoll, N.Y.: Orbis Books, 2000.

Farajaje-Jones, Elias. "Breaking Silence: Toward an In-the-Life Theology." In *Black Theology: A Documentary History, Vol. 2: 1980–1992*, edited by James H. Cone and Gayraud S. Wilmore. Maryknoll, N.Y.: Orbis Books, 1993.

Farley, Edward. *Theologia: The Fragmentation and Unity of Theological Education.* Philadelphia: Fortress Press, 1983.

Farley, Reynolds, and Walter R. Allen. *The Color Line and the Quality of Life in America.* New York: Oxford Univ. Press, 1989.

Fassett, Thom White Wolf. "Where Do We Go From Here?" In *Defending Mother Earth: Native American Perspectives on Environmental Justice,* edited by Jace Weaver. Maryknoll, N.Y.: Orbis Books, 1996.

Felder, Cain Hope. *Troubling Biblical Waters: Race, Class, and Family.* Maryknoll, N.Y.: Orbis Books, 1989.

______, ed. *Stony the Road We Trod: African American Biblical Interpretation.* Minneapolis: Fortress Press, 1991.

Fernández, Eduardo C. *La Cosecha: Harvesting Contemporary United States Hispanic Theology [1972–1998].* Collegeville, Minn.: Liturgical Press, 2000.

Fox, Michael W. *The Boundless Circle: Caring for Creatures and Creation.* Wheaton, Ill.: Quest, 1996.

Fraser, Nancy. "Talking About Needs: Interpretive Contests as Political Conflicts in Welfare-State Societies." *Ethics* 99, no. 2 (January 1989): 291–313.

Freire, Paulo. *Pedagogy of the Oppressed, 20th Anniv. Ed.* Translated by Myra Bergman Ramos. New York: Continuum, 1994.

Frye, Northrop. *The Great Code: The Bible and Literature.* San Diego: Harcourt Brace, 1982.

Fukuyama, Francis. *The End of History and the Last Man.* New York: Free Press, 1992.

García, Ismael. *Dignidad: Ethics through Hispanic Eyes.* Nashville: Abingdon Press, 1997.

García-Rivera, Alejandro. *The Community of the Beautiful: A Theological Aesthetics.* Collegeville, Minn.: Liturgical Press, 1999.
Gebara, Ivone, and Maria Clara Bingemer. *Mary: Mother of God, Mother of the Poor.* Maryknoll, N.Y.: Orbis Books, 1989.
Gilkes, Cheryl Townsend. "A Conscious Connection to All That Is: The Color Purple as Subversive and Critical Ethnography." In *Embracing the Spirit: Womanist Perspectives on Hope, Salvation, and Transformation,* edited by Emilie M. Townes. Maryknoll, N.Y.: Orbis Books, 1997.
Gilson, Anne Bathurst. *Eros Breaking Free: Interpreting Sexual Theo-Ethics.* Cleveland: Pilgrim Press, 1995.
Goatley, David Emmanuel. *Were You There? Godforsakenness in Slave Religion.* Maryknoll, N.Y.: Orbis Books, 1996.
Goizueta, Roberto. *Caminemos con Jesús: Toward a Hispanic/Latino Theology of Accompaniment.* Maryknoll, N.Y.: Orbis Books, 1995.
______. "U.S. Hispanic Popular Catholicism in Theopoetics." In *Hispanic/ Latino Theology: Challenge and Promise,* edited by Ada María Isasi-Díaz and Fernando Segovia. Minneapolis: Fortress Press, 1996.
González, Justo. *A History of Christian Thought: From the Beginning to the Council of Chalcedon,* rev. ed. Nashville: Abingdon Press, 1970.
______. "Prophets in the King's Sanctuary," *Apuntes* 1, no. 1 (1980): 3–6.
______. *Mañana: Christian Theology from a Hispanic Perspective.* Nashville: Abingdon Press, 1990.
______. *Santa Biblia: The Bible Through Hispanic Eyes.* Nashville: Abingdon Press, 1996.
______. "The Alienation of Alienation." In *The Other Side of Sin: Woundedness from the Perspective of the Sinned-against,* edited by Andrew Sung Park and Susan L. Nelson. New York: SUNY Press, 2001a.
______. *Mapas para la historia futura de la iglesia.* Buenos Aires: Kairos, 2001b.
______. *The Changing Shape of Church History.* St. Louis: Chalice Press, 2002.
Gorsline, Robin H. and Daniel T. Spencer. "Putting Our Bodies on the Line: Markers for Justice. Continuing the Conversations Between Lesbians and Gay Men in Religion." *The Journal of Men's Studies* 4, no. 3 (February 1996): 291–309.
Goss, Robert E. *Jesus Acted Up: A Gay and Lesbian Manifesto.* San Francisco: HarperSanFrancisco, 1993.
______. "Erotic Visionaries and Freedom Fighters For a New Sexual Reformation." In *Queering Christ: Beyond Jesus ACTED UP.* Cleveland: Pilgrim Press, 2002.
Gottwald, Norman K. *Tribes of Yahweh: A Sociology of the Religion of Liberated Israel, 1250–1050 B.C.E.* Maryknoll, N.Y.: Orbis Books, 1979.
Grant, Jacquelyn. *White Women's Christ and Black Women's Jesus: Feminist Christology and Womanist Response.* Atlanta: Scholars Press, 1989.
______. "Black Theology and the Black Woman." In *Black Theology: A Documentary History, vol. 1: 1966–1979,* edited by James H. Cone and Gayraud S. Wilmore. Maryknoll, N.Y.: Orbis Books, 1993.

______. "Subjectification as a Requirement for Christological Construction." In *Lift Every Voice: Constructing Christian Theologies from the Underside,* edited by Susan Brooks Thistlethwaite and Mary Potter Engel. Maryknoll, N.Y.: Orbis Books, 1998.

Gregory of Nyssa. "Against Eunomius." In "Select Writings and Letters of Gregory, Bishop of Nyssa," translated by William Moore and Hery Austin Wilson, in the *Nicene and Post-Nicene Fathers, Vol. V, Bk. I, 14.* Grand Rapids: Eerdmanns, 1988.

Grenz, Stanley. *The Social God and the Relational Self: A Trinitarian Theology of the Imago Dei.* Louisville: Westminster John Knox Press, 2001.

Grey, Mary. "Where Does the Wild Goose Fly To: Seeking a New Theology of Spirit for Feminist Theology." *New Blackfriars* (1991): 89–96.

Griffin, Horace. "Giving New Birth: Lesbians, Gays and the 'Family': A Pastoral Care Perspective." *Journal of Pastoral Theology* 3 (Summer 1993): 88–98.

______. "Revisioning Christian Ethical Discourse on Homosexuality: A Challenge for the 21st Century." *Journal of Pastoral Care* 53, no. 2 (Summer 1999): 209–19.

______. "Their Own Received Them Not: African American Lesbians and Gays in Black Churches." *Journal of Theology and Sexuality* (Spring 2000): 88–100.

Guardiola-Sáenz, Leticia S. "Borderless Women and Borderless Texts: A Cultural Reading of Matthew 15:21–28," *Semeia* 78 (1997): 69–81.

______. "Border-crossing and Its Redemptive Power in John 7:53–8:11: A Cultural Reading of Jesus and the Accused." In *John and Postcolonialism: Travel, Space and Power,* edited by Musa Dube and Jeffrey Staley. New York: Sheffield Academic Press, 2002.

Gutiérrez, Gustavo. *The Power of the Poor in History.* Translated by Robert R. Barr. Maryknoll, N.Y.: Orbis Books, 1984.

______. *We Drink from Our Own Wells: The Spiritual Journey of a People.* Translated by Matthew J. O'Connell. Maryknoll, N.Y.: Orbis Books, 1985.

______. *A Theology of Liberation: History, Politics and Salvation.* Translated by Caridad Inda and John Eagleson. Maryknoll, N.Y.: Orbis Books, 1973, 1988.

______. "Toward a Theology of Liberation." In *Liberation Theology: A Documentary History,* edited by Alfred T. Hennelly. Maryknoll, N.Y.: Orbis Books, 1990.

______. *The God of Life.* Translated by Matthew J. O'Connell. Maryknoll, N.Y.: Orbis Books, 1991.

______. *Las Casas: In Search of the Poor of Jesus Christ.* Translated by Robert R. Barr. Maryknoll, N.Y.: Orbis Books, 1993.

Hardin, Garret. "Living on a Lifeboat." *BioScience* 24, no. 10 (October 1974): 561–69.

Harris, James H. *Pastoral Theology: A Black-Church Perspective.* Minneapolis: Fortress Press, 1991.

Harrison, Beverly Wildung. *Our Right to Choose: Toward a New Ethic of Abortion.* Boston: Beacon Press, 1983a.

______. *Making the Connections: Essays in Feminist Social Ethics.* Boston: Beacon Press, 1983b, 1985.

______. "Forward." In *Welfare Policy: Feminist Critiques,* edited by Elizabeth M. Bounds. Cleveland: The Pilgrim Press, 1999.

Hart, H. L. A. "Are There Any Natural Rights?" *Philosophical Review* 64 (1955): 175–91.

Harvey, Van Austin. *A Handbook of Theological Terms.* New York: Macmillan, 1964.

Hayes, Diana L., *Hagar's Daughters: Womanist Ways Of Being In The World.* Mahwah, N.J.: Paulist Press, 1995.

Hayes, Diana L. and Cyprian Davis, eds. *Taking Down Our Harps: Black Catholics in the United States.* Maryknoll, N.Y.: Orbis Books, 1998.

Hegel, G. W. F. *The Phenomenology of Mind.* Translated by J. B. Baillie. New York: Harper & Row, 1967.

Hennelly, Alfred, ed. *Santo Domingo and Beyond: Documents and Commentaries from the Fourth General Conference of Latin American Bishops.* Maryknoll, N.Y.: Orbis Books, 1993.

Heyward, Carter. *Our Passion for Justice: Images of Power, Sexuality, and Liberation.* New York: Pilgrim Press, 1984.

______, ed. *God's Fierce Whimsy: Christian Feminism and Theological Education.* By the Mud Flower Collective. New York: Pilgrim Press, 1985.

______. *Coming Out & Relational Empowerment: A Lesbian Feminist.* Audiocassette. Wellesley, Mass.: The Stone Center; 1988.

______. *Touching Our Strength: The Erotic as Power and the Love of God.* San Francisco: Harper and Row, 1989.

______. "Heterosexism: Enforcing Male Supremacy." In *Redefining Sexual Ethics: a Sourcebook of Essays, Stories, and Poems,* edited by Susan E. Davies and Eleanor H. Haney. Cleveland: Pilgrim Press, 1991.

______. "Embodying the Connections: What Lesbians Can Learn from Gay Men about Sex and What Gay Men Must Learn from Lesbians about Justice." In *Spirituality and Community: Diversity in Lesbian and Gay Experience,* edited by J. Michael Clark and Michael L. Stemmeler. Las Colinas, Tex.: Monument Press, 1994.

______. *Saving Jesus from Those Who Are Right: Rethinking What It Means to be Christian.* Minneapolis: Fortress Press, 1999.

______. *God in the Balance: Christian Spirituality in Times of Terror.* Cleveland: Pilgrim Press, 2002.

Hill, Reneé. "Who Are We For Each Other? Sexism, Sexuality and Womanist Theology." In *Black Theology: A Documentary History, Vol.*

2: 1980–1992, edited by James H. Cone and Gayraud S. Wilmore. Maryknoll, N.Y.: Orbis Books, 1993.

______. "Disrupted/Disruptive Movements: Black Theology and Black Power 1969/1999." In *Black Faith and Public Talk: Critical Essays on James H. Cone's* Black Theology & Black Power, edited by Dwight N. Hopkins. Maryknoll, N.Y.: Orbis Books, 1999.

Hinkelammert, Franz. *El grito del sujeto: del teatro-mundo del evangelio de Juan al perro-mundo de la globalización.* San José, Costa Rica: Departamento Ecuménico de Investigaciones, 1998.

Hirabayashi, Lane Ryo, Akemi Kikumura-Yano, and James Hirabayashi, eds. *New World, New Lives: Globalization and People of Japanese Descent in the Americas and from Latin America in Japan.* Palo Alto, Calif.: Stanford Univ. Press, 2002.

Hobsbawm, Eric. *Age of Extremes: The Short Twentieth Century, 1914–1991.* London: Michael Joseph, 1994.

Hodgson, Peter. *God's Wisdom: Toward a Theology of Education.* Louisville: Westminster John Knox Press, 1999.

Hoig, Stan. *The Sand Creek Massacre.* Norman, Okla.: Univ. of Oklahoma Press, 1961.

Holm, Tom. "Patriots and Pawns: State Use of American Indians in the Military and the Process of Nativization in the United States." In *The State of Native America: Genocide, Colonization and Resistance,* edited by M. Annette Jaimes. Boston: South End, 1992.

Hood, Robert. *Must God Remain Greek?* Minneapolis: Fortress Press, 1990.

hooks, bell. *Feminist Theory: From Margin to Center.* Boston: South End Press, 1984.

Hopkins, Dwight N. *Black Theology USA and South Africa: Politics, Culture, and Liberation.* Maryknoll, N.Y.: Orbis Books, 1989.

______. *Down, Up & Over: Slave Religion and Black Theology.* Minneapolis: Fortress Press, 1999.

______. *Introducing Black Theology of Liberation.* Maryknoll, N.Y.: Orbis Books, 1999.

______. *Shoes That Fit Our Feet: Sources for a Constructive Black Theology.* Maryknoll, N.Y.: Orbis Books, 2000.

Horner, Tom. *Jonathan Loved David: Homosexuality in Biblical Times.* Philadelphia: Westminster Press, 1978.

Hume, David. *The Natural History of Religion.* London: A. & C. Black, 1956.

Hunt, Mary E. *Fierce Tenderness: A Feminist Theology of Friendship.* New York: Crossroad, 1991.

______. "Opposites Do Not Always Attract: How and Why Lesbian Women and Gay Men Diverge Religiously." In *Spirituality and Community: Diversity in Lesbian and Gay Experience,* edited by J. Michael Clark and Michael L. Stemmeler. Las Colinas, Tex.: Monument Press, 1994.

Ignatiev, Noel. *How the Irish Became White.* New York and London: Routledge, 1996.

Irarrázabal, Diego. *Inculturation: New Dawn of the Church in Latin America.* Maryknoll, N.Y.: Orbis Books, 2000.

Isasi-Díaz, Ada María. *En la Lucha/In the Struggle: Elaborating a Mujerista Theology.* Minneapolis: Fortress Press, 1993.

______. *Mujerista Theology: A Theology for the Twenty-First Century.* Maryknoll, N.Y.: Orbis Books, 1996.

______. "Solidarity: Love of Neighbor in the 21st Century." In *Lift Every Voice: Constructing Christian Theologies from the Underside,* edited by Susan Brooks Thistlethwaite and Mary Potter Engel. Maryknoll, N.Y.: Orbis Books, 1998.

Isasi-Díaz, Ada María, and Yolanda Tarango. *Hispanic Women: Prophetic Voice in the Church.* San Francisco: Harper and Row, 1988.

Jaimes, M. Annette, and Theresa Halsey. "American Indian Women: At the Center of Indigenous Resistance in North America." In *The State of Native America: Genocide, Colonization and Resistance,* edited by M. Annette Jaimes. Boston: South End, 1992.

Jiménez, Pablo A., and Justo L. González. *Púlpito: Preaching with an Accent.* Nashville: Abingdon Press, 2003.

Jones, Major. *The Color of God: The Concept of God in Afro-American Thought.* Macon, Ga.: Mercer University Press, 1987.

Jones, William R. *Is God a White Racist?* New York: Anchor/Doubleday, 1973.

Joyce, James. *A Portrait of the Artist as a Young Man.* New York: Viking Press, 1962.

Jüngel, Eberhard. *God as the Mystery of the World: On the Foundation of the Theology of the Crucified One in the Dispute Between Theism and Atheism.* Translated by Darrell L. Guder. Edinburgh: T&T Clark, 1983.

Kant, Immanuel. *Perpetual Peace and Other Essays.* Indianapolis: Hackett, 1985.

Kaufman, Gordon. *In Face of Mystery.* Cambridge, Mass.: Harvard Univ. Press, 1993.

Kelsey, David. *To Understand God Truly: What's Theological about a Theological School.* Louisville: Westminster/John Knox Press, 1992.

Kidwell, Clara Sue, Homer Noley, and Tink Tinker. *A Native American Theology.* Maryknoll, N.Y.: Orbis Books, 2001.

Kien, Ing. *Phka Chhouk Kampuchea (Lotus Flower of Cambodia).* Paris: Edition Anakota, 1977.

Kim, Jung Ha. *Bridge-Makers and Cross-Bearers: Korean-American Women and the Church.* Atlanta: Scholars Press, 1997.

______. "But Who Do You Say That I Am?" (Matt 16:15): A Churched Korean American Woman's Autobiographical Inquiry." In *Journeys at the Margin: Toward an Autobiographical Theology in American-Asian*

Perspective, edited by Peter C. Phan and Jung Young Lee. Collegeville, Minn.: The Liturgical Press, 1999.

King, Martin Luther, Jr. *Stride Toward Freedom.* New York: Harper and Row, 1958.

______. *Strength to Love.* Philadelphia: Fortress Press, 1963.

______. *A Testament of Hope: The Essential Writings of Martin Luther King, Jr.,* edited by James M. Washington. San Francisco: Harper and Row, 1986.

Kingston, Maxine Hong. *The Woman Warrior: Memoirs of a Girlhood Among Ghosts.* New York: Knopf, 1975.

______. *China Men.* New York: Ballantine Books, 1980.

______. *Tripmaster Monkey: His Fake Book.* New York: Vintage Books, 1990.

Kirk-Duggan, Cheryl. *Exorcising Evil: A Womanist Perspective on the Spirituals.* Maryknoll, N.Y.: Orbis Books, 1997.

Knitter, Paul F. "Beyond a Mono-religious Theological Education." In *Shifting Boundaries: Contextual Approaches to the Structure of Theological Education,* edited by Barbara G. Wheeler and Edward Farley. Louisville: Westminster John Knox Press, 1991.

Kogawa, Joy. *A Choice of Dreams.* Toronto: Canadian Publishers, 1974.

______. *Jericho Road.* Toronto: Canadian Publishers, 1977.

______. *Obasan.* Boston: David Godine, 1982.

______. *Itsuka.* New York: Viking Penguin, 1992.

Kolmar, Wendy, and Frances Bartkowski, eds. *Feminist Theory: A Reader,* Mountainview, Calif.: Mayfield, 2000.

Koyama, Kosuke. *Waterbuffalo Theology.* Maryknoll, N.Y.: Orbis Books, 1974, 1999.

______. *Mount Fuji and Mount Sinai: A Critique of Idols.* Maryknoll, N.Y.: Orbis Books, 1984.

Kusmer, Kenneth L. *Down and Out, on the Road: The Homeless in American History.* New York: Oxford Press, 2002.

Kwasikwakye-Nuako. "The Akan People, Ancestors and Christmas: Toward Indigenizing Christianity in Africa." *Voices from the Third World* 25 (December 2002): 175–204.

Kwok Pui-lan. *Chinese Women and Christianity, 1860–1927.* Atlanta: Scholars Press, 1992.

______. *Discovering the Bible in the Non-Biblical World.* Maryknoll, N.Y.: Orbis Books, 1995.

______. *Introducing Asian Feminist Theology.* Cleveland: Pilgrim Press, 2000.

LaCugna, Catherine Mowry. *God for Us: The Trinity and Christian Life.* San Francisco: HarperSanFrancisco, 1991.

Lee, Charles. "Evidence of Environmental Racism." *Sojourners* (February-March 1990): 21–25.

Lee, Jung Young. *A Theology of Change: A Christian Concept of God in Eastern Perspective.* Maryknoll, N.Y.: Orbis Books, 1979.

______. *Embracing Change: Postmodern Interpretations of the I Ching from a Christian Perspective.* Cranbury, N.J.: Univ. of Scranton Press, 1994.

______. *Marginality: The Key to Multicultural Theology.* Minneapolis: Fortress Press, 1995.

______. *The Trinity in Asian Perspective.* Nashville: Abingdon Press, 1996.

______. *Journeys at the Margin: Toward an Autobiographical Theology in American-Asian Perspective.* Collegeville, Minn.: Liturgical Press, 1999.

Libânio, João B., and Maria Clara L. Bingemer. *Escatologia Cristã: O Novo Céu e a Nova Terra.* Petrópolis, Brasil: Vozes, 1985.

Liew, Tat-Siong Benny, ed. "The Bible in Asian America." *Semeia* 90/91. Williston, Vt.: Society of Biblical Literature, 2002.

Lincoln, C. Eric, and Lawrence Mamiya, *The Black Church in the African American Experience.* Durham, N.C.: Duke University Press, 1990.

Long, Charles H. *Significations: Signs, Symbols and Images in the Interpretation of Religion.* Minneapolis: Fortress Press, 1986.

Long, Ronald E. "Toward a Phenomenology of Gay Sex: Groundwork for a Contemporary Sexual Ethic." In *Embodying Diversity: Identity, (Bio)Diversity, and Sexuality,* edited by J. Michael Clark and Michael L. Stemmeler. Las Colinas, Tex.: Monument Press, 1995.

López-Sierra, Héctor E. "Crítica a la epistemo[teo]logía desde el Caribe afro-antillano de habla hispana." *Apuntes* 19, no. 3 (Fall 1999): 84–95.

Lowe, Lisa. "Heterogeneity, Hybridity, Multiplicity: Marking Asian American Differences." *Diaspora* 1, no. 1 (Spring 1991): 24–44.

Loya, Gloria Ines. "The Hispanic Woman: Pasionaria and Pastora of the Hispanic Community." In *Frontiers of Hispanic Theology in the United States,* edited by Allan Figueroa. Maryknoll, N.Y.: Orbis Books, 1992.

Lucas, Lawrence. *Black Priest/White Church: Catholics and Racism.* New York: Random House, 1970.

Lyotard, Jean-François. *The Postmodern Condition: A Report on Knowledge.* Minneapolis: Univ. of Minnesota Press, 1984.

Machado, Daisy. "The Writing of Religious History in the United States: A Critical Assessment." In *Hispanic Christianity within Mainline Protestant Traditions: A Bibliography,* edited by David Maldonado, Jr. and Paul Barton. Decatur, Ga.: AETH, 1998.

Maduro, Otto. "Notes Toward a Sociology of Latina/o Religious Empowerment." In *Hispanic/Latino Theology: Challenge and Promise,* edited by Ada María Isasi-Díaz and Fernando Segovia. Minneapolis: Fortress Press, 1996.

Maldonado, David, Jr., ed. *Protestantes/Protestants: Hispanic Christianity within Mainline Traditions.* Nashville: Abingdon Press, 1999.

______. *Crossing Guadalupe Street: Growing up Hispanic & Protestant.* Albuquerque: Univ. of New Mexico Press, 2001.

Martey, Emmanuel. *African Theology: Inculturation and Liberation.* Maryknoll, N.Y.: Orbis Books, 1993.

Matovina, Timothy, and Gerald E. Poyo, eds. *¡Presente! U.S. Latino Catholics from Colonial Origins to the Present.* Maryknoll, N.Y.: Orbis Books, 2000.

Matsuoka, Fumitaka. *Out of Silence: Emerging Themes in Asian American Churches.* Cleveland: Pilgrim Press, 1995.

Matthiessen, Peter. *Sal Si Puedes: Cesar Chavez and the New American Revolution.* New York: Random House, 1969.

McAfee Brown, Robert. *Spirituality and Liberation: Overcoming the Great Fallacy.* Louisville: Westminster/John Knox Press, 1988.

______, ed. *Kairos: Three Prophetic Challenges to the Church.* Grand Rapids: Wm. B. Eerdmans, 1990.

McCunn, Ruthanne Lum. *Thousand Pieces of Gold: A Biographical Novel.* Boston: Beacon Press, 1981.

McDaniel, Jay B. *Of God and Pelicans: A Theology of Reverence for Life.* Louisville: Westminster/John Knox Press, 1989.

McFague, Sallie. *Metaphorical Theology: Models of God in Religious Language.* Philadelphia: Fortress Press, 1982.

______. *Models of God: Theology for an Ecological, Nuclear Age.* Philadelphia: Fortress Press, 1987.

______. *The Body of God: An Ecological Theology.* Minneapolis: Fortress Press, 1993.

______. *Super, Natural Christians: How We Should Love Nature.* Minneapolis: Fortress Press, 1997.

McNeill, John. *The Church and the Homosexual.* Kansas City: Sheed Andrews and McMeel, 1976.

Mercer, Joyce Ann. "Liberation." In *Dictionary of Feminist Theologies,* edited by Letty Russell and J. Shannon Clarkson. Louisville: Westminster John Knox Press, 1995.

Merchant, Carolyn. *Radical Ecology: The Search for a Livable World.* New York: Routledge, 1992.

______. *Earthcare: Women and the Environment.* New York: Routlege, 1995.

Miguez-Bonino, José. *Doing Theology in a Revolutionary Situation.* Philadelphia: Fortress Press, 1975.

______. *Towards a Christian Political Ethic.* Philadelphia: Fortress Press, 1983.

Mitchell, Mozella. "Women at the Well: Mahalia Jackson and the Inner and Outer Spiritual Transformation." In *Embracing the Spirit: Womanist Perspectives on Hope, Salvation, and Transformation,* edited by Emilie Townes. Maryknoll, N.Y.: Orbis Books, 1997.

Min, Anselm Kyungsuk. "Solidarities of Others in the Body of Christ: A New Theological Paradigm." *Toronto Journal of Theology* 14 (1998): 239–54.

______. "Dialectical Pluralism and Solidarity of Others: Towards a New Paradigm." *Journal of the American Academy of Religion* 65, no. 3 (Fall 1997): 587–604.

______. "From Autobiography to Fellowship of Others: Reflections on Doing Ethnic Theology Today." In *Journeys at the Margin: Towards an Autobiographical Theology in American-Asian Perspective,* edited by Peter C. Phan and Jung Young Lee. Collegeville, Minn.: Liturgical Press, 1999.

Mollenkott, Virginia Ramey, and Letha Scanzoni. *Is the Homosexual My Neighbor? Another Christian View.* San Francisco: Harper and Row, 1978, 1994.

Moltmann, Jürgen. *The Church in the Power of the Spirit: A Contribution to Messianic Ecclesiology.* Minneapolis: Fortress Press, 1993.

______. *The Coming of God: Christian Eschatology.* London: SCM Press, 1996.

______. "Is There Life After Death?" In *The End of the World and the Ends of God: Science and Theology on Eschatology,* edited by John Polkinghorne and Michael Welker. Harrisburg, Pa.: Trinity Press International, 2000.

Morse, Merrill. *Kosuke Koyama: A Model for Intercultural Theology.* Studies in the Intercultural History of Christianity Vol. 17. Frankfurt: Peter Lang, 1991.

Mosala, Itumeleng J. *Biblical Hermeneutics and Black Theology in South Africa.* Grand Rapids: Wm. B. Eerdmans, 1989.

Muñoz, Ronaldo. *The God of Christians.* Translated by Paul Burns. Maryknoll, N.Y.: Orbis Books, 1990.

Murray, Robert. *Symbols of Church and Kingdom: A Study in Early Syriac Tradition.* London: Cambridge University Press, 1975.

Mveng, Englebert. "Third World Theology–What Theology? What Third World?: Evaluation by an African Delegate." In *Irruption of the Third World: Challenge to Theology,* edited by Virginia Fabella and Sergio Torres. Maryknoll, N.Y.: Orbis Books, 1983.

Niebuhr, H. Richard. *Christ and Culture.* New York: Harper 1951.

Niebuhr, Reinhold. *The Nature and Destiny of Man, Vol. 1.* New York: C. Scribner, 1941–43.

______. *Faith and History: A Comparison of Christianity and Modern Views of History.* New York: C. Scribner, 1949.

Novak, Michael. *Unmeltable Ethnics: Politics and Culture in American Life,* 2d ed. New Brunswick, N.J.: Transaction Press, 1996.

Oduyoye, Mercy Amba, and Musimbi R. A. Kanyoro, eds. *The Will to Arise: Women, Tradition, and the Church in Africa.* Maryknoll, N.Y.: Orbis Books, 1992.

Olazagasti-Segovia, Elena. "Judith Ortiz Cover's Silent Dancing: The Self-Portrait of the Artist as a Young, Bicultural Girl." In *Hispanic/Latino Theology: Challenge and Promise,* edited by Ada María Isasi-Díaz and Fernando Segovia. Minneapolis: Fortress Press, 1996.

Omi, Michael, and Howard Winant. *Racial Formation in the United States: From the 1960s to the 1980s.* New York and London: Routledge, 1986.

Ortega y Gasset, José. *Ideas y creencias.* Madrid: Revista de Occidente, 1942.

Panikkar, Raimon. *The Intrareligious Dialogue.* New York: Paulist Press, 1978, 1999.

Panos Institute. "We Speak for Ourselves: Social Justice, Race, and Environment," 1990.

Paris, Peter J. *The Spirituality of African Peoples: The Search For A Common Moral Discourse.* Minneapolis: Fortress Press, 1995.

Park, Andrew Sung . *The Wounded Heart of God: The Asian Concept of Han and the Christian Doctrine of Sin.* Nashville: Abingdon Press, 1993.

______. *Racial Conflict and Healing: An Asian-American Theological Perspective.* Maryknoll, N.Y.: Orbis Books, 1996.

______. "A Theology of Transmutation." In *Journeys at the Margin: Towards an Autobiographical Theology in American-Asian Perspective,* edited by Peter C. Phan and Jung Young Lee. Collegeville, Minn.: Liturgical Press, 1999.

Pedraja, Luis G. *Infinity in Finitude: The Trinity in Process Theism and Eberhard Jüngel.* Ph.D. diss., University of Virginia, 1994.

______. *Jesus Is My Uncle: Christology from a Hispanic Perspective.* Nashville: Abingdon Press, 1999.

Peters, Tiemo Rainer, and Claus Urban, *Ende der Zeit? : die Provokation der Rede von Gott : Dokumentation einer Tagung mit Joseph Kardinal Ratzinger, Johann Baptist Metz, Jürgen Moltmann und Eveline Goodman-Thau in Ahaus* (Mainz : M.-Grünewald-Verlag, c1999).

Phan, Peter C. "Betwixt and Between: Doing Theology with Memory and Imagination." In *Journeys at the Margin: Towards an Autobiographical Theology in American-Asian Perspective,* edited by Peter C. Phan and Jung Young Lee. Collegeville, Minn.: Liturgical Press, 1999.

______. "A Common Journey, Different Paths, the Same Destination: Method in Liberation Theologies." In *A Dream Unfinished: Theological Reflections on America from the Margins,* edited by Eleazar S. Fernandez and Fernando F. Segovia. Maryknoll, N.Y.: Orbis Books, 2001.

Phelps, Jamie T., ed. *Black And Catholic: The Challenge and Gift of Black Folk. Contributions of African American Experience and Thought to Catholic Theology.* Milwaukee: Marquette Univ. Press, 1997.

Pineda, Ana María. "Oral Tradition of a People." In *Hispanic/Latino Theology: Challenge and Promise,* edited by Ada María Isasi-Díaz and Fernando Segovia. Minneapolis: Fortress Press, 1996.

Pinn, Anthony B. *Why Lord? Suffering and Evil in Black Theology.* New York: Continuum, 1995.

______. *Varieties of African American Religious Experience.* Minneapolis: Fortress Press, 1998.

Pixley, Jorge. *La resurrección de Jesús, el Cristo: Una interpretación desde la lucha por la vida.* Managua, Nicaragua: CIEETS, CEDEPCA & CCM, 1997.

Pixley, Jorge, et al. *Por un mundo otro: alternativas al mercado global.* Quito, Ecuador: Consejo Latinoamericano de Iglesias, 2003.

Plato. *The Republic.* Translated by Richard W. Sterling and William C. Scott. New York, Norton, 1985.

Polkinghorne, John, and Michael Welker, eds. *The End of the World and the Ends of God: Science and Theology on Eschatology.* Harrisburg, Pa.: Trinity Press International, 2000.

Prichard, Rebecca Button. *Sensing the Spirit: The Holy Spirit in Feminist Perspective.* St. Louis: Chalice Press, 1999.

Prucha, Francis Paul. *Americanizing the American Indian: Writings of the Friends of the Indian, 1880–1900.* Boston: Harvard Univ. Press, 1973.

Quasten, Johannes, and Joseph C. Plumpe, eds. *Ancient Christian Writers: The Works of the Fathers in Translation.* Vol. 6. Westminster, Md.: The Newman Press, 1961.

Raboteau, Albert J. *Slave Religion: The "Invisible Institution" in the Antebellum South.* New York: Oxford University Press, 1978.

Rasmussen, Larry L. *Earth Community, Earth Ethics.* Maryknoll, N.Y.: Orbis Books, 1996.

Ray, Stephen G. *Do No Harm: Social Sin and Christian Responsibility.* Minneapolis: Fortress Press, 2003.

Recinos, Harold. "The Barrio as the Locus of a New Church." In *Hispanic/Latino Theology: Challenge and Promise,* edited by Ada María Isasi-Díaz and Fernando Segovia. Minneapolis: Fortress Press, 1996.

______. "Popular Religion, Political Identity, and Life-Story Testimony in an Hispanic Community." In *The Ties that Bind: African American and Hispanic/Latino/a Theologies in Dialogue,* edited by Anthony B. Pinn and Benjamin Valentin. New York: Continuum, 2001.

Redkey, Edwin, ed. *Respect Black: The Writings and Speeches of Henry McNeal Turner.* New York: Arno Press, 1971.

Rieger, Joerg. *Remember the Poor: The Challenge to Theology in the Twenty-First Century.* Harrisburg, Pa.: Trinity Press International, 1998.

Riggs, Marcia. *Awake, Arise, Act: A Womanist Call to Black Liberation.* Cleveland: Pilgrim Press, 1994.

Rivera-Pagán, Luis N. *Essays From the Diaspora.* México, D. F.: Centro Luterano de Formación Teológica, Publicaciones El Faro, Lutheran School of Theology at Chicago, Centro Basilea de Investigación, 2002.

Roberts, J. Deotis. *Liberation and Reconciliation.* Philadelphia: Westminster, 1971.

______. *Africentric Christianity: A Theological Appraisal for Ministry.* Valley Forge, Pa.: Judson Press, 2000.

Rodríguez, Jeanette. "Sangre llama a sangre: Cultural Memory as a Source of Theological Insight." In *Hispanic/Latino Theology: Challenge and*

Promise, edited by Ada María Isasi-Díaz and Fernando Segovia. Minneapolis: Fortress Press, 1996.

Rodríguez, José David, and Loida I. Martell-Otero, eds. *Teología en Conjunto: A Collaborative Hispanic Protestant Theology.* Louisville: Westminster John Knox Press, 1997.

Rodríguez-Díaz, Daniel R., and David Cortés-Fuentes, eds. *Hidden Stories: Unveiling the History of the Latino Church.* Decatur, Ga.: AETH, 1994.

Romero, C. Gilbert. *Hispanic Devotional Piety: Tracing the Biblical Roots.* Maryknoll, N.Y.: Orbis, 1991.

Rooks, Charles Shelby. *Revolution in Zion: Reshaping African American Ministry, 1960–1974/A Biography in the First Person.* New York: The Pilgrim Press, 1990.

Roth, Joshua Hotaka. *Brokered Homeland: Japanese Brazilian Migrants in Japan.* Ithaca, N.Y.: Cornell Univ. Press, 2002.

Ruether, Rosemary Radford. *Liberation Theology: Human Hope Confronts Christian History and American Power.* New York: Paulist Press, 1972.

______. *New Woman, New Earth: Sexist Ideologies and Human Liberation.* New York: Seabury, 1975, Boston: Beacon Press, 1995.

______. *Sexism & God-talk: Toward a Feminist Theology.* Boston: Beacon Press, 1983, 1993.

______. *Gaia and God: An Ecofeminist Theology of Earth Healing.* New York: HarperCollins, 1992, 1994.

______. *Women Healing Earth: Third World Women on Ecology, Feminism, and Religion.* Maryknoll, N.Y.: Orbis Books, 1996.

Rusch, William G. *The Trinitarian Controversy.* Philadelphia: Fortress Press, 1980.

Said, Edward. *Culture and Imperialism.* New York: Alfred A. Knopf, 1993.

Saiving, Valerie. "The Human Situation." In *Womanspirit Rising,* edited by Carol Christ and Judith Plaskow. New York: Harper & Row, 1979.

Sandel, Michael J. "The Encumbered Self." In *Morality and Moral Controversies: Readings in Moral, Social, and Political Philosophy,* 5th edition, edited by John Arthur. Prentice Hall: Upper Saddle River, 1999.

Sandoval, Moisés. *On the Move: A History of the Hispanic Church in the United States.* Maryknoll, N.Y.: Orbis Books, 1990.

Sano, Roy, ed. *Amerasian Theology of Liberation: A Reader.* Berkeley, Calif.: Pacific and Asian Center for Theology and Strategies, 1973a.

______. *The Theologies of Asian Americans and Pacific Peoples: A Reader.* Berkeley, Calif.: Pacific and Asian Center for Theology and Strategies, 1973b.

Sartre, Jean-Paul. *Nausea.* New York: New Directions Books, 1959.

Schaup, Joan. *Woman: Image of the Holy Spirit.* Denville, N.J.: Dimension Books, 1975.

Schüssler Fiorenza, Elisabeth. *Bread Not Stone: The Challenge of Feminist Biblical Interpretation.* Boston: Beacon Press, 1984.

______. *But She Said: Feminist Practices of Biblical Interpretation.* Boston: Beacon Press, 1992.

______. *Discipleship of Equals: A Critical Feminist Ekklesia-logy of Liberation.* New York: Crossroads, 1993.

Schüssler Fiorenza, Francis. "Theological and Religious Studies: The Contest of the Faculties." In *Shifting Boundaries: Contextual Approaches to the Structure of Theological Education,* edited by Barbara G. Wheeler and Edward Farley. Louisville: Westminster/John Knox Press, 1991.

Scroggs, Robin. *The New Testament and Homosexuality.* Philadelphia: Fortress Press, 1983.

Segovia, Fernando F. "Reading the Bible as Hispanic Americans." In *The New Interpreter's Bible: Genesis to Leviticus, vol. 1,* edited by Leander E. Keck. Nashville: Abingdon Press, 1994.

______. "In the World but Not of It: Exile as Locus for a Theology of the Diaspora." In *Hispanic/Latino Theology: Challenge and Promise,* edited by Ada María Isasi-Díaz and Fernando Segovia. Minneapolis: Fortress Press, 1996.

______. *Decolonizing Biblical Studies: A View from the Margins.* Maryknoll, N.Y.: Orbis Books, 2000.

Segundo, Juan Luis. *Our Idea of God.* Maryknoll, N.Y.: Orbis Books, 1973.

______. *The Liberation of Theology.* Maryknoll, N.Y.: Orbis Books, 1976.

Sheridan, Vanessa. *Crossing Over: Liberating the Transgendered Christian.* Cleveland: Pilgrim Press, 2001.

Sierra Club. "A Place at the Table." *Sierra* (May/June 1993): 51–58, 90–91.

Smith, Bill. "Liberation as Risky Business." In *Changing Conversations: Religious Reflection & Cultural Analysis,* edited by Dwight Hopkins and Sheila Devaney. New York: Routledge, 1996.

Smith-Christopher, Daniel L.. *A Biblical Theology of Exile.* Minneapolis: Fortress Press, 2002.

Sobrino, Jon. *Christology at the Crossroads: A Latin American Approach.* Translated by John Drury. Maryknoll, N.Y.: Orbis Books, 1978.

______. *Jesus in Latin America.* Translated by Robert R. Barr. Maryknoll, N.Y.: Orbis Books, 1987.

Solivan, Samuel. *Orthopathos: Prolegomenon for a North American Hispanic Theology.* Ph.D. diss., Union Theological Seminary, New York, 1993.

______. "The Holy Spirit-Personalization and the Affirmation of Diversity: A Pentecostal Hispanic Perspective." In *Teología en Conjunto: A Collaborative Hispanic Protestant Theology,* edited by José David Rodríguez and Loida I. Martell-Otero. Louisville: Westminster John Knox Press, 1997.

______. *The Spirit, Pathos and Liberation: Toward an Hispanic Pentecostal Theology.* Sheffield: Sheffield Academic Press, 1998.

Song, Choan-Seng. *Third-Eye Theology: Theology in Formation in Asian Settings.* Maryknoll, N.Y.: Orbis Books, 1982, 1990.

______. *Tell Us Our Names: Story Theology from an Asian Perspective.* Maryknoll, N.Y.: Orbis Books, 1984.

______. *Theology from the Womb of Asia.* Maryknoll, N.Y.: Orbis Books, 1986

______. *Jesus, the Crucified People.* New York: Crossroad, 1990.

______. *Jesus and the Reign of God.* Minneapolis: Fortress Press, 1993.

______. *Jesus in the Power of the Spirit.* Minneapolis: Fortress Press, 1994.

______. *The Believing Heart: An Invitation to Story Theology.* Minneapolis: Fortress Press, 1998.

______. "Five Stages Toward Christian Theology in the Multicultural World." In *Journeys at the Margin: Toward an Autobiographical Theology in American-Asian Perspective,* edited by Peter C. Phan and Jung Young Lee. Collegeville, Minn.: Liturgical Press, 1999.

Spencer, Daniel T. *Gay and Gaia: Ethics, Ecology, and the Erotic.* Cleveland: Pilgrim Press, 1996.

Stannard, David E. *American Holocaust: Columbus and the Conquest of the New World.* New York: Oxford University Press, 1992.

Stanton, Elizabeth Cady, ed. *The Woman's Bible.* New York: European Pub. Co., 1895, 1898.

Stevens Arroyo, Antonio M. *Prophets Denied Honor: An Anthology of the Hispanic Church in the United States.* Maryknoll, N.Y.: Orbis Books, 1980.

Stewart, Dianne. *The Evolution of African Religions in Jamaica: Toward a Caribbean Theology of Collective Memory.* Ph.D. diss., Union Theological Seminary, New York, 1997.

______. *Three Eyes for the Journey: African Dimensions of the Jamaican Religious Experience* . New York: Oxford Univ. Press, 2002.

Stone, Ken, ed. *Queer Commentary and the Hebrew Bible.* Cleveland: Pilgrim Press, 2001.

Sugirtharajah, R. S., ed. *Asian Faces of Jesus: Faith and Cultures.* Maryknoll, N.Y.: Orbis Books, 1993.

______. *The Postcolonial Bible.* Sheffield: Sheffield Academic Press, 1998.

Sugirtharajah R. S., and Cecil Hargreaves, eds. *Readings in Indian Christian Theology, vol. 1.* Belgium: International Academic Publishers, 2001.

Tamez, Elsa, ed. *Through Her Eyes: Women's Theology from Latin America.* Maryknoll, N.Y.: Orbis Books, 1989.

______. *Against Machismo: Rubem Alves, Leonardo Boff, Gustavo Gutiérrez, Jose Miguez Bonino, Juan Luis Segundo and Others Talk About the Struggle of Women.* Yorktown Heights, N.Y.: Meyer Stone, 1987.

Taylor, Mark. *The Executed God: The Way of the Cross in Lockdown America.* Minneapolis: Fortress Press, 2001.

Terrell, JoAnne Marie. *Power in the Blood? The Cross in the African American Experience.* Maryknoll, N.Y.: Orbis Books, 1998.

Tertullian. *Tertullian's Treatise Against Praxeas.* Edited by Earnest Evans. London: S.P.C.K., 1959.

Thiong'o, Ngugi wa. *Decolonizing the Mind: The Politics of Language in African Literature.* London: James Currey; Nairobi: Heinemann Kenya; New Hampshire: Heinemann, 1986.

Thurman, Howard. *Jesus and the Disinherited.* Richmond, Ind.: Friends United Press, 1976, 1981.

Tillich, Paul. *Theology of Culture.* New York: Oxford Univ. Press, 1959.

Tinker, Tink. "The Integrity of Creation: Restoring Trinitarian Balance." *Ecumenical Review* 41 (1989): 527–536.

______. *Missionary Conquest: The Gospel and Native American Genocide.* Minneapolis: Fortress Press, 1993.

______. "Spirituality, Native American Personhood, Sovereignty and Solidarity." In *Spirituality of the Third World: A Cry for Life,* edited by K.C. Abraham and B. Mbuy-Beya. Maryknoll, N.Y.: Orbis Books, 1994.

______. "American Indians and Jesus: Reflections Towards an EATWOT Christology." *Voices from the Third World* 18 (December 1995): 115–134.

______. "Spirituality, Native American Personhood, Sovereignty, and Solidarity." In *Native and Christian?: Indigenous Voices on Religious Identity in the United States and Canada,* edited by James Treat. London and New York: Routledge, 1996.

______. "Jesus, Corn Mother, and Conquest." In *Native American Religious Identity: Unforgotten Gods,* edited by Jace Weaver. Maryknoll, N.Y.: Orbis Books, 1998.

Townes, Emilie. *In a Blaze of Glory: Womanist Spirituality As Social Witness.* Nashville: Abingdon Press, 1995.

Trible, Phyllis. *Texts of Terror: Literary-Feminist Readings of Biblical Narratives.* Philadelphia: Fortress Press, 1984.

______. *God and the Rhetoric of Sexuality.* Philadelphia: Fortress Press, 1978.

Trimiew, Darryl. *God Bless the Child That's Got Its Own: The Economic Rights Debate.* Atlanta: Scholars Press, 1997.

Villafañe, Eldin. *The Liberating Spirit: Toward an Hispanic American Pentecostal Social Ethic.* Grand Rapids: Wm. B. Eerdmans, 1993.

Volf, Miroslav. "Enter into Joy Sin, Death, and the Life of the World to Come." In *The End of the World and the Ends of God: Science and Theology on Eschatology,* edited by John Polkinghorne and Michael Welker. Harrisburg, Pa.: Trinity Press International, 2000.

______. "The Final Reconciliation: Reflections on a Social Dimension of the Eschatological Transition." In *Theology and Eschatology At the Turn of the Millennium,* edited by James Buckley and L. Gregory Jones. Oxford, UK: Blackwell, 2001.

______. *Exclusion & Embrace: A Theological Exploration of Identity, Otherness, and Reconciliation.* Nashville: Abingdon Press, 1996.

Walker, Alice. *The Color Purple.* New York: Harcourt, Brace, Jovanovich, 1982.

______. *In Search of Our Mothers' Gardens: Womanist Prose.* New York: Harcourt, Brace, Jovanovich, 1983.

Walker, Theodore, Jr. *Empower the People: Social Ethics for the African-American Church.* Maryknoll, N.Y.: Orbis Books, 1991.

Walzer, Michael. *Spheres of Justice: A Defense of Pluralism and Equality.* New York: Basic Books, 1983.

Warren, Karen. *Ecofeminist Philosophy.* Lanham, Md.: Rowman and Littlefield, 2000.

Warrior, Robert. "Canaanites, Cowboys, and Indians: Deliverance, Conquest, and Liberation Theology Today." In *Christianity and Crisis* (1989): 261–65.

______. "Canaanites, Cowboys, and Indians: Deliverance, Conquest, and Liberation Theology Today." In *Voices from the Margins: Interpreting the Bible in the Third World,* edited by R. S. Sujirtharajah. Maryknoll, N.Y.: Orbis Books, 1989.

______. "Canaanites, Cowboys, and Indians: Deliverance, Conquest, and Liberation Theology Today." In *Native and Christian?: Indigenous Voices on Religious Identity in the United States and Canada,* edited by James Treat. London and New York: Routledge, 1996.

Weber, Eugen. *Apocalypses: Prophecies, Cults, and Millennial Beliefs through the Ages.* Cambridge, Mass.: Harvard Univ. Press, 2001.

Weems, Renita J. *Just a Sister Away: A Womanist Vision of Women's Relationships in the Bible.* San Diego: LuraMedia, 1988.

Welartna, Usha. *Beyond the Killing Fields: Voices of Nine Cambodian Survivors in America.* Palo Alto, Calif.: Stanford Univ. Press, 1993.

West, Cornel. *Prophesy Deliverance: An Afro-American Revolutionary Christianity.* Philadelphia: Westminster Press, 1982.

Westra, Laura, and Peter Wenz. *Faces of Environmental Racism: Confronting Issues of Global Justice.* Lanham, Md.: Rowman and Littlefield, 1995.

Whitehead, Alfred North. *Adventure of Ideas.* New York: Free Press, 1933, 1961.

Wiesel, Elie. *All Rivers Run to the Sea: Memoirs.* Translated by Jon Rothschild. New York: Knopf, 1995.

Wilkins, David. *American Indian Sovereignty and the U.S. Supreme Court: The Masking of Justice.* Austin: Univ. of Texas, 1997.

Williams, Delores S. "Womanist Theology: Black Women's Voices." In *Weaving the Visions: New Patterns in Feminist Spirituality,* edited by Judith Plaskow and Carol Christ. New York: Harper & Row, 1989.

______. "Womanist Theology: Black Women's Voices." In *Yearning to Be Free: Liberation Theologies in the U.S.,* edited by Mar Peter-Raoul, Linda Rennie Forcey and Robert Fredrick Hunter. Maryknoll, N.Y.: Orbis Books, 1991.

______. *Sisters in the Wilderness: The Challenge of Womanist God-Talk.* Maryknoll, N.Y.: Orbis Books, 1993.

______. "Sin, Nature, and Black Women's Bodies." In *Ecofeminism and the Sacred,* edited by Carol Adams. New York: Continuum, 1994.
Williams, Robert. *The American Indian in Western Legal Thought: The Discourses of Conquest.* New York: Oxford Univ. Press, 1990.
Wilmore, Gayraud S. *Black Religion and Black Radicalism: An Interpretation of the Religious History of the African Americans.* Maryknoll, N.Y.: Orbis Books, 1983, 1998.
Wilmore , Gayraud S., and James Cone. *Black Theology: A Documentary History, 1966–1979.* Maryknoll, N.Y.: Orbis, 1979.
Wilson, William Julius. *The Truly Disadvantaged: The Inner City, the Underclass, and Public Policy.* Chicago: Univ. of Chicago Press, 1987.
______. *When Work Disappears: The World of the New Urban Poor.* New York: Vintage Books, 1997.
Wimberly, Edward P., and Anne Streaty Wimberly. *Liberation & Human Wholeness: The Conversion Experiences of Black People in Slavery and Freedom.* Nashville: Abingdon Press, 1986.
Wimbush, Vincent L. *African Americans and the Bible: Sacred Texts and Social Textures.* New York: Continuum, 2000.
Wood, Charles M. *Vision and Discernment: An Orientation in Theological Study.* Atlanta: Scholars Press, 1985.
Woods, Robert. *Christ and the Homosexual.* New York: Vantage Press, 1959.
Yeats, William Butler. "The Second Coming." In *The New Oxford Book of English Verse, 1250–1950,* edited by Helen Gardner. Oxford: Oxford Univ. Press, 1972.
Young, Josiah Ulysses, III. *A Pan-African Theology: Providence and the Legacies of the Ancestors.* Trenton, N.J.: African World Press, 1992.

Index

A

E

F

M

N

O

P

T

V

W

Y

Printed in the United States
23413LVS00004B/43-306

9 780827 214484